P9-EDV-298

SOCIAL INTERVENTION:
THEORY AND PRACTICE

AUGUSTANA UNIVERSITY COLLEGE
LIBRARY

SOCIAL INTERVENTION: THEORY AND PRACTICE

Edward M. Bennett
Editor

Studies in Health and Human Services
Volume Eleven

The Edwin Mellen Press
Lewiston and Queenston

Library of Congress Cataloging-in-Publication Data

Social intervention, theory and practice.

(Studies in health and human services ; v. 11)
Bibliography: p.
Includes index.
1. Social change--Case studies. 2. Operant
behavior--Case studies. 3. Community development--Case
studies. I. Bennett, Edward M., 1939- . II. Series.
HM101.S6932 1987   303.4'84'0926   87-24005
ISBN 0-88946-136-8

71959

This is volume 11 in the continuing series
Studies in Health and Human Services
Volume 11 ISBN 0-88946-136-8
SHHS Series ISBN 0-88946-126-0

Copyright © 1987 The Edwin Mellen Press

All rights reserved. For information contact:

The Edwin Mellen Press   The Edwin Mellen Press
P.O. Box 450   P.O. Box 67
Lewiston, New York   Queenston, Ontario
USA 14092   CANADA L0S 1L0

Printed in the United States of America

CONTENTS

AUGUSTANA UNIVERSITY COLLEGE
LIBRARY

Part IV

COMMUNITY ECONOMIC DEVELOPMENT APPROACHES
TO SOCIAL INTERVENTION

To my parents, Adele and Fred Bennett,
whose enduring support and unconditional love,
nurtured in me the strength to challenge
and to stand up to the forces
of oppression and repression.
Also, to my aunt Lil
in celebration of her 89th birthday
and her joie de vivre.

PREFACE

As the reader will see in the text of the book itself, the theory and practice of social intervention are inextricably linked to the problem of innovation and to the creation of new settings. By definition, change *of* the system demands the collaboration of a group of people in a planned deliberate activity over a sustained period of time to either create a new setting or to transform an existing one.

However, our knowledge of how to effect social change is either incomplete or misleading. For one thing, the scholarly literature contains a minimum amount of information on the topic of social intervention in general and on the process of social intervention in particular. For example, Bennett and Foy's recent content analysis of 1,130 articles selected in three year clusters over the period 1971-1985 from three scholarly journals which have a close historical relationship to the topic area revealed that only 3% of the articles addressed the *process* of social intervention. For another, a major obstacle in the meaningful study of social intervention has been the unwillingness of social scientists to either function together in multidisciplinary teams to address what is in essence a multidisciplinary problem area, or to pair up with practitioners working on social intervention projects in joint ventures (which could have valuable reciprocal action and research benefits), or to address the limitations of the logical positivist traditions of their university bases. Until such time that social scientists can come to grips with these problems they will continue to fall short of their potential as an intellectual and social force.

A central goal of this book therefore is to stimulate the reader to consider these issues and the possibilities for alternative behaviours. The approach to the topic is multidisciplinary (and at times interdisciplinary). As well, a conscious effort was made to integrate theory, research and practice and to invite contributions from practitioners in the field and from practice-oriented academicians. If we are to advance in our understanding of social intervention, such reciprocal exchanges between academics and practitioners must be encouraged. It is my hope that these observations will be useful to others and that my belief in the richness resulting from this collaborative approach will be confirmed by the reader and the critic alike.

A collection such as this is not possible without the help and support of many people. I would like to express my gratitude to Mary Sehl who was of inestimable value as copy-editor and to Rachelle Longtin who typeset the book in a superb manner. Thanks also to Heather Smith Fowler who copy-edited three chapters in Mary's absence and to Gwen Richardson who assisted me and the contributors in proofreading the final draft for reproduction errors. I am grateful to Thomas Hueglin, Joseph W. Lella, Patrick O'Neill and Geoffrey Nelson who each commented on earlier drafts of individual chapters. Thanks also to the students in my graduate seminar on social intervention for their helpful comments on seven of the book's chapters. Also, my appreciation to Stephen Berger for his friendship and his willingness to discuss the topic of social intervention with me and to Sandra Woolfrey who has been a most helpful critic.

I would also like to acknowledge the contributions of Burton Blatt who left us all too soon and Seymour B. Sarason who has been a friend and mentor for over twenty years. My years with Burt at Boston University and with Seymour at the Yale Psychoeducational Clinic, in ways far more inumerable than they ever realized, provided the foundation for what follows.

Finally, I am grateful to the Research Office of Wilfrid Laurier University for providing me with a Short Term Research Grant and a Book Preparation Grant which made the preparation of this book possible.

Edward M. Bennett

Newton, Ontario
June, 1987

Part I
INTRODUCTION

Edward M. Bennett

1
SOCIAL INTERVENTION: THEORY AND PRACTICE

INTRODUCTION

The central purpose of this book is to examine the nature of social intervention with particular emphasis on the process of how it is introduced and implemented. Social intervention refers to the interference with or alternation of ongoing societal relations. Process refers to the way change is initiated, develops, and endures in the social world.

As noted by Parsons (1951), it is necessary to distinguish clearly between processes of change *of* the system and processes of change *within* the system. Our purpose in this volume is to examine processes of change *of* the system and not that which occurs within a system which itself remains unaltered. Change of a system involves a shift or a transformation from trying to solve problems within a system which itself remains unchanged to a higher logical level of problem-solving which considers changing the assumptions, values, structural relations, and rules governing the system itself. Solutions oriented toward altering the premises and patterns of existing structural arrangements and practices are referred to by Watzlawick, Weakland, and Fisch (1974) as "second-order change." Solutions that accept the system's premises are referred to as "first-order change," and by definition are not considered to be instances of social intervention.

Unfortunately, many social-change efforts commit an error of conceptualization by attempting a first-order-change solution to a problem which can be solved only from the next higher logical level (second-order change of the system). The result is that things remain the same and the status quo is preserved. Watzlawick et al. (1974) provide a simple abstract example (see Figure 1) which helps make this point clear. Figure 1 contains a grouping of line dots which are to be

13

connected without lifting your pencil from the paper. The reader who has never before attempted this problem is advised to try it before reading further.

FIGURE 1

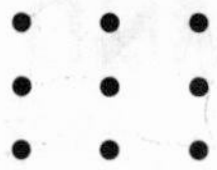

Most people who attempt this problem try to solve it with a first-order-change solution. The basic premise they apply is that the dots comprise a square and therefore the solution must be discovered within the square.

Regardless of the combination of four lines the problem-solver may attempt, the outcome will leave at least one unconnected dot. That is, their first-order-change solution cannot solve the problem. The solution requires a quantum jump, changing the self-imposed assumption that the dots compose a square. The solution requires leaving the field by stepping outside the box and moving to a different logical type by changing one's assumptions *about* the dots as noted in Figure 2.

FIGURE 2

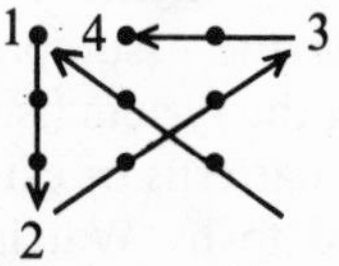

The solution of the nine-dot problem (Watzlawick et al., 1974, p. 27).

As we can readily see from this abstract example, the solution requires a change of the assumptions, rules, or premises governing the system as a whole; referred to by the authors as second-order change.

What we are emphasizing here is the importance of getting people to notice their assumptions and to examine them as part of an intervention strategy. The power of this strategy is evidenced in Myrdal's (1944) publication *An American Dilemma* in which his analysis pointed out Americans have within them both democratic and racist ideologies. It is this contradiction that he then posits as an available opening for positive change.

Further, Weick (1984) argues that social science is best equipped "to address how problems get defined in the first place. A shift away from outcomes toward inputs is not trivial, because the content of appropriate solutions is often implied by the definition of what needs to be solved" (p. 40).

On the nature of change of the system, our position is that it can involve a multitude of within-system changes. As Sarason (1972) observes, even revolutionary forms of change necessitate many within-system transformations. It is too easy to underestimate the resources which are needed and the time frame which is required for cultural transformation to occur.

Weick (1984) asserts that to avoid leaping the limits of bounded rationality (and becoming overwhelmed), larger social problems must be recast into smaller, less arousing problems. Lindblom (1959) and Weick (1984) demonstrate the value of attempts to recast larger social problems into a series of small problems and efforts to achieve modest results. Because it is in the nature of social problems to only achieve partial results and because social problems don't remain solved forever (Sarason, 1978), practitioners can expect to endlessly repeat the problem-solving process.

However, it is only by changing our conceptualization about the problem (by reframing the problem) that we can avoid the failure of first-order-change strategies which will never solve the task. We shall return to the subject of second-order change in our case-study illustrations.

APPROACHES TO SOCIAL CHANGE

There is an extensive literature in the modern field of social change. One major segment of approaches to change includes a range of interventions which have been pioneered by industrial and organizational psychologists (Argyris, 1962, 1970; Bennis, Benne, Chin, & Corey, 1976; Lawrence & Lorsch, 1967; Lippitt, Watson, & Westley, 1958). Generally using Empirical-Rational and Normative-Re-educative strategies, these change agents consider society and its organizations to be basically sound but periodically in need of adjustment and re-alignment. Empirical-Rational strategies include: basic research and education, personnel selection and replacement, systems analysis, applied research and diffusion of data, utopian thinking, and perceptual and conceptual reorganization. Normative-Re-educative strategies include: improving problem-solving and methods of realizing and fostering growth in persons within the system (Bennis et al., 1976).

The strategies of change noted above provide a useful knowledge base and set of tactical skills. However, because such strategies are used to maintain organizations' and society's underlying goals, values and beliefs and prevailing social, political, and economic orientations, they are not instances of social intervention. Rather, such approaches have been classified as: Social-Technician and Traditional Social Reformer (Goldenberg, 1978) or Professional-Technical (Crowfoot & Chesler, 1974).

In relation to the solution of social problems, Goldenberg (1978) refers to the Social-Technician as the guardian of the system who is used to silence community discontent or unrest. He describes the Traditional Social Reformer as the eternal middleman or broker who never works for the empowerment of the community, views change as eminating from the top down, and encourages the oppressed to be patient, and to accept relatively small changes or concessions. Further, Goldenberg feels that the Social Technician and Traditional Social Reformer both wish to perpetuate their own positions of leadership, status, and financial gain and will never seek to empower the community to provide for their own direction or obtain change for themselves. Similarly, Crowfoot and Chesler (1974) note that the Professional-Technical perspective does not seek to change society. They attribute a lack of motivation to work at societal change to the increased intellectual and operational risks and the view that such tasks are beyond the Professional-Technician's expertise.

In contrast to the Social Technician and Traditional Social Reformer, the Social Interventionist is interested in change *of* the system. The Social Interventionist therefore seeks to change or interfere with society's usual modes of thinking and behaving, including its ideology and conceptualization of people and social arrangements. The term social intervention refers to social actions which are designed to effect change in social institutions. It implies cooperative or collaborative activities between people or interest groups to effect change *of* a social system.

DOES SOCIAL INTERVENTION MEAN PROGRESS?

Social intervention activities involve value questions regarding both the means and ends of the social intervention activity. The underlying value explicated in this volume is the use of social intervention activities in relation to instances where society's institutions have been *repressive* and/or *oppressive*. The criterion for success is the degree to which there has been movement to reduce these conditions and whether the strategies employed are creating social processes and structures which provide the marginal person with greater access to goods and services and movement toward a psychological sense of community.

On Oppression

We use the term oppression to refer to "a state of continual marginality and premature obsolescence" (Goldenberg, 1978, p. 3). According to Goldenberg (1978), four structures comprise and spawn the experience as follows:

1. containment, which serves to restrict and narrow the scope of physical or psychological possibilities (e.g., an Indian Reserve);
2. expendability, which assumes that specific groups of people are expendable and replaceable without any loss to society as a whole (e.g., the underclass in modern society or people in third world countries);
3. compartmentalization, which prevents people from living an integrated lifestyle (e.g., little or no relationship between one's life interests and one's work);
4. ideology, which refers to the interpretation schema—the structure which shapes an individual's responses to their conscious experiences. In oppressive circumstances, the ideology is designed to encourage the victims to interpret their shortcomings as a function of unchangeable personal deficits. For example, the ideology of native inferiority governed and has continued to govern most of the relationships which the dominant white culture has with native persons and their communities. The most devastating aspect of this ideological structure is that it has encouraged native people to identify with the message and to view themselves as personally deficient (Bennett, 1982). Goldenberg (1978) has appropriately labelled this phenomenon "the doctrine of personal culpability."

On Repression—Alienation and Anomie

The term repression refers to those instances in which society's institutions are constrictive and contribute to the alienation (estrangement from self) and anomie (lack of mutual interdependence) of its members. As suggested by Mills (1959), it is important in the above to distinguish between personal troubles of the milieu and public issues of the social structure.

Troubles have to do with the private matters of individuals, the limited areas of social life of which we are aware. *Issues* transcend the range of private matters of individuals and have to do with the organization of many such local environments and the way they form the institutions and the larger structure of social and historical life (Mills, 1959). Our concern here is with public issues.

ALIENATION AND ANOMIE—THE PUBLIC ISSUES

It is rare to meet anyone who does not feel prey to the profit motive and the idea that man's social destination will take care of itself. The sense one almost always obtains is that the fact of life for many is the experience of estrangement from self, others, and environment—a pattern of hopelessness and helplessness that continually subverts the desire "to become," and is symptomatic of the problem of alienation (Fromm, 1941, 1955). For some, the process is involuntary and continual—they do not feel able to earn goods and services. For others, it is more voluntary—they may feel threatened by violence or possible unemployment, and feel helpless to do anything. Both types of individuals feel psychologically separate from the society with which they are physically joined. This lack of mutual interdependence with others is referred to as anomie (Durkheim, 1933; Landecker, 1951; Merton, 1957). Consider your own environment. When was the last time you were invited to contribute to the solution of a community problem or felt needed by others? Although you pay taxes and are entitled to vote, do you influence the direction of community life? Anomie is more often presented as a social-structural attribute, while alienation is an individual phenomenon resulting from structural situations. Ironically, there are few concepts which can shed as much light on the process of the development of physical, emotional, and mental energies and the organic integration of people, as those of alienation and anomie. It seems paradoxical that concepts depicting lack of fulfillment, physical and mental debasement, human denial and misery, and deteriorated social relationships would be most meaningful in providing insight for the prevention and resolution of these issues and the restitution of human wholeness. Nevertheless, one way to obtain insight into human development is to better understand what limits it. Furthermore, inherent in the root of these concepts is our relation to our environment and to other people.

Historically, the explanations of both concepts are rooted in the work situation. Work in the context of this volume is viewed as a person's activity in relation to his or her environment. It can therefore be a child's relationship to events in school, a housewife's activity in the home, etc. For Marx (1906) the process of alienation occurs as an individual is not able to control either his work situation or the products of that work. It entails loss of self and the transformation of people into an object or commodity. One situation in which this occurs is when labour is divided—a condition which Durkheim first thought would lead to an interdependence of parts and functions and to social ties based on this interdependence. Instead, Durkheim (1933) observed a state of normlessness and deteriorated social relationships, where people no longer had normative definitions to guide them in their actions. He called this unhealthy development "anomie." Durkheim and Marx both came to advocate worker control over their environments and social relations. They viewed this control as leading to human fulfillment and social integration, and lack of this control as leading to an absence of social integration, or anomie and feelings of personal alienation.

In light of the human misery which is caused by anomie and alienation, Sarason (1974) regards a *psychological sense of community* as the overarching criterion for what a community should be. He defines the concept to mean "a readily available, mutually supportive network of relationships upon which one could depend and as a result of which one did not experience sustained feelings of loneliness that compel one to actions or adopting a style of living masking anxiety and setting the stage for later and more destructive anguish" (p. 1).

The experience of marginality and the absence of a psychological sense of community have a particular relevance for social intervention activities. For one thing, the social interventionist's goal is to alter the policies and behaviours which spawn oppressive or repressive situations. For another, within a bottom-up approach to social change the process of involving marginal people in actions to direct their lives and their environments are necessary steps in the process of restoring people to their human wholeness.

The priorities with regard to change for the oppressed are: altering consciousness, organization and mobilization to achieve greater power, and access to goods and services. For the repressed the priorities are: altering lifestyle and interpersonal and community relations toward mutual exchange and shared control; and organizing to reduce dehumanizing bureaucracy, and to reduce or eliminate institutional practices destructive to the natural ecology (Bennett, 1970; Crowfoot & Chesler, 1974; and Goldenberg, 1978).

PERSISTENCE AND CHANGE

The French proverb, "the more things change, the more they remain the same," points to the paradoxical relationship between persistence and change. As Watzlawick et al. (1974) indicate, there have been "theories of persistence or theories of change, not theories of persistence *and* change" (p. 2).

This conception is fundamental to the theory and practice of social intervention. The social interventionist viewing a public issue must ask, "What is the issue about and how does it persist?" and "What will it take to change it?"

For example, as Berger (1985) observes, throughout the new world clashes of culture and values have occurred between the dominant society and native peoples. Since the discovery of the new world, people have sought wealth at the frontier, wealth to enrich the metropolis. In North America today the drive is to extract energy and resources, most often without regard for the world of native or indigenous people. Witness the following statement by John Armstrong, chairman of Imperial Oil, in 1980, "The Canadian oil industry should be moving into the most promising Atlantic and Arctic properties like an army of occupation" (cited in Berger, 1985, p. 102).

The public issue in this instance is our inclination to expand the industrial machine to the limit of our frontiers without considering the use of restraint or the damage to the natural and social ecology. The resolution of the problem, "What will it take to change it?" begins by asking the questions: "Can we get along with a smaller proportion of the world's non-renewable resources?; and are there other energy alternatives?

In short, the persistence of the phenomena observed during the last 400 years will continue unless we redefine or reframe the problem, thus inducing a *new* definition of the same situation. In this instance the stakes are quite high, as Berger (1985) observes:

> So we stand on the leading stage of history, driven by forces that require greater and greater use of energy, and greater consumption of dwindling resources. Can we change directions? Upon the answer to that question depends the future of each nation, of our environment, and of mankind itself (p. 111).

APPROACHES TO INTERVENTION

The interventions described in this book cluster around three types of approaches. They are: (a) cultural, ideological and educational, (b) legal, policy and political and (c) community economic development. Although each of the interventions described in the book emphasizes one of these approaches, one intervention may simultaneously include more than one approach. By definition, instances of social intervention to some degree involve a cultural-ideological transformation. Each approach is briefly defined below.

Cultural, Ideological and Educational Approaches

The goal here is to change the underlying ideology and institutionalized roles and relationships within educational settings. In this volume the primary focus will be on post-secondary educational settings. The underlying ideology and practices are the means which provide the interpretive scheme for our experiences. It is the means by which people and their social institutions maintain either enabling or disabling social, political, and economic conditions. Ideology mediates society's most important structures and shapes our responses to events which penetrate our consciousness. Consciousness-raising which is an important step in social intervention, includes altering ideology. Ideology is fundamental to all social intervention approaches and as you shall see, is a significant factor in social change.

Educational settings both follow and reflect the existing social order. Thus, as Dewey (1939) has observed, they participate in the determination of a future social order. Regarding the involvement of educational settings in the production of social change, Dewey identifies three possible directions of choice.

> Educators may act so as to perpetuate the present confusion and possibly increase it. That will be the result of drift, and under present conditions to drift is in the end to make a choice. Or they may select the newer scientific, technological, and cultural forces that are producing change in the old order; may estimate the directions in which they are moving and their outcome if they are given freer play, and see what can be done to make the schools their ally. Or, educators may become intelligently conservative and strive to make the schools a force in maintaining the old order intact against the impact of new forces (p. 694).

It is our belief that ideological revolutions are possible and in line with Dewey (1939) we believe our educational settings have a central role to play in the construction and reconstruction of the social order in relation to the movement of its social forces.

Legal, Policy and Political Approaches

The relationship between law, social policy, politics, and social intervention is a complex one. In this volume we will examine social intervention activities based on legal and social policy reforms designed to restructure the patterns of relationships between people and groups. Of interest in these case studies is the interactive relationship between law, social policy, politics, and society.

There are serious difficulties associated with the use of law and social policy to create social change. No law or policy reform can develop independently of, or remain unaffected by the social, political, and economic environments of their time. While central authority can have a great deal of influence in developing legal and social reforms, the events of recent decades have underlined the resource, knowledge, and authority constraints in attempting to prescribe and implement policies to resolve complex social problems.

What will become evident from the case studies is the importance of viewing policy formulation as a collaborative and incremental process which includes citizens, decision-makers, and experts.

The collaborative-incremental approach is based on the ideas provided by Grinnell (1969), **Lindblom** (1965) and **Lindblom** and Cohen (1979), and is consistent with the premises previously outlined. The approach redefines the relationship between citizens, experts, and decision-makers and between policy knowledge and organization. The error of the traditional approach to policy-making and implementation is that it limits the involvement of the ordinary citizen and ordinary knowledge in the problem-solving process and fragments the problem-solving roles of the major actors.

The proposed integrative collaborative approach allows people with direct experience with the problem (e.g., service providers and consumers), to collaborate with other experts (e.g., social scientists and decision-makers) in problem solving, policy making, and policy adjustment. It is through these transactions that individuals, organizations, and communities develop the capacity to implement solutions and refine the process.

Community Economic Development Approaches

This is a means of revitalizing the economic life of communities or even larger organizational units such as a region or state. It provides an opportunity for a community to control a vital element in its survival and development—its economy. Thus, it provides a key source of community and societal advancement.

Community economic development stresses community rather than individual ownership of property. Often this is a practical response to the reality that many people do not have the capital to become owners of businesses or other property. Unlike a capitalist approach to ownership which is a reward by itself, ownership is viewed as a means to achieving other community ends such as the provision of services, the creation of jobs, and an increased sense of community.

Community economic development can be seen as a proactive

response to overcoming the destructive doctrines of Personal Culpability and Social Darwinism. That is, successful community economic development, by definition, is based on the competence of people including their ability to cooperate, thus negating the notions of "survival of the fittest" and "poor people are inferior people."

The selection of case-study material for inclusion in this volume was based on the desire to provide the reader with a range of conceptual and practical experiences. The theme, change *of* the system (second-order change) is consistent across all content. The treatment of topics includes a description of the process and an evaluation of the intervention. The success of the intervention must ultimately be measured by its goals, processes, and outcomes for those whose lives are most affected by the outcomes. Following our underlying premises, success can be measured to the extent there is a meaningful relationship between the intervention, the needs of the people, the direction they would like to go, and how they are going there.

The treatment of topics is not to establish that there is one best way to effect change of social systems. Given the nature of the project, the variation and imprecision of the issues to be dealt with, and the multiple authors and disciplines contributing to the volume, my goal instead has been to emphasize the theme of social intervention and to define it clearly for the purposes of this book.

To maximize consistency in both the theme and focus of the case-study material, the contributors were encouraged to consider the following items as guidelines for their analyses:

(a) The goals and purpose of the intervention;

(b) a description of the intervention;

(c) the processes of interaction which took place during the period of intervention;

(d) the processes of member involvement and how the intervention addressed their problems;

(e) the outcome(s) of the intervention such as the impact on the target group and groups within the broader community;

(f) an evaluation of the intervention's success and/or failure; and

(g) a discussion of implications and lessons for social-intervention theory and practice.

PLAN OF THE BOOK

The primary focus of part two of the book is on cultural, ideological and educational approaches to social intervention. In chapter two Stephen Berger explores the dialectical relationships between social change worker, organizational base and the people the social interventionist wishes to work with. Key conceptual issues such as time, who owns and controls the setting, and whether or not one is dependent on the setting for one's livelihood are explored for a variety of organizational bases and are then particularized to the sociology of the university as an organizational base for social intervention.

Chapters three through five illustrate the use of higher education as a base for social intervention with a particular emphasis on cultural-ideological reform and training. Chapter three by David Osher and Ira Goldenberg describes the ten year history of the School of Human Services (SHS), one of the very few alternative post secondary educational settings *created* for human service para-professionals who are from racial and ethnic minority groups. The SHS is a unique program in relation to the multitude of alternative higher education programs that were formed as a result of the civil and social unrest of the 1950s and '60s. On the basis of the typology established by Grant & Riesman (1978) the SHS fits within the telic reforms—those attempts to change undergraduate education and redefine its goals. What is unique about the SHS is that it is one of the few examples of the radical reform model (Foy, 1987) and one of the only settings which has survived for a period of more than three to five years. The authors' description of the creation of this important setting examines the vicissitudes of "muddling through" this process of creation and illustrates the potency of ideology, commitment and passion to social intervention.

Chapter four by Edward Bennett and David Hallman describes the process of educational reform within an existing university setting as well as the use of the university as an organizational base for social intervention. The chapter demonstrates the centrality of *practice* in education to cognitive change in the student, and to transforming and influencing ideological and cultural forces to produce change in human service systems.

Chapter five by Mary Reidy, Louise Lévesque and Maurice Payette discusses how a group of university-based educators and an organizational development consultant intervened to transform the ideology and program of a nursing care setting. Their case study illustrates the combined power of ideology, in-service training and action research to social intervention.

Part three of the book is on legal, policy and political approaches to social intervention. Chapters six and seven focus on political approaches. Specifically, both chapters describe the development of citizens' coalitions as vehicles for social reform. Bruce Tefft's chapter describes the creation of an advocacy coalition to influence policy and system reform at the provincial level in Manitoba, Canada. David Hallman's chapter on the Nestle boycott is a process-oriented description of the creation of an international citizen-based social movement to reduce the exploitation and oppression of mothers and infants in developing countries—an account of a battle between a David and a Goliath. The chapters illustrate the importance of resource mobilization (Jenkins, 1983) to social movements as a political and organizational tool and as an aid to perserverance in problem-solving, a critical issue in social intervention.

Chapters eight and nine focus on legal approaches to social intervention. Chapter eight by Gail Czukar illustrates the benefits of a mediating organization to ensure the effective use of law in social change. This is particularly true in the case study of the Advocacy Resource Centre for the Handicapped (ARCH), where the controlling influence is the disabled population. Chapter nine by Patricia Hughes provides an interesting contrast to Gail Czukar's chapter. Dr. Hughes carefully documents the hazards and drawbacks of employing legal mechanisms of social intervention *without* the accompanying meaningful involvement of, or ownership by the setting most affected by the problem of abortion—the pro-choice movement.

The final chapter in part three of the book examines the social, professional and political forces which have influenced mental health policy reform in the Province of Québec in the past 25 years. The chapter written by Françoise Boudreau is a provocative case study of the problem of persistence and change, the definition of social problems, and the psychosocial politics of system reform.

Part four of the book is on community economic development (CED) approaches to social intervention. As I have noted earlier in the chapter, CED can serve as a vital means to overcoming the destructive forces of personal culpability and Social Darwinism, and as a key source of community and societal advancement. The chapters in this section of the book give serious attention to the nature, scope and practice of CED.

Chapter eleven by Swack and Mason establishes the philosophical and conceptual context for CED and examines why it compares favourably to traditional social welfare policy attempts and conventional economic alternatives. The chapter includes a discussion of major CED approaches including community land trusts and loan funds, as a means by which a community can obtain control over their own resources.

Chapters twelve and thirteen by Christina Clamp examine the Mondragon system of worker co-operatives, as a detailed case study example of a substantial experiment in CED that is more than 25 years old. Established in 1956, the Mondragon system is acknowledged as the most successful example of worker co-operatives and community-based economic self-help. Chapter twelve presents the history and structure of the Mondragon system of worker co-ops and discusses how it serves the broad goals of humanism, social justice, democracy and economic well-being. Chapter thirteen describes how the complex system of more than 165 co-operatives is managed and how it has responded to the forces of time and change, including the recession of the 1970s and the early '80s. In combination the two chapters provide an outstanding illustration of the efficacy of large-scale approaches to worker co-operatives and CED. As well, they help us to understand the cultural and ideological forces which drive them and the discipline, commitment, organization and skill which are required to make them work.

Chapter fourteen by Alexander Lockhart illustrates that community-based economic development in the Canadian North compares favourably to conventional economic development on three process variables critical to the attainment of social health and community well-being: economic viability, social viability and political viability (Matthews, 1976, 1983). On the basis of his comparative analysis and years of CED experience, Dr. Lockhart emphasizes the importance of shifting from "band-aid" approaches to CED to large-scale ventures such as Mondragon. Harrington's (1984) incisive exposé of the new American poverty, juxtaposed with the material in part four of this volume, provides a strong argument for government, labour and the mainstream sources of venture capital to more seriously consider a major adjustment to community-based thinking and development.

This concludes the introduction to the book. I hope the collection serves to inspire and stimulate the reader as it did myself, to consider alternative ways of thinking about social problems and the theory and practice of social intervention, and to increase the probability of creating successful solutions.

REFERENCES

Argyris, C. (1962). *Interpersonal competence and organizational effectiveness.* Homewood, IL: Dorsey Press.

Argyris, C. (1970). *Intervention theory and method.* Reading, MA: Addison-Wesley.

Bennett, E.M. (1970). *A social systems approach to health planning in rural communities.* Unpublished doctoral dissertation, Case Western Reserve University, Cleveland, Ohio.

Bennett, E.M. (1982). Native persons: An assessment of their relationship to the dominant culture and challenges for change. *Canadian Journal of Community Mental Health, 1*(2), 21-31.

Bennis, W., Benne, K.D., Chin, R., & Corey, K.E. (1976). *The planning of change.* New York: Holt, Rinehart & Winston.

Berger, T.R. (1985). Energy resource development and human values. In E.M. Bennett & B. Tefft (Eds.), *Theoretical and empirical advances in community mental health* (pp. 101-112). New York: Edwin Mellen Press.

Crowfoot, J.E., & Chesler, M.A. (1974). Contemporary perspectives on planned social change: A comparison. *Journal of Applied Behavioural Science, 10* (July/August), 278-303.

Dewey, J. (1939). Education and social change. In J. Ratner (Ed.), *Intelligence in the modern world: John Dewey's philosophy* (pp. 691-696). New York: The Modern Library.

Durkheim, E. (1933). *Division of labor in society.* New York: Free Press.

Foy, M. (1987). *An outcome evaluation of a post-secondary educational program for minority group paraprofessionals.* Unpublished thesis proposal, Wilfrid Laurier University. Waterloo, Ontario.

Fromm, E. (1941). *Escape from freedom.* New York: Rinehart & Co.

Fromm, E. (1955). *The sane society.* New York: Holt, Rinehart & Winston.

Goldenberg, I.I. (1978). *Oppression and social intervention.* Chicago: Nelson-Hall.

Grant, G., & Riesman, D. (1978). *The perpetual dream: Reform and experiment in the American College.* Chicago: The University of Chicago Press.

Grinnell, S.U. (1969). *An integrative process for urban and socio-technical problem-solving.* Cleveland: Engineering Design Center and Organizational Behavior Groups, Case Western Reserve University, Cleveland, Ohio.

Harrington, M. (1984). *The new American poverty.* New York: Holt, Rinehart & Winston.

Jenkins, J.C. (1983). Resource mobilization theory and the study of social movements. *American Review of Sociology, 9*, 527-553.

Landecker, W.S. (1951). Types of integration and their measurement. *American Journal of Sociology, 56*, 332-340.

Lawrence, P.R., & Lorsch, J.W. (1967). *Organization and environment.* Homewood, IL: R.D. Irwin.

Lindblom , C.E. (1959). The science of "muddling through." *Public Administration Review, 19*, 79-88.

Lindblom., C.E. (1965). *The intelligence of democracy.* New York: The Free Press.

Lindblom, C.E., & Cohen, D. (1979). *Usable knowledge: Social science and social problem solving.* New Haven: Yale University Press.

Lippitt, R., Watson, J., & Westley, B. (1958). *The dynamics of planned change.* New York: Harcourt & Brace.

Marx, K. (1906). *Capital I.* Chicago: Charles H. Kerr & Co.

Matthews, R. (1976). *"There's no better place than here": Social change in three Newfoundland communities.* Toronto: Peter Martin.

Matthews, R. (1983). *The creation of regional dependency.* Toronto: University of Toronto Press.

Merton, R.U. (1957). *Social theory and social structure.* Glencoe, IL: The Free Press.

Mills, C.W. (1959). *The sociological imagination.* New York: Oxford University Press.

Myrdal, G. (1944). *An American dilemma: The negro problem and modern democracy.* New York: Harper & Row.

Parsons, T. (1951). *The social systems.* New York: The Free Press.

Sarason, S.B. (1972). *The creation of settings and future societies.* San Francisco: Jossey-Bass.

Sarason, S.B. (1974). *The psychological sense of community.* San Francisco: Jossey-Bass.

Sarason, S.B. (1978). The nature of social problem-solving in social action. *American Psychologist, 33,* 370-380.

Watzlawick, P., Weakland, J., & Fisch, R. (1974). *Change: Principles of problem formation and problem resolution.* New York: W.W. Norton & Co.

Weick, K.L. (1984). Small wins: Redefining the scale of social problems. *American Psychologist, 39*(1), 40-49.

Part II
CULTURAL, IDEOLOGICAL AND EDUCATIONAL APPROACHES TO SOCIAL INTERVENTION

Stephen D. Berger

2

HIGHER EDUCATION AS A BASE FOR SOCIAL INTERVENTION: COMPARATIVE ANALYSIS

INTRODUCTION

Those of us who work in colleges or universities are most conscious of the difficulties these settings present for working for social change. Others of us, not so located, sometimes find ourselves jealous of the freedom and resources for social change work we presume exist in colleges and universities.

It may be useful to examine the characteristics of different organizational bases from which to work for social change and their strengths and weaknesses. For those of us who work in universities, or are contemplating doing so, it may also be useful to understand more clearly the difficulties as well as the opportunities inherent in that base, so we may use it more effectively. This article speaks to both goals, the comparative analysis of organizational bases for social change, and the particular nature of higher education as a base.

I should add some information about what is not in this article. The article is focused on the structural problems of doing social change work in different organizational bases, and does not deal with the problems and ambivalences of the individual social change worker. Given its focus, it also talks as if only social change workers were active and everyone else—friends, enemies, powerful people, etc.,—were passive, or reactive. While this is obviously not so, to take

Author's Note: My thanks for Verne McArthur for very stimulating comments on a very different earlier version of this paper, to Ira Goldenberg for great help on the previous draft of this version, and to Ed Bennett for suggesting the idea. Verne McArthur and David Osher also gave helpful feedback on a previous draft on this version.

31

all of this into account would go far beyond the scope of the article. Except for a few hints, this article does not deal with the larger political, economic and historical contexts within which our social change work occurs. Finally, the style of the article is addressed primarily to social change workers, particularly younger social change workers. It is written to try to codify some of what I have learned about organizational bases for social change, which may be helpful to other people.

BASES OF SOCIAL INTERVENTION

A base of social intervention is an organization in which we are located for substantial portions of our daily time, and from which we try to engage in social change activities. This can be our full-time job, it can be our voluntary participation, it can be where we are students.

How we relate to our organizational base depends, first of all, on two issues: (a) Do we control it? and (b) are we dependent upon it for our salary? If we control our organizational base, we don't have to worry too much about legitimizing our social change efforts as part of our work, but we have to be very concerned about maintaining the organization. Conversely, if we do not control our organizational base, we may be able to let others worry about maintaining the organization, but we may have to worry about legitimizing our social change efforts *within* the organization itself.

If we are dependent on the organization for our salaries, then we do not have to be distracted from our organizational work by the necessity of earning money, but the organization has a stronger hold on us. If we are not dependent on the organization for our money, we have to be concerned about getting money elsewhere, which usually means holding down a job, since few of us are independently wealthy. Generally, this is the difference between having an organizational base which is composed of full-time paid employees and one which is a voluntary organization.

Granting that each of these considerations is important, what happens if we cross-classify them?

		Control of Organization	
		Yes	No
Nature of	Paid	1	2
Organization			
	Voluntary	3	4

Examples of case 1, in which we control the organization and are paid, are organizations for training community organizers, like the Industrial Areas Foundation and the Midwest Academy, and independent educational organizations like the Highlander Folk School, etc. In such organizational bases, the central focus of one's time and energy frequently is doing the things that make the necessary money to get the jobs paid and keep the organizations going. Whether or not these money-making activities are the social change activities we want to carry out becomes a central tension in the organization. Suppose, for example, our community organizer training group wants to train poor people in selected communities, but the Federal Government is no longer into community organizing and the foundations want to focus on job training? Or suppose we are a community education group who thinks the major issue is environmental pollution, but there is only money for job development (or the reverse)?

Thus the central organization problem for case 1 bases is maintaining one's chosen mission as an organization. Much talent, time and energy will need to be continuously devoted to this issue, even at the price of not doing what we want to do.

Case 2, in which we do not control the organization but our work is paid, is exemplified by working for most colleges or universities. I will return to this in a little while. Case 3, in which we control a voluntary organization, may be exemplified by many community-based volunteer organizations that are started by one's own group. In this case, resources are not a direct issue, since we earn our money elsewhere, and the major issues to be addressed usually are gaining support and resonance from the external world, including getting people to join and stay in the organization. To the degree that the activities of the organization are seen as confrontive or radical or ideologically pure, there may be difficulties in gaining such support. Sometimes the organization then retreats into its own enclave of members and immediate supporters in the face of a hostile world. If on the other hand, the group finds resonance in its environment, then other people will want to get involved. Often those who come later have different expectations, have had different experiences, and want different things. This can create a generational tension within the organization between the founders and the late-comers. In the extreme, a power struggle for control of the organization can ensue. (Some of this is discussed in Seymour Sarason's *The Creation of Settings and the Future Societies* (1972).)

Case 4, correspondingly, could involve joining a voluntary organization already in existence and which has not been started or controlled by one's own group. (In some ways this is the situation just discussed, seen from the point of view, not of the founders, but of the later joiners.) If we envision these as relatively small voluntary organizations, then case 4 circumstances may be ones in which we start by trying to legitimate something different from what the organization has been doing. This often rapidly escalates into a battle, either for control of the organization, or to exclude us as outsiders.

What does this little exercise tell us so far about the strengths and weaknesses of different bases from which to work for social change? 1. When we control our own organizations (cases 1 and 3), enormous amounts of time, energy and talent will go into issues of starting and maintaining the organization, that is, obtaining the resources and support necessary for the organization to operate, such as money, people, support, good will, access, and so forth.

In the "easiest" of cases (what we might call external sponsorship), resources and sometimes also support are easily forthcoming because significant forces in the external world have already been persuaded and are only looking for people to carry out their desires. It is important to stress how unlikely this is, especially to folks who were engaged in social change in the War on Poverty era, when the Federal Government was (in extreme cases) practically begging to give money away for projects even approximately appropriate (Matusow, 1984, chapters 4, 9). On the other hand, sometimes we feel uneasy about external sponsorship: we fear being co-opted and we worry that we are insufficiently radical if relatively powerful people want to sponsor what we want to do. While co-optation needs to be worried about, sponsorship, I suggest, should not be rejected out of hand.

The second easiest case is one in which it is somewhat difficult to obtain the necessary resources and support, but the activities to obtain them are the same as, or at least congruent with, the social change activities one wants to undertake. Community organizing activities may sometimes be of this type.

The more difficult case is the one in which obtaining the necessary resources and support can only be done at the price of deflection from our mission. In process terms this can happen if all the organization's energy is devoted to obtaining the resources necessary to function. It can also happen if the resources are obtained only to do something different from what we wanted to do.

For example, if we are building a school, we may find that we spend an inordinate amount of time recruiting students (the process problem), and then discover that the students we are able to recruit and whom we need to pay the bills, are different from the ones we wanted to serve.

Finally, the most difficult case is one in which the environment is or becomes so hostile that the organization's energy is devoted to resisting actual external attack. In that case, too, the degree to which we can carry out the social change activities we had envisioned is minimized.

To repeat, the first generalization about the strengths and weaknesses of organizational bases is that where we control our own organizations (cases 1 and 3), enormous amounts of time, energy and talent will go into issues of starting and maintaining the organization, and this may mean some deflection from our desired social change activities. The problem is more difficult in case 1, in which we need monetary resources for salaries, than in case 3, in which we are not expecting to be maintained through this work.

The second generalization about organizational bases is:

2. In the case in which we do not control our own organizations, then time and energy will need to be devoted to legitimizing our social change activities. In the extreme, this will require a fight to control the organization. This case usually involves a trade-off: the organization allows us to do some of what we want to do, on the condition that we also do some of what it wants us to do. (This is true even where we control the organization: we have to devote some of our time and energy to organizational maintenance.) Thus the balance of this trade-off becomes criticial in assessing the usefulness of the organization as a base for social intervention.

If we think of the amount of time we are able to (overtly or covertly) negotiate for social change activities as our "social change time"—time not gobbled up by the organization for its own ends—then a potential base is attractive if it has more such time. This is one of the things that makes the university attractive to outsiders: teachers and students appear to have a lot of time available for social change work. Many other potential bases seem to have much less social change time.

So far, I have assumed that we can talk about different organizational bases for social intervention efforts without dealing with the kind of social intervention we want to do. Obviously, at some point it makes a difference what we want to try to do.

TYPES OF SOCIAL INTERVENTION

In the context of our concern for the strengths and weaknesses of different organizations as bases for social intervention, we would like to know whether the type of social intervention we undertake makes a difference in choice of organization? Or, in a given organization base, what impact will be made on our social intervention efforts?

I am not aware of a really good typology of social intervention efforts. I will therefore proceed once again by raising some obvious issues and hoping to draw some not-quite-so-obvious conclusions from them. I will, however, make use of some distinctions raised by Ira Goldenberg in *Oppression and Social Intervention* (1978).

Even without a good typology, we know enough about social intervention to assert that the following issues are important:

1. What *kind* of change are we trying to achieve? Do we seek changes in what people and organizations do, or changes in how people think and feel, and what they value?
2. Is the style of interaction between us and the people we are trying to change collaborative or confrontive?
3. Is our work focused more on working with the folks we see as on our side, or on the people we see as our opponents, or on those we see as in power but not on our side?
4. Are the people we want to work with mostly like us (in terms of class, gender, race, and ethnicity) or are they significantly different from us?
5. Are the people we want to work with already organized in groups or organizations?
6. Do we control the setting and circumstances in which we interact with people?
7. Do our efforts have legitimacy from institutionalized power sources?
8. How big a change, in how big a system, are we trying to make?

Issue 1. What *kind* of change are we trying to achieve. Do we seek changes in what people and organizations do, or changes in how people think and feel, and what they value?

I think of this as the consciousness-raising issue. While there are many different ways of doing consciousness-raising, they all require a place and time to confront one's internal conflicts between the past and what one wants to be in the present. This phase of work is focused inward at least, and requires time and skills to help it to happen.

It also makes a lot of difference whether or not the people whose consciousness we are trying to change want that change to happen themselves. It's one thing if the people we are working with our like ourselves and we all come together because we feel a need to change ourselves (women's consciousness-raising groups, for example). (This issue is very closely related to the third and fourth issues: Are we working with friends or enemies, and with people like us or different from us?) It's very different if we are black and want to change the consciousness of white segregationists.

In fact, it was precisely out of thinking about such problems that people fighting prejudice and discrimination in the 1950's decided to focus on getting actions changed *as a strategy* for getting consciousness changed (Clark, 1953). The issue was changing prejudice and discrimination, and the strategy was closely connected to the social-psychological theory of cognitive dissonance (Festinger, 1957) which implied: don't try directly to get a segregationist to change how he thinks, but rather try to get a change in what he does. Over time, he'll adjust his thinking to what he is doing.

Put another way, if we are dealing with opponents and we frame the issue in consciousness-raising terms, then we are saying you have to change how you think and how you feel. Said at all confrontively, however, this is likely to provoke defensiveness. (This relates to issue 2: is our style collaborative or confrontive?) Being defensive, the response is likely to be confrontive. The situation, then, is likely to become a power struggle, in which the short-term issue then is simply relative power.

Issue 2. Is the style of interaction between actors and targets of change collaborative or confrontive?

Social change, like all work, affects one's position, prestige, circumstances, and so forth. If the social change work I do gets me and the people I work with involved in confrontation with a target group, then that target group may try to get back at me by pressuring my organization. If our folks control the organization, then they may try to hurt our organization. If we don't control it, they may try to get the organization to stop us, or get rid of us.

Sometimes the issue does not have to be drawn in such symbolic oppositional terms. Yet we have a somewhat dangerous *preference* for defining issues in terms of opposites or differences in values. For example, we will often seek to define our social intervention efforts in terms which *require* a change in values of our opponents: we will say that we seek a change "of the system," or a "second-order change." We do this, obviously, in response to experiences (and charges) of having sought too little, or having been co-opted, or having sold out, or generally having been insufficiently radical. In so doing, we define as the most important reference group those whom we assume to be more radical. And, if they are our most important reference group, then it matters less how we are seen by our opponents, who are not only less radical but positively conservative or reactionary. If we offend these opponents, well, this simply reaffirms our radicality.

But the point, presumably, was to induce or persuade or provoke or pressure those opponents to change. The strategic and tactical issues then, should focus on how best *to do that*, rather than how best to seem radical.

When dealing with opponents, it is generally more effective to focus on changing actions, with rhetoric which stresses *commonality* of values. This was the strategy, for example, in the civil rights movement, in which people sought to change segregated and discriminatory statutes and practices by reference to a rhetorical framework of a common commitment to democracy and equality. (Myrdal's approach in *An American Dilemma* (1944) stressed and legitimated such an approach.)

On the other hand, issues of consciousness-raising are often terribly important when dealing with those we see as our friends, allies, and partners. Why is that? Because it is necessary to expose and deal with those parts of ourselves which inhibit our ability to act passionately, effectively and humanely in creating a better world.

It is necessary, for example, to deal with all of the passivity, self-blame and terror that is part of having been oppressed and victimized. That is why Paulo Freire (1973) starts with exercises to allow people to discover their activity, their competence and their creativity. We discover analogous phenomena in every major example of consciousness-raising.

Issue 3. Is our work focused more on working with the folks we see as on our side, or on the people we see as our opponents, or on those we see as in power but not on our side?

All social change efforts involve both working with our own folks and with the people who aren't with us. The issue I'm raising here is the issue of relative balance. When women get together to form consciousness-raising groups, for example, they are more focused on working among themselves. When women get together to form a lobbying organization to get the Equal Rights Amendment (ERA) passed, they are more focused on people in decision-making positions, who cannot, in general, be assumed to be already among the convinced (compare Freeman, 1975; Ferree and Hess, 1985).

The circumlocutions I've just gone through, both in the phrasing of the issue and in the example, suggest that I may be confusing two somewhat different issues: (a) working with presumed friends rather than presumed enemies, and (b) working with people in decision-making positions as opposed to working with those who are not. If we cross-classify these, we get:

		Working with	
		Friends	Enemies
Working with People	In Decision-Making Positions	1	2
	Not	3	4

What this shows me is that my phrasing of the question suggested I was considering only case 3 (friends not in decision-making positions) and case 2 (enemies in decision-making positions). I had implicitly assumed that the folks with me were out of power (the powerlessness assumption) and that the folks in power were against me (the assumption that the system is against me). While both of these may happen, they do not exhaust the possibilities. Furthermore, the dichotomy "you're either with me or against me," while having New Testament roots, among others, often is neither accurate nor helpful. Surely there are often people who are initially neither the one nor the other.

These conceptual limitations stem from the assumption that we try to do different things with people we see as either actual or potential friends than with people we do not see as friends. (We have to deal with them, either because they are active enemies, or because they participate in decision-making and have some power.)

The crucial question, then, is what do we do that is different with each group of people? The answer is that we seek to persuade friends, not only to agree with us, but to go on to become actively involved with us and to become part of us. We will then expect a further active commitment to activities necessary to work towards our ends. On the other hand, we seek not to persuade but to oppose enemies. That is, by and large we do not seek to change their minds but rather to counter and to minimize their effects *on others*, and we seek to get decision-makers to make the decisions we want them to make (whether or not they are *persuaded* by us).

This suggests that activities among friends make up the bulk of social intervention efforts, when we count time and energy, considering, for example, that the preparation for a hearing, or a march, or voter registration, is much more lengthy than the actual event. If that is so, then two issues need to be raised about an organizational base: (a) Does it permit (and even encourage) the lengthy commitment of time and resources to working with potential and actual friends; and (b) does it tolerate, permit, and even encourage the opposing of enemies and the attempt to get decision-makers to act?

Issue 4. Are the people we want to work with mostly like us (in terms of class, gender, race and ethnicity) or are they significantly different from us?

To follow directly on the previous discussion, do the people we see as friends see us as friends? Or is there extensive work to be done before they will even consider talking with us and listening to us?

Issue 5. Are we working with already organized groups or organizations?

What I have in mind here is the degree to which our change efforts must involve encouraging and motivating people to join in, or whether we can assume that in some sense people are already "in" and we can focus on what we want to get done.

The reason I stress this criterion is that it has to do with how much concerted *time* we must plan to put in. Organizing efforts involve a lot of hanging out time—being with people, becoming acceptable to them, drawing them out, suggesting, persuading, and so forth. To the degree that our change work involves this kind of organizing, it requires a lot of social change time, which many bases lack.

Issue 6. Do we control the setting and circumstances in which we interact with people?

This is the "turf" issue. It relates to the first issue of legitimacy, in that controlling setting and circumstances usually involves having legitimacy, but it also involves who comes to whom, and who wants what from whom.

To give an example: if my setting is the university, and if I can legitimately get the people I want to work with to be my students, then I have the ability to do my work, with legitimacy and power, within my organizational time, (i.e., my job). This enhances my ability to concentrate on that work. (It obviously also raises the problem of status and power in my relationships with the people I am working with.)

Issue 7. Do our efforts have legitimacy from institutionalized power sources?

This really has to do with how people perceive us as we try to act as agents of social change, with whether we can ask for support because our legitimacy can be presupposed or whether we first have to earn our legitimacy with the people we want to work with. Union organizers in the 1930's used the passage of federal legislation to say to people, "FDR wants you to join the union," (Alinsky, 1970, chapter 4). I interpret this as the organizers' attempt to improve their legitimacy by claiming a tie to President Franklin Delano Roosevelt.

Some organizers, in line with their commitment to democratic self-organization, try to define their legitimacy as only coming from the people they are trying to help organize. This ignores the fact that people always characterize outsiders in some fashion; if we do not try to influence how people perceive us, then they will do it anyway, without our influence. Thus we may be seen as kids, students, radicals, Communists, or whatever.

I am saying it is harder to work for change when one is without legitimacy, than if one has legitimacy. To the degree that bases for social intervention confer, add to, detract from or destroy legitimacy, then they have a significant impact on our work.

Legitimacy, of course, does not have to be defined in terms of the larger society. The organizers I mentioned were attempting to derive legitimacy from FDR. Black ministers in the Civil Rights Movement, on the other hand, used the legitimacy which came from their positions in the black church, not from the larger white society. Similarly, legitimacy can come from already established and respected change agents when these have already developed a positive reputation, as in "He's an Alinsky organizer;" "She's a feminist;" "So-and-so vouches for them."

It is also true that legitimacy is not all-or-nothing. Sponsorship by an institution may give you legitimacy with one group, while simultaneously denying it with another. If you work for Harvard University, you gain access and legitimacy with some, but lose it with others.

Issue 8. How big a change, in how big a system, are we trying to make?

I left this one for last, deliberately. It is the one we are inclined to place first, and then it crowds out all other considerations.

Obviously, the bigger the change you want, the longer it takes to make it, on the average. The more people you are trying to effect, the longer it takes. Thus, the bigger the change you want to make, the more you need a base of operations that gives you a lot of social change time.

Beyond that, whether one says one is trying to get at the root causes of oppression, or one says one is trying to achieve second-order change, or in the older political language one simply says one is trying to "change the system," it is implied that the social changes we want to help get made are big, difficult, and significant. Some go further, and denigrate any social change efforts that are not big enough, as in "That's just a band-aid;" "You're just helping the system to adapt opposition."

Furthermore, any base of social intervention which has legitimacy in the larger society may be denigrated as automatically undermining significant social change efforts. For example, one view might be that the university is just a part of the capitalist system and if you work there they're just co-opting your efforts, or using you.

While there is something to all of this, it can all too easily lead to a purest-of-the-pure position. I prefer not to put such emphasis on the presumed nature of the system one wants to change. I believe this overstates the situation (which is often more fluid than our language suggests) and serves to make it harder for us to expect to succeed, while we congratulate ourselves on our radicality.

We've talked about organizational bases and the impact they have for different forms of social intervention work. What does this mean for working out of the college or university as a base?

THE UNIVERSITY AS A BASE FOR SOCIAL INTERVENTION

How does the university work as a base for social intervention efforts, and how may we try to use it better?

The college or university is an example of what I called case 2 earlier in the chapter, in which we do not ourselves control the university, but in which we work within it as teachers.* (Students working for social change from a university base are in a different situation, more like case 4, since they do not generally get their subsistence from the university. I will therefore discuss students separately from teachers.) Typically, we are not responsible for obtaining the resources to maintain the institution, though as teachers we will be expected to teach our classes, advise our students, and so forth, in such ways as to encourage students to stay and to advise others to come, and we may be expected to submit research grant proposals which provide institutional overhead to our university.

Social Change Within the Classroom

I indicated earlier that the typical problem of case 2 organizational bases is legitimizing social change work. It follows that the easiest way to legitimize social change work from a university base is to have it take place in the classroom and thus be included in one's job description. Therefore, we have to ask "What kind of social change

---

*A more complete discussion would also look at members of university-based institutes, administrators, etc.

work is that?''; ''How does one do that?''; and ''What are the problems with that?''

There are a variety of social change activities you can try to do in the classroom. You can try to give people information they don't have; you can try to give people information that contradicts what they have been told or taught; you can try to teach people to see how things are interrelated and work together as systems. Each of these activities is important and each may to some degree raise consciousness, but each of these tends to be limited in that they tend to be ''knowledge about'' rather than concrete ''knowledge of,'' including knowledge of how to do things. Second, they tend not to touch upon the ways people have been previously harmed and have internalized that harm.

For example, many people have been scarred by their previous educational experiences. Overtly and covertly they were told they were stupid, unable to learn, and shouldn't even try. For instance, almost everybody learns that learning is something you do alone, as an individual, and that it's cheating to work with other people, who are not to be trusted and will steal your work.

It is very hard for people to learn effectively in the classroom when they are carrying around that kind of emotional baggage. Indeed, we could argue that the first social change effort in the classroom must be to try to get that baggage out into the open, to allow people to discover and examine it, ask how and why it got there, and what might be the social functions of its being there. Finally, people must be allowed to decide what they want to try to do with that baggage.

This kind of education as consciousness-raising—in the sense of discovering what has been built into us and why and how we want to relate to it—is a criticial form of classroom social change work, and very difficult to do. It contradicts everything we have learned to expect will happen in the classroom. It is frightening for both students and faculty. Students may not feel they are learning and faculty may not feel they are teaching or ''covering the curriculum.'' It is difficult because much of the baggage is the result of education, and however advanced and self-consciously critical we may feel we are, we may not notice how well we have assimilated the nature of educational institutions and how much we reproduce their features even as we criticize some of them.

Thus, we need to take the time to work through what we are trying to do, that is, what kinds of social change we are trying to accomplish in the classroom. As we do that, we need to recognize that this way of thinking—as if teachers were the active ones and the students merely passive and needy—is inadequate, undialectical, and part of the problem rather than the solution. I talk below about student social change activities. We need to find ways of talking about interaction between teachers and students.

This discussion obviously relates to the issues of what kind of change we want to make and who we want to work with, which appear earlier in this paper. It is implied here that in the classroom we are working with at least potential friends and that the kind of activity we are focusing on is consciousness-raising.

But how do you get your classroom teaching focused on social change? There are two sides to the question: (a) How do you use classes, courses, and programs for social change or get curriculae oriented to social change approved; and (b) how do you get the people you want to work with into your classes, courses and programs as students?

(a) There are relatively few places in the university in which you can get courses and programs explicitly devoted to social change. Offhand, I know only of community organization programs in social work, and community psychology programs, although there may be a few others. Beyond that, we must frame courses and programs in ways which are acceptable to our universities, and which still allow us to do social change work within them. For example, the group I work with does this through programs aimed at training human service workers. I believe there is potential for social change curriculae in psychiatry, psychology, sociology, law, political science, social work, and even perhaps economics—broadly speaking, in the social sciences.

The issue, however, is getting courses and programs approved in which one can do as much social change work as possible. It's easier in a community psychology course, harder in an experimental psychology course; easier in a social movements course, harder in an urban sociology course; easier in a community organizing course, harder in a casework course; easier in a community psychiatry course, harder in a psychopathology course, and so forth. So how do you get courses and programs approved?

The first answer here is to accumulate power. It's easier if you have tenured or senior professors as part of your group, easier if there are more of you, and easier if you control the course, program and degree requirements, easiest if you are a separate program. (Then, however, you would begin to become responsible for maintenance issues like income, numbers of students, retention, and expenses.) If it makes sense in terms of your social change goals to do at least some of your work in the classroom, there are short-, medium-, and long-term organizational strategies you should pursue to increase your numbers of faculty and their rank, and to control course and program requirements and definitions.

(b) In some ways the more difficult question is how to get the "right" people into the classroom as your students. This is more, or less difficult depending on who the people are with whom you want to work. The basic problems tend to be money and time: the people we usually want to work with often need to work full-time and don't have the money for tuition.

Thus, you may find you need to get involved in the logistics of education, that is, when classes are offered, and how. At the School of Human Services, New Hampshire College, for example, we have weekend classes once a month in order to accommodate the people we want to reach, and as a result, have created a class session which lasts 6-7 hours. This has required adaptation on all of our parts. You will also need to get involved in student recruiting, student selection, and financial aid decisions, if you want to get the people you want to work with as your students.

Unfortunately, many of the people you want to work with may not want to earn degrees, or can't afford the money or the time. You are likely, therefore, to end up only working with a fraction of the people you initially wanted to work with. The usual student recruiting processes also separate people from each other: each student applicant is treated as a separate individual. This individualizing and separating is taken for granted in the academic world, but tends to work against organizing efforts, in which we typically want to encourage people to see themselves as part of a group.

You are also unlikely to have a class composed solely of the people you wanted—there are likely to be many students in the classroom who are there for different reasons than the ones you are interested in. Once there, of course, those students have as much right as anyone else to push for what they want out of their education.

This raises an abstract issue about social intervention—the characteristics of the site of social change activity and its inhabitants. In the earlier discussion about social intervention issues, I implicitly assumed that social change work takes place only with the people you choose to work with at that time. If you are trying to work with friends, you work only with friends, and likewise, if you choose to work with enemies you work only with them. It is easy to realize this is not likely to be the case. Although, we may seek to work with friends, there may be enemies present as well (consider F.B.I. infiltration, for example). In the case of the classroom this is particularly sticky because the arrangement that brings us together is that of teacher and student, implying ethical and legal obligations on our part to act as teachers even towards students who act as enemies.

There are some ways of trying to minimize this problem. Sometimes you can try to make it a condition of acceptance into the program that students possess similar values. Social work schools, for example, can legitimately require commitment to social work ethics and values.

Other characteristics of the university as a base for social intervention can determine the kinds of work that can or cannot be done in the classroom. Class work tends to be limited by time constraints, class frequencies are determined by extrinsic schedules, and neither of these may correspond to the time needs of the social change effort itself. There are also process issues: specifically what social change processes are possible in the classroom? Ethical concerns about what is allowable in the classroom are also relevant. (This gets mixed up with grading issues, but also has to do with privacy, and legitimacy issues which arise from the professional limits that should be placed on teachers' power.) Further, the norms and standards of certain groups and social classes shape what is allowed in the classroom, as seen by the notions that one can teach facts but not values, and that the classroom is and should be apolitical. Related are issues about overt accreditation standards and the sometimes covert ways they may be applied. Finally, there is the degree to which the educational process in the classroom gets shaped by the encompassing educational program in which it occurs, which may well have aims different from social change.

Social Change Outside the Classroom

In addition to, or instead of attempting social change within the classroom, research efforts are another set of social change activities which faculty members can undertake within the normal boundaries of their job, since in most universities they are required to conduct and publish research to keep their jobs. The difficulties with these activities concern:

(a) How to frame social change work in research terms, and
(b) how to get that research accepted and valued as academically respectable and appropriate research.

Since research is usually neither created nor controlled by people with an explicit social change focus, we have to deal with the ways in which research is usually defined and evaluated by the larger institution. There are some real difficulties here, which I will only sketch out so as not to overstretch the boundaries of this chapter. These difficulties have to do with expectations about what good research looks like, and underlying that, expectations of what knowledge is, and what is appropriate knowledge.

I believe most of the social sciences work from a conception of knowledge which focuses on what *is*, on defining and understanding the essential nature of individuals, groups, organizations and institutions, and on finding their "causes." Typical questions are: "What *is* the family?"; "How many families of what kinds are there?"; "What are the causes of this many families of this (these) kind(s)?" Social scientists do *not* tend to ask process questions such as "How does this family work?" 'What are the people in this family trying to do with it, and what happens when they do those things?"

Put more abstractly, the favored approach tends to be static and essentialist; instead of seeking to understand processes of change, it focuses on what is the essential nature and cause of static structures. If you start from this kind of question about essences, then the major questions you will ask related to change will be of the following forms: (a) How does this essence come into existence?; (b) How does this essence go out of existence?; (c) What factors cause this essence to come into existence?; (d) What factors cause the maintenance or decline of this essence?

I imagine this sounds like you have wandered into a philosophy course and you may be wondering what this has to do with anything specific. Let's take as an example the education of minority children, which appeared to have been dealt with in the famous and extensive Coleman-Campbell study from the mid-1960s of the determinants of educational success and failure of public school students (Coleman & Campbell, 1966). However, the first thing Coleman and Campbell did was to factor out the effects of parents' social class by using multivariate procedures, predicting performance on the basis of class variables, and then calculating the residuals from those predictions. Thus, Coleman and Campbell did not look at the nature of the educational institutions until *after* they had factored out the results of social class. As a result, there is no way, methodologically, they could investigate how schools deal with children of different class backgrounds (Ryan, 1971, 44-54). Rather than look at processes of interaction between schools and teachers and students of different social classes and races, they simply asserted that the social class of parents determines school performance. In policy terms, of course, this shifted the discussion away from what schools do, what they should be doing, and how to change them, and encouraged cynicism and apathy by implying that schools don't matter because it is the parents' social class that determines educational performance.

For the social interventionist, the critical issue is what the processes of interaction are between students and schools, such that some children do well and others do poorly, as dealt with, for example, in Ray C. Rist's careful observational study, *The Urban School: A Factory for Failure* (1973). As social change agents, the knowledge we want to gain is process-oriented, rather than essentialist, since we are interested in *how* change happens and how to help bring about the kinds of changes we want. We are less interested in knowing about the effects, or end product than we are in how the end state is brought about—in evaluation, this is analogous to the difference between summative and formative research.

Yet this kind of knowledge is hard for many university researchers to understand and value. Furthermore, university researchers tend to value research which is based on theory and which is experimental or quasi-experimental in procedure. But in many cases we know so little about change processes that it is difficult to frame studies theoretically and it is inappropriate to adopt experimental or quasi-experimental procedures. Rather, what we need is solid, detailed description of the processes of real social change, to give us more to look at and think about. Such descriptive work is often not valued. In the extreme, it may be written off by the university as "journalism"—never mind that journalistic accounts are sometimes far more revealing, intelligent and significant than some social-science accounts.

Therefore, if you want to use your position as a researcher in the university to do social change work in which the goal is increasing relevant knowledge about social change, you are likely to have to put in a lot of time and energy into legitimizing your work, which may well include having to write and publicize methodological critiques which try to legitimize the kind of work you want to do and which you think is useful and necessary.

Of course, there are other ways of using the research part of one's job, especially when the focus is not on doing new research for publication but on applied research as community service. Here there are creative things one can do to work with community people on social change projects, as may be evidenced by the work of Julian Rappaport and his colleagues and the University of Kansas Community Technology Project (Fawcett *et al.*, 1984).

A third way of using a university teaching position for social change is in relation to student projects and to field placements. These have the great potential advantage that they are outside the classroom, out in the community. They may allow the faculty member to get out into the community, to help arrange, provide liaison to, and supervise these projects and placements. They certainly allow and legitimize students being out in the community. Bennett and Hallman's chapter in this volume demonstrates graphically how effective projects and placements can be as social change efforts.

The difficulties of using field placements for social change include trying to juggle the logistics of the work of teacher and student, both on campus and in the community, as well as program and university expectations which push the projects and placements in different directions than social change. For example, many social work field placements provide agencies with students who wish to learn what workers do in their positions, rather than working to change those. Publicity may also be generated by social change work, which the university and the program view as negative and unwelcome.

There are other possibilities for university-based faculty working on social change, each of which are limited by the time constraints of one's job—working informally with students outside of the classroom, working with other members of the university outside of the classroom such as in unions, and social change efforts outside of the university. These three kinds of activities usually must be squeezed into one's schedule, since they are not usually official parts of one's work.

In short, there are a variety of ways in which faculty members can do social change work, some of which can be part of one's official work, and some of which are usually outside of it. These often tend to require legitimation from the institution, and are often enhanced if they are part of special programs which are oriented toward social change. To achieve these, time and energy are required—success is far more likely if a variety of people co-operate to achieve them. Thus, social interventionist efforts using the university base are much more likely to be continuous and successful if they are based on the co-operative efforts of a variety of people over a relatively long period of time.

However, there is much in the recruitment and socialization of faculty members, and in the nature of faculty work, which militates against such cooperation. Faculty generally learn to work alone, and to compete with each other. Thus, the possibilities inherent *in the setting* conflict with the *modes of acting* which people are likely to do in that setting. In fact, the very form of the question I have been working with—the use of the university as a base by individual social change agents—is an individualistic form of analysis, which places individual social interventionists in a setting we do not control.

One way to try to deal with this problem is to try to develop a long-term co-operative effort among a variety of people, which aims both at getting more control over the specific work situation and directing it more towards social change efforts, and at dealing differently with a setting under external control and individual activity. The people I work with, the School of Human Services at New Hampshire College exemplify one such effort. (See chapter by David Osher and Ira Goldenberg in this volume.) Such efforts, of course, have strengths and weaknesses of their own.

Student's Involvement in Social Change

Let me now discuss the use of the university as a base for social change by students. For students, the university is usually a voluntary organization in the sense that it does not provide their subsistence, yet students pay tuition to it and expect to get an education and a degree in return. If that degree is seen as a step in a career ladder, then participating in the educational program may be compared to working, even if one is not being paid for the work. As an organizational base for social change, the university, from a student's point of view, is a mixed form. The mixture seems to depend on two things—the student's other responsibilities and social embeddedness, which often depend on the age of the student, and whether or not the educational program is an undergraduate or a graduate program. I would therefore like to differentiate among younger students, graduates, and older students—not because their social change efforts are mutually exclusive, but because the variables of age and program level can influence the type of social change work they choose and their participation in it.

Younger students. Social change work done by young students seems to take several forms. The first is involvement outside the university on issues in the larger world, for which university studies may provide a wider perspective, a feeling of protection (by their college or university location), and a tradition of student activism. Examples abound, of which black student sit-ins in 1960 and student anti-war efforts throughout the 1960s may be the best known.

A second form of social change efforts by younger students are those which are institutionally sponsored (at least by a part of the institution) and represent an activity which goes beyond the time-span of the individual student's membership at that institution. These efforts are often connected with religious or charitable groups within the university. In my own personal history, I became aware of this possibility by considering the nature of Phillips Brooks House at Harvard University, an organization which places students in community organizations and institutions.

Third, there are social change efforts which arise out of the classroom and which are in part faculty-induced. (There are other faculty-induced efforts as well: I witnessed efforts in the 1960s to induce students to protest the war, in which the efforts took place at speeches and meetings outside of the classroom.) Finally, there are social change efforts which are focused on the setting itself: efforts, for example, to deal with rape and sexual harassment on campus, efforts to deal with racism on campus, etc.

An important kind of student social change effort focused on the setting can be students' effects on their faculty and administrators. In overt and subtle ways, students may "radicalize" their teachers and administrators, though they may also frighten them into moving to the right. Sometimes this effect can be achieved as simply as by changing the role of the class as audience, or by changing the proportions of that audience. If you have been teaching in an all- or predominantly-male setting, introducing significant proportions of women may make you conscious of the ways you have taken on the sexism of the setting. Similarly, the racial composition of the classroom can make an enormous difference, as can the presence of significant numbers of gay people, older adults, poor people, and people from other countries. Often, however, this change is neither easy nor simple.

To a degree, young college students are open to the possibility of engaging in social change efforts not only because of the idealism of youth, but because they are often not yet tightly embedded in the adult world of connections, obligations, relationships and controls. In addition, young people in college, especially young people in colleges with high prestige, define themselves as both competent and responsible, which, coupled with the sense of not being tightly tied into the adult world, may make them more willing to act.

The ebb and flow of studies plays a significant role in the social change activities of students, particularly those efforts which are not classroom-based. To the degree that students work primarily by cramming at mid-term and finals times, to that degree they are more free and more available at other times, for other activities, including the possibility of social change activities.

In my experience, this means that student social change efforts—especially by undergraduates—tend to be intermittent and episodic. They can be extremely intense for a relatively short period (a month to six weeks) and then tail off for a time. I have come to think of student participation as wavelike, although I am not at all sure that this characteristic of participation is limited to students.

Finally, student social change efforts are bounded roughly by the time period of the student's presence in college, unless specific arrangements with the organization or institution are made to mediate the transition beyond the college and to maintain participation during that transition. Thus, student social change efforts will be more effective on projects which are more short-term than long-term.

Graduate students. Very generally, graduate students tend to form more cohesive groups than do undergraduates, because their work is focused in one department, rather than being spread across an entire collegiate curriculum. Graduate students tend to work together, socialize together, to some extent even live together more than undergraduates do. This means that graduate students, if they become involved in social change work, may be more cohesively and continously organized than undergraduates. It is this, I believe, as well as higher organizational rank, which explains the central role of graduate students in social change efforts such as the Berkeley Student Revolt of the 1960s.

Graduate students may also play a central role by virtue of being close to activist faculty, on the one hand, and activist undergraduates on the other. This depends, however, on the degree to which they are economically able to be present on campus most of the time. When I was a graduate student in the early 1960s, I (and most of my fellow students) received a tuition scholarship and only had to work very part time to earn enough to live on. As scholarships, fellowships and grants decline, and tuition charges rise, this may be less possible. I do not know whether many graduate students are still able to "hang out" as we were able to 25 years ago.

Another strong influence on graduate students is the relationship to faculty members. Some schools and some departments create a situation in which graduate students focus very much on a single professor, working for that person on a grant and with that person on a project. In such circumstances, those students tend to socialize only or primarily with the other students working with the same professor. Other graduate departments have much more distanced faculty-student relationships, in which students become much more dependant on each other to survive and prosper as students. My hypothesis would be that activist professors have more influence on their graduate students in the first circumstance, but so would non-activist faculty influence *their* graduate students away from social change activities. However, my hypothesis is also that graduate students as a larger group are more likely to engage in concerted activities in the second circumstance.

Graduate students, are more likely to engage in social change activities which they see as related to their discipline or to the university setting, particularly if they work for the university as well (as graduate assistants, for example). Thus, issues of on-campus military and military-related recruiting, university involvement in defense research, as well as sexism and racism, have been particularly likely to draw interest and involvement from young graduate students.

So far I have been talking about younger students, in which not only their age but their structural lack of assimilation into adult structures are characteristic. What about older students?

Older students. Older students, first of all, are more likely to be focused on their studies and to be more highly motivated than are younger students. They have not simply gone on in school, but have been elsewhere in the world, usually working and raising children. When they return to school, it is usually a struggle because of all the other things going on in their lives, so they are likely to focus on their studies and wish to get done as quickly as possible.

They are also likely to be ambivalent and mistrustful of schools—often they have had earlier educational experiences in which they felt put down, or were not encouraged to feel they were good at school. But since then they may have experienced their own competence in the adult worlds of work and home, and may therefore demand that the educational institution treat them as competent adults.

Social change activities by older students, therefore, are likely to arise either directly out of their studies (to the degree to which their studies encourage such activities) or out of experiences with the institution, in which students feel they need to work to change the educational institution itself.

CONCLUSION: USING THE OPPORTUNITIES WHILE RESISTING THE BLANDISHMENTS

So far, I have discussed the university as an organizational base from the point of view of the social interventionist, its opportunities and constraints. The university, however, is not a passive tool of social interventionists' actions. As an active organization of activities, as a set of rewards and punishments and as a setting for careers, the university also tends to shape how people who work within it (or seek to) see themselves and therefore think and act.

This is particularly obvious with regard to faculty members who have a long-term involvement with colleges and universities, stretching back to their college and graduate school experiences as well as forward to their future career contingencies. Unless one is very careful or very lucky, or both, the university may very well socialize you out of your intention to function as a social interventionist. I remember a fellow who entered graduate school with me, who came with a reputation as a "heavy" activist, having been a student leader at Berkeley. Within a year he was asking me how I could justify being involved in political activities, rather than being engaged in study and research. And while I do not know how he saw the changes he was going through, he ended up working for the Rand Corporation making a reputation testifying against busing as a means of achieving school integration.

How does this kind of thing happen? I would sketch the process as follows: graduate school socializes people into thinking of themselves as professional members of an academic discipline, and as professional researchers. Research and related activities become the primary ways of acting as a professional. This is reinforced by the process of writing the Ph.D. dissertation. As a junior faculty member, one's time tends to be taken up with working on classes and publishing research to get tenure. If one succeeds in getting tenure, one has usually internalized the academic discipline's definitions of what is knowledge, what are appropriate ways of defining problems, and what is appropriate research. In addition, one's departmental colleagues tend to become one's primary local reference group, as one's disciplinary colleagues tend to become one's primary larger reference group. As a result, actions and ambitions tend to be defined in departmental and disciplinary terms. The status of one's university also becomes important to people: one's career tends to become defined in terms of attaining and maintaining a high-level position in a high-status university. Finally, high-status universities tend to have high-status contacts in the outside world, and if one plays one's cards right, one will be able to become a part of that network. This may bring consulting contracts, board memberships, government projects, testifying before legislative committees, and sometimes even more inside membership in the networks of decision-makers.

Thus, while the university may offer a variety of opportunities for social interventionist work, it is often the case that these opportunities do not get well used, because potential social interventionists get deflected along the way. The university is a very powerful socializing and rewarding and punishing mechanism, which usually is not particularly supportive of social interventionist efforts.

Our ability to use the possibilities of the university as an organizational base for social change depends largely, therefore, on our ability to resist the seductions, to tolerate or evade the punishments (or both), and still put out the constructive energy needed to realize the opportunities. If we organize and help each other, and if we assist and pass on our knowledge to students and younger faculty, we may increase our ability to use the university as an organizational base for social intervention.

REFERENCES

Alinsky, S. D. (1970). *John L. Lewis*. New York: Vintage Books (originally 1949).

Clark, K. B. (1953). Desegregation: An appraisal of the evidence. *Journal of Social Issues, IX*, 4, 2-76.

Coleman, J. S., *et al.* (1966). *Equality of educational opportunity*. Washington, D.C.: U.S. Government Printing Office.

Fawcett, S. B., *et al.* (1984). Creating and using social technologies for community empowerment. In J. Rappaport, C. Swift & R. Hess (Eds.), *Studies in empowerment*. New York: Haworth Press, 145-171.

Ferree, M. M. & Hess, B. B. (1985). *Controversy and coalition: The new feminist movement*. Boston: Twayne Publishers.

Festinger, L. (1957). *A theory of cognitive dissonance*. Stanford: Stanford University Press.

Freeman, J. (1975). *The politics of women's liberation*. New York: David McKay.

Freire, P. (1973). Education as the practice of freedom. In *Education for critical consciousness* (pp. 1-84). New York: Seabury Press.

Goldenberg, I. (1978). *Oppression and social intervention*. Chicago: Nelson-Hall.

Matusow, A. J. (1984). *The unraveling of America*. New York: Harper and Row.

Myrdal, G. (1944). *An American dilemma*. New York: Harper and Brothers.

Rist, R. C. (1973). *The urban school*. Cambridge, MA: MIT Press.

Ryan, W. (1971). *Blaming the victim*. New York: Pantheon Books/Vintage Books.

Sarason, S. (1972). *The creation of settings and the future societies*. San Francisco: Jossey-Bass.

David Osher
and
Ira Goldenberg

3

THE SCHOOL OF HUMAN SERVICES: A CASE STUDY IN SOCIAL INTERVENTION AND THE CREATION OF ALTERNATIVE SETTINGS

The story of the creation of the School of Human Services is a tale of two colleges and two eras and, as is so often the case in attempts at social intervention, it is a story whose ending is far from being known. It is also a story of ongoing struggle and continuing tension, a story that cannot be fully appreciated unless one begins to understand the broader socio-political context within which change occurs and the internal dynamics that invariably affect the process of change itself. The purpose of this chapter is to attempt a descriptive analysis of both these phenomena, on the assumption that unless and until social interventionists begin to understand both the macro and micro levels of the change process, victories will have no form and defeats will have no meaning.

FRANCONIA: AN EXPERIMENT IN A NEW TIME

Like so many of the schools and colleges that came into being during the latest upsurge of the experimental education movement, Franconia College was born at a time of widespread and righteous questioning of the goals, curriculum and processes of higher education in the United States. It was also a time when "easy money," a sense of political legitimacy, and a growing disaffection with existing models of education accompanied the principled criticism of most social institutions. And the criticisms of higher education were more than a little cogent: colleges had indeed become little more than factories for processing human beings. Curriculae were more often than not "irrelevant" to the perceived needs and interests of students and students had very little to say about the course of their own development and education. Faculty were judged, not on the basis of their effectiveness and creativity as teachers, but according to criteria that placed a heavy premium on publications, the ability to attract research monies and a willingness to play the highly politicized and demeaning "tenure game." The atmosphere of most colleges and universities had become a mosaic in which the exercise of power and unbridled competition betrayed any possible sense of "community." Moreover, educational institutions had purposely separated themselves from the broader social, political and economic context of which they were nominally a part.

Franconia College's response to this catalogue of horrors was both predictable and imperfect, and served to highlight many of the contradictions it would one day be forced to confront. On the "predictable" side of the ledger was the school itself. It was a small school in keeping with the prevailing motif that "small is beautiful." It was an informal school where first names and a tolerance for diverse lifestyles underscored an abiding commitment to individuality. It was a school where the humanities and the creative and performing arts—"the windows to the soul"—assumed centre stage, no longer muted or condemned to second-class citizenship by the onslaught of an unchecked science and questionable technology. It was a school committed to community, a place in which "town meetings," consensus and participatory democracy would replace top-down, authoritarian and manipulative decision-making as the principal governance structure. And it was a school whose rhetoric spoke to the core yearnings of its alienated vanguard for a world in which freedom, justice, beauty and meaning would one day assert dominion over the forces of greed, bigotry and oppression.

But it was also an "imperfect" school, whose people and principles bore the unmistakable scars of an inability to transcend or fully confront the very society found so wanting. Widespread and earnest political discussions were only rarely translated into collective action. Each life was its own "political statement," and the commitment to "doing your own thing" (so long as it didn't hurt anyone or impinge on anyone else's freedom) resulted in a brand of individualism that was neither profoundly different from nor fundamentally antagonistic to the elitist mentality of the much-reviled "traditional" academic institutions. It was also a setting whose internal divisions resulted from the multiple definitions of reality and the varying personal motives that drew people to its midsts.

For many of its faculty, Franconia was a refuge, a place to be creative and develop positive relationships with students without the constrictions of traditional academic modes—a Black Mountain College (Duberman, 1972). For others, the setting represented an opportunity to do serious work and interdisciplinary exploration in a reasonably supportive and tolerant atmosphere (a somewhat avant-garde Oxford). And for some, Franconia provided the opportunity to translate the rhetoric of community into programs and policies that spoke directly to the social, economic and political aspirations of the disenfranchised—a Highlander School (Adams, 1975). This latter group, distinctly in the minority in 1975, would eventually come to create the School of Human Services.

Other problems, some of a long-term nature, served to debilitate and further weaken Franconia, problems which in their own ways only highlighted the setting's internal dilemmas. Lacking an endowment, bankrupted in 1968, and refinanced in 1974, Franconia did not have the financial resources to withstand the enrollment decline of the post-Vietnam years. Its "traditional" student body of relatively wealthy, white, alienated post-adolescents and somewhat older working-class students was shrinking. Furthermore, Franconia was politically and educationally controversial and lacked the establishment support needed to withstand the new onslaught of educational reaction which Ira Shor describes in *Culture Was* (Shor, 1986). A 10-day attack by a Governor and a statewide newspaper, for example, had led to the loss of a $500,000 grant to share resources with a local school system.

Another problem was that the local town and its people, never fully involved in or supportive of Franconia, tolerated its existence with the same tensions that define most "Town-Gown" relationships. With some very important exceptions, Franconia College was "that place up on the hill" populated by some strange-looking people, mostly "outsiders," who had neither been born nor raised in the North Country, nor would ever really be accepted as part of its culture, traditions and values. The town's rock-ribbed conservatism was no friend of Franconia, fueled as it had been by years of isolation, economic stagnation and the muted anger that so often seethes within the heart of many overly-romanticized but marginal rural communities. Neither was the State of New Hampshire, whose motto, "Live Free Or Die," served to mask and elevate an institutionalized and uncaring Social Darwinism to the level of human virtue.

Finally, there was Franconia's Board of Trustees itself, a group that provided Franconia and its surrounding community with a

AUGUSTANA UNIVERSITY COLLEGE
LIBRARY

glimpse of "another world." Wealthy and educated, they were a cross-section of the bankers, landowners, insurance interests and aging aristocracy who ruled the North Country. For all its peculiarities, youthful foolishness and annoying excesses, to them Franconia was a sometimes tolerable problem-child—so long as it remained economically viable and did not, as it had done once before in 1967-1968, become too politically controversial. Franconia was a local creation (although not in its radical form) which still brought "culture" to the North Country. And as alien as it had become to some, it contributed to the local economy.

In summary, Franconia College in the Summer of 1975 was a uniquely innovative, but troubled setting. The previous year or two had seen the return of hard times: a revolt against one President had empowered a faculty and student body and alienated the Board at a time when diminishing resources and deep-seated philosophical differences among faculty and staff and students—bridgeable in good times—could explode to produce a community divided along political, professional, educational and personal lines. The incoming President faced declining enrollments, political controversy, larger-than-projected deficits, reduced borrowing ability, increasing costs and growing Board unrest, and all of these problems were amplified by an active "rumor mill" that pervaded every nook and cranny of the institution. Franconia's long-term financial and political problems and ever-competing visions of itself were now placed in bold relief: Franconia confronted a financial crisis of catastrophic magnitude. Sooner or later, choices would have to be made—and some of them would be very painful.

THE PROBLEM: EDUCATION IN SOCIETY

Historically, the practice of progressive social intervention has always oriented itself toward dealing with the consequences of an oppressive system in one of two ways—by curbing its most flagrant excesses or by broadening its responsiveness. The development and implementation of the Human Services Program at Franconia College was an attempt to create an alternative setting capable of dealing with both of those sets of activities. Specifically, the Program was designed to challenge and redress the exclusion of disenfranchised groups such as para-professional human service workers from higher education in America.

Elitism and Exclusion

As one of society's primary formal institutions, the role of the educational system has always been three-fold: to socialize people into a society's existing value system; to control the passage of people into society; and to prepare people to function at different levels in the economy. It exercises its leverage through the legitimizing and credentialing functions it performs (Collins, 1979).

Like the other socializing and legitimizing institutions in our culture, the educational system does not operate in a vacuum. Its validity, indeed its very existence, depends on the degree to which it mirrors and perpetuates—by what it includes and excludes in its curriculum, pedagogy, and learning environment—the values (and historical biases) that lie at the foundation of the society it represents. If, as is the case in the United States, the cultural imperative revolves around the acquisition of goods and power within a white male "Anglo-conforming" context (Gordon, 1978), then the educational system itself must both reflect and support this view of the world.

To retain its validity and to fulfill its destiny, the educational establishment must function as the handmaiden of the prevailing social ethos. And if the consequences of history, intent and chance have combined to produce a society whose oppressive fabric depends upon the systematic exclusion (or containment) of whole groups of people on the basis of class, race and sex, then the responsibility for both perpetuating and masking this reality falls upon society's formal social institutions, including its educational system. Thus, it should come as no surprise to find that in each formal social institution whose functions directly influence the passage of people through "the system," we find the same groups detoured from full participation in the existential struggle. Poor people, people of colour and women consistently emerge as the victims of whatever policies and practices dominate the day-to-day decisions of our major social institutions, especially the educational system. The pattern is simple, complete and so consistent as to defy any interpretations predicated on the acceptance of chance as the appropriate explanatory principle. If the entire educational system is suspect, its effects on the poor, minorities and women have been particularly devastating.

Regardless of its genesis or the varying dynamics that guide it, the result of this state of affairs is the exclusion of vast numbers of people from the economic and intellectual possibilities of higher education and their subsequent relegation to positions of continuing personal, social and political powerlessness. In a credentials-conscious society, there is no better tool with which to perpetuate the servitude of the poor, minorities and women than to deny them access to a system historically mandated with tasks of defining and providing (or withholding) professional legitimation. Nowhere has this been more true than in the field of human services.

Human Services and the Para-Professional

The field of human services was born during the now overly-romanticized and overly-maligned days of the 1960s. The personnel needs posed by both the U.S. War on Poverty and the community mental health movement brought a new service provider into fields previously only populated and completely dominated by professionals. The para-professional entered the field of Human Services not because of any deeply felt need to open the field to newcomers. Nothing could be further from the truth. They were recruited because of two basic realities: the first was that existing modalities of treatment (i.e., psychotherapy) proved almost totally ineffective in meeting the needs of poor people. The second reality was that mental health professionals, even in the face of mounting evidence documenting the severe limitations of traditional theory and practice, were either unable or unwilling to abandon their sacred cows and explore alternative ways of dealing with a society structured so as to continually produce untold numbers of victims. And there were literally thousands and thousands of people to "treat." Enter the non- or para-professional.

The emergence of the para-professional as a soldier in the War on Poverty or as a neighbourhood-based resource person in community mental health centres, welfare offices, schools and manpower programs was greeted with all the enthusiasm usually reserved for those prepared to do the work others will not or cannot do. Lauded for their "indigenousness" and praised for their energy, commitment and motivation, para-professionals entered the breach and proceeded to demonstrate their competence as counselors, community organizers, administrators, teachers and community leaders. The fact that many of them came from the same neighbourhoods as their clients, had usually experienced firsthand the debilitating and dehumanizing consequences of poverty, racism and sexism, and were sometimes loathe to perpetuate a "blaming the victim" mentality created a host of interesting and often unanticipated situations. Here were people initially hired to serve in the middleground between the mental health establishment and the local populace who sometimes questioned both the assumptions and purposes of their work. Expected to ensure domestic tranquility and defuse community unrest, they often joined with their clients to confront some of the very institutions whose policies and practices created the backdrop for unabated suffering. But whether they engaged in social activism or restricted themselves to providing sensitive and responsive service, para-professionals established themselves as competent human service workers.

By the mid-1970s, despite their demonstrated competence and 10-year record of accomplishments, para-professionals not only remained mired, but found themselves increasingly vulnerable in the no-man's land maintained for expendables. Low paid, often powerless to effect policy in their own agencies, and increasingly under the continual supervision of professionals, human service workers were caught in the grip of their "non-career" status. Constantly reminded that they were non-professionals and held no college degrees, human service workers remained vulnerable to the ups and downs of public funding and private philanthropy. Always the first ones fired during times of retrenchment and the last ones hired during times of plenty, para-professionals could not win for losing. The fact that most of them came from lower-class backgrounds and were members of minority groups or were women, only underscored the oppression. Denied by economic circumstance, colour or sex the opportunity to attend college at the usual time of life, human service workers could now be punished and kept in their place by a convenient reliance on the very standards they were previously prevented from attaining. The classic Catch-22 situation worked to perfection. Should one ever want an impressive example of the manner in which an exclusionary society operated, one need look no further than the life and times of the para-professional.

THE HUMAN SERVICE PROGRAM

Most programs that emerge from a social interventionist perspective have no clearly identifiable birthday. Neither is their parentage all that clear. Such was certainly the case with respect to the Human Service Program.

The handful of Franconia College faculty and administrators who developed the Human Service Program were initially united more by a shared ideology and analysis of society than by any long history of having worked together as a group. Some were already at Franconia in 1975 and had been involved in the experiments and struggles that had dominated the setting's internal life for several years. Others had arrived with the new administration. Some had extensive experience in the War on Poverty and the community mental health movement and had worked for many years with para-professionals. Others were veterans of the Civil Rights struggle and the anti-war movement. They were sociologists, psychologists, historians and educators by training. They were socialists, activists and radicals by inclination.

Much is made of the soul-searching agony that surrounds and accompanies the creative process. Such was not the case in the initial conceptualization and development of the Human Service Program. Rather, given a shared analysis of the function and contradictions of higher education in the United States and given some shared experience at Franconia, the task of designing a new program that would challenge conventional education "wisdom" was more of an exercise in joy than a laborious process of self-discovery.

Goals and Ideology

The goals and ideology of the Program were clear:

* To provide educational access, professional legitimation and quality education to those previously excluded from higher learning and to do so in a way which minimized the domesticating and "cooling out" functions of post-secondary education (Freire, 1986; Clark, 1960; Shor, 1980);
* To develop a program that was committed to the concept of social change and that would challenge the "blaming the victim" orientation that dominated most educational and professional programs in the field of human service; and
* To enable faculty and students, as colleagues, to collectively examine shared issues of oppression and actively engage themselves in efforts to combat its debilitating impact on people and communitites.

The program's design was premised on a number of critical assumptions:

• That education is a political process;
• That adults learn effectively when they struggle with material independent of faculty;
• That students learn from each other and that learning takes place both in and out of the classroom;
• That students learn best when their teachers share experience with them, respect them, and are able to connect materials—no matter how abstract—to peoples' past, present, and future.

Structure and Curriculum

Given its conceptual framework, it was not too difficult to design a structure that would support the Human Service Program's goals and objectives. In terms of curriculum, it meant developing opportunities for collective analysis, skill enhancement and the application of knowledge to problems that were both real and of ongoing community concern. Thus was born the Core Curriculum, the Elective Curriculum and the Thesis (later changed to the Project in Community Development and Change in order to underscore the importance of collective as opposed to individual empowerment). The Core Curriculum was intended as a medium for students and faculty, independent of agency affiliation, to examine the issues and contradictions that define the field of human services. Organized in terms of certain recurring themes (e.g., professionalism; the family and community; class, race and sex; social control; and social change), the Core Curriculum sought to focus attention on the common threads and experiences that define an oppressive social structure. The Elective Curriculum, composed of a host of specific courses in the areas of counselling, community organizing, administration, advocacy and research, was designed to enable students to pursue and become more skilled in the variety of areas that comprise the range of human service and community action activities. The Thesis was reserved for the application of knowledge to problems of direct community import, and institutionalized the Program's commitment to the sharing of knowledge and the translation of theory into action.

With respect to the self-imposed mandate to provide access and legitimation to those previously either discouraged or excluded from higher education, the Human Service Program made four crucial fiscal and structural decisions. First, the Program was designed in such a manner as to reduce or eliminate the financial burden of participation. This was done by setting its tuition at a level equal to the maximum existing Basic Educational Opportunity Grant (BEOG) available to low-income students. Since it was assumed that most of its potential students would be human service workers occupying positions at the lowest end of the pay scale, this policy would either eliminate or substantially reduce the ability to pay as a barrier to college attendance. In addition, "paper scholarships" and liberal tuition payment plans were implemented to further ease the financial drain on a student's resources. The operating fiscal theory was a simple one: the Program would seek solvency through volume rather than individual cost.

Second, the Program was structured and organized so that

students attended classes two full, 8-hour days a month—one weekend day on campus, and one weekday in their communities. One full, 8-hour day of classes each month for each of the Core and Elective courses. The Thesis portion of the required curriculum could be done as an Independent Project under faculty supervision. Since it was anticipated that most of its students would be married or have significant family responsibilities, the notion of adopting the traditional 2 or 3 evening-per-week, per-course continuing or adult education model was rejected. Given the distance students would be traveling, coupled with the emotional and physical drain of full-time human service work, the evening school model was both inappropriate and potentially destructive. Rather than increase the separation of students from their families, the Program's classroom structure was organized to minimize such separation and students were encouraged to bring their partners and children with them to the College.

Third, the Program took very seriously the notion that the knowledge derived from full-time experience in the field was, or should be, translatable into college credit and advanced academic standing. Credit for life experience and CLEP tests (i.e., standardized exams to evaluate a student's ability to demonstrate knowledge and competence in specified areas related to individual college courses) were already a fixed part of the adult education landscape. What the Human Service Program would do was broaden that landscape in ways that spoke to the critical nature of relevant experience as a powerful aspect of the educational process and, thereby decrease the exclusionary character of college education. Thus, it would now become possible to have at least two years' advanced standings at an accredited, undergraduate degree-granting Program, even if one had never attended college in the past. A process was developed that enabled people to document the nature and implications of their work in a manner that demonstrated both an understanding of the meaning of those experiences and a grasp of the contradictions and issues they posed.

Finally, the Program placed heavy emphasis on the fact that its students were not just older "traditional" students: they were people who would enter Franconia College with very different needs and often conflicting motives—and the Program would have to deal with those realities. Some would enter accompanied by the "baggage" of having been told or made to feel that they were incapable of handling college-level work; for them the Program had to provide the support needed to overcome such feelings. Others would be attracted to the Program because it appeared to be a quick, easy and relatively inexpensive way of getting the kind of academic "union card" that could be translated into personal job security and economic mobility, or both; for them the Program had to address the contradictions of education as a vehicle to individual advancement as opposed to group empowerment. And still others would be drawn to the Program because of its rhetoric concerning social change and the need to alter the oppressive character of society; for them the Program would have to remain true to itself and the meaning of its own existence.

Of final importance in the elaboration of the Human Service Program was the commitment to use the Program and its education base as a vehicle for addressing broader issues of oppression, empowerment and social change. Of primary importance here was the history of many so-called innovative programs, a history which all too often indicated the tendency of programs to become complacent, to revert back to elitist modes of thinking and acting, to resurrect minimalist expectations of themselves and traditional expectations of faculties, and to slowly but surely become little more than mirror images of the programs and settings once deemed so fraudulent. To guard against this ever-present potential for self-destruction (as well as because no real resources were available) the Program was structured in a manner consistent with the notion of an underpopulated behaviour setting (Barker, 1960): faculty and administrators were defined as "workers" and expected, in addition to teaching, to assume responsibility for marketing the Program, recruiting students, providing students with the academic and personal support needed to succeed, engaging in relevant community projects, handling specific administrative tasks and developing new programatic resources. While perhaps not totally realistic, the working assumption was a simple one: a sense of "community" could not be achieved through simplistic rhetoric and the posturing that passes itself off as political ideology—it requires hard work and both the willingness to reject traditional role definitions based on a conception of academicians as a privileged class and the ability to replace these definitions with an ethic more consistent with the concept and process of struggle.

THE PROCESS

It would not be true to assume that the agenda of Franconia College's new President in 1975, the people he brought with him, or the faculty and administrators already at the College centred around the desire to create a separate School of Human Services or to transform the liberal arts college into a School of Human Services. The opposite is closer to being correct: the Human Service Program came into being as part of the process to either save Franconia or extend its life. It was initially hoped that the new revenue it might generate would ease Franconia's financial problems. Only in 1978, when it became clear that Franconia was beyond the pale and that its demise would signal the end of the fledgling Program, were efforts undertaken to salvage the Human Service Program from the abyss that would finally claim Franconia College.

Although the Human Service Program was conceptualized during the 1975-76 academic year, most of the energy that year was devoted to saving Franconia College by reducing expenses, fundraising, broadening the base of the Board of Trustees, grantsmanship, attempts to resolve internal divisions, and efforts aimed at convincing the community as a whole that Franconia's financial crisis was not only real but required drastic action. A program of voluntary salary cuts and labour performed, again on a voluntary basis, by Franconia's faculty, students and staff failed to significantly reduce the deficit or its attendant cash flow problems. Although Franconia's budget and budget processes were opened up to the community, many continued to believe that the crisis was a manufactured one—and when the reality of the situation finally sank in, the community again fell prey to the divisiveness that had marked the preceding years. The creative and performing arts faculty, who always defined Franconia College as an arts centre, called for reductions in the social sciences and education. The social science and education faculty, weary of the demands of the setting's "artistes," called for reductions in the arts curriculum and faculty. Most saw "fat" in the administration and felt righteous in their indignation that administrators (whose entire reason for being, presumably, was to raise money for the faculty and its programs) had failed Franconia through incompetence or more likely, nefarious intent. And the Board of Trustees, finally aware of the severity of the situation and the possibility of impending disaster, began distancing itself from Franconia while at the same time calling upon the administration to provide "forceful leadership" and make the "hard decisions." It was in the context of this maelstrom of competing emotions that the Human Service Program was implemented in 1976.

Implementation: 1976-1977

All attempts to develop new or alternative programs in education institutions require legitimation both from the setting itself and from those who hold the fiduciary responsibility for its welfare, its Board of Trustees. Normally, this legitimation process is a long and arduous affair. Faculty usually display a curious intellectual preciousness when approached with new ideas and programs that either smack of unanticipated consequences or could conceivably intrude upon their domains and tip the delicate balance of interests that characterize most academic settings. It is at such times that concerns about an institution's "mission," its "standards" and its "traditions" are raised with both passion and purpose. Change is always a potential enemy, novelty is a potential threat, and usually the only way to handle such situations is through time, patience and proof that the new program will neither interfere with, challenge or otherwise encroach upon other peoples' turf and resources. At such times to be conservative and to go slow is to be responsible—and most faculty are ever so "responsible" when it comes to protecting their own interests. Similarly, Boards of Trustees, though not nearly as "responsible" as academicians, harbour their own concerns about new programs. More often than not, new programs pose new resource demands, and those who are ultimately held responsible for an institution's fiscal sobriety are loathe to redistribute existing resources, especially when those resources are limited and the proposed program cannot project a timely infusion of new and sufficient amounts of revenue to provide a reasonable level of comfort.

In the case of the proposed Human Service Program the usual drawn-out legitimation process was unusually short, and for a very good reason that had not been overlooked by the Program's creators. A drowning swimmer cannot endlessly debate the shape, quality or colour of a potential life-preserver. To be sure, the faculty raised the usual (and some unanticipated) concerns. The new Program would bring undetermined numbers of adult students into a setting traditionally reserved for adolescents—would this not alter the basic "character" of the setting? The new Program would be professionally oriented—would this not subvert Franconia's established mission as a liberal arts college? The new Program would be run on weekends—would this not place additional use and financial burdens on an already-shaky facility? And the Program would be run at a tuition-rate much lower than the one currently being charged to full-time students—would this not create unnecessary tensions and animosities between students?

The answer to most of these questions was "Yes," but the answers were framed in ways to appease and mollify the faculty. But it was the unanticipated questions that proved far more revealing. The new Program would bring unknown numbers of blacks and other minorities to the North Country—was this a wise and responsible thing to do? The faculty's concerns were echoed by many members of the Board of Trustees, and often in more blatant ways, but the Program's advocates asked for no money and promised a new source of income. And in the end this argument proved persuasive. However threatening the Human Service Program was, it was an offer the Board of Trustees just couldn't refuse.

The real problems attendant to the Program's implementation fell on the shoulders of its creators. In addition to their full-time faculty and administrative duties at Franconia College, the "little band of rebels" would now assume the total responsibility for the Program's development: they would do all the teaching, recruiting, student support and administration required by the Program, at no pay and without any relief from their other obligations to the College. Perhaps this was an offer that should have been refused, but the Program's creators were in no position to play hard to get.

Even today, some 11 years after the Program's implementation, it would be difficult to convey the sense of purpose and mission that bound the Program's creators to each other. However difficult and long the road might be, they shared a dream that infuses its dreamers with a kind of exhuberance and passion usually reserved for the very young. We mention this not because of any need to retrospectively romanticize or extoll the virtues of the Program's creators, but because it highlights a critical, often trivialized, and overlooked aspect of social intervention: the practice of change is a passionate affair.

Having been granted its necessary if half-hearted legitimation by the College, the Program's early days were predictably filled with hectic and often disorganized activity. The highway between Franconia, New Hampshire and New Haven, Connecticut became a lifeline for the new Program. Since most of the Program's potential students worked in human service programs and agencies in Connecticut, the 5-hour car ride from Franconia to New Haven became a time for planning, strategizing, sharing fears and enough comic relief to fill several *Saturday Night Live* shows. Huddled in cars, some of which had no heat, the Program's teachers/recruiters/administrators would leave Franconia at 4:00 a.m. for a day of teaching and marketing the Program in a city 300 miles away. They would not return until the next morning, just in time to assume their regular duties at Franconia—and they would repeat this ritual over and over again. The reason for focusing attention on New Haven (and later Boston, Massachusetts) was simple: some of the Program's creators had lived in the city and had worked with many of its human service agencies and staffs for several years before coming to Franconia College. The Program sought its students from those settings that knew and trusted them, and this pattern of recruiting (and of relying on word-of-mouth to spread the story of the Program) would characterize the Program's early years.

The Human Service Program's first incoming class of 70 or so students arrived at Franconia College for its first weekend class in the Summer of 1976. The Program had completed that part of its journey that stretched between an idea and a reality. A much longer road lay ahead.

Relocation: 1977-1978

It would be nice to be able to say that the success of the Human Service Program saved Franconia College. Unfortunately, not only was this not the case, but the argument could be made that the Program's implementation and early development actually hastened the demise of Franconia. Three factors conspired to transform any hope of salvation into what it really was, a fantasy. First, there was the condition of Franconia itself. The onset of the 1976-77 academic year brought with it nothing but increased turmoil and financial pain. Traditional, full-time student enrollment continued to decline. The previously negotiated decrease in Franconia's borrowing power with its lead bank created conditions in which freezes, cost reductions and lay-offs were commonplace. Local vendors, previously held at arms' length, were appropriately concerned and began clamoring for monies long owed them. Fund-raising and new grants failed to produce enough money to offset Franconia's cash-flow problems. And the rumor mill, the ever-present rumor mill, was working overtime. Stories of impending death and disaster filled the air like so many glowing sparks from some roaring summer campfire.

Second, there was the Human Service Program. It had, indeed, brought numbers of new students to the College, but the numbers were not nearly enough to compensate for the decline in traditional, residential student enrollment, and the lower tuition paid by the Human Service students was slow in arriving. And third, there was the "community impact" of the new Program and its students. The students were, indeed, different. Most of them were black, older and either unprepared or unwilling to become a part of the setting's culture. Indeed, many were taken aback by Franconia's unkempt look—they had their own images of what colleges should look like and how they should be run. Sloppiness and gentle disrepair might be O.K. for "spoiled, rich kids," but those were certainly not the kind of trappings that engendered awe in people who saw colleges and universities as stately places of pomp and circumstance. The clash of cultures was only heightened by the widespread perception that the Program's creators—and other faculty who had become enthused by the program—were neglecting the "real" Franconia and spending most of their time worrying about the outsiders, intruders and usurpers of Franconia's history and traditions. Liberal rhetoric about equality, liberation and justice was one thing, but abandoning the College for "that element" was another. But the bottom line was clear: the new Program was a living Rorschach. It provided everyone with whatever experiences were needed to fulfill personal prophecy.

Despite its own developmental problems and the unabating turmoil that gripped Franconia, the Human Service Program grew. The message was out: there was now an accredited, degree-granting Program that met the needs of experienced, adult human service workers. By the end of the 1976-77 academic year, there were over 90 students in the Program. More cars were now hitting the roads, highways and turnpikes between the inner-cities of New Haven and Boston and the postcard quietude of the White Mountains of New Hampshire. On October 2, 1977, the Human Service Program held its first Commencement Ceremonies. Honorary Degrees bestowed upon Kenneth B. Clark and Muhammad Ali underscored the Program's arrival on the academic landscape. The Program's first graduates, surrounded by their parents, children and sometimes grandchildren, received their diplomas under the gray and rainy skies of an unseasonably cold Autumn day. Some laughed, a few cried, no one was untouched. For a few short moments, everything made sense.

Three other events in the Fall of 1977 sealed the fate of both Franconia College and the Human Services Program. The first event involved accreditation. While many relatively privileged residential students and their iconoclastic faculty did not view accreditation as important—many, in fact, had opposed accreditation in 1971—the "seal of approval" meant a great deal to those who had not had the choice of entering college when they were young, particularly when they were attending a non-traditional program. Given the symbolic importance of accreditation, and the administration's view of the Program as the vanguard of the emergent Franconia, and given the unique and controversial nature of the Program, its creators chose to highlight the Program rather than hide it or place it at the periphery of the College in the 1977 accreditation study and visit. Their choice proved fortunate, since the visiting team separately reviewed and praised the new program in their report. They did so in part because the review team and the director of accreditation were good and open people—the type of allies that pathbreakers need to find and work with. They also did so at a time when accreditors were at the height of their commitment to acknowledge the strengths as well as weaknesses in non-traditional programs, an openness which proved to be somewhat short-lived (Aronowitz & Giroux, 1985).

The second event involved the banks. In a memorable meeting held at the central offices of the lead bank, and after reviewing with its bankers the desperate nature of the institution's fiscal situation, Franconia focused attention on the growth and development of the Human Service Program. It had grown to about 60 full-time students, was generating cash flow and since its creators weren't being paid for the work of running and teaching the Program, it was actually producing a profit. A proposal was made that would allow the College to use these profits in order to develop the Program more quickly and efficiently. The rationale was a simple one: if the profits were put back into what appeared to be a viable, resource-producing venture, it was conceivable that over time, the Program could begin to generate the kind of revenues necessary to support the rest of Franconia. An alternative proposal was also placed before the bankers: sell off unneeded assets and use the resulting capital to support its more promising programs, including the Human Service Program. Both proposals were rejected. The banks would apply any and all profit to the retirement of Franconia's debt and would not sanction the sale of parts of Franconia. What was abundantly clear was that Franconia, its educational mission notwithstanding, was working for the banks.

The third event was just as critical. As one of only a handful of 4-year colleges and universities in the State, Franconia College was a member of the New Hampshire College and University Council, a consortium of senior educational institutions that engaged in longterm planning, educational policy development and information sharing. Another member of the consortium was New Hampshire College, a private business school located some 100 miles south of Franconia College in Manchester, New Hampshire. Its President, an entrepreneur and businessman of no small talent, had become enamoured with the "goings on" at Franconia College. He was particularly intrigued with the Human Service Program, and after several visits to Franconia indicated his concern that this promising Program not succumb if and when Franconia College went "belly up."

In the Winter of 1977, upon learning of the College's demise, he initiated negotiations and indicated his desire to bring the Human Service Program, "lock, stock and barrel," to New Hampshire College. To be sure, there were alternatives. Preliminary interest in the Program had been expressed by another public institution in the State and a private one in Massachusetts. But what New Hampshire College offered was speed and the assurance that students currently in the Program would not lose a day of class time as a function of the Program's relocation. The President's overall proposal was both simple and complete. New Hampshire College would hire and give raises in salary to all the Human Service Program's faculty. In addition, it would provide the Program with space and allow it to develop in any way the Program saw fit. In return, the Program would commit itself to running "in the black" and refrain from being "too outrageous." Financially, the relationship would work as follows: the Human Service Program would get 50% of each tuition dollar it generated and would use this money to pay faculty and staff salaries, while New Hampshire College would get the other 50%. Out of this money, it would pay for faculty and staff fringe benefits, the Program's overhead, and any and all other expenses associated with running the Program. Any monies left at the end of New Hampshire College's expenses were the College's profit, and the Human Service Program would have no priority claim on this money. The proposal was framed as a "teach-out plan," a temporary situation that would enable New Hampshire College's President to bring a Human Service Program into a Business College with minimal opposition. It was expected, however, that if the arrangement appeared to be working, the teach-out phase of the plan would be but a prelude to the Program's formal annexation and its eventual development as a School in its own right at New Hampshire College.

The waning days of the Fall, 1977 semester at Franconia College were brutal and painful ones. A College was dying and taking with it the hopes and dreams of many of its people. The lingering death scene was in no way brightened by the knowledge that a part of Franconia might continue intact. If anything it made things worse. Although efforts would be mounted to place Franconia's students in appropriate educational settings, and help would be offered to the remaining faculty, the reality of the death of Franconia College was all that really mattered.

Growth and Stabilization: 1978-1985

The term "culture shock" is an overused and often simplistic way of referring to the clash between different environments, values and life styles. In the case of New Hampshire College and the Human Service Program the use of the term is both appropriate and, if anything, an understatement. If the Program represented a shift in the prevailing ethos of Franconia College, it was nothing short of a radical departure in the life and times of New Hampshire College.

New Hampshire College was a college "on the move." Founded as a proprietary school for the training of secretaries and bookkeepers almost 50 years before, the College was still a reasonably small and manageable private institution that had only recently shed its proprietary status. The legal shedding of this status had not changed the prevailing perception (or the functional reality) of the College as an entrepreneurial, profit-oriented, family-run business. Upon the death of the College's founder his wife took over as President, and when she grew too old to handle the running of the place on a day-to-day basis her son ascended to the position. Relatives and old friends of the family dotted the landscape as members of the faculty and administration. Leaders of one of the State's most powerful and prestigeous law firms, again old friends of the family, ran the Board of Trustees and handled much of the College's legal and financial affairs. Located in Manchester, New Hampshire—home of the notorious Manchester Union-Leader, arguably the most powerful daily voice for the most reactionary elements of American society—the College mirrored, both ideologically and stylistically, the political and educational conservatism of its environs. The President took great pride in the fact that he was neither an educator nor an academician. He was a "mover and a shaker," a man with a keen eye for new business and marketing opportunities whose energy level and entrepreneurial zeal were as boundless as his ability to manipulate events and people. He loved and possessed New Hampshire College; it was his entire life and reason for being, and the shadow of his accomplishments, triumphs, faux pas and foolishness provided the College with its own daily charm and a healthy dose of continual embarrassment.

In 1978 New Hampshire College was an institution that was growing rapidly and searching, with almost equal fervour, for the academic imprimaturs and social legitimacy usually denied proprietary institutions. In truth, the College was not a "heavy" intellectual setting. Its residential students generally brought with them undistinguished high school careers and low SAT scores; its faculty was neither particularly eminent in terms of credentials nor productive in terms of research and publications. It was a teaching, "hands-on" business college and its motto, "At New Hampshire College We Mean Business," accurately summed-up the setting's image and conception of itself. But it was also a College that was both financially sound and expanding. In addition to its residential Program it offered an MBA and had developed a network of Continuing Education Centers (evenings schools) that stretched across the entire State and reached as far as Puerto Rico. And it had only recently moved into a brand new campus bought and built entirely out of operating funds and hard cash. It was, in short, a College "on the make." Whatever lingering sense of inferiority it felt about being a second-rate educational institution was amply offset by the reality that it was growing while other small colleges and universities were closing. Thus, it could indulge itself in the kind of intellectual pretentiousness befitting a setting that thrived and flourished during hard times.

As one might imagine, the introduction of the Human Service Program into New Hampshire College was anything but an occasion for mass celebration on the part of most of the College's faculty and administrators. Neither was the Program brought into the setting in a manner that would inspire anyone in the ways of participatory democracy. Grumbling, resistance, even the righteous outrage of many faculty members only underscored the finality of Presidential power at New Hampshire College. The faculty's concerns were clear, and not too dissimilar from those raised at Franconia College only a few years before. The Program was bringing activists, social change folk, people who questioned the profit motive, even socialists into an education bastion committed to capitalism and the virtues of free enterprise. The Program would bring "transients" (i.e., non-residential, adult students) onto a campus specifically designed and built to meet the needs of adolescents. The Program would tarnish the College's image by enveloping it in the aura of a failed institution. The Program and its people just didn't "fit," "feel right" or "make sense" at New Hampshire College.

In response to this predictable reception, the Program's creators made a number of critical strategy decisions concerning a response to the situation. Unlike the case at Franconia College, the Program would not beg, seek or grovel for acceptance. To be sure, the Program wanted to remain, at least temporarily, at New Hampshire College. What better cover could there be for the Program, especially during its developmental period, than that of a College whose avowed conservatism and fiscal stability might serve to both shield the Program from unnecessary visibility and provide it with the time and space in which to establish its own educational legitimacy and an alternative base of community support? But in order for this to happen the Program could not initially devote any significant amount of energy to the time-consuming exercise of winning the hearts and minds of the unconvertible. Instead, the decision was made to adopt a set of tactics based on the assumption that the vast majority of New Hampshire College's faculty were a comfortable and relatively powerless lot, could not take on their President in open rebellion and would, sooner or later, get back to the business of teaching and pursuing lucrative outside consulting arrangements. This assumption, together with an analysis of the nature of the setting and its history, was translated into a posture that was taken over and and over again whenever meetings were held to debate the wisdom of the Program's relocation at New Hampshire College. In essence, this posture was composed of the following elements: first, the Program would confront the College's faculty and actually highlight the ideological and political differences that existed between them, and point to the presumed commitment to academic freedom and educational pluralism that formed the assumptive bedrock of higher education in America. Second, the Program would challenge the faculty's concern regarding academic standards and stature—and trot out its own elitist trappings, credentials and achievements; and, finally, the Program would make clear its own reservations about being at New Hampshire College, enunciating its strong concerns that the College might not prove good enough for the Human Service Program, its students and its staff. In terms of the immediate rebellion, the tactics worked: there was none, and within a relatively short period of time the College's faculty, some still mumbling and grumbling, having taken their principled stance and exercised whatever symbolic passions were called for, receded into the primordial forest of traditional faculty concerns about overload and night-school teaching rates, course loads and fringe benefits. Although some would eventually become supportive of and even involved in the Program, most would not. But as a whole, the College's faculty would never play a decisive role in the Program's fortunes.

The following years were years of enormous growth and necessary stabilization. After a short period of time as a department within the School of Business, the Program became a School in its own right, with its own Dean, governance structure, faculty and staff. Between 1978 and 1985 the School of Human Services grew from a student body of approximately 80 to well over 700 full-time students. A new Associates Degree Program was started to meet the needs of welfare recipients, as were new Undergraduate Concentrations in Labor and Criminal Justice. An International Program in Human Services was launched. An entire Graduate Program was developed with Specializations in Counseling and Community Psychology, Community Organizing and Advocacy, Administration and Gerontology. A separate Program in Community Economic Development was established and an MSW Program was implemented. The School of Human Services, still primarily tuition-driven, was producing over $3,000,000 of cash-flow, and the "50-50" arrangement negotiated in 1978 enabled the School to hire sufficient numbers of new faculty and staff to at least keep pace with its growth.

In addition to the growth of its programs and student body, the School added campuses to its list of holdings. Fulfilling a promise made during the dying days of Franconia College, it returned to the North Country and opened a small satellite Program in Littleton, New Hampshire, several miles from the defunct Franconia College. To reduce the traveling burdens the College's location imposed on many of its Massachusetts- and Connecticut-based students, the School opened a campus in New Haven, Connecticut. And finally, responding to the needs and relationships developed through its Program in Community Economic Development, the School implemented an educational site in San Juan, Puerto Rico.

During this same period of time the School began to seek and obtain the "soft monies" needed to support some of its educational Programs and social change activities. Grants from the U.S. Department of Labor were used to explore issues of youth employment; the Ford Foundation provided support for the School's Community Economic Development Program and students; and a variety of other public and private grants were obtained to support the School's work in the areas of hunger, aging and economic development. All told, the School of Human Services was able to generate over $1,000,000 in non-tuition sources of support for its Programs and projects. These projects, and the hearings, forums, research programs and conferences they enabled the School to organize, became an integral part of the School's efforts to use its own setting as a vehicle for networking about issues of significant community concern.

Questions of achieving appropriate academic and professional recognition were also of importance during this period of time, and the School of Human Services succeeded in obtaining such legitimation. It was favorably reviewed, both as a distinct entity and in the context of New Hampshire College as a whole, by appropriate regional and national accrediting associations. One of these reviews termed the School a "model for the country." The School's New Haven campus, after an extensive and often acrimonious review by the Board of Higher Education of the State of Connecticut, was awarded a license and permitted to operate as part of an out-of-state institution. A similar license was granted sans acrimony, to the School's Community Economic Development Program by the Council of Higher Education in Puerto Rico. A longitudinal follow-up study on graduates of the School's Baccalaureate Program yielded data that were more than a little encouraging: 45% of the School's graduates applied to Graduate Schools and 92% of those applying were accepted. Fifty-five percent of the School's graduates chose not to apply to Graduate Schools—they averaged $3910 in salary increases during the year following graduation. And finally, in 1984, the School of Human Services received the Regional Award of Recognition as an "outstanding institution" from the National Organization of Human Service Educators. If the School had ever been concerned about the external world's view of its quality and emminence as an educational setting, those concerns could now be laid to rest.

At the same time that the School of Human Services was growing and earning professional and academic recognition, significant efforts were undertaken to stabilize and provide the School with a greater sense of internal coherence and organization. Activities directed toward creating a more standardized process of awarding advanced standing resulted in greater administrative uniformity; curriculum refinement of both the Core and Elective Curriculae resulted in greater educational consensus; and given the proliferation of Programs, a process of de-centralization was undertaken to provide faculty and staff with a greater sense of personal ownership and accountability. Serious attention was given to the marketing of the School's various Programs, and long-range fiscal and program planning became an area of intense, ongoing activity. The School of Human Services had grown quickly and dramatically and, as is so often the case in such situations, it could become a victim of its own success.

In summarizing the School's growth and development we do not wish to convey the picture of life at New Hampshire College as a bed of roses. Nothing could be further from the truth. The years between 1978 and 1985 were rarely placid and free of conflict. New Hampshire College was, and remained, a fundamentally anti-intellectual institution whose concerns for profit were always more in harmony with the objectives of a factory than those of a college or university. Annual budget battles, continual threats of cuts, and periodic attempts to alter the "50-50" arrangement were an ever-present reality.

In addition, the School of Human Services' social change activities always provoked reactions from other parts of the College, its administration and the Board of Trustees. Each new Program, every conference held, even its separate commencement ceremonies continually drew the critical attention of suspicious and often hostile colleagues. Efforts always seemed to be being mounted to improve the fit between the School of Human Services and the College's Undergraduate and Graduate Schools of Business, efforts aimed at "toning the School down" and "smoothing its rough edges" so that it was more a part of the administrative, bureaucratic, political and educational milieu of New Hampshire College. Each new assault had to be dealt with, thereby taking time and energy away from the School's primary mission. And each new mini-crisis generated fears and instability with the School itself.

No, it would be very misleading to portray the years between 1978 and 1985 as years of exuberance unencumbered by trauma and travail. Contradictions abounded and the unavoidable implications of those contradictions were a matter of daily concern and debate. The School of Human Services was the proverbial "stranger in a strange land," a political and educational alien in a fortress of conservatism. Its own growth and success only served to underscore the lingering contradictions of this existence.

Crisis and Choice: 1985-present

As previously indicated, any attempts to fully appreciate the purpose, process and practice of social intervention require an understanding of two sets of related issues: the character of the broader context in which change occurs and the internal dynamics that come to define the setting that serves as the vehicle for change. The School of Human Services is no exception to this rule.

In 1985 the frenzied, hustling, "on-the-make" world of New Hampshire College began to crumble. During its days of unrestrained and unreflective growth the College had overextended itself. This fact, coupled with declining enrollment of its typical students, decreased federal support for higher education, the absence of any significant endowment, and the realities of being a highly leveraged institution combined to create a climate of extreme apprehension and unrest. The bankers, once one of the College's main sources of comfort and security, were growing wary and not a little distrustful of the rosy figures being offered as the basis for renegotiating the College's debt service and borrowing authority. The College had begun running unprojected deficits the size of which could no longer be covered by "paper transfers" and creative accounting. The Undergraduate School of Business, the College's flagship, was the principle offender, and the apparent surpluses generated by the School of Human Services, the Graduate School of Business and the College's Continuing Education Centers were no longer sufficient to cover the flagship's losses.

And there were other problems. The College's new campus, built but a few short years before, began showing the unmistakeable signs of faulty design and construction. Dorms were imploding on themselves and a multi-million dollar sports complex was found to have serious structural defects. Even the College's most recent acquisition, a campus which housed both the School of Human Services and the Graduate School of Business, was discovered to be in an alarming state: several of its buildings contained unacceptable and illegal levels of health-endangering asbestos. The projected costs of repair and renovation were staggering. A state-of-the-art computer system, both a critical part of the College's administrative procedures and a source of educational and business pride to the institution, was found to be functionally wanting and financially draining. It neither reduced costs nor increased efficiency. If anything, it had succeeded in plunging the College into a new administrative and fiscal morass.

And, finally, there was the President himself. His commitment of significant amounts of money to marketing the College internationally had produced highly questionable income and expense numbers and his reliance on external efficiency experts to reduce operating expenses proved both costly and disruptive to the institution's day-to-day functioning. These failures, so unusual and out of character for a man whose entrepreneurial instincts had rarely disappointed the College, only served to heighten long-smoldering concerns about the President's penchant for behaving in ways that embarrassed the College and its Board of Trustees.

The anxiety that began to descend upon and weave its way throughout the College also made itself felt in the School of Human Services, but in a slight-different manner. More than ever before, the School was treated as a "cash cow" whose sole reason for being was to produce surpluses to cover a multitude of sins in the rest of the institution. New threats and questions concerning the School's appropriateness as a part of New Hampshire College were raised whenever the School sought the resources needed to maintain the quality of its Programs. Reorganizations and periodic re-alignments of staff within the College as a whole were invariably translated into decreased services and personnel for the School of Human Services. The word had gone out: New Hampshire College and its flagship were in trouble, and all auxiliary enterprises would be expected to do whatever was deemed necessary to right the ship.

External crises always exact a toll from ongoing settings and often serve to heighten whatever contradictions exist within the settings themselves. And this was certainly the case in the School of Human Services. The School of Human Services in 1985 was a very different setting from the Program that had been transplanted to New Hampshire College some seven years before. To begin with it was, of course, much bigger, both in terms of the number of programs it ran and the number of people it employed. Even its student body had begun to reflect the differences that changes in government funding, respectability and economics bring about in educational settings: many more students were traditional in terms of most socio-economic indicators save age. Some of the School's earlier faculty and staff had departed and had been replaced by others, and these people, together with the many new faculty and staff who joined the School during its seemingly endless period of growth, were not a part of the School's early history either at Franconia College or New Hampshire College.

They were the School's second and third generation and had neither experienced nor shared in the trials and tribulations of the "old days." For them the past, however increasingly romanticized with the passage of time, could never be a part of direct experience. Theirs was not a panorama of "struggle in the mountains" beyond Franconia Notch. Their concerns were appropriately focused on the current and future existence of the School, and their experiences and expectations of the School of Human Services were as distinctive and valid as were those of the School's creators. If the School of Human Services was coming under siege it was not history that would save it, it was the people currently inhabiting the setting.

A second issue concerned the structure of the School itself. As previously indicated, the School's growth brought with it the need to de-centralize many of its Programs. Simplistic, top-down administrative structures may suffice during the early days of a setting when it is intimate and small, but it is not a structure that fuels creativity nor, in the long run, supports the sense of participatory ownership so critical to the enterprise of social change. But even partial de-centralization is a two-edged sword: while it fosters intimacy and relationship-building in smaller groups, and provides the context for the kind of unity of purpose that often results in excellence, it can also tend to separate people and programs from each other and foster the privatization of group concerns and individual agendas. When a setting is threatened or begins to perceive itself as under siege, these agendas and concerns invariably surface, and whether cloaked in personal, political or programatic garb, they often mirror the needs and aspirations of sub-groups, not the setting as a whole.

And as always, there was the issue of ideology. Progressive settings are often notorious for their ability to seek refuge in endless ideological debates when confronted with danger. Purity of thought and consensus are usually the sine qua non of action. Patience, support for the deliberative process and the collective ability to persistently focus in on the relevant issues, strategies and options are difficult and often time-consuming activities. At such times ideology, even a generally shared ideology, can serve to heighten existing contradictions rather than help to resolve them. Legitimate but rarely-discussed concerns for personal safety, security and stability invariably muddy the ideological waters, and the result is a weakened setting at a time when the setting should be at its most united, disciplined and organized best.

There are no enduring kinships or friendships where vested professional and business interests are concerned. In the summer of 1986, after another year of declining College fortunes and new revelations about the extent of the College's mounting fiscal woes, the President was effectively dismissed, along with several of the College's top administrators. The new leader was a member of the College's current Board of Trustees and had served as its Chairman for many years.

Within a reasonably short period of time the Chancellor's basic intentions and view of the world became quite clear. By both word and deed he enunciated a three-part agenda. First, it was a time for patience, sacrifice, trust and good will. To be sure, the College had its share of problems, but it was a sound and strong place, and with a steady hand at the helm and confidence in its future it would emerge from its difficulties healthier and more vibrant than ever before—hard times were only a prelude to better times. Second, it was the Undergraduate and Graduate Schools of Business, those parts of the College that most accurately and faithfully reflected its traditions and history, that were and would always be at the heart of the institution's existence and meaning. And third, there were real and legitimate questions about the appropriate role, if any, of a School of Human Services at a Business College. The School of Human Services had achieved and contributed a great deal to the College and it was a "fine place filled with good, bright and hardworking people," but an "open mind" must be kept regarding its future and the very best interests of both the School and New Hampshire College as a whole.

As indicated at the very beginning of this chapter, the ultimate story of the School of Human Services is far from over. What is clear are the choices that currently confront the School. What is unclear is the choice the School will make and, given that choice, whether the School and its people will be able to implement its choice in a manner that enables it to remain true to its mission and together as a setting.

First, there is the choice of "accommodation." To some, a future away from New Hampshire College holds little appeal. For all its difficulties, contradictions and turmoil, New Hampshire College is a familiar place and a known quantity. It has been negotiated in the past and can be negotiated in the future. To be sure, changes might have to be made and new financial and institutional compromises worked out, but that is a price worth paying for the opportunity to continue some of the School's programs in a relatively uninterrupted manner. Better to deal with a known adversary than an unknown quantity. And besides, what assurances and guarantees could one ever get that the School's people, its faculty and staff—people with families, kids in school, mortgages to pay, survival needs and community ties—would be able to count on jobs if the School did not remain at New Hampshire College? Accommodation might well limit the School of Human Services' impact and the ability to pursue some of its social change goals, but it might also enable the School, or at least some of its programs, to remain fully functional.

A second choice is relocation. Relocation would involve seeking a formal affiliation with another college or university. And there is much to recommend this option. The School of Human Services is in many respects a "plum" and would easily enhance any educational institution's fiscal and academic status. It is a fully-accredited and professionally-recognized School that generates over $3,000,000 dollars of annual cash flow and throws off somewhere in the neighborhood of 14% profit. Given the current situation confronting many institutions of higher education, the School could bring with it the kinds of programs, reputation and resources that would substantially add to another setting's stability and viability. This is leverage of an attractive kind, the kind of leverage to be used in selecting an affiliation based on greater educational and philosophical commonalities. Some favor this option.

And, finally, there is the option of independence, of committing itself to a program, process and timetable whose goals are nothing short of etablishing the School of Human Services as a separate, free-standing independent college in its own right. This option, the argument goes, is the School's ultimate and most natural destiny. Born as an alternative to existing models of adult education, the School of Human Services would never fully realize its potential unless and until it controls its own fate and is no longer called upon to bend to the will of other masters. If self-determination is a critical part of all liberation struggles, why should not the School of Human Services first become what it exhorts others to be? Some favor this approach, fully aware of the anxiety, uncertainty and instability that usually attends all movements for selfhood.

At the point of this writing the School of Human Services is engaged in the kind of internal debate and dialogue out of which a choice must emerge. It is, as one might imagine, a difficult and often painful process. Ideology invariably conflicts with practicality, the personal and political are joined, and every conceivable contradiction that defines our lives and the lives of the settings we become a part of emerges, naked and raw like some demon from the Abyss. And one way or another the demon must be met and exposed for what it really is—a mirror of ourselves, our beliefs, our passions and our imperfections. What ultimately hangs in the balance is more than the fate of the School of Human Services, it is the meaning of struggle itself.

LESSONS AND IMPLICATIONS FOR THE PRACTICE OF SOCIAL INTERVENTION

The field and practice of social intervention is still in its infancy. It is at a stage of development where the greatest disservice possible would be a premature push for closure. However discomforting the lack of closure may be, the reality of the situation calls for continuing differentiation, as opposed to the tendency to precipitously define (and confine) the field within existing and comfortable frames of reference. The premature push for closure invariably retards the attempt to develop anything more than novel approaches to the handling of symptoms. Options are reduced, creative thinking suffers, and problems (as well as solutions) become defined narrowly and with little self-critical analysis. The reality of the practice of social intervention is that we are always learning little things both about ourselves and the process of change. It is these many little things that may one day serve to provide us with the comfort and arrogance needed to christen and proclaim a "field." At the present time, however, it might be wiser and more appropriate that we contribute to the development of that field by trying, as it were, to slow it down at least long enough for more little things to pile up. What follows are some of the little things we have learned (or re-learned) from the experience and reality of the School of Human Services.

Passion and Community

The practice of social intervention is a passionate affair—it always has been and always will be. But passion, we are told, is a dangerous thing and not to be trusted: it blurs reality, substitutes affect for thought, and can serve to seriously distort the world as it actually exists. We are warned about the self-deluding quality of passion, and much of our lives is spent learning how to control, deny or enslave it. What we are rarely taught (and even more rarely experience) is the liberating quality of passion, the manner in which it can ennoble us and bring us closer to that most precious of human experiences—the feeling of being uniquely and wonderfully alive.

It would be a mistake of enormous proportions to restrict our understanding of passion to its negative and potentially debilitating aspects, but that is exactly what we are all too-prone to do, especially as professionals. In point of fact, one could make a good case for the opposite interpretation: the absence of passion is what renders our commitment to community more rhetorical than real. Passion need not be unreflective or uncritical, especially when tied to the process of creating a new or alternative setting. At such times it can prove both unifying and can serve as a vehicle for examining issues and problems often overlooked or relegated to obscurantist discourse. Real, hard work coupled with a shared commitment to clearly-enunciated and value-based principles are the true building blocks of community. All else is rhetoric and posturing. "Burn out" is the problem to be feared, not passion.

We may well be approaching the time when the teaching of passion ought to occupy our minds and thoughts. Perhaps too much energy has already been spent reifying the virtues of objectivity and disinterest in the process of social change. For the creators of the School of Human Services community was achieved through a combination of passion and hard work. As the philosopher John Ruskin once put it: "When people are rightly occupied, their amusement grows out of their work, as the colour-petals out of a fruitful flower."

Timing and Tactics

The *Old Testament* as well as a popular folk song state that "There is a time for every season under heaven." The creation of alternative settings is no exception to this wisdom. The real issue is one of recognizing the appropriate season and selecting the appropriate planting strategies and tactics.

Under the assumption that most attempts at social intervention grow out of a profound critique of the politics, policies, and practices of existing institutions, then both the timing and tactics of intervention become part and parcel of that analysis. Consider the issues raised by Marx, de Tocqueville and Marris: no matter how open people and institutions are, change is threatening; no matter how insular an institution may seem, it may contain within it the seeds of or space for innovation.

In the case of the School of Human Studies—a program always seeking to be a part of an already existing or established setting—several guidelines emerge. First, alternative settings and programs can often be more easily developed in institutions that are weak, troubled or engulfed in situations of ongoing crisis. However discrepant the goals and politics of the Human Services Program may have been to the conservatives at Franconia College, they were in no position to thwart its development and implementation. When survival is at stake even the devil can be wrapped in Faustian possibilities.

Second, alternative settings can become a part of and can thrive at institutions with which they have little in common so long as two conditions are met: 1) the larger institution is at a point in time in its own development where what the innovator has to offer is wanted—in this case money and prestige; and 2) the larger institution's leaders possess and are prepared to use their authority to guarantee entry.

And third, how an alternative organization chooses to confront a new setting and people with values it neither shares nor aspires to may very well be different from how it presents itself to institutions with which it shares some common values. At Franconia College, the creators of the Human Service Program dealt with dissonance by "selling" it; at New Hampshire College they chose to stonewall it. Mere time and words—"education," if you will—never suffices to convert the inconvertible when issues of basic ideology and core values are involved.

New Skills for the Unskilled

We generally associate the field of social intervention with the social sciences and the helping professions. Whether or not this is in fact the case or even historically accurate is certainly a matter for debate. But even assuming the validity of the statement, the reality of the practice of social intervention, be it in the form of the creation of alternative settings or in terms of the work involved in fundamentally changing existing settings, is that skills are needed which are not generally associated with the helping professions. Principle among these are those related to business, administration and economics. Again, it is a situation in which good ideas and intentions, even creative conceptual solutions to problems of enormous human import, can (and often do) either fall helplessly by the wayside or fail to come to fruition because of a lack of the skills necessary to translate ideas into programs. In the past we have relied on the hiring of outside technicians or other experts to handle money issues and the more mundane aspects of an enterprise, reserving for ourselves the clinical, community, research and programatic areas of concern, the "really important stuff."

The fact of the matter is that there are no mundane or important parts of the practice of social intervention. Issues related to money and the conduct of a setting's business are neither apolitical nor should they be viewed as ancillary to a setting's mission. Marketing issues, the difference between a budget and cash-flow, the difference between fixed and variable expenses, and the differences between gross, net and net-net income are critical to a setting's success, as are questions of how to leverage money, refinance debt and make economic projections. It may make sense to delegate the responsibility for such work on a day-to-day basis to accountants, comptrollers and business managers, but it makes no sense at all for practitioners of social intervention to be "babes in the woods" when it comes to understanding the realities of the economic environment. Bad economics, not bad politics or pedagogy killed Franconia; attention to economics created needed space for the School of Human Services.

The time may well have come for courses and seminars in business to be a formal part of the preparation of social interventions. Our experiences at the School of Human Services certainly reinforce and support the wisdom of such an approach.

Socialization and the Generation Gap

Like all settings, alternative settings generally go through at least four distinct periods of development. There is a creative period usually characterized by all the frenzy and missionary zeal that usually accompanies the birth of a newborn child. This is followed by a period of growth and stabilization, a time when the setting, if it survives, begins to both "flex its muscles" and "clean up its act." Then there is the unavoidable time of crisis, a period during which the setting, whether or not it is externally threatened, cannot avoid coming to grips with its own contradictions. And finally, depending on how it has resolved the question of its own existence, there comes a time of renewal or death. Stretching across this entire panorama are people, and it is a setting's people who ultimately determine its fate.

The reality of a setting's life-cycle means that different people will join and leave it at different and unpredictable points in time. That is a given. What is not a given, and what often serves to undermine a setting's ability to deal with its own meaning and identity, is the manner in which new people are introduced and socialized into the setting. This is an absolutely critical issue, especially for settings that define themselves in opposition (or as an alternative) to others. Not all can be present at the moment of creation—does this make them less worthy to determine the future? Some were present at the creation—does that make them prone to resist change? The questions are indeed both real and serious, and the answers are far from clear.

It is clear that settings need to take their own history seriously enough so that the past is neither allowed to become a mythical and insurmountable obstacle to the future nor automatically relegated to the dung heap of outworn ideas and outmoded practices. We tend to be an ahistorical people, socialized to look mainly to the present and the future, and we are generally taught to fictionalize the past in ways that allow us to discard it.

Settings committed to the ongoing struggle for social justice cannot afford the luxury of taking their own histories lightly. If all that is past is prologue, then it is absolutely critical for every succeeding generation of a setting's warriors to appreciate the context or arena of the struggle they have joined. To understand the past is not to revere it, but to learn from it; to ignore the past is not a demonstration of our freedom, merely a statement of our foolishness. It is unclear, certainly from our own experiences, that our practice of social intervention has succeeded in providing its second and third generation of people with an accurate and helpful understanding of the history and meaning of the School of Human Services.

EPILOGUE

The School of Human Services is now 11 years old, not a small accomplishment at a time when the half-life of most alternative settings is less than a third of that. It has already had a significant impact on its students, its graduates, its staff, the communities it serves, and on aspects of the educational social service and social development systems. Its students, however remain exceptions. Fewer poorer students and fewer minority students are attending colleges and universities. And the ranks of the poor have become greater, not less. It would be foolish to pretend to know what lies ahead for the School of Human Services. It may live and change and prosper to the beat of the different drums of those who come to possess it; it may die the premature death of a setting that comes to despise itself; or perhaps worst of all, it may remain the same, never transcending the dreams of its many creators.

Editor's Note: A critical underlying issue in Osher and Goldenberg's chapter is reflected in the question—Owning vs. Renting?

One of the lingering contradictions in all efforts to create alternative settings is the frequency with which they are both born into and often remain a part of the very institutions whose values and politics they profess to attack. No less curious are the rationales we develop for remaining a part of basically antagonistic settings: we can outwit them, or change them, or remain untouched and unblemished by them. It is a situation akin to that of an isolated and poor tenant who continually professes to be able to seduce, cajole, threaten or manipulate the landlord into doing his or her bidding. In the final analysis, tenants are tenants and landlords, even nice ones, always possess the power and resources required to define the quality of the tenant's life.

Sooner or later the practice of social intervention will have to come to grips with the absolute limits of the interventionist agenda itself. For those of us involved in the creation of alternative settings the limits of that agenda are becoming harder and harder to avoid. Why do we always seem to be renting apartments rather than owning buildings? Why continually go through the agonizing process of creating alternatives that can be rendered impotent or transformed into exercises in futility by capricious landlords? Are we frightened by the prospects of ownership? Have we ourselves become so much a part of the system that we equate freedom with misfortune? Can it really be that those of us who teach about liberation are in need of liberation ourselves?

We shall return to the heart of such questions in part four of the book in our consideration of community economic development alternatives.

REFERENCES AND SOURCES OF INFORMATION

Adams, F. (1975). *Unearthing seeds of fire: The idea of highlander*. Winston-Salem, NC: Blair.

Aronowitz, S. & Giroux, H. (1985). *Education under seige*. South Hadley, Ma.: Bergan & Garvey.

Barker, R.G. (1960). Ecology and motivation. In M.R. Jones (Ed.), *Nebraska Symposium on Motivation*. Lincoln: University of Nebraska Press.

Blau, P. (1960). Orientation towards clients in a public welfare agency. *Administrative Science Quarterly*, V, 341-361.

Bowles, S. & Gintis. H. (1976). *Schooling in capitalist America*. New York: Basic Books.

Clark, B. (1960). The cooling out function in higher education. *The American Journal of Sociology*, 65, 569-576.

Clark, K.B. (1967). *Dark ghetto*. New York: Harper & Row.

Cloward, R., & Epstein, I. (1967). Private social welfare's disengagement from the poor. In G. Brager & F. Purcell (Eds.), *Community action against poverty*. New Haven: College and University Press. 40-63.

Collins, R. (1979). *The credential society*. New York: The Academic Press.

Duberman, M. (1972). *Black mountain: An exploration in community*. New York: E.P. Dutton & Co.

Erickson, F. (1975). Gatekeeping and the melting pot. *Harvard Education Review*. 45, 44-70.

Freire, P. (1972). *Pedagogy of the oppressed*. New York: Seabury.

Freire, P. (1986). *The politics of education*. South Hadley, Ma.: Bergan & Garvey.

Giroux, H. (1983). *Theory and resistance in education*. South Hadley, Ma.: Bergan & Garvey.

Goffman, E. (1961). *Asylums*. Garden City, N.Y.: Doubleday.

Goldenberg, I. (1978). *Oppression & social intervention*. Chicago: Nelson-Hall.

Gordon, M. (1978). *Human nature, class, and ethnicity*. New York: Oxford University Press.

Mannheim, K. (1936). *Ideology & utopia*. New York: Harcourt, Brace and World.

Marris, P. (1974). *Loss & change*. London: Routledge & Kegan Paul.

Martin, W. (1971). Essay review: Academic values and mass education. *Harvard Education Review*, XLI, 568-574.

Osher, D. (1984, spring). Consistency of assumption in education innovation. *Human Services Education*.

Osher, D. & Berger, S. (1978). *The life & death of Utopia College*. Cambridge: Harvard University Institute of Educational Administration.

Riessman, F. & Popper, H. (1968). *Up from poverty*. New York: Harper and Row.

Ryan, W. (1971). *Blaming the victim*. New York: Vintage.

Sarason, S. (1972). *The creation of settings and the future of societies*. San Francisco: Jossey-Bass.

Sennett, R. & Cobb, J. (1972). *The hidden injuries of class*. New York: A. Knopf, Inc.

Shor, I. (1980). *Critical teaching and everyday life*. Boston: South End Press.

Shor, I. (1986). *Culture wars*. London: Routledge & Kegan Paul.

de Tocqueville, Alexis (1955). *The ancien regime and the French revolution*. Garden City, N.Y.: Doubleday.

Edward M. Bennett
and
David Hallman

4

THE CENTRALITY
OF FIELD EXPERIENCE
IN TRAINING
FOR SOCIAL INTERVENTION

INTRODUCTION

The purpose of this chapter is to describe some of the educational practices which the authors have found to be helpful in educational/training initiatives in social intervention.

In the writers' experiences, the preparation of social interventionists requires both instruction in very specific skills for very specific tasks (e.g., assessment, consultation, and intervention), and at the same time involving the students in social intervention practice experiences and raising their awareness of the complexities of social problems and the implications for social intervention. For the social interventionist, learning to think critically involves being able to analyze situations and to develop effective strategies in response to problems. Because the business of social intervention is viewed as a means of social advance, reconstruction, and reorganization of social system forces, training/educational strategies must include processes to both involve and influence social groups and systematic forces without directing or controlling them. As indicated in chapter one, social intervention activities involve value questions regarding both the means and ends of the social-intervention activity. A fundamental goal of second-order change is the need to ensure that individuals and groups have the power to influence the direction of their lives and of their social institutions. The underlying value explicated in this volume is the use of social-intervention activities to reduce conditions of oppression and to create social processes and structures which provide the marginal individual with greater access to goods and services and movement toward a psychological sense of community. Students need to be exposed to these value questions and taught how to implement them. Moreover, when you commit yourself to serious practicum training then the projects are both real social change efforts *and* training projects. The art is to juggle both aspects simultaneously.

How can one do this within a university environment? As Berger observes in Chapter two of this volume, the easiest case is when the social-change activity is legitimized as part of one's job description. In the university environment, this means to have it take place as part of one's legitimate educational responsibilities either in the classroom or in the field in coursework, research, and service—either as student or faculty.

How do you do that? Berger notes there are two sides to the question: (a) how do you mount social-change-oriented classes or use your classes for social-intervention work, and (b) how do you obtain the faculty and students you want to work with?

In our case the first task was made easier because the first author was hired as a community-oriented psychologist. As such, he was generally able to teach at least one social-intervention-oriented class. As well, he has been able to frame his other courses in a community psychology context and in this way introduce students to community psychology principles and experiences.

Moreover, as our department's solitary community-psychology course expanded to become a program and new faculty members were hired, we were able to legitimize and protect their social-change interests in similar ways. For example, in one instance we employed two faculty members whose job descriptions included a part-time resource exchange commitment with the local board of education and an emphasis on action research in prevention and community development (Nelson, Bennett, Dudeck, & Mason, 1982).

We now have a program which will allow us to do social-change work. The conceptual and ideological underpinnings of our work contain many of the elements necessary to social intervention as follows: emphasis on the optimal and just distribution of services to meet the needs of individuals and communities; a collaborative approach to community research and development; emphasis on the identification and utilization of strengths and the promotion of individual competence and community well-being; the valuing of diversity and cultural relativity; the valuing of a social-ecological-historical perspective; and commitment to social and community intervention as a means of solving individual and community problems (Bennett, 1970;

Rappaport, 1977; Sarason, Levine, Goldenberg, Cherlin, & Bennett, 1966).

The second task—getting people you want to work within your program—is more difficult. Our experience with this question suggests that you find people with potential and with diverse complementary skills and interests and work with them. On the faculty side, the people you may wish to hire may be unacceptable to your colleagues or to the administration. For example, although community psychology is based on a multidisciplinary perspective, department colleagues often resist efforts to hire academics from disciplines outside of psychology. Frequently those applicants who are academically acceptable have had limited experience in social-intervention work. In regard to our graduate-student applicants, there are relatively few places where as undergraduates they can get courses or programs which introduce them to social intervention. Our strategy, therefore, has been to be as selective as possible in student and faculty recruiting as well as to develop program strategies to increase the program's emphasis on social intervention.

One of the successful strategies has been the students' community practicum and research experience. First introduced in 1971 at both the undergraduate and graduate levels, the practicum has been a critical element in social-intervention education, training, and research, for both students and faculty.

In this chapter, we shall focus our discussion of training/educational processes on the student practicum. In particular, we shall discuss the use of the practicum as a means to facilitate second-order cognitive change in the student and to encourage student social-intervention initiatives.

WORKING PRINCIPLES

In their practica, students learn to apply and test the theory offered in their course work, by functioning as research-consultants. The theoretical basis for the practicum experience is derived from John Dewey's discussion of educative practices as a *source*. In short, Dewey (1929) argued that educational practices (such as a practicum experience) provide the *subject matter* for research and development problems. Further, they provide the ultimate *test* of such research and development.

Students' actual experiences in the research-consultant role are guided by several general principles[1].

1. Prevention and whenever possible, primary prevention, is a

main thrust of the practicum as it is identified as a key concept in community psychology.

2. Within this preventive focus, students are helped to understand their environment, themselves, and to use their own resources effectively. Using a process consultation approach (Schein, 1969, p. 9), the instructor helps the students in their practica to: "perceive, understand and act upon process events which occur in the client's environment." The instructor assumes that the students can learn to use their own resources effectively. In line with Mills (1959), the student must become familiar with clients, their social relationships and activities, and the organizational and community structures of which they are a part. At the same time that students become aware of their own values they are taught not to impose their values on how the client system should operate, but rather to help the client system in self-help (self-diagnosis and self-intervention). The student and the client system must learn to identify where problems originate and how to solve problems. Within these experiences, it is hoped the students will undergo a metamorphosis in their thoughts and actions in relation to people and their social systems. In other words, a second-order cognitive change.

3. Within their activities, students learn concepts and develop skills in consultation, community assessment, program evaluation, field research, and community organization and development. Students are taught to understand how groups, organizations and communities operate and to learn how to assist people and their settings to identify problems and social forces which must be influenced in order to solve their problems. In other words, they learn how to do social-intervention work.

4. Students are expected to develop a multidisciplinary view of the particular practicum issue by becoming engaged with the theory and practice of other disciplines. The latter emphasis is easier said than done. The great majority of textbooks, periodicals, and educational programs are not multidisciplinary in their orientation. Nevertheless, it is an important task to attempt to increase the students' knowledge and experience of multidisciplinary approaches. It is not assumed that the student can master all disciplines, but rather that the most valid approach to social intervention is a multidisciplinary one and this dictates the approach to education and training.

5. A collegial relationship between students and faculty in the development of the practicum experience is encouraged and emphasized. Our own experience with student practica has indicated that students who are interested in social-intervention activities benefit most from group projects which include other students and faculty

member(s). Such collaborative involvement provides the student prac-
titioner with role models as well as increased opportunities to clarify
and to work through interpersonal and task interactions in the field.
As well, by processing the task and interpersonal interactions in the
field, the student practitioners will learn to be able to identify
problems in their own activities (self-diagnosis) and subsequently to
take action to reduce or eliminate the problem (self-intervention). This
self-help oriented approach will help them to improve their relationships with one another, their task effectiveness, and empower them to
become more effective in the field setting.

6. The practicum should provide the possibility of developing an
acceptable thesis project. An overarching issue is the desirability of
combining research with consultation and providing the student with a
longer-term and improved experience by developing a viable thesis
project from the practicum activity. The development of a thesis from
a practicum experience also strengthens the bridge between the roles
of practitioner/consultant and researcher/scientist.

Settings can be chosen which allow the students to obtain several
kinds of social-intervention experiences as follows:

1. The student works as a temporary but integral part of the organization. For example, one student's practicum experience involved
   him as a staff member in a new community residence for mentally
   retarded adults. The student observed difficulties in the program's
   operation which seemed to stem from a conflict between the
   perception of goals and values held by the staff, residents, parents,
   and the advisory committee. These difficulties made communication between the groups very difficult and led to stereotyping of
   one group by the other and increased disparity of perception between them. With the support of all four groups, the student's
   practicum project evolved to become an action-research thesis project which assessed the development of the community residence as
   a system of interacting elements, including the perceptions of the
   four groups. These data were then fed-back to the groups and used
   as a means of self-diagnosis and as a step to change the underlying
   problems.

2. The student operates as an outside consultant on a contractual
   basis. For example, a school of human services, based upon
   meeting the needs of adult human-service workers who had been
   implicitly or explicitly denied access to college education wished to
   evaluate their ten-year performance from the primary perspective
   of its graduates. The school contracted with the practicum supervisor and a graduate student to explore the feasibility of the project
   (a one-term practicum experience). A high participatory approach

was taken whereby the student worked collaboratively with the College's Dean and various members of the staff and faculty to assess the project's feasibility. The practicum phase of the activity introduced the student to program-evaluation skills and methods and provided her with a hands-on experience in developing a research-consultation project. Because the pedagogy of the school of human services was the pedagogy of the oppressed it provided a first-hand exposure to a program which itself was a social intervention.

The conclusion of the practicum experience was marked by an agreement to conduct a thesis research project with two main objectives as follows: (a) to assess the impact of the school of human services upon their graduates in relation to nine program goals and (b) to assist the school in building and maintaining a coalition with its graduates. A first draft of an evaluation proposal designed for the School of Human Services was prepared. The proposal partially fulfilled the requirements of a program-evaluation course as well as the practicum course and provided a foundation for the student's thesis research proposal. The student's practicum advisor shifted his role responsibility from practicum supervisor to thesis supervisor.

3. The student works in a worshop or conference experience. For example one student conducted process evaluations on planning meetings and conferences held by an organization involved in the evolution of the Nestle boycott, in relation to the infant-food controversy. The practicum evolved to become a thesis to: (a) document the evolution in Canada of the infant-food formula controversy (1978-1984), and (b) propose a model to improve our understanding of similar social actions in the future.

4. The student is involved in an unsolicited intervention. For example, a practicum involvement with refugees with housing problems led to an action-research thesis in which the student aided the community in self-diagnosis and self-intervention resulting in an effort to create a multi-ethnic cooperative housing community. The student describes the process by employing ethnographic research techniques to document the intervention and evaluates the program by using content analysis techniques.

As training/educational experiences, the above examples illustrate several types of practica experiences and how the practicum can evolve into a thesis project which is concerned with a social-intervention initiative. The thesis often documents the richness of the blend of the students' conceptual awareness of problems of oppression and their social-intervention-oriented, action-research, assessment, consultation and community development interests and skills.

SUPERVISION AND EVALUATION

The guidelines for practicum supervision and evaluation are as follows:

1. The student has an active role in selecting a practicum project to meet his/her interests, skills, and needs. At the start of the academic term, practica options are listed and discussed between students and the faculty. Occasionally students initiate their own practica. A student may explore more than one practicum option during the pre-entry phase of the selection activity. The student is encouraged to decide on a practicum project within a few weeks of the start of the term.

2. Each student has one faculty member as a supervisor. A faculty member may supervise more than one student and may also work with a group of students as a team. Additional faculty may be involved as members of a team or as consultants to the student or to a group project, as needed.

3. The faculty supervisor and student draw up a contract outlining the goals of the practicum and the responsibilities of each party early in the practicum. In the case of a group project, the goals and responsibilities of individual parties as well as those of the team are defined. These goals and responsibilities are evaluated at the conclusion of both minor and major work cycles and redefined as necessary.

4. Within the first few weeks of the practicum, the student and client (agency) draw up a formal contract or at least a letter of intent outlining the goals of the project and the duties and responsibilities of both parties. These goals and tasks are evaluated at the conclusion of work cycles and redefined as necessary. There is provision in the contract for either party to terminate the relationship if the project is not working out and cannot be redefined to meet mutual interests. For example, one student entered a clinical setting with an interest in helping the setting to define a community focus to their work. After a period of three months it was apparent that the agency's support for the community emphasis was lacking and the student negotiated to terminate with the setting and to select a different project.

5. Supervision is conducted on a weekly basis and in the case of team projects, students and faculty will often meet as a group. A

minimum of one hour per week is devoted to supervision. In the case of a social-intervention project, student and faculty collaboration as team members in the field will often be considered a necessary part of the supervision/training process. Linking with the student in a meaningful way at various stages of an intervention project is critical to the student's skill development and to the success of the innovation. The amount of time a single intervention project may demand can put a strain on both student and faculty unless the project can simultaneously serve other organizational responsibilities. The easiest way is when the various aspects of a student's curriculum can be integrated with the practicum training sequence. Such integration of course work simultaneously allows the student to combine theory with practice and makes it physically and psychologically possible for the student to mount a social-intervention project. Similarly, faculty members must receive some form of teaching credit for supervising practica and thesis activities. In short, providing meaningful assistance to students working on social-intervention projects is demanding work and in order for such a program to thrive on a long-term basis, appropriate teaching credit must be assigned.

6. Practica are evaluated on a pass-fail basis. The student writes a report at mid-year and again at the conclusion of the year. The faculty supervisor writes a brief evaluation of the student's progress at mid-year and a final evaluation at the end of the year. The purpose of the student report is to promote a log of the practicum experience. Keeping a log is a useful way to chronicle a practicum. It provides the students with an opportunity to review their progress over time and can aid in bringing various aspects of the project into perspective. Finally, the log can provide a useful data base in the development of a thesis project.

STUDENT PRACTICUM AT THE UNDERGRADUATE LEVEL

The strong motivation of most students enrolled in psychology courses to become associated with diverse community settings and their clients as a form of experiential enrichment of classroom instruction, coupled with the community's desire for additional human resources, offers the potential for a valuable exchange between the university and other human service settings in the community. During the academic year 1971-72, a field placement program was introduced in the undergraduate psychology program at Wilfrid Laurier University. Approximately 150 students from developmental, exceptional, social, and organizational psychology courses did two hours per week of course-related volunteer work in the community. The field placement program was expanded steadily as follows: 1,000 students in 1971-1975; 1,250 students in 1976-1980; and 1,750 students in 1981-1986. During the 1985-1986 academic year, 393 students enrolled in 11 psychology courses were placed in 67 different community settings. Important factors in the program's development have been the employment of a field supervisor commencing in 1973 and of graduate-student teaching assistants whose roles over the years have included: supervisory responsibilities; liaison between student, setting, and instructor; process consultation with the setting, student, and instructor; and leadership in facilitating social-intervention activities.

We feel that the incorporation of a field placement option in some courses and a requirement in others has constituted an important social intervention. Our periodic evaluations of the program suggests the field placement experience has had an important influence on student lives. For example, in a 1981-1982 evaluation based on a sample of approximately 300 students, 87.3% reported they learned new skills (31.4% reported they learned interpersonal skills); an overwhelming majority of the volunteers felt they learned a moderate amount or much about themselves (87.3%); and 55.1% reported learning a moderate amount to very much about the client population. The agencies suggested students learned much (50.0%) to very much (39.3%) about the client population. Most students felt their placements helped them to apply what they learned in class (69.6%) (Charbonneau, 1982).

The students' field-placement diaries provide a further source of evaluative information. A random selection from a population of 162 student diaries collected over a period of five years were content analyzed[2] (Bennett, 1986). The content analysis assessed changes in students' expression of needs and changes in the response of the field setting over the course of the field-placement experience (September to April).

The categories of needs were derived from Alderfer's (1972) existence, relatedness, growth theory; Maslow's (1954) hierarchy of needs; and Murray (1938). Existence-oriented needs included: comfort level in setting, comfort level with client, feelings of conflict in setting, ability to relate to client, and ability to work with client. Growth-oriented needs included: personal achievement and direction, goal setting and attainment, application of theory, and reciprocative feelings with clients. Community response included: sharing in decisions, sharing in planning, asking for opinion, giving responsibility, and continued request for volunteers.

The students whose diaries were assessed related to one of seven field settings associated with a course in mental retardation. Each diary was broken into 10 time slots for the content analysis. A 1-5 scale was used, with 1 being very positive and 5 being very negative.

As can be seen in figures one through three, the changes over time are highly significant with an increase noted in student satisfaction of their existence and growth-centred needs and with their experiences in the field setting. This appears to be a good predictive model. Ninety-three percent or greater of the variance was accounted for and the obtained F was greater than the critical F at an alpha level of .001. Inter-

FIGURE 1

Existence-Oriented Needs

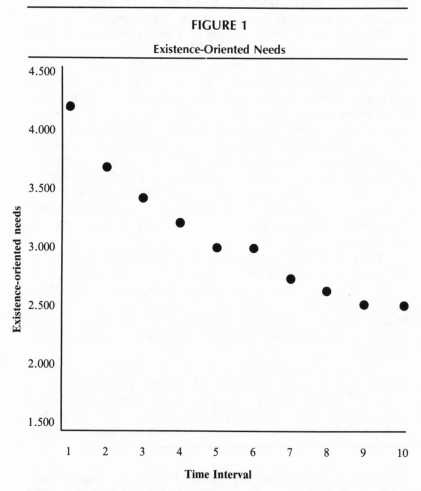

$E(Y) = 4.125067 + (-.1865394)X_1$ $F(1,8) = 111.17833$ R Squared = .93287
Source: This figure appeared in Bennett (1986).

rater reliability was .80. In short, these data provide strong support for this form of learning experience (Bennett, 1986).

The most innovative part of the practicum experience can arise when students are offered regular opportunities to process their field experiences. It is in such instances where one can facilitate a change in the student's cognitive and conceptual orientation and where the student learns to function as an agent of social intervention.

We shall attempt to describe these two strategies for training in social intervention in relation to student practica experiences with persons who had been labelled mentally retarded and their settings. The

FIGURE 2

Growth-Oriented Needs

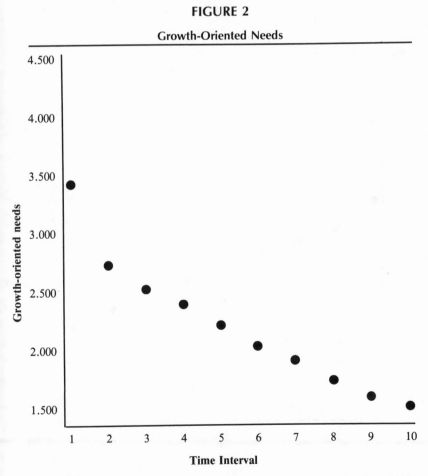

$$E(Y) = 3.275067 + (-.1878121)X_1 \quad F(1,8) = 115.16534 \quad R \text{ Squared} = .93505$$
Source: This figure appeared in Bennett (1986).

students were enrolled in an undergraduate course which one of the authors offered on the topic of mental retardation. The specific emphasis of the course content was "educating for work with retarded persons." In the course, the issue of how people are prepared for work with retarded people encompassed: (a) the relationship between the content and experiences of such preparation and the functions required of workers in their daily activities and (b) the relationship between these training processes, the local milieu in which they occurred, and the larger societal context. The problem we addressed was a formidable one. We felt that although psychologists and educators know

FIGURE 3

Community Response

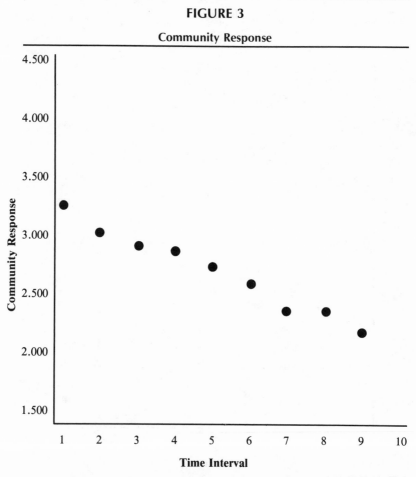

$E(Y) = 3.282533 + (-.1237879)X_1$ $F(1,8) = 301.81911$ R Squared = .97418
Source: This figure appeared in Bennett (1986).

a fair amount about the conditions which enhance or impede learning and development, they knew very little about how to utilize this knowledge in creating such conditions in ongoing social systems such as the school or broader community. Using the research literature as an operational indicator of the "state of the field" we found considerable evidence to support this view. A major focus of our social intervention activities therefore, was to define a process to reduce the gap between our knowledge of those conditions which facilitate human development and their implementation in "educating for work with retarded persons."

In other words, our goals included an interest in helping the students and community to define the nature of the social problem and to increase their problem-solving capabilities and the community's problem of resources in addressing it. We took a transactional approach (Sameroff, 1975) within a social-systems framework (Bronfenbrenner, 1979). Sixty-five undergraduates enrolled in the course that first year.

In introducing the course we used a process-consultation approach (Schein, 1969), and employed graduate students in what has since been labelled an Educational Pyramid Model (Seidman & Rappaport, 1974). These students met bi-weekly with the undergraduates to help them process their experiences. The graduate students would then meet as a group with the course instructor to process their own experiences. The second author was a graduate student who supervised the students in the case study material which follows. He attended class sessions with regularity and participated in the field settings with the undergraduates. His process-consultation work with the undergraduate students was as much a training experience in social intervention for him as it was for them.

We were first interested in defining what the content of such a course meant to those who had enrolled. On the basis of these data and the instructor's images of the content concerns of the field, individual and group learning goals were established with short-range objectives and evaluation landmarks to determine progress. On this basis the problems were regularly evaluated and redefined and appropriate action steps determined, taken, and evaluated. A high value was placed on utilizing the ongoing experiences, field or otherwise, as data for generating theories, hypotheses, and activities. We regularly examined the relationship of the student (subject) to the content (mental retardation) and situation (community and social historical perspective).

The two strategies for training which we employed were efforts to facilitate: (a) a change in the cognitive and conceptual framework of the students and (b) a dynamic exchange between the students and ongoing social systems directed toward influencing change in the ongoing social forces.

THE STUDENT AS CHANGING: CHANGE IN THE STUDENT'S COGNITIVE AND CONCEPTUAL ORIENTATION

The change was accomplished by two interdependent processes: (a) the introduction of new information and (b) the use of feedback and the discussion of experience as a means of making sense of one's thoughts, observations, and feelings. In other words, students were constantly exposed to situations or perspectives they had never before encountered and at the same time, asked to recognize and accept their thoughts and feelings which were in turn reflected on and discussed in order to utilize these experiences as a vehicle for learning and change.*

When a new experience is introduced into the consciousness of our students they characteristically start to deal with it in the same terms as they dealt with related experiences in the past. If however, there is an element of uniqueness in the experience itself or in the perspective in which the experience is presented, and if that element of uniqueness is identified and discussed so that the student becomes conscious of it, then there is likely to be something of a modification of the approach or response set of the student to incorporate the new information and respond in a manner consistent with the new learnings. The student will now come to the next situation with a slightly altered disposition or mind. The more personally relevant and valued the new experience is, the more it is likely to effect change in the individual. There is a general freeing of the imagination where not only are more alternatives envisaged for the specific situation, but the facility for the identification of alternatives is strengthened.

The changes with which we were concerned occurred at three levels. The first level concerns what an individual thinks and feels about a particular conceptual issue like mental retardation or the

---

* It is important to note that students were encouraged to accept their thoughts and feelings. Although others may have shared contrasting experiences, the differing views were not imposed on an individual. Change is an individual decision which has been described as "unfreezing" and "refreezing" (Lewin & Grabbe, 1945) and "breaking frame" and "reframing" (Goffman, 1974). To evaluate overtly another person's thoughts or feelings made more difficult the process of self-examination and reflection because it would generally result in individuals feeling the need to defend their positions.

nature of the educational experience. The second is more basic and in-volves how individuals examine situations and conceive of problems and solutions—that is, their way of thinking. The third level is the way in which they approach situations, and activate and test the alter-natives they have identified. Dramatic changes occurred in the students at all three levels. Although there is frequent interaction and overlap among these, the examples in this section of the chapter focus on the first two levels of change. The next section, "The Student as a Change Agent," deals with the third.

In the course, "Educating for work with retarded persons," students were exposed to more than just the subject matter of retarda-tion but to mentally retarded individuals. Their initial reactions were often horror and despair with the sentiment being expressed that these retarded children seemed totally helpless and hopeless. For some students this was a traumatic experience characterized by fear, repul-sion, and guilt. To illustrate their experiences, including the changes noted over time, the excerpts which follow were selected from the diaries of several of the students enrolled in the course.

Margaret: The one experience that had the most extreme effect on

Margaret:

The one experience that had the most extreme effect on me, outside the classroom, was my visit to the custodial home for retarded children. The main reason for this was that I absolutely had no idea what to expect there. I had never seen a hydrocephalic before or a mentally retarded patient who was unable to respond in any way. I was shocked, and frightened, and sickened by what I saw. At this point, I felt they were completely justified in just putting these children away and forgetting about them.

Pat:

On October 28, I had my first visit to the custodial home for retarded children. There were to be two visits, one in the morning and one in the afternoon . . . . I happened to be talking to someone who had been to the morning tour and she proceeded to tell me all about it. She was telling me all the worst things she had seen there and this really upset me as I had never even heard of half the things she was describing to me. She told me about children with huge heads, which later I learned to be hydrocephalics, also children who are just like freaks of nature such as a child with two heads (one growing out of the top of the first one).

Well I must admit, that this was almost sufficient information to stop me from going. But then I thought about it and figured that it would be better for me as a person to see these things that happen in life and not to just ignore them as if they weren't there. So I mustered up all the courage I had and went on the tour. Even though I had an idea of what I was going to see it was still a great shock to actually see them. As I went through from ward to ward I felt like I was in some kind of zoo. I could not have possibly imagined in my mind how awful these children looked or how tragic was their state if I had not seen it . . . it also made me feel rather useless for I could not imagine what could be done for children like these.

Jane:

To be quite honest, I was frightened by many of the children. Some of the children were ugly to look at and to listen to and when they would grab onto me, I really was afraid of them. I knew it was a cruel and very wrong way to feel about these children but I couldn't help feeling that way.

After a year's experience in direct contact with retarded children all three changed their perspectives considerably.

Margaret:

Through my work at the day care centre and from hearing the experiences of other students, I was soon able to see that those children at the custodial home need not be in the lifeless state many of them are in. It's hard to realize the hidden potential in each retarded child until you work with them.

Pat had a similar experience. Despite her initial reactions, Pat chose the custodial home for her field work. Listen to her in April.

Pat:

All the children I worked with came to mean a great deal to me and it makes me wonder a lot what will become of them in future years. I feel that quite a few of them could be helped if enough time, attention, money, and love was put into looking after them and teaching them . . . this is where I feel our group helped these children. Most of the people in our group had one or two children they spent most of their working hours with and this could only benefit the child . . . .
To me it was extremely enriching, sometimes frustrating and heartbreaking but it was to me one of the most worthwhile and important things that I have ever done in my life.

The changes that Jane experienced were equally dramatic and significant for her personally.

Jane:

The more I interacted with the children, the more I realized that they were just the same as normal children—they had the same wants and needs: like candy and getting into mischief; enjoy going to movies, skating, playing hockey, going to the ice-follies, love, affection and to get attention, etc. Each one of these children has a unique personality, and they have names and that's something that I wasn't emotionally aware of before I started this course.

In short what can I say except that they are handicapped in certain respects; but this handicap does not make them any less human, perhaps in some cases it even makes them more human. I sincerely believe that this feeling is the most important thing I could possibly have learned during the entire year and it is something that cannot be experienced through books but can only be experienced personally.

In the above we see how Margaret, Pat, and Jane considerably changed their concepts of retardation and their views of how to approach the problems of retardation. Their experiences in "real world settings" were highlighted by an increased understanding of the person who is called mentally retarded, and most importantly, the meaning and value of a relationship with a mentally retarded person.

True, the attitudes of many students changed in regard to retardation as a result of close, sustained contact with a retarded person. But beyond that, many of them experienced the joy, frustration, and satisfaction of having a personal, meaningful relationship with another human being. At that level, the fact that their friend was retarded was totally insignificant.

Arnold:

Our relationship has raised many questions; and the only way to answer them is to have them happen. Most certainly Steve has taught me to communicate and realize that there is someone else in the world who is vital to my existence . . . . Therefore, I can truly say that life has changed; maybe not as drastic as night and day but it has changed for the better.

To arrive at this depth of human understanding it was first necessary for the students to come to grips with their own feelings of ambivalence toward the retarded. The meaning of this struggle should not be underestimated as an important step in the growth of students. The value in this struggle and their experience in the real world was recognized as an important aspect of the educational process.

The theoretical framework of the course was that of social systems organized to meet human needs. This perspective was consciously integrated in our relationship with various field settings and facilitated the process whereby the students worked with retardation in a broader context. A number of aspects of the course warrant comment here because of their significance for the change process experienced by so many of the students. First of all, the integration of field work was critical. As testified by these few quotes from their diaries, many of the students' learnings were related directly to their active relationships with retarded persons and institutions. Involvement in the setting was complemented by regular opportunities to discuss their experiences. This dual process allowed them both the direct experience and the chance to come to grips with its emotional significance for themselves and to better understand its meaning conceptually.

The second important factor about the course format was that it did not attempt to provide the students with quick easy answers to the bold questions they were facing in the settings, nor would it provide precise definitions for the problems they encountered. In this way it more accurately reflected both the complexity of life and the true state of our knowledge within substantive areas. The students were forced to struggle with many very difficult questions for which there aren't easy answers, and to learn how to deal with the ambiguity and contradictions that surround the problems. By having a course structured so they had to define their own goals and struggle with the problems of evaluating progress toward these goals, they learned new ways of thinking that were to prove important in their working effectively in the settings.

Margaret:

I have learned about causes and symptoms of mental retardation from my other courses. The one thing I appreciated most about this course is that it has greatly broadened my view of retardation by introducing ideas on community relations, family relations, environmental factors and attitudes toward mental retardation in general. It's like looking at the topic in a completely new and more meaningful way . . . . All year I felt the classes were so unstructured that I couldn't possibly learn anything. Now I realize that if we had spent all our class time learning facts about mental retardation the whole point behind the course would have been lost. In class we can learn that a child with a certain I.Q. may be severely retarded or trainable. But from outside experience I have learned that such a statement is not as cut and dry as it appears. A child may be tested and the results will give him a certain I.Q. but that child's I.Q. may have been reduced because of a short attention span or because of perceptual problems. A child's I.Q. is not set, but results from so many factors. This course has made me realize just how many things can help a retarded child . . . . Studying mental retardation from a text seems to alienate the mentally retarded, referring to them as a group isolated from normal society. The approach we have been using this year has made me realize they are very much a part of our society and that it is not possible to draw a line and separate society into normal and abnormal.

Mary:

I have personally found this course a very worthwhile venture. In no other course, have I gained so much practical experience and knowledge about a subject area. When I first started this course, I was afraid it was not what I had expected. And it turned out that it was not. Fortunately it was not. For I feel now that a course in mental retardation cannot be something which is learned about merely in lectures, for the whole field of knowledge in this area lies in the field settings and in the practical work. You can only begin to understand something by becoming completely involved in it.

These are just a few illustrations from the diaries of the students of how they saw themselves changing. The changes were significant because it wasn't just a matter of them learning some facts, they became involved in an issue personally and they changed as persons. In addition, the diaries confirm Dewey's theory on the power of practice.

To make sense of the transition in the students' methodological orientation we can contrast two approaches to problem-solving: episodic empiricism and cumulative constructionism, both of which have been conceptualized by Bruner (1962). In the former approach, the student makes no attempt to identify patterns or relations among the factors of the problem situation. Instead they make haphazard stabs at solutions. In contrast, cumulative constructionism involved conscious effort to utilize reason and imagination to identify relations among the factors and visualize as many different combinations as possible. As students became immersed in a conscious programming of field experiences and absorbed information, they moved from a haphazard and random approach to problem solving to a greater appreciation of the figure-ground relationships and situational relativity. In other words, they became sensitive observers increasingly appreciative of an incremental and cumulative building process in relation to problems with a meaningful view of the context as well as the particulars.

Among the outcomes of such changes in the orientation of an individual are a much greater appreciation of the future and an awareness of the multiple consequences of problems in society and of projected alternatives for action. Operationally, this means that an individual comes to realize he or she is rarely locked into situations and courses of action from which there is no escape but that there are alternatives if the imagination is exercised and effective problem-solving skills utilized. They then come to feel and experience that they can have a more potent hand in determining the nature of their future as well as that of their community. One of the more important meanings of the above is that they have become more free, for freedom consists of an awareness of the existence of alternatives and the ability to act on this awareness. In the section that follows, we discuss some theories and experiences related to the development of students as proactive agents of change.

THE STUDENT AS AN AGENT OF CHANGE

The university has been a focus of the movements of social change and has been under great pressure to acknowledge its interdependence with the broader society. As some members of the university community became more critically sophisticated in their analyses of the social and natural ecology, they realized the shallowness of the belief that the university's virtue is one of intellectual detachment from the world. The university was not isolated from society but very much a part of it, supporting and encouraging the very dehumanization and depotentiation that had been identified in the world community. The belief was even more disturbing when it became apparent that the calls for academic detachment from sociopolitical affairs were often operational indicators of the alienation and anomie of many academics. Moreover some social scientists who were in a position to be actively and helpfully involved abdicated their responsibility to study social problems and to find solutions. Thus for those who were aware of the problems and actively seeking solutions, there were two inter-related battles: (a) to confront the university where it was organized to support an inequitable distribution of power and resources in society, and (b) to help it accept its responsibility to better the welfare of mankind in the local community and beyond.

Our program at the university focused primarily on the latter issue. The potential of students as change agents initially found expression in the field of services for retarded persons. The students spent the year involved as groups in one of the six different settings with which we had an active relationship, or they worked individually in other settings of their choice. The intent of the course was to focus on their experiences in the settings, helping them to understand their own reactions to retarded persons and the staff, and equipping them to help staff members develop their understanding of and effectiveness in working with retarded children. To describe their activities as change agents we will briefly outline two case studies that draw on the experiences of students in two of these settings.

Case Study A

Institution A was a residential home for profoundly retarded children where the care was primarily custodial with only a minimal amount of programming: physiotherapists circulated throughout the wards dividing their attention among approximately 120 children, 20 of whom spent a few hours daily in a school program on the premises. The other children received attention only when the staff could spare some time from their chores of feeding, laundering, and cleaning, or when volunteers were present. The majority of the children had been diagnosed as profoundly retarded and an attitude of resignation and hopelessness pervaded the home. The administrators had not been exposed to alternatives for habilitation and believed that nothing could be done to help these children. The children's problems were perceived as organic—problems for which there was no solution—and the children were expected to live out their lives rolling around in their beds and staring at the ceiling. This attitude was accepted by the staff who tended to work mechanically and impersonally with the children, saying not a word to them as they were fed, and generally regarding them as "vegetables" devoid of human feelings and potential for growth. The children were condemned to lives as "vegetables" not as a function of their retardation, but on the basis of the preconceptions of the administrators and staff which negated the possibility of effective and stimulating programs that could help the children learn and develop.

Twelve students were introduced to this setting as volunteers. Their first experience involved a tour of the institution.* Some had no previous contact with mentally retarded persons and their initial exposure to this institution was depressing and traumatic. Some experienced an immediate repulsion and horror at the sight of some retarded children, especially the hydrocephalics. However, these anxieties were largely overshadowed by their reactions to staff who seemed to relate to the children with indifference and sometimes callousness. During the initial tour of the setting, the students were remarkably restrained and conveyed none of their feelings to the staff lest the administrators become alarmed and refuse them the opportunity they wanted to work in the home throughout the year. Follow-

---

* Because we anticipated severe cultural shock, we took a good deal of effort to prepare students for this first encounter. In addition, a student supervisor accompanied them on the tour. Included in this preparation was ample warning not to offer evaluative statements of what they were experiencing during the tour, as difficult as that might be. Opportunities for processing in small group sessions away from the setting were made available immediately after their visit.

ing the tour, the group met for a very emotional discussion during which they shared their anger and resentment at the inhuman conditions in which the children were living. The students were shocked by what they had seen and determined to do something about it.

Their determination was a critical element in their involvement in that institution. Obviously there were more pleasant settings in which they could have worked, but on the basis of what they had seen and heard they felt morally compelled to stay in Institution A. They realized that it wasn't always going to be possible to move rapidly ahead with changes and expect encouraging enthusiasm and the support of administrators and staff. Besides, the healthier institutions were already blessed with more enlightened leadership and less in need of student/volunteer efforts and concern than settings where there was far less awareness of the development potentials of the children and where resistance to change was greater. In other words, even though their involvement would be more difficult and discouraging in a less developed institution, there was at the same time a greater need for it.

Initially, most students did not perceive the activation of change as a focus of the course. Having had all their educational experience in very traditional academic contexts, most of them enrolled in the course to "learn about" mental retardation by lecture and textbook. When the students realized field work was to be a major focus of the course, they saw it primarily as an opportunity for volunteer service where they could be doing something useful and at the same time learning more about retarded persons. This was especially the case in settings that seemed to have quite progressive programs. But for those who entered Institution A, the more difficult setting, this service orientation was accompanied from the beginning with a determination to "do something" about the place. The total absence of program for most and the ensuing sense of hopelessness with regard to the development of the children engendered a very conscious concern in the student volunteer for providing alternatives for what was happening.

The students' relationships with the children were personally relevant because of the sense of responsibility they felt for them. The learning experience was more total because the students had the rare opportunity of experiencing unconditional concern for others in what they did for and with those children.

The students thought of several strategies for involvement: working with the institution as a whole, concentrating their attention on a single ward, or focusing on specific children. The administrators had thoughts of their own with regard to the involvement of students. They were very proud of Ward C which had the most advanced children. Since some of these children were able to speak and thus more rewarding to work with, the administrators, their staff, and visitors to the home spent a lot of time in Ward C, in contrast to the little attention that was shown children in less developed wards. The administrators tried to encourage the students to work in this ward and initially some of the students accepted their suggestion believing that children in other wards were indeed helpless and hopeless. But after extensive discussion as a group with the faculty member and student supervisor the students came to realize that doing so would only serve to reinforce and perpetuate the perspective at the home (i.e., only Ward C children could be helped and thus merited attention, but all the others were quite hopeless, work with them being a waste of time). Because of the anger they came to feel for the staff and administrators who they viewed as irresponsible in the treatment of the children the students cared for, their initial reaction was to want to expose publicly the incompetence and destructiveness of the home. It took many weeks for them to become committed to the view that the only effective way to change the attitudes of the administrators and staff and bring about a better learning environment for the children was to be able to demonstrate that the hopeless were not hopeless. To accomplish this they decided to concentrate of Ward F whose children were generally regarded as without potential. If through their attention and work, the children in this ward could be shown to develop, the administrators would be led to reassess their previous conceptions and perhaps even adopt a new and more positive attitude toward the children in the entire home. The least the students expected was that in playing and in other ways caring for the children as children and not as "retardates," the staff could be influenced to perceive and react to the children as human beings. That was the least that was expected; much more was hoped for.

It was important throughout the year to always be cognizant of the attitudes, reactions, and behaviour of the administrators and staff. It was encouraging that the students realized very early that it would not be sufficient to devote all their attention to the children and neglect the staff. Such an approach would have been self-defeating to the broader purpose of improving the learning and living environment of the institution. To ignore the conscious building process with the staff and administration would have only provided a handful of children with some extra attention for a few hours a day over a period of eight months, the time when the students were present. To have a real impact on the institution, the students recognized that they had to have an effect on the behaviour and way of thinking of those who were around the children constantly and who would be there long after their involvement was completed. Working on that level of awareness was one step removed from direct service to the children but it made the difference between being volunteers and being change agents, between short-term and long-term effects.

Each of the 12 students spent from two to five hours there weekly. The schedule was staggered so that there was at least one and usually two or three students working in the ward daily. Their activity focused primarily on playing with and exercising the children and included assisting the staff in some of their duties, especially feeding. Every other week, in addition to the regular class meetings, the group would meet as a whole to talk about their experiences, share their observations, and discuss any new developments pertaining to the children and the way the staff was relating. The emerging pattern was imitation: that is, the students modelled certain behaviour which the staff then assimilated into their own repertoire. Students would initiate a new activity, for example, taking a child out of the crib and playing with him on the floor or singing and talking to a child while feeding her. These were simple, constructive activities that the staff could, but were not performing, mostly because of their limited view of the children's potential. However, after watching the student for awhile and seeing the positive results the activity had on the child, the staff would begin to copy the student. As the students consciously developed the process, it produced some of the changes in the direction the students had hoped.

The manner in which the children were fed and the diet itself was a source of great concern among the students. On the basis of the philosophy that these children were somehow not really human because of their retardation, the staff and administration felt it didn't really matter what the children ate as long as it filled them and kept them alive. As a consequence, they were primarily fed starches and a whole meal might consist of soggy, mashed potatoes. They received very little food of any nutritional value and in combination with constant heavy sedation and a history of little exercise with the ensuing atrophy of their muscles, the children were consistently listless and very underdeveloped. The staff concluded the children could not profit from exercise because of their physical condition but they failed to realize the factors that accounted for the children's condition. The low subsistence diet had been in effect for as long as any of the staff members could remember and they never thought to question it. Some of the students quietly introduced an alternative by arranging to get some baby food from the kitchen and feeding it to the children at their regular meal times. Many of the children visibly responded with great enthusiasm seeming to note the change in taste. Children who had previously been very fussy eaters suddenly became co-operative. When the staff saw the favourable results of the new diet, they began to think more consciously of diet consideration for other children. Now they were conscious of an alternative that had not previously existed.

This experience provided the staff with the opportunity to take some initiative independent of their administrators, something the students had never before observed. By their own apathy, lack of awareness, and a certain degree of intimidation by the administrators, the staff had grown into the position of not making any decisions concerned with the functioning of the ward but only carrying on the traditional procedures in unthinking ways.

Our students had not entered into a contract to be change agents in this setting but rather were there to be volunteer-helpers. This, however, did not limit their effectiveness in being able to influence the direction of the program or to increase staff awareness and capability. Their own concerns for the children were honest and primary motivators for wanting others to both see and hear what *their children* were capable of. In other words, they were determined to see that their children were not abused, not only maintained, but provided with development-oriented programming. It was as though they had taken on the life-death struggle for their young. In contrast, too often we have seen the more formally contracted change agent with greater skills and a stronger conceptual base have less influence because he or she was lacking in the authentic commitment for the lives of the client system or those with whom he or she was involved. In addition, a formal contract for a change agent sometimes unwittingly creates the psychological atmosphere which gives him/her the major responsibility for planning and effecting the change.

Our students because of their role relationship as volunteers in the setting were not viewed as miracle-worker-experts, there to perform some magical change. While they did not have the authoritative support as expert, their role as change agent became easier because of the absence of a barrier of unrealizable expectations generally placed on the expert consultant. Their authentic commitment to the children and the successful changes that occurred were more than ample forms of authoritative support which influenced staff members to take cognizance of the program alternatives. None of this is to say that the more formal change agent cannot effectively deal with the problems noted above. In fact, they can deal with the dependency problems associated with being perceived as a miracle worker if they help the client system to both recognize the issue and its potential pitfalls as well as to collaborate in addressing it. The issue of the change agent being able to relate to the client system in a personally committed way is a more difficult problem. In the course we concerned ourselves with this problem by discussing the essential conditions that underly the development of authentic relationships that are mutually enhancing.

One factor that affects all change agents is the level of awareness the client system has of their problems and the need for change. The administration and staff of Institution A had a very low level of awareness of the changes that were needed, feeling the home was well run and they were doing as much as they could for their children. The contrast between their acceptance of the situation and the students' horror of the dehumanizing environment was apparent from the beginning. Given the level of awareness of the administrators and staff, for the students to confront them with the dichotomy of their perceptions would be too threatening to the administrators and would effectively bar us from the institution. The students generally swallowed their comments while they were at the home. This minimized the possibility of discussing many of the concerns of the students openly and honestly with administrators and staff.* If the problems of the home could have been openly recognized and consciously studied by administrators, staff, and students together, the process of change would probably have been more effective. The path of modelling behaviour as a means for effecting change is a very arduous one. It enabled us to influence change in both staff and children and through the process of these relationships to develop sufficient authoritative support to initiate a more open feedback discussion with administration and board members by the end of the year. The students took elaborate precautions to make this meeting nonthreatening: it was held in the home where the administrators, staff, and the board representative would feel more secure, and a carefully written document describing the "concerns" of the students was distributed in advance. Unfortunately, the personnel of the home felt too insecure to examine the concerns or to see them as suggestions for improvements and change, and instead viewed them as criticisms and proceeded to rationalize or deny them. Some suggestions were too strongly supported by data to be ignored; most notably that the prescription and dispersement of medication for several children had been handled ir-

---

* There are other change agents (e.g., Argyris, 1970) who would not work with systems that they assessed to be closed to open confrontation. Our perception of the problem was that an open reality check would have been defended against whereas the incremental introduction of new information by the modeling of new behaviour with the children would allow us to remain in the system and still introduce change. It is important to point out that this patterning of behaviour was developmentally oriented and introduced under conditions of psychological success (Lewin, 1948).

responsibly by the attending physician. Not only did he respond to the cases cited with great immediacy, but shortly thereafter he reviewed every one's prescription. It is not clear whether the concerns expressed resulted in any attitude change on his part regarding the usage of medication for behavioural control. It is clear that he responded quickly and with grave concern to the issue of dispensing medication in dangerous and illegal quantities. This is an example where, due to the danger to the lives of the children involved, an immediate change was of greater importance than attitudinal change of the doctor although this too was a desired outcome. In terms of the latter, a large part of the discussion at the meeting centred on the possibilities for reducing or eliminating medication for all children except those who required it to control various forms of epilepsy. Even though they had a difficult time hearing some of the more painful comments, the trust engendered during the course of the year was sufficient that the administration was receptive to our involvement in a subsequent year.

To summarize our involvement in Institution A, described as a closed system, at a minimum some significant changes occurred in some of the children and with some staff. More important perhaps is the perspective that in a difficult complex system such as this, meaningful change can only occur over a long period. An invitation to return and make possible such continuity was a very important outcome. Furthermore, our involvement in Institution A came as society was becoming increasingly aware of the developmental potential of mentally retarded children. Subsequent to our involvement, others including the state authorities responsible for monitoring care at the facility became more interested in it. Over time many changes have occurred there including developmental programming for all children. It is a very different institution today than it was when we first became involved.

Case Study B

Institution B forms an interesting contrast to Institution A. It was a large hospital-school operated by the government and one of the more progressive in the province. It had a highly developed program and was attempting to integrate the children into the community and to involve community members as volunteers in the institution. The administrators welcomed the involvement of our students from the beginning of the year. After extensive negotiation the administrators of Institution B viewed our students as more than just a ready source of more volunteers but as an opportunity to have some thoughtful and constructive feedback on a regular basis. To reiterate some of the content discussed in the entry process, the factors which combined to prompt them to envisage the students playing this role included:

1. it was an organized group coming from a university setting where they were regularly engaged in discussion concerning the broader conceptual issues related to mental retardation and society;
2. the students would be at the institution regularly and would thus become familiar enough with the setting to make intelligent comments from an outsider's perspective and could participate with some continuity in the programming;
3. the initial contacts between the administrators and the faculty member and students were positive enough to generate the kind of mutual respect and trust necessary if the students were to function as change agents.

During the year, the students were involved in almost every segment of the program and regularly gave feedback on what they were observing to some of the administrators and staff. These feedback sessions were generally held at the end of each day that the students were at the Centre. This added to the spontaneity of the observations and provided an immediate opportunity for them to be discussed. This process culminated at the end of the year when the group wrote a paper compiling their observations and synthesizing the major suggestions for change that had developed over the year. This formed the basis for discussion at a final evaluation meeting and resulted in some action steps for planned change. Based on the positive experience of both the field setting and the university, arrangements were made to continue and expand student involvement for the following year.

SUMMARY

A couple of general comments are probably in order regarding involvement of students as agents of change in service institutions. One of our basic assumptions is that more can be gained by collaborating with the various interest groups, be they administrators, staff, parents, or whatever, than by imposing values, beliefs, and changes on them. This assumption is predicated on the belief that one cannot significantly change a situation unless one can alter and develop the ideas and attitudes of those directly involved in the situation. It serves no purpose in the long run if you accomplish a short-term, immediate change while leaving the perspective of those in the situation untouched, as intransigent as ever. The process of how a change is introduced is as important therefore as the content of the change.

In terms of end states, our intention was always to work ourselves out of a job rather than to create situations where all change was dependent on our presence. We were aware from the beginning that students would not be in the same setting forever, and thus they were responsible for helping the personnel develop skills so that the organization could retain a dynamism and continue changing after the departure of the students. In addition, it is those personnel who are there on a daily basis who are in the best position to meet the basic program needs identified as part of the planned change process. Their involvement and commitment to identifying these needs and implementing the change are essential conditions for a successful realization of the defined goals.

Students can be particularly effective as change agents because of the outside perspective they bring to a situation. In both institutions described, it was the fact that they were not a part of the day-to-day operation that allowed them to seek alternatives the staff weren't able to envisage. Students are particularly good resources in this respect because they are coming from a university setting where they have the opportunity to discuss with a wide variety of faculty and students the issues and problems that they are encountering in the field. Therefore, when they enter the field situation, they come with not only their own resourcefulness but that of the university community of which they are a part.

Also, because of their numbers, they have the manpower resources to offer some very concrete, visible, and needed help immediately. Because of this, there is not the loud silence or question generally asked of the change agent during the early weeks or months; "We know you're spending time here but what do you actually do?" In contrast, the function the students serve by being extra hands is valued and allows them the opportunity over time to work and share observations and alternative ideas with others in the setting. They're generally viewed as low-profile participants and their effectiveness can be felt through the incremental, ongoing, and very often subtle changes introduced into the system. It becomes so much a part of the system, it very often goes unrecognized until many months have gone by and the cumulative effect is noted.

The student practicum provides a valuable structural arrangement to assist students to refind themselves and to extend such mastery to others in their social environment. Through a series of small wins (Weick, 1984) over a period of many years it can also provide the bases for systemic change.

NOTES

1. The principles and design of the practicum experience at Wilfrid Laurier University have evolved over a period of fifteen years. Its development has been influenced by the program's faculty, field supervisors, and students.
2. The authors would like to acknowledge the assistance of Richard Gerson, John D. Clark, and Cheryl Norry in the analysis of these data.

REFERENCES

Alderfer, C.P. (1972). *Existence, relatedness, and growth*. New York: The Free Press.

Argyris, C. (1970). *Intervention theory and method*. Reading, MA: Addison-Wesley.

Bennett, E.M. (1970). *A social systems approach to health planning in rural communities*. Unpublished doctoral dissertation, Case Western Reserve University, Cleveland, OH.

Bennett, E.M. (1986). *A social history of community psychology at Wilfrid Laurier University*. Paper presented at the Annual Meeting of the Canadian Psychological Association, Toronto.

Bruner, J. (1962). *On knowing*. Cambridge, MA: Belknap Press of Harvard University Press.

Bronfenbrenner, U. (1979). *The ecology of human development*. Cambridge, MA: Harvard University Press.

Charbonneau, G. (1982). *Evaluation of WLU field placement program for psychology undergraduates*. Waterloo, ON: Wilfrid Laurier University. Unpublished manuscript.

Dewey, J. (1929). *The sources of a science of education*. New York: Horace Liveright & Co.

Goffman, E. (1974). *Frame analysis: An essay on the organization of experience*. New York: Harper & Row.

Lewin, K., & Grabbe, P. (1945). Conduct, knowledge and acceptance of new values. *Journal of Social Issues, 1*(3), 53-63.

Lewin, K. (1948). *Resolving social conflicts*. New York: Harper & Row.

Maslow, A. (1954). *Motivation and personality*. New York: Harper & Row.

Mills, C.W. (1959). *The sociological imagination*. New York: Oxford University Press.

Murray, H.A. (1938). *Explorations in personality*. New York: Oxford University Press.

Nelson, G., Bennett, E.M., Dudeck, J., & Mason, R.V. (1982). Resource exchange: A case study. *Canadian Journal of Community Mental Health, 1*, 55-63.

Rappaport, J. (1977). *Community psychology: Values, research and action*. New York: Holt, Rinehart and Winston.

Sameroff, A.J. (1975). *Concepts of humanity in primary prevention*. Paper presented at the Vermont Conference on the Primary Prevention of Psychopathology, Burlington, VT.

Sarason, S.B., Levine, M., Goldenberg, I.I., Cherlin, D., & Bennett, E.M. (1966). *Psychology in community settings: Clinical, educational, vocational and social aspects.* New York: J. Wiley & Sons.

Schein, G. (1969). *Process consultation: It's role in organization development.* Reading, MA: Addison-Wesley.

Seidman, E., & Rappaport, J. (1974). The educational pyramid: A paradigm for research training and manpower utilization in community psychology. *American Journal of Community Psychology, 2,* 119-130.

Weick, K.E. (1984). Small wins. *American Psychologist, 39*(1), 40-49.

Mary Reidy
Louise Lévesque
and
Maurice Payette

5

A PARADIGM SHIFT IN NURSING CARE FOR THE CHRONICALLY ILL AGED: CONCEPTS, TRAINING AND RESEARCH

The age pyramid in North America has in recent years undergone dramatic change. Repercussions are evident in all major aspects of our society, but none so much as within the health system. Not only has chronic illness become the major health problem of the elderly, but at the same time, the population of the "old-old," who are particularly vulnerable to such chronic illness, has increased. The elderly's escalating need for health care is seen by those responsible for health services, planners, administrators and health professionals alike, as a highly undesirable state of affairs and as a distinct and pressing difficulty which can be resolved by strategies already known within the health system. The most favoured strategy in recent years has been the creation of an ever-increasing number of long-term facilities where, for the most part, the care system continues to reflect that favoured in the acute hospital, but with the further constraint of restricted financial and human resources. This multiplication of facilities constitutes a familiar, accepted, and often effective response to most of the usual

Acknowledgements: Preparation of this chapter was facilitated by Research Grants from the Ministère des Affaires Sociales du Québec and National Health Research Development Programme of Canada No. 6605-1699-04. Members of the research team at the Faculté des sciences infirmières, were Louise Lévesque, Mary Reidy, Evelyn Adam and Denyse Latourelle.

difficulties and needs which arise within the health system. However, this solution not only seems to have failed to resolve the difficulty of caring for the chronically-ill elderly, but in fact, has further contributed to, and intensified this difficulty.

The crisis and cure orientation which responds well to episodic, acute, and short-term illnesses, fails to take into account the characteristics of either chronic illness or the aging process. Such an orientation is in great part responsible for the lack of personalized care and the atmosphere of dehumanization found in many long-term care settings. In mishandling care for the increasing number of chronically-ill elderly, a true problem has been created and maintained; there now exists an impasse, a situation in which an ever-increasing allotment of resources has failed to alter growing dissatisfaction among care givers, families, and the elderly themselves.

Public and private long-term care hospitals and nursing homes are the most common institutions providing care for the chronically ill, functionally-impaired, or socially-isolated elderly. A type of subculture seems to have evolved particular to these long-term care institutions. The norms and standards of this "care culture" are essentially traditional and conservative, little touched by nursing professionalism, advanced education or research, and greatly ignored by the developments of other para-medical professions and by the technological advances of the medical science of our capitalist society. At its worst, it is custodial and punitive, viewing the patient as marginal to our modern productive society, and subsequently providing care that can only be judged inhumane. At its best, it reflects the prevalent values of a nursing-care system where known physical needs are met in a perhaps kindly, but routine fashion. Within this culture, the ideal nurse is decisive, confident, tidy, well organized, technically well trained, dependable, and respectful. These values are held and reinforced in her[1] maternalistic relationship with residents and by the authoritarianism of the doctors and her superiors. The doctor is a powerful and paternalistic, but often distant figure. The resident is dependent and powerless in a controlled, controlling, and not necessarily benevolent environment.

In contrast, nursing functions in the acute-care unit are necessarily divided between the dependent role (i.e., providing delegated medical care) and the independent role (i.e., functions which are specific to nursing and are nursing responsibilities). While the doctor remains the most powerful member of the multidisciplinary team, the nurse as a team member is called upon to provide professional, autonomous, and responsible nursing care. For the most part, this integrated effort meets the needs of the acute-care patient.

Two months of intensive observations of long-term care units by a geriatric nursing research team[2] supported views frequently noted in the literature (Lévesque, 1980) and confirmed opinions held by both the public and professionals. Our team noted that certain elderly residents deteriorated rapidly upon admission to long-term care institutions and that the reason for placement was frequently psychosocial, caused by insufficient familial support and a lack of community resources. We also found that care was often custodial, and the medical model had been carried over from the acute setting. The doctor tended to maintain his power, but reduce his function; he tended to see residents regularly but infrequently, for their medical conditions were usually chronic but controlled. Nurses tended to take the dependent nursing role with little recognition of or preparation for the complex needs of a very special population.

In analysing our data, two paradoxes seemed to arise. First, institutionalization tended to meet the resident's physical needs, while ignoring those falling within the psycho-social and rehabilitative spheres, despite the psycho-social reasons associated with institutionalization. Secondly, the nursing staff, while making maximum effort, provided care that was neither effective, efficient, nor self-satisfying. This pattern of nursing practice suggested to our research team the need for an approach which would help nurses to reframe the nursing-care paradigm. The approach, subsequently developed and implemented, focused on the quality of life of the aged person in the long-term care setting, and on the orientation of and care given by the nursing team. The theory of change and concept of reframing proposed by Watzlawick, Weakland and Fisch (1974) provided the conceptual basis for our analysis. This analysis included a detailed description of the already existing custodial paradigm, and led to the development of an alternative model—a holistic nursing paradigm (see Table 1). To make possible the shift from one paradigm to the other, the research team saw the need not only to conceptualize the nursing approach based on the holistic paradigm, but also to develop a training program which would prepare nurses to implement this approach. Such an implementation requires a logical shift and implies second-order change.

The text which follows presents a theory of change, the nursing-care paradigm shift, and two case studies of planned change interventions which incorporated this nursing-care approach. Study 1 focuses on the development of the approach and Study 2 focuses on the training program and the systems-oriented change it produced.

TABLE 1

Nursing Care Paradigm Shift

Elements		Paradigms	
		Custodial	Holistic
Conceptions and values	About human nature	Mind-body separation	Mind-body perspective
	About the aging person	Continuous decline	Change
	About the sick person	Object of care	Person
	About goals	Efficiency	Self-actualization
System of nursing care	Focus	Physical	Bio-psycho-social
	Orientation	Non-explicit, disease	Explicit, adaptation
	Organization of work	Mechanistic-ritualistic	Responsive to patient needs and habits
	Interaction with environment	Iatrogenic	Prosthetic
Nursing personnel characteristics	Attitudes	Fatalistic	Optimistic
	Emotional reaction	Avoidance	Positive expression
	Focus of interelationship	Instrumental alone	Expressive/ instrumental
	Preparation	Not relevant to geriatric care	Relevant to geriatric care
	Ability	The accomplishment of tasks	The resolution of adaptation problems

A THEORY OF CHANGE

Watzlawick et al. (1974) propose a theory of change which encompasses principles of problem formation and resolution. They maintain that these principles can be formulated at a level general enough to be applied to various types of problems, regardless of the size or level of the social system involved (Watzlawick et al.). The authors propose a basic distinction between a difficulty and a problem. A difficulty is simply an undesirable situation which may either be resolved by common sense, or tolerated because no solution is known to exist. A problem, however, is an impasse, a dead end or a situation which, when not remedied, becomes further aggravated. The authors propose levels of change based on this distinction. On the one hand, a difficulty requires only first-order change, that is, change that remains within the frame or the system manifesting the situation. On the other hand, a problem can only be resolved by second-order change, that is, change that modifies the rules of the game which define the situation.

Whether the situation is personal, interpersonal, organizational, or social, second-order change is a qualitative jump which produces an effective and definitive solution. One of the main postulates of this theory of change is as follows: one may lock oneself into a vicious circle of false solutions which resolve nothing or which in themselves become the problem. By restricting oneself to a specific logical level one limits oneself to first-order change when in actuality second-order change is required, because the system's structure itself must undergo change. One applies "more of the same," when in fact one must modify one's logical perspective. Resolution or termination is *meta* to the system. To correct this error, it is necessary to effect a radical shift in the way the situation is perceived and decoded; it is essential to focus less on the content of the problem and more on its frame of reference. Watzlawick et al. (1974) call this operation "reframing," and define it as follows:

> to reframe, then, means to change the conceptual and/or emotional setting or viewpoint in relation to which a situation is experienced and to place it in another frame which fits the "facts" of the same concrete situation equally well or even better, and thereby changes its entire meaning (p. 95).

As Lefebvre (1982) observed, it is sometimes necessary to make a logical "shift" in order to view a situation in a larger context. Reframing is such a "shift." It is action- rather than origin-oriented, and makes an appeal to intuition and creativity at the same time as it permits more rigorous conceptualization (Watzlawick et al., 1974).

Objects are usually seen as belonging to one class. Once a certain class membership is accepted as reality, it often seems impossible to conceptualize an object as belonging to any other class. It is for this reason that reframing is such an effective tool of change. Having perceived an alternate class membership, one does not remain trapped within the impasse of the former view of reality. The reframed problem gives rise to effective solutions, albeit paradoxical or contrary to common sense solutions.

A NURSING-CARE PARADIGM SHIFT

Observations, consultations, the theory of change of Watzlawick et al. (1974), and a literature review, supported by the team's experience, formed the basis for a planned change from a custodial to an holistic nursing paradigm. The term paradigm is used here in the sense of "a framework of thought, a scheme for understanding and explaining certain aspects of reality" (Ferguson, 1980, p. 26). The orientation that has prevailed in long-term care settings and which has in itself become a problem, may be termed custodialism. The principal components of custodialism are basically negative and therapeutically pessimistic as compared to those of holism. The holistic paradigm central to the team's intervention implies a global optimistic response to the existing potential of residents. Reframing from custodialism to holism involves a change in conceptions and values, in the system of nursing care, and in the characteristics of the nursing personnel.

These elements are summarized in Table 1. Some of the more important implications of each of the paradigms for long-term care residents are presented below with illustrations drawn from our experiences.

Conceptions and Values

Care givers' concepts of human nature, the aged, and the process of aging in large part determine the type of interaction which the aged person experiences. If one separates mind and body and views aging as a gradual and unitary process of physical and psychological decline, where all functions are likely to be involved and all elderly are likely to experience the same decrements, custodialism necessarily prevails (Zarit, 1980). The presence of chronic illness supports this conception of the aged, and institutionalization can only imply a final journey toward death. An alternate point of view leads one to realize that while the risks of decline increase with old age, the level and rate of change varies considerably, and intervention must be particular to the individual. When aging is associated not only with deterioration, but also with growth, and when positive change is linked with appropriate intervention, one sees the care of the elderly from a different point of view.

The aged resident, when custodialism prevails, becomes a passive object of care, an object that is manipulated in a depersonalized way. They are encouraged to play the sick role, the only legitimate social role left to them. It should be realized that the "loss of instrumental roles is one of the most destructive aspects of becoming an institutionalized person" (Lawton, 1974, p. 78). Alternatively, the resident may be seen as a person with idiosyncratic life experiences. They have had, and with help can, continue to maintain a variety of social roles and family relationships despite institutionalization. Nurses can then see the importance of the family and appreciate the difficulty of having a family member in long-term care.

On the one hand, aged residents are perceived as weak, disabled, and dependent, requiring a highly structured and controlled setting where safety and over-protection predominate. They are rarely consulted about their concerns, wishes, or suggestions and have little opportunity to express themselves, to answer questions, to make choices or decisions. They occupy the lowest position in a status hierarchy and have no power.

On the other hand, a conceptual shift to the holistic paradigm enables recognition of individual potential and quality of life through patient and family participation in the decision-making and care processes.

The System of Nursing Care

In reframing, not only must the focus of nursing care be shifted from the merely physical to the bio-psycho-social, but change must also be effected in the orientation of care. A care model which is not explicit, but which retains residual traces of the medical model, becomes cure-oriented and supports a patient/professional relationship in which "the patient is dependent and the professional is the authority" (Ferguson, 1980, p. 247). However, elderly residents with controlled medical conditions, when viewed within the ecological context, require interventions of a psycho-social nature and not just sophisticated technical and medical expertise. The custodial paradigm, which focuses on disease and the deficiencies associated with it, not only neglects functional rehabilitation but also reinforces a pessimistic view of the situation which is demoralizing to staff and residents alike.

An explicit nursing model such as the Roy (1976) adaptation model, provides a framework which helps nurses to systematically identify resident problems, and ensures a common conception of care upon which objectives and interventions can be based. It encourages contributions from various levels of staff, facilitates the supervision of the nursing team, and favours cooperation and team work.

When the focus of care remains physical and disease-oriented, and the principle of work organization mechanistic, the environment tends to become inherently iatrogenic: the treatment becomes the cause of disease, especially at the social and psycho-social level. Staff members often prefer to carry out tasks themselves rather than to motivate or encourage residents to help themselves. This in turn leads to the phenomenon of excess disability, or the discrepancy between functional disability and actual physiological limitations (Barton, Baltes, & Ortech, 1980; Kahn, 1972).

In contrast, within the holistic paradigm, collaborative identification of health objectives and the formulation of care plans by staff, residents and family is viewed as a crucial process which both takes advantage of and encourages the development of the resident's potential. Further, nurses understand the importance of an environment which minimizes dependency and ensures a way to cope with functional deficiencies (Brody, 1977). Residents capitalize on their resources by making use of the prosthetic aspects of the milieu or of specific prosthetic devices complementary to their residual abilities.

Nursing Personnel Characteristics

The nursing staff operating within the paradigm of custodialism tends to adopt a fatalistic attitude toward the ill elderly. Such an attitude produces a Rosenthal (1966) effect or self-fulfilling prophecy. The more one believes in the inevitable decline and lack of rehabilitative potential of the elderly, the more one will expect steady deterioration, lack of functional ability, and loss of autonomy, and the more it will, in fact, occur.

The emotional impact of the aging process daily confronts staff members. To protect themselves emotionally, many develop defence mechanisms, the most common of which is avoidance. This emotional reaction protects staff members who tend to have difficulty maintaining even limited contact with clients and family members. Communications remain task-oriented and relationships instrumental. There is little mutual encouragement, positive reinforcement, or understanding among the staff.

Within the holistic paradigm, however, the role of nurses is to foster adaptation, and to be conscious of the patient's potential for rehabilitation thus encouraging an optimistic and hopeful attitude, rather than avoidance of residents. Nurses realize that effective care is based on attentive listening, validation of perceptions, and the feeling of confidence and mutual trust which are part of a cooperative relationship. In order to maintain such an optimistic attitude toward the aged resident, staff members must feel free to express the emotional reactions and feelings they experience in caring for these residents. The positive expression of emotion requires support from the rest of the nursing staff, which will also aid in managing tensions in both the group and individuals (Johnson & Martin, 1965). Both the helping relationship with the resident and the supportive interactions of staff members are in turn facilitated by an open, supportive environment.

Nurses, from the custodial point of view, do not seem aware of their lack of preparation despite the fact that they feel at a loss to deal with many situations, and they do not know, or feel the need to know, how to interpret or to utilize psycho-social information to plan interventions. The nurse within the custodial framework develops and values abilities specific to the accomplishment of tasks, whereas the holistic approach favours abilities related to fostering the adaptation of aged residents. Furthermore, the holistic paradigm being global as well as complex, requires both specific and extensive professional knowledge of geriatric care.

TWO CASE STUDIES

Case Study 1

Observations and subsequent analyses of nursing practice led our research team to develop, implement, and systematically evaluate an holistic nursing approach.

After obtaining research grants from the federal and provincial (Québec) governments, we received permission to conduct a one-year evaluative research project in a 500-bed long-term care hospital in Montreal. The first phase of this project was to develop the components of the approach; the second was to implement the approach and to evaluate its effects.

A. *First Phase: Development of the Components of the Nursing Approach.* The first component of our approach is the nursing model conceptualized by Roy (1976).[3] It is based on Helson's adaptation-level theory and was chosen because of its holistic orientation and its strong concern for psycho-social as well as biological factors. A nursing model is essential because it provides the mechanism of intervention if not the specific strategies, and it clarifies for nurses their role in the health team.

Roy (1976) views the goal of nursing as client adaptation. Adaptation is defined as a positive response to stimuli, that is, one which preserves bio-psycho-social integrity. The nurse sees her client as an adaptive system which responds in four adaptive modes to internal and external stimuli. The nurse's role is to facilitate adaptation. Her intervention focuses on the stimuli (focal, contextual and residual) which provoke responses (behaviours) in each of the four modes.

The first of the adaptive modes is bio-physiological. The three others are psycho-social. They include self-concept, role function, and interdependence modes. The nurse collects data on each mode regarding client behaviours (responses) and the provoking stimuli. Behaviours are judged as adaptive (positive responses) according to two criteria. First, a given behaviour provoked by a given stimulus must preserve the bio-psycho-social integrity of the client. Second, behaviours provoked by one stimulus must not be so intense that the client has no energy to respond to complementary stimuli.

The nurse plans her intervention as the increase, decrease, maintenance, or elimination of the stimuli, manipulating the focal stimulus first (if possible), and the contextual and residual stimuli next. Once the intervention is completed, client behaviours are evaluated (i.e., have adaptive behaviours been maintained and non-adaptive ones modified?). In order to provide care based on this conceptual model, the nurse uses the systematic nursing process or problem-solving method derived from the model. Clinical tools necessary to the nursing process were developed specifically for use in this study.

The second component of our approach is the helping relationship. Nurses, of all health professionals, are best placed to give natural psycho-social aid and support. Regardless of the conceptual framework which guides them in the practice of their profession, the helping relationship is essential to the role of nurses. It is particularly so within the context of the holistic paradigm. Therefore, sensitizing staff members to the importance of a helping relationship and helping them to develop appropriate attitudes and abilities is given high priority. We utilized a program which was directed toward nurturing natural psychological skills, rather than preparing professional psychotherapists. As part of this program, the nurse learns to explore her own feelings and to bring clients to explore their feelings in the client-nurse interaction. The nurse also learns the importance of using open-ended rather than closed questions, and of not only reflecting on the content of client communications, but also identifying the feelings underlying their words.

The third component of our approach consists of strategies which have been reported in the literature as effective in the manipulation of stimuli often encountered in geriatric settings. While there are many such strategies, those selected for the initial implementation, and introduced to the nursing staff were: interventions with residents and their families as family units, reminiscence groups, and sensory stimulation. Others, such as reality orientation and bladder retraining, were seen as possible additions once these initial ones were mastered.

Only the family-intervention strategy will be discussed in this text, since the others are well known and easily accessible in the literature. Family intervention is important within our paradigm, and this particular strategy was developed specifically for this project by a member of the research team.[4]

Roy (1976) perceives the family as one of the key stimuli contributing to either the adaptive or non-adaptive behaviour of the elderly resident. Coping adequately with the institutionalization of an elderly member is often a long and painful process for a family. Both the family as a unit and the elderly person must come to terms with changes in the nature of respective responsibilities, with the reality of living in two settings, and with the realization that family relationships must be interpreted within in a new context.

The intervention (Latourelle, 1985; Latourelle & Lévesque, 1985) is based on the explicit assumption that the family is an ongoing interactional system and that the understanding of that system necessitates direct observation during family interaction (Minuchin, 1974; Watzlawick et al., 1967). The main intervention parameters are: helping family members verbalize their perceptions of the situation and to acquire a realistic viewpoint; helping them identify and explore their feelings about the current situation; supporting them in their efforts to bring about changes in their roles and relationships; keeping them adequately informed of the sick member's state of health; teaching them how they might be more helpful during visiting hours; and informing them of, and referring them to, community resources.

The pivotal point of the intervention occurs when the family identifies one of its current "problems." By observing and sustaining the family as it works through a problem, the nurse is in a position to see its members interact, and is thus able to focus on the process. In other words, she concentrates on what is happening at a given time, in a given place and context (Satir, 1967). The nurse's way of relating to the sick person, becomes a model for the family. She helps family members apply their experience to other family "problems" which affect their elderly hospitalized relative.

B. *Second Phase: The Trial and Evaluation.* The design was traditional: quasi-experimental, with pre- and post-tests and non-equivalent experimental and comparison groups. Fifty-nine participants from three experimental units and 62 participants from three comparison units within a long-term care hospital were part of the sample (mean age: 74.7).

The four main tasks associated with the second phase of this study included: the preparation of clinical nurse specialists, preparation of training sessions for the nursing and para-nursing personnel, the implementation and evaluation of the approach.

Four nurse specialists were trained to implement the approach and to participate in training sessions with the regular unit staff. These nurse specialists were expected to hold advanced degrees in nursing science and to assume a nursing role appropriate to the holistic paradigm, but which would be difficult to conceive within the framework of custodialism. The theoretical and clinical background (i.e., gerontological nursing) of these clinicians ensured they possessed expertise in the science of nursing.

The training sessions were provided concurrent with the implementation of the approach in order to gain the active collaboration of the nursing staff. They were expected to reinforce and complement the planned intervention of the clinicians.

The actual implementation of the approach, excluding the pre- and post-tests and the information session with hospital authorities and head nurses, took approximately eight months. The first three weeks allowed the clinicians to become acquainted with staff and residents. During the next 3 months, the nurse specialists' major role was to "try out" the approach by giving direct care to a certain number of residents, who often required complex care. In doing so, they acted as models for the rest of the staff. A secondary role included elements of teaching, supervising, and consulting. A series of workshops were organized, the themes of which were later explored in clinical meetings on the units, in terms of applicability to resident care. Support, encouragement and information were freely provided. Thus, the clinicians learned to function effectively while using the new approach, and began to help other staff members to reframe the nursing care they provided.

Three and one half months of active collaboration followed the training period. The clinicians continued in their roles as direct care providers, and the staff worked with them and in some instances "tried out" the approach themselves. While the clinicians still performed certain formative tasks, they did so to a lesser extent. During the last three weeks they prepared to depart from the units, and tried to assure continuity in the care of the residents.

The final task of this phase was the evaluation. Despite a tendency toward positive change among residents in areas such as autonomy in activities of daily living, social activities, and locus of control, only two variables showed significant positive change for the experimental group. These were a decrease in the number of p.r.n. drugs (i.e., medication given on demand) distributed each week and an increase in affiliative support among residents. No significant differences were found in staff attitudes toward patient rehabilitation, or in the quality of communication.

These results must be interpreted in light of clinical realities. The trial period was too short; the approach was not implemented as intensively as anticipated because a larger than expected proportion of the clinicians' time was required for staff formation, leaving less time for direct intervention; and finally, active collaboration from the staff came much later than expected, with the result that the whole nursing team implemented the approach for only a limited period of time.

From descriptive data and process measures, however, we found certain changes had occured. A large proportion of the staff had learned both the Roy (1976) model and how to use the clinical tools, and by the end of the project they tended to favour continued application of the approach. A task force including staff members was formed to maintain the approach and to begin its implementation in other units of the hospital.

From the descriptive data we also learned of other factors explaining the process and results, including: a level of staff preparation lower than expected, an attitude of defeatism and enormous emotional difficulties among the staff resulting from their daily confrontation with aging and chronic illness, the importance given to routine, poor leadership, conflict over roles and tasks among care givers, and lack of support among members of the team.

By the end of the project, the staff on the experimental units had begun to accept the approach and wished to maintain it. On the other hand, they realized how far the type of change to be effected went beyond their usual activities. They were being asked to change their conceptual, emotional and value orientation. We had effected "unfreezing"—beginning the change process but not allowing enough time for the process to be completed and for re-integration to occur.

Taking into account the statistical trends shown by the results and the amassed descriptive data, we concluded that the results were sufficiently positive to allow continued refinement and modification of the nursing approach. However, we also concluded that a subsequent implementation would require the inclusion of specific strategies for planned change, and a well developed training program for the personnel. Furthermore, the general quasi-experimental design seemed too limited in terms of both the monitoring and control of the implementation process. An action-research design would seem to be more viable, flexible, and appropriate.

Case Study 2

As the above research project drew to a close, the project director was approached by a group of nurses working in a long-term care hospital in Quebec City. Frustrated by their inability to resolve the difficulties of geriatric care, having known the director as a professor of geriatric nursing, and having heard by word of mouth of the intervention just described, they asked for help. They returned to their director of nursing with information provided by the research team about our nursing approach.

TABLE 2

Overview of the Training Program

Learning Objectives	Methods of Evaluation(s)	Outcomes
1)To analyse staff attitudes toward aging, the aged person and chronic illness;	a) Scale-Attitude Toward Rehabilitation (D'Amour, 1980) b) Critical incidents	a) no significant difference be-fore-after b) content analysis indicated trend toward more positive at-titude
2)To understand and to take into account in the planning of care, certain bio-psycho-social modifications associated with the aging process and chronic illness;	a) critical incidents b) clinicians' reports of clinical meetings for plan-ning of care	a) content analysis indicated trend toward increased under-standing b) clinicians consensus of in-creased utilization in planning over time
3)To understand the main elements of the nursing adaptation model and how it can guide clinical practice;	a) auto-evaluation scale of comprehension of (6) ele-ments of the model	a) significant difference (p. ‹.001) before-after
4)To follow the steps of the systematic nursing process which derive from the nursing model;	I. Auto-evaluation scale of a) ability to accomplish (8) activities associated with the systematic nursing process b) accomplishment of (8) activities associated with the systematic nursing process c) accomplishment of (10) interventions associated with key problems of adaptation II. Content analysis of a sample of nursing his-tories, synthesis forms and care plans	I. a) significant difference (p. ‹.001) before-after b) significant difference (p. ‹.004) before-after c) significant difference (p. ‹.02) before-after II. Content analysis indicated tendency toward increasing ability to follow steps
5)To use certain clinical tools such as the nursing history, synthesis form, and the nursing care plan;	I. Count of a) the proportion of nur-sing personnel who used all clinical tools b) the proportion of clients for whom clinical instruments were used II. Content analysis of a sample of nursing his-tories, synthesis forms, and care plans	I. a) all nurses had completed at least one series of clinical tools b) approximately 50% of residents had series com-pleted—each ward devel-oped a schedule to complete the series for all residents II. A content analysis of a sample of these tools indicated that they tended to be completed in an appropriate way

6)To be able to establish an interpersonal relationship derived from an holistic approach toward the person;	a) b)	auto-evaluation scale (6 item) of abilities in the helping relationships auto-evaluation of – self transparency – relation of self	a) b)	significant difference (p. <.001) before-after values not available but director of "Helping Relationship Workshop" reported a trend toward positive change
7)To interact with the client's family, informing them of the care plan, explaining life at the centre, and helping them make visits more pleasant and therapeutic;	a) b)	observation and identification of family interaction (6 items) interaction with family (4 items)	a) b)	significant difference (p. <.031) before-after significant difference (p. <.030) before-after
8)To assume, as a part of the interdisciplinary team, a specific nursing role and to interact with the other members of the team in a complementary way.	a)	critical incidents of team participation and case presentations during interdisciplinary clinical team meeting	a)	content analyses indicated active participation and a trend toward differentiation of roles and tasks from other medical and para-medical practitioners

Shortly thereafter the director of nursing contacted the research team and formally asked for help to better prepare his staff to meet the exigencies of geriatric care. The situation was discussed in detail. Our research team proposed that a nursing sub-system try to implement, under realistic conditions, the approach we were in the process of refining. The nursing administration in turn proposed a contract whereby the research team would undertake an intervention of planned change which incorporated the approach, and would evaluate the effects of the change process.

The general objective of this second intervention of planned change, stated in the language of change theory (Watzlawick et al., 1974), was to reframe the conceptions and values, the system of care, and the nursing characteristics of the members of the hospital nursing sub-system from a custodial to an holistic paradigm of geriatric care.

This project was different in aim from the preceding one. In the first case study the team undertook a research project with a quasi-experimental design, with the aim of evaluating the effects of a new nursing approach. This subsequent study was a type of action-research which consisted of helping a whole sub-system undergo second-order change by means of a formal training program, and analyzing the change effected.

The complexity of the anticipated second-order change could only be effected through a training program which was in itself complex. The training program was based on the experiences of our first study, but was developed and modified according to the needs expressed by the nursing care personnel, the characteristics of the staff, and the clinical situation of a predominently geriatric clientel. The hospital housed 300 residents in six long-term care units, a readaptation unit, and a day hospital. Approximately 360 members of the nursing care team—the nurses, auxillaries and aids of the day, evening and night shifts, participated in the training. The input of other sub-systems of the hospital, such as the union and the departments of medicine, social work, and physiotherapy, was important to the functioning of the nursing sub-system, was also important to the change process.

The specific learning objectives of the training program are presented in Table 2 along with the method and the results of the evaluation. These results will be discussed later in this text.

The objectives of this intervention involve changes in attitudes, knowledge and behaviour. Consistent with an action-oriented intervention they were developed in collaboration with the nursing staff. It may be noted that objectives 3-8 were addressed to the professional nurse, though all members of the nursing team were involved to different degrees in the process of care.

General Principles and Pedagogical Strategies. Within the training program, we placed the accent on developing abilities, thinking rather than memorizing, and learning by doing. We were conscious that the staff would undergo major changes, questioning even their professional values. For this reason, we tried to establish a learning climate which permitted them to feel at ease and to express their feelings, opinions, and needs. Further, we took into account their actual level of knowledge and ability, and their perceptions of the work situation. We encouraged their collaboration and involvement by participative methods, and valued their intuitive knowledge as well as the acquisition of new professional behaviour.

In order to facilitate the shift from one paradigm to the other, we hired four clinical nurse specialists and a clinical coordinator. These clinicians assumed educational functions, and for the most part, carried out these functions and did their teaching on the care units. They reinforced, or in certain cases re-explained, theoretical concepts introduced during workshops, while at the same time, helping the staff to integrate such notions into daily practice. They accompanied and supported the staff through various learning experiences, and when necessary, acted as role models in giving direct care to patients. The nurse specialists' function in the work situation was, we believe, pedagogically essential, considering the magnitude, complexity, and diversity of the cognitive and emotional reframing necessary to change paradigms.

In order to provide the content basic to certain cognitive reframing, two series of workshops were organized. The aim of the first series was to help the personnel to learn to establish a helping relationship[5] (see Objective 6, Table 2) by developing a receptive attitude including empathy, authenticity, and respect, and by communicating this attitude through listening, reformulation, reflection, validation, exploration, and feedback (Chalefour, 1982).

The second series focused on aging; professional skills, values, and attitudes; the Roy (1976) model (as discussed in Case Study 1); and the systematic nursing process which is derived from it. The steps of this process include: the identification of adaptive and non-adaptive behaviours and the environmental stimuli affecting these behaviours, the formulation of objectives, the planning of an intervention to maintain or modify stimuli, execution of the intervention, and assessment to determine if adaptive behaviour has been maintained and if non-adaptive behaviour has become adaptive. On the whole, the small-group format and the discussions, role playing, and use of actual clinical situations in the workshops rendered the learning of new professional behaviour less threatening.

The change initiated in the workshops was reinforced and accelerated by meetings of the nursing team on each care unit, under the supervision of the nurse specialist. Certain themes generated by current care situations were discussed in depth, and specific clinical problems and difficulties relating to the use of the systematic nursing process were explored. Clinical tools, the nursing history form for analysis and synthesis of data, and the nursing care plan were perfected, and care was planned with the help and support of the clinicians.

Systems-Oriented Change. All second-order change implies modification of the system; it may take the form of new strategies of organization or communication, new rules of organizational behaviour, or a reformulation of the institutional mission or objectives. In the case under discussion, the implementation of a nursing approach had an organizational impact not only on the nursing sub-system, but also on the other sub-systems of the long-term care hospital.

Very early in the change process it was necessary to redefine the roles of the different care givers within the nursing sub-system and to reorganize tasks and the time allocated to them. It also became urgent to undertake the work of team-building, to bring care givers to a level of consensus, to better use their respective resources, and to reach a higher level of efficiency in their work. The preparation for, and animation of regular team meetings, which became an important task of the head nurse, required the support of the clinical nurse specialist.

Each team had to learn to interact in a positive and constructive way both within their own group and with other professionals in the centre.

Many sub-systems, in addition to nursing, were affected more or less directly during the course of the intervention (e.g., the administrators, para-medical professionals, employees' union, resident committees, residents' families). The collaboration of these groups proved to be indispensible to the success of the project. From the beginning the research team made a point of meeting with representatives of these groups to explain the objectives and implications of the project and to examine different modalities of collaboration.

Many factors contributed to rendering these organizational changes positive and long-lasting. Most important was a strategy of prevention. On the one hand, this approach consisted of adequately informing, at the right time and by the right means, all those persons or groups affected by the intervention. An appropriate circulation of information during the course of any change process can prevent misunderstandings, problems and certain resistance. The feeling of being threatened by the activities of the planned intervention were attenuated as the study progressed.

On the other hand, it would be naive to expect that the change anticipated in the implementation of such an intervention would not provoke resistance. We wished to change the structure of the nursing system itself, a system which functions as a sub-system of an institution. For many within both the nursing sub-system and other interrelated sub-systems, the hoped-for changes appeared paradoxical and even inappropriate. Throughout the period of implementation, we monitored the positive and negative forces and tried to identify obstacles as rapidly as possible. We encouraged change, recognizing and accepting resistance as a necessary condition of change, and even incorporating such resistance in a positive fashion into the change process.

The quality of the relationship which developed between the university research team and the different care givers was also important to the success of the intervention. A reciprocal recognition of ability and expertise, the pursuit of common goals for change, and an appropriate sharing of responsibilities rendered the relationship truly cooperative. Among those at the centre who collaborated closely with the project were the director of nursing and his assistant, the head nurses, and the psychologist responsible for the development of professional services within the centre.

During the course of the study, the research team relied upon the services of a consultant in organizational development. The role of this consultant was to coach the research team members, including project directors, clinicians, and coordinator, as they considered the organizational dimensions of the project and anticipated the systemic impact of their activities. With this support, they assumed the role of change agents, dealt with crucial incidents, and functioned as a recognized support group to the nursing personnel. The staff brought to the study a willingness to solve their problems, and a readiness for change. The university team, coming from outside the system and with an expertise in geriatric care, brought a new perspective to the care problem that had so frustrated the hospital staff.

This planned change intervention lasted approximately one year. The first phase, lasting about one month, gave the nurse specialists a chance to get acquainted with the setting, to be known, and to make known the nature of the project. The objectives were to establish mechanisms of participation and exchange between the research team, the nursing personnel, and the institutional milieu; to identify learning needs and the resources to be mobilized; and to clarify the mode of implementing the training program. During this period, the nurse specialists gathered information on the organizational structure, the functions and roles of the nursing care-givers, the type and content of interaction between care-givers and residents, residents' adaptation problems and the related stimuli, and the nature of the relationship between the families and care-givers.

The second phase, requiring seven to eight months, began with workshops on the helping relationship for all levels of the nursing team. Once a climate of confidence had been created and the helping relationship was strengthened and reinforced, formation of the nursing model and the systematic nursing process was possible. Other workshops on the family and specific nursing strategies were alternated with periods of clinical application under the guidance of the nurse specialists. This allowed the care givers to apply the systematic nursing process, to use the clinical tools developed for the nursing approach, and to concretize the theoretical notions presented to them. At their request, great emphasis was placed on clinical practice, and head nurses began to identify other needed nursing strategies and to plan for their introduction during a follow-up phase of the project.

The final phase of the intervention, which lasted about one month, was a period of consolidation, evaluation, and formalization of follow-up mechanisms to ensure the stabilization of the paradigm shift. For example, during this period the nurse specialists helped the staff to seek as a resource person the psychologist responsible for professional relations within the institution. His function was to facilitate the process (i.e., small-group dynamics, leadership, development of criteria or indices for evaluation of nursing services, etc.). A second follow-up mechanism was to develop a realistic plan or schedule for the completion of all nursing histories and revised nursing-care plans. Another was the elaboration of a reference manual on various aspects of the program (i.e., the Roy model, the systematic nursing process, etc.). This manual still serves as a reference point for staff who are familiar with the program, and as a starting point for the orientation of new staff. The elaboration of these and other strategies was a collaborative effort between the departing research team and the personnel within the milieu, who assumed responsibility for the follow-up phase.

THE IMPACT OF THE INTERVENTION OF PLANNED CHANGE

Questions concerning the impact of planned second-order change can perhaps be approached at two levels. First, we may ask if reframing did indeed occur; and secondly, whether such reframing resolved the problem at hand. A systematic evaluation, based on data from staff, administration, and residents, was carried out to determine if the learning objectives of the program were attained. Table 2 presents these objectives and a summary of the method of evaluation and the outcomes.

The evaluation included a series of auto-evaluation scales developed by the research team and/or clinicians (for which nominal and content validity was assured), critical incidents collected by the clinicians and submitted to content analysis, and a count of events or reports of events collected by the clinicians. The methodology included descriptive, pre-post-test, and repeated measures designs. At no time was a control group used.

The study differed from Case Study 1 in that it was an appropriate and economical form of program evaluation in keeping with an action-research orientation and limited financial resources.

The consistency of positive outcomes (see Table 2) served as evidence that the project's objectives were for the most part attained and that this, in turn, resulted in the type of conceptual shift desired. Such reframing seems most definitely to have led toward problem resolution.

A further sign that second-order change had been achieved, was the type of learning realized by a significant number of the nursing personnel. Using Argyris' (1982) distinction between single-loop and double-loop learning, we examined the shift in level of learning which had taken place. In single-loop learning, "the actor learns only within the confines of what is acceptable" or in other words "many of the hypotheses or hunches that people generate will become self-sealing or self-fulfilling" (Argyris, 1982, p. 88). On the other hand, double-loop learning "allows us to examine and correct the way we are dealing with any issue and our underlying assumptions about it" (p. 159). In this type of learning "people will confront the validity of the goal or the values implicit in the situation" (p. 88). We found clear indications of double-loop learning from the analysis of critical incidents and from the clinicians' observations that members of the nursing team had changed their assumptions about the goal of nursing care, their roles, and the potential of their patients.

Impact on the Nursing Subsystem

The impact on the nursing sub-system was a direct reflection of the change effected in the three elements of the nursing-care paradigm (Table 1). The new ways in which nursing personnel handled patient care were evidence that they had begun to perceive themselves, their patients, and patient care differently. The reframing from the custodial to holistic paradigm implies a shift in conceptions and values. The nurses and para-nursing personnel began to speak more respectfully about their patients, and to spend more time speaking with them and to respond better to their spiritual needs and religious aspirations. Further, residents and families became more active in care planning, both informally and through participation in the multidisciplinary team.

When the resident is seen as a person, the staff will begin, as did these nurses, to interest the family in the care of their hospitalized relative. A pamphlet was developed and given to families at the admission of each resident. The aim was to reduce feelings of guilt, to encourage collaboration, and to make family visits more satisfying. This, coupled with a discussion of the patients' care plans, seems to have been associated with better resident/family relations and a reduction in the number of complaints to the administration concerning care.

The system of nursing care, as such, is also an integral part of the care paradigm. The focus of care became bio-psycho-social rather than merely physical, and was based on the assessment of individual residents and on their perceptions of their needs. After participating in the program, nurses were more conscious of the importance of their professional work and could better define their professional role. Sensitized to the importance of flexible and supportive leadership, the nurses began to give a more systematic orientation to the care process, and began to better assume their responsibility as team leaders. The other members of the nursing team, nursing auxillaries, aides, and orderlies, felt more involved in decisions relating to care and developed a greater sense of the value of their participation in team meetings. The nursing team generally recognized personal, professional, and clinical benefits from the changes they were experiencing, and felt an appropriate return from their investment of time and energy.

Important changes related to the third element of the paradigm—the nursing personnel characteristics—were noted. Increased abilities, particularly those directly associated with the analysis of patient needs and subsequent interventions, were noticeable. Staff members' interest intensified as their skill in completing nursing care plans according to the nursing model, augmented.

An impact was also felt on the functioning of the interdisciplinary team. The regular use of clinical nursing tools (e.g., the nursing history and nursing care plan) better prepared the nurses to participate at a professional level, and increased the complementarity of the interdisciplinary team members. In becoming more conscious of their specific professional role and identity, as defined by the nursing model, the nurses better comprehended their place in the team. As the team began to function better, the quality of the meetings and team spirit improved. Closer contacts began to develop between individual professionals within the different disciplines (nurses, physiotherapists, occupational therapists, pharmacists, etc.).

Informal feed-back and feed-back exercises carried out by the clinicians during workshops and on the wards indicated, on the part of the personnel, satisfaction with their learning and personal growth, feelings of optimism, better relations with patients, and more contact with families. Because they viewed situations differently, the nurses themselves were different.

Impact Observed at the Institutional Level

Major and important change in the nursing care sub-system of a long-term care institution cannot help but have an impact on the institutional system, and even perhaps on the global health system.

The hospital administration sought and obtained money for the position of a clinical nurse-specialist. One of the nurse-specialists from the program was hired to develop and fill the new post. Her goal was to maintain and reinforce the changes already attained, to help reinforce the learning already achieved, and to help the staff to continue to develop skills and strategies to meet the specific needs of their patients. Particular attention was paid to the development of nursing sub-programs in neurological and readaptation nursing.

The creation of a quality-of-care committee was among the most important and interesting realizations for the institution. This permanent committee functions as consultant to the director of nursing care and has as its mandate, the development and implementation of mechanisms to assure the quality of nursing care. It also makes recommendations for staff formation in order to prepare nursing team members to better respond to patient needs. It is composed of nurses, nursing auxillaries, aides, orderlies, and nursing administrators or supervisors.

Recreation committees were also organized on several units and many organized activities have already been planned with the collaboration of the residents and their families. The environment was also made more stimulating. For example, under the direction of a committee of aides, old songs were collected from the residents and staff, and residents began to sing together; a reminiscence day became an established event; mirrors and clocks were placed in patients' rooms, gardens were cultivated, and birds appeared on several units.

The impact has not only been felt within the nursing sub-system and hospital organization as a whole, but the planned intervention has had certain direct and indirect repercussions on the larger health sub-system. The hospital has become a living example for other long-term care units or institutions, and it now invites administrators and care-givers from other hospitals to visit and observe. The hospital has also begun to make arrangements to receive students of various disciplines for practicum and fieldwork experiences.

The research team has published reports and articles describing the intervention and has presented papers at various meetings and conferences. These have included meetings with representatives of the department of the provincial health ministry responsible for planning and providing long-term care, meetings with care-givers and nursing or hospital administrators, and multidisciplinary scientific conferences. We have also published and allowed, in selected milieux, the use of certain of the clinical and evaluation tools. Permission to use these tools depends upon the preparation and experience of the care-givers, and their familiarity with the approach and/or the underlying model. It may be granted to clinicians or care-givers who participated in one of the studies we have presented, who have been prepared in a nursing masters program at our university, or who have been specially coached.

Each member of the research team is a professor in the faculty of nursing, and integrates aspects of these studies in courses, seminars, and directed studies with graduate students. Courses include, either directly or indirectly, content (care of the geriatric client or their family), process (how to implement or facilitate change), or methodology (research tools or design) generated by the intervention. Among these are: two seminars and one course on the care of geriatric clients, courses on program development, research methodology, clinical nurse specialization, and family dynamics and woman's health. We estimate that more than a hundred graduate students in the past two years, have been exposed to, if not influenced by, some aspect of our intervention.

The provincial ministry of health funded a project to explore the possibility of the systematic implementation of the intervention within a variety of other long-term settings in the province, by means of a team of consultants. The protocol developed was rejected, however, on two counts. First, it did not fall within the governmental educational policy currently in force, concerning staff of long-term care institutions, and second, it was considered too expensive to implement. Nevertheless, the sub-departments of the ministry responsible for long-term care hospitals and nursing homes have asked for continued consultation and are ready to fund specific projects carried out by our research team. In addition, a long-term care hospital in Montreal, partially with internal development funds and partially with funding from the ministry of health, has begun replication of our intervention of planned change. The project will differ from that presented in Case Study 2 in that the conditions of implementation are even more realistic. A special project team of nurse clinicians from within the institution itself, rather than from the university, will be responsible for the change process, with consultation from the university research team. This implementation will take into account our earlier experiences and certain recommendations we believe are important for any future replication. These recommendations are discussed below.

DISCUSSION

A critical assessment of the implementation process in these two studies has convinced us that certain changes would be appropriate in the design of a replication program. We do not suggest the introduction of new program components, but rather a refinement, intensification, or more explicit development of certain already existing elements. First, a better appreciation of the change situation, through a well planned diagnostic process would allow program directors to better anticipate the effect on the whole system. While such a process was tried with a certain degree of success on our part, a more developed and far-reaching "diagnosis" paired with appropriate strategies of planned change would further facilitate the change process and ensure the desired reframing.

A second recommendation is more specific to the process of the training program. The head nurses should be better prepared in advance, not only in terms of the cognitive content and strategies inherent to the holistic paradigm and the nursing approach, but also in leadership skills. With such advance preparation they could be more quickly involved in the training program. They could support and reinforce the change process initiated by the nurse specialists and act as leaders in the promotion and adoption of the holistic approach.

The third recommendation concerns the content of the program. We tried during the implementation to help the staff increase its skills in using certain clinical strategies for the manipulation of stimuli, in order to facilitate the continuing adaptation of clients. However, the nursing personnel were unable to completely master the "family care" strategy (described earlier). In the time allowed, we were unable to either complete the training process for this strategy, or to work with the staff in identifying and learning other strategies. Such a process would be possible in a longer program or could be built into a more formalized follow-up of the training program on the part of the institution.

The fourth recommendation is closely related to this idea of a formal follow-up of the training program. The planning and development of our program included the concept of maintenance and consolidation, in order to continue the evolutionary change process we had set in motion. The setting can assume responsibility for itself but it requires means, structures, resources, and a knowledge of change strategies. For this reason we recommend that even greater importance be given at a very early stage to this aspect of planning.

A fifth recommendation would combine the process evaluation of the second case study with the outcome evaluation of the first. Verification on a longitudinal basis would indicate whether or not the conceptual shift on the part of the personnel indeed helps the residents.

In summary, Watzlawick et al.'s (1974) principles of problem resolution, which we have already discussed, were applied with a four-step procedure:

1. a clear definition of the problem
2. an investigation of the solutions attempted so far

3. a clear definition of the concrete change to be achieved
4. the formulation and implementation of a plan to produce this
   change (p. 10).

We indeed faced a true problem, one which was more than just a difficulty and was reaching an impasse. We were able to identify and describe the problem, which was perhaps intensified by the intricacy of the situation and by the types of solutions already attempted. However, the principles of change proved appropriate and were applied. We used the results achieved by this method, as our criteria of effectiveness. Watzlawick states:

> . . . the handling of many fundamental social problems—e.g., poverty, aging, crime—is customarily approached by separating these difficulties as entities into themselves, as almost diagnostic categories, referring to essentially quite disparate problems and requiring very different solutions. The next step then is to create enormous physical and administrative structures and whole industries of expertise, producing increased incompetence in ever vaster numbers of individuals. We see this as a basically counter-productive approach to such social needs, an approach that requires a massive deviant population to support the raison d'être of these monolithic agencies and departments (p. 159).

We, for our part, handled the problem in a unified and global fashion. We did not create new or costly physical or administrative structures, but rather looked at the situation as it existed from a different point of view. We accepted that the objective circumstances or the limits and constraints of the situation, whether the health problems of the resident or the number and type of regular personnel, would continue to be beyond our control. The real cost of the implementation of such a training program is difficult to compute in terms of human energy, but the necessary monetary investment can be calculated directly from the salaries paid to the four clinical nurse specialists and the coordinator over a period of about one year. The benefits accrued are manifold for personnel and residents alike. We believe that we have effected second-order change in a problem situation.

In conclusion, it should be stressed that while it seems we have found a way to resolve a problem that had not responded to ordinary or usual responses, in fact, we have proposed a solution to a problem that should have been prevented. The first step in such a prevention process would be to recognize that the care of the long-term geriatric resident is very complex. Neither these residents nor the personnel engaged to care for them can continue to be seen as "second-class" in our "hi-tech" culture, by those responsible for the planning and financing of health care. Geriatric care givers require a high level of preparation. They need to know! A large body of scientific knowledge concerning the care of the aged has already been developed and is easily accessible; it contains extensive contributions from medicine, nursing, and other para-medical disciplines. Administrators must understand the needs of their clients, know the characteristics of a staff capable of meeting these needs, and implement the work conditions essential to high quality care. Perhaps it is now time to plan a second-order change at a higher level within the health care system.

NOTES

1. It is acknowledged that nurses are both male and female but will be referred to, in the present text, as "she."
2. Faculté des sciences infirmières, Université de Montréal; the team consists of four professors with expertise in geriatric care, model development, evaluation, or family dynamics.
3. The adoption of the conceptual model was under the direction of E. Adam, Professor, Faculté des sciences infirmières, Université de Montréal.
4. D. Latourelle, Professor, Faculté des sciences infirmières, assumed the responsibility for the development and implementation of the nursing intervention with the family.
5. J. Chalifour, Professor, Département des sciences infirmières, Université Laval, Quebec City, assumed responsibility for the development and training of the nursing personnel in the "helping relationship."

REFERENCES

Argyris, C. (1982). *Reasoning, learning and action*. San Francisco: Jossey-Bass.

Barton, E.M., Baltes, M.M., & Orzech, M.J. (1980). Etiology of dependance in older nursing home residents during morning care: The role of staff behavior. *Journal of Personality and Social Psychology, 38* (3), 423-431.

Brody, E.M. (1977). *Environmental factors in dependancy*. In N. Exton-Smith & E.G. Evans (Eds.), *Care of the elderly* (pp. 81-95). New York: Grune & Stratton.

Chalifour, J. (1982). Relation d'aide en soins infirmiers: Une réalité souvent ignorée. *Union Médicale du Canada, 3* (7), 620-625.

D'Amour, D. (1980). Ideology of nursing care staff toward the rehabilitation of an attitude scale. *Nursing Papers, 12* (2), 17-30.

Ferguson, M. (1980). *The aquarian conspiracy*. Los Angeles: J.P. Tarcher.

Johnson, M.M., & Martin, H.W. (1965). A sociological analysis of the nurse role. In J.K. Skipper & R.C. Leonard (Eds.), *Social interaction and patient care* (pp. 29-39). Philadelphia: J.B. Lippincott.

Kahn, R.L. (1971). Psychological aspects of aging. In I. Rossman (Ed.), *Clinical geriatrics* (pp. 107-113). Philadelphia: J.B. Lippincott.

Latourelle, D. (1985). Working with the family and its hospitalized chronically ill member. In M. Stewart, J. Innes, S. Searl, & C. Smillies (Eds.), *Community health nursing in Canada* (pp. 348-362). Toronto: Gage Pub. Ltd.

Latourelle, D., & Lévesque, L. (1985). Intervenir auprès du malade chronique hospitalisé et de sa famille. *Canadian Journal of Mental Health/Revue Canadienne de Santé Mentale, 4* (1), 90-102.

Lawton, M.P. (1974). Coping behavior and the environment of older people. In A.N. Schwartz & I.N. Mensh (Eds.), *Professional obligations and approaches to the aged* (pp. 67-73). Springfield, Ill.: Charles C. Thomas.

Lefebvre, G. (1982). *Le coeur à l'ouvrage*. Montréal: Centre Interdisciplinaire de Montréal. Les éditions de l'Homme.

Lévesque, L. (1980). Rehabilition of the chronically ill elderly: A method of operationalizing a conceptual model for nursing. In R.C. Mackay & E.G. Zilm (Eds.), *Research for nursing practice: Proceedings of the national research conference* (pp. 19-30). Halifax.

Minuchin, S. (1974). *Families and family therapy*. Cambridge, Mass.: Harvard University Press.

Rosenthal, R. (1966). *Experimenter effects in behavioral research*. New York: Appleton-Century-Crofts.

Roy, C. (1976). *Introduction to nursing: Adaptation model*. New York: Prentice Hall.

Satir, M. (1967). *Conjoint family therapy: A guide to theory and technique*. Palo Alto, California: Science and Behavior Books.

Watzlawick, P., Helmick-Beavin, J., & Jackson, D.D. (1967). *Pragmatics of human communication: A study of interactional patterns pathologies and paradoxes*. New York: Norton Press.

Watzlawick, P., Weakland, J.H., & Fisch, R. (1974). *Change: Principles of problem formation and problem resolution*. New York: Norton Press.

Zarit, S.H. (1980). *Aging and mental disorders*. New York: The Free Press.

Part III
LEGAL, POLICY
AND POLITICAL APPROACHES
TO SOCIAL INTERVENTION

Bruce Tefft

6

ADVOCACY COALITIONS AS A VEHICLE FOR MENTAL HEALTH SYSTEM REFORM

INTRODUCTION

This chapter is a case study of the Community Coalition On Mental Health (CCOMH), a nongovernmental coalition of 32 service agencies, advocacy organizations, self help groups, professional associations, and health care unions in Manitoba, Canada. Formed in 1984, CCOMH supports comprehensive, community-based mental health services through advocacy, public education, and applied research. The author was its co-founder and initial Chair. The chapter is organized as follows. First, the environment or setting for the case study is described, including the status of the mental health system in Manitoba prior to 1984. Development of the Coalition is then reviewed within the framework of resource mobilization theory (Jenkins, 1983), a prominent sociological theory of social movements. Finally, the Coalition's effectiveness and future prospects are discussed.

ENVIRONMENT

The Province of Manitoba

Manitoba is a moderate size province located in the geographic centre of Canada. Its population of slightly over one million is clustered mainly in the southern one-third of the province, with approximately 685,000 residing in the capital, Winnipeg. Outside its largest city, the predominantly rural countryside is dotted by small towns, Manitoba's economy is fueled primarily by agriculture, mining, transportation, light industry, and small business. While its diversification makes the economy highly stable, it does not generate great wealth. Consequently, Manitoba is considered a "have not" province and depends heavily on transfer payments from the federal government to maintain adequate human services. Its accumulated deficit per capita is among the highest in Canada and is rapidly becoming a serious constraint on social policy initiatives.

The political life of Manitoba is dominated by two parties. The New Democratic Party (NDP), generally considered left-centre in its orientation, has governed for 14 of the last 20 years, including the period covered by this case study. The right-wing Progressive Conservative (PC) Party formed the government during the remaining six years. The Liberal Party, occupying the centre of the political spectrum, presently holds only one seat in the provincial legislature after years without any.

On the face of it, the political balance described above would appear to augur well for innovative, progressive mental health services. Liberal governments are usually more favorably disposed toward reform-minded social policies than conservative governments. However, such is not the case in Manitoba, largely due to an idiosyncratic combination of local circumstances. For the entire period the NDP has been in office during the past 20 years, their Minister of Health has been the same conservative politician. A former mortician, he has been able to achieve and hold a senior portfolio even though he is far to the right of the party mainstream. His unlikely hold on power stems from an ability to repeatedly carry a key ethnic riding in Winnipeg, the party's traditional electoral base. When seriously challenged regarding his conservative policies, the Minister of Health threatens to leave the NDP, thereby jeopardizing the party's capacity to govern. However unsophisticated, this tactic is extremely effective in terms of keeping critics at bay. Predictably, the Minister has surrounded himself with senior officials who share his conservative views and shape the information he receives in such a way as to reinforce those views. Thus, the department most responsible for mental health services in Manitoba is widely regarded as a conservative island in a much more liberal, even socialist lake.

The Manitoba Mental Health System

Governance. Manitoba is divided into eight regions, with integrated health and social services delivered within this regional structure. However, effective control of health and mental health services is heavily centralized in Winnipeg, where planning, policy development, the setting of standards, and budgeting all take place. The key government decision makers regarding mental health, in order of influence, are the Minister of Health, the Deputy Minister of Health, the Assistant Deputy Minister (Mental Health), the Provincial Psychiatrist, and the Director of the Mental Health Directorate. Proposals to regionalize governance of the mental health system have not been well received by this management group, which in turn has badly alienated rural regions. With considerable justification, rural constituencies believe that mental health decisions made in Winnipeg have not well recognized their needs. The validity of this belief may be judged in part by the distribution of mental health services across the province (see below).

Allied with the formal governance structure is an informal system of influence dominated by organized medicine in general and psychiatry in particular. These constituencies have routine, low-cost access to key mental health decision makers and are frequently asked for advice regarding policy issues, a privilege not afforded any other interest group. For example, the Provincial Psychiatrist and the Head of Psychiatry at one of the major teaching hospitals are seen by the Minister of Health as the natural leaders in the mental health field and are granted a high degree of credibility. It often appears as if the interests of their discipline and base institutions are distinguished poorly if at all from the interests of mental health service recipients and other affected groups.

Services. Mental health services in Manitoba are centralized geographically in Winnipeg and are predominantly medical and institutional in nature. Two large mental hospitals (now called mental health centres) were constructed in the late 1800s and contained a peak patient population of 2700 in the 1950s. Since then their census has gradually declined to approximately 800, in keeping with deinstitutionalization across North America (Kiesler, 1982; Richman & Harris, 1983). Still, in terms of their size, historic significance, and annual cost, they dominate the mental health landscape like monuments to a bygone era. One is located in western Manitoba, the other just northeast of Winnipeg. Their primary functions are long-term hospitalization (often for psychogeriatric patients), forensic psychiatry, and intermediate-term hospitalization of residents from rural catchment areas. A much smaller (40 beds), newer mental health facility is located in the extreme southeastern portion of the province. While also called a mental health centre, in reality it functions as a regional facility providing comprehensive services to a distinct religious and ethnic population.

In addition to the mental health centres, Manitoba has approximately 250 general hospital psychiatric beds, all in Winnipeg. Roughly 60% are located in two large teaching hospitals, with the remainder divided between four smaller hospitals throughout the city. While intended for acute care, these general hospital beds are often occupied by chronically mentally disabled persons due to a severe lack of supportive community services. Further, residents of rural Manitoba requiring acute care are usually sent to Winnipeg because appropriate services are unavailable in their communities. The net result is a bed occupancy ratio which nearly always approaches and, at times, even exceeds capacity. Negative media attention to this apparent bed shortage and calls for new bed construction are commonplace.

Community mental health services, by far the most poorly developed sector of the formal mental health system, include approximately 100 community mental health workers attached to the eight health regions. Their activities vary tremendously from region to region. Workers in Winnipeg are overloaded with chronic clients and spend much of their time attempting to maintain them in the community through medication and crisis intervention. Workers in rural Manitoba do not experience this burden to nearly the same extent and, therefore, have more freedom to provide a broader range of treatment services. However, their low numbers and the vast catchments for which they are responsible preclude anything but brief treatment.

A second component of community mental health services is residential care for the chronically disabled. Residential care includes a variety of situations, from intensive, supervised treatment in a family-like setting to large, impersonal board and care homes providing only basic physical necessities. In total, there are approximately 725 residential care spaces in Manitoba, the vast majority of them in Winnipeg. Most are funded through the Department of Community Services rather than the Department of Health.

Personal care homes are sometimes overlooked as another major segment of the mental health system. Roughly 2,200 individuals, or some 25% of the entire population of personal care home residents, are classified as having a primary psychiatric diagnosis (Mental Health Working Group, 1983). They require more intensive, specialized care than most other residents and, for this reason, are not always welcomed by operators. However, personal care homes represent a large and rapidly growing mental health resource.

Finally, medical services for patients with a primary diagnosis of mental disorder are provided by both psychiatrists and nonpsychiatric physicians. These services primarily consist of psychotherapy and ad-

TABLE 1
Manitoba Mental Health Expenditures For Fiscal Year 85/86[1]

Sector	Expenditure ($000)	Percent
Mental Health Centres	36,197.6	23.8
General Hospitals	54,380.9	35.7
Community Mental Health	6,034.9	3.9
Personal Care Homes	42,555.0	28.0
Medical Services	13,025.8	8.6
TOTAL	152,194.2	100.0

[1]Source: Mental Health Services Division, 1986

ministration of psychotropic drugs, and account for a majority of episodes of care each year. Nearly all psychiatrists in the province live and practice in Winnipeg.

Expenditures. The pattern of services described above strongly suggests that mental health expenditures in Manitoba are heavily weighted toward medical and institutional services. Examination of aggregated Department of Health figures for the fiscal year 1985-1986 in Table 1 confirms this suggestion. These figures reveal that, based on a budget of $152.2 million, 87.5% of all mental health expenditures in 1985-1986 went to some form of institutional care and another 8.6% went to medical services, leaving only 3.9% for community mental health. Remembering that the vast majority of medical and institutional services are concentrated in Winnipeg, these figures also clearly indicate how well founded is the perception of rural Manitobans that centralized decision making has been detrimental to their interests.

In conclusion, the mental health system in Manitoba is comprised of two very different realities. Rural regions have few services and are starved for resources. Despite evidence that rural community mental health teams do excellent work and can reduce the frequency of costly psychiatric hospitalization, they have precious little in the way of resources with which to work. Institutionalization at a mental hospital or Winnipeg general hospital is often the only alternative. On the other hand, Winnipeg is relatively rich in mental health resources. Unfortunately, they are utilized very inefficiently due to a glaring paucity of community mental health services within the city and an equally striking lack of rationalization and coordination of existing services.

Barriers To System Reform

This bleak picture of the mental health system in Manitoba raises the obvious question of how this situation could occur. In other words, what processes or dynamics have contributed to the creation and maintenance of a system so obviously imbalanced both geographically and in terms of service type? Although the absence of hard data precludes any definitive answers to this question, the following are almost certainly contributing factors. Some are readily generalizable to other jurisdictions while others are more unique to Manitoba.

Adherence to values supporting institutionalization. Manitoba has one of the highest rates of institutionalization in Canada, not just of the mentally disabled but of other health disability groups and the elderly (Roch, Evans & Pascoe, 1985). This pervasive response to human distress is rooted in the value system of decision makers within and outside of government. Essentially, it reflects authoritarian, socially restrictive, and bureaucratic values tempered with varying degrees of benevolence depending on the client group in question. Competing values such as normalization, social integration, and community control have been, for the most part, either ignored or dismissed.

Lack of commitment to rational planning. Rational planning of health services, including mental health services, has never been a priority within the Department of Health. Planning typically has been viewed as busywork for bureaucrats between real jobs, a stalling tactic when political pressure to take disagreeable action becomes uncomfortably high, or a form of on-the-job retirement for senior officials. In the early 1970s, attempts by the Mental Health Directorate to rationally plan and implement system reform were met with intense hostility at the highest levels of the Department. When the Directorate staff kept pressing forward with their proposals, they were either fired or frustrated to the point of resigning, and the Directorate was disbanded altogether for nearly ten years.

Professional isolation and inbreeding. Despite being in the centre of Canada, Manitoba is isolated professionally. Correctly or not, it is seen as a relatively undesirable province in which to live, and consequently, tends not to attract professionals or students seeking postgraduate training from outside the province. Therefore, the important process of cross-fertilization of professional knowledge and values is seriously attenuated. Traditional ways of thinking and acting have not been vigorously challenged. Moreover, isolation has encouraged Manitoba professionals to view the province as somehow different from other jurisdictions and to resist innovative approaches proven effective elsewhere.

Fragmentation of system governance. Earlier we stated that governance of the mental health system is highly centralized, in that ultimate funding authority rests with the Department of Health. Paradoxically, however, governance is also fragmented in the sense of there being multiple, almost independent points of accountability. This is most apparent with regard to the general hospitals in Winnipeg, which are the most costly component of the mental health system.

Hospitals are funded through the Manitoba Health Services Commission (MHSC), a semi-independent arm of the provincial government, not unlike a crown corporation in the economic sector. MHSC has its own board of directors, staff, and funding review mechanisms. While strategic policy direction is established by the Department of Health, MHSC has broad discretion in implementation. Thus, accountability by the Department is seriously eroded. In fact, the Department often uses the autonomy of MHSC as a shield when it wishes to protect itself from embarrassing or uncomfortable decisions regarding hospital services.

System fragmentation also results from the fiercely independent stance of many general hospital boards, who believe government should simply provide funding and allow them to run their facility as they see fit. Rationalization and coordination of services with other hospitals is a distinctly secondary goal.

Similar levels of fragmentation exist regarding mental health centres, personal care homes, and even the community mental health program. In reality, the mental health "system" in Manitoba is not a system at all but rather, at best, loosely connected collection of service facilities and programs, each competing for resources and struggling to maintain its autonomy.

Lack of systemic information. Manitoba is the only province which does not report system-wide information on mental health services to Statistics Canada. Until 1983, the province did not even have a comprehensive accounting of its mental health expenditures. No mechanisms are available to routinely gather provincial mental health statistics. The failure to develop such mechanisms can be viewed as a logical corollary to the system fragmentation and lack of commitment to rational planning. Systemic information is regarded as difficult to obtain and largely unnecessary. Further, its absence makes it more difficult for critics to challenge traditional practices and argue for reform.

Exclusive linkages between psychiatry and government. These linkages, described previously, would be acceptable were it not for their exclusive nature. Psychiatry has an important and valid perspective on delivery of mental health services. However, the interests of psychiatry and the public are not necessarily the same. Other mental health disciplines, as well as various community groups, also have valuable perspectives on service issues. Unfortunately, these perspectives have tended to be ignored or greatly discounted in mental health policy decisions. Psychiatry brings with it undeniable biases and vested interests which, unchallenged by alternative points of view, have helped create the extreme system imbalance seen in Manitoba.

Absence of effective community advocacy. If government has discounted other, more community-oriented professions and groups, it has done so in part because there was little political cost involved. Community advocacy has been sporadic, unsophisticated, unorganized and, therefore, ineffective. Advocacy for community-based mental health services is made more difficult by public stigma toward the mentally disabled, exacerbated by sensationalist media coverage of violent or bizarre behavior by people with a psychiatric history.

In conclusion, the several barriers to system reform discussed above have proven over the years to be very difficult to influence, much less overcome. As a result, by the early 1980s, reform-minded constituencies had grown cynical and discouraged. Despite deplorable conditions within the mental health system, the prospects for meaningful change appeared dim. Then, a watershed was reached which rekindled energy and hope.

The Mental Health Working Group

In 1982, an informal coalition of three community organizations began organizing a task force from the voluntary sector to review mental health services in Manitoba. Their goal was to focus public attention on the inadequacy of current services and to generate public support for reorientation of the mental health system toward comprehensive, community-based services. Negotiations with the Department of Health were undertaken to determine if the task force could be a cooperative effort of the public and voluntary sectors. After several meetings the Department refused, declaring that it would establish its own internal study group without community representation. Their mandate would be defined narrowly as developing recommendations to improve the efficiency of the current system. No fundamental changes were contemplated.

At this point the coalition chose strategically to pursue representation on the government study group, believing that access to con-
fidential information and the resources of government were more important than attempting to carry on alone. The coalition was also concerned that the government study would be a whitewash and later used
to resist second-order reform. Again the Department refused to
cooperate. Intensive political lobbying by the coalition was then initiated through an existing network of supporters in the New
Democratic Party, eventually reaching all the way to the Premier.
After several months, the Minister of Health agreed to appoint six
community members nominated by the coalition to the task force, on
the condition that they sit as individuals rather than as organizational
representatives. The author was one such individual. Six governmental appointees and a psychiatric consultant (the aforementioned Head
of Psychiatry) were also named, giving birth to the Mental Health
Working Group (MHWG). The mandate of the MHWG was
renegotiated to be much more open-ended, namely "to examine the
structure and content of existing provincial mental health programs
and provide viable options for future development." Work was begun
in March, 1983 and a final report (Mental Health Working Group,
1983) submitted to the Minister in November of that same year. The
reader is referred to this document for details regarding the process or
methodology employed.

The findings of the Working Group were solidly in line with what
critics of the mental health system had been saying for years.
However, this was a blue-ribbon, government-sanctioned panel of experts, which could not be easily ignored or dismissed. The final report
strongly recommended major structural modifications, including:
(a) regionalization of planning and governance, (b) redress of im-
balances between institutional and community services and between
urban and rural areas, (c) phasing out of the two large mental health
centres, (d) consolidation of mental health administration to enhance
accountability, (e) improved program standard setting and monitoring, and (f) reorientation of professional training programs. Importantly, the report presented a clear statement of progressive principles
and policies to guide future development of mental health services.

Rather than respond immediately, the Department of Health attempted to regain control of the reform process by appointing a panel
of six hand-picked individuals from psychiatry and the bureaucracy to
study the Working Group recommendations. The panel held in-
camera hearings to receive feedback from interested parties. Despite
predictable opposition from psychiatry and the mental health centres,
the public response was overwhelmingly positive. Thus, the Minister

had little choice but to reluctantly endorse the MHWG report in November, 1984. However, he endorsed it only "in principle" without indicating which specific recommendations were being accepted or rejected. The Minister also made it clear that recommendations would be implemented only with new (as opposed to reallocated) mental health funds, knowing full well that new money would be in very short supply for the foreseeable future. Again, this extremely guarded response can be seen as an attempt to regain control of the reform process by avoiding firm commitments and establishing serious barriers to implementation.

In the next six months, few if any important recommendations were acted upon. Momentum for reform was dissipating and it appeared that the Mental Health Working Group report would suffer the fate of so many other, long-forgotten government studies. However, the report had mobilized, if temporarily, a large number of community groups in support of its overall thrust. This suggested that collaboration of a more enduring nature might be possible. Remembering the success of a small, informal coalition, the author and the Executive Director of the most prominent mental health advocacy group in the province, the Manitoba Division of the Canadian Mental Health Association (CMHA), discussed initiation of a larger, more formal collection of organizations to work for implementation of the MHWG report. Thus began the Community Coalition On Mental Health. Before describing its development, however, an appropriate theoretical framework will be briefly presented.

RESOURCE MOBILIZATION THEORY

Resource mobilization theory (Jenkins, 1983) is a relatively recent conceptualization of the deliberately political process by which social movement organizations (SMOs) mobilize to establish control over resources. Within this framework, societal conflict arises when non-dominant groups with relatively few resources (i.e., with grievances) challenge, through collective action, dominant groups with relatively many resources. Resource mobilization theory views social movements as a normal process of social and political life. It emphasizes the "continuities between (social) movement and institutional actions, the rationality of movement actors, the strategic problems confronted by movements, and the role of movements in social change" (Jenkins, 1983, p. 528).

Social movement organizations must have both an ideological and material base in order to achieve their objectives. The former refers to a coherent understanding of their grievances that shows them to be illegitimate products of institutional actions and subject to change. The latter refers to assets, tangible and intangible, that can be pooled and directed toward mobilization. Organization is seen as the mechanism by which SMOs convert minimal resources into effective collective action to take advantage of opportunities presented by the larger social and political environment. Success is measured by short-term and long-term changes in relevant public policies, alteration of decision-making elites, and changes in the distribution of socially valued goods, or all of these.

Resource mobilization theory is particularly appropriate for this chapter because of its focus on the processes underlying social movements. For example, it regards the existence of grievances as a relatively unchanging or static feature of societal relations. It attributes considerable importance, however, to the process by which grievances are redefined and contribute to mobilization. Similarly, the theory perceives organization as a dynamic process of matching structure with tasks to be performed. This chapter is primarily about the process of coalition-building and its functioning. Resource mobilization theory introduces a helpful degree of order to phenomena that might otherwise appear chaotic.

COALITION FORMATION

From a resource mobilization perspective, social movement formation entails specific strategic tasks. Organizers must identify a "cleavage issue" or grievance on which to focus attention. They must also articulate an ideology that challenges the dominant ideology by presenting an alternative explanation for the grievance. Rank-and-file participants of a social movement must then be mobilized by combining resources, by organizing, and by taking advantage of opportunities for collective action. How these tasks were accomplished in the Manitoba context is described next.

For the sake of clarity, events have been simplified and made to appear more linear than was actually the case. Community development and social action on a large scale are inherently multidirectional, dynamic processes. Coherence is more often imposed externally than self-evident. Therefore, this account should be regarded as more similar to the minutes of a meeting than a transcript.

Cleavage Issue

A cleavage issue is one that separates a nondominant group (i.e. the challenger) experiencing hardships, from a dominant group (i.e., the target) believed to control the societal structures producing these hardships. Essentially, it consists of one hardship that is defined as a grievance, ascribed critical importance, and adopted as sufficient justification for challenging the target group. An adequate cleavage issue must be readily understandable and appear persuasive or valid to both the nondominant group and potential allies such as sympathetic elites or the general public, thereby giving them a symbol around which to rally. Moreover, to the extent that the structures requiring change are deeply entrenched and stoutly defended, a cleavage issue ideally should focus on a point of relative vulnerability and yet go right to the core of the problem. In this sense, identifying the best cleavage issue for a social movement is analogous to identifying the best point and angle at which to strike an uncut diamond.

Several potential cleavage issues were available to organizers of the Coalition, including all of the serious mental health system deficiencies discussed previously. A major consideration in selecting an issue was the anticipated diversity of interests of Coalition members. It would have to meet all of the above criteria and also have broad appeal to many qualitatively different organizations.

For several reasons, the cleavage issue chosen was lack of comprehensive, community-based mental health services. First, it was easily understood. In rural regions, people had only to look around them to observe the absence of such services. In Winnipeg, the same observation could readily be made but with the added contrast of extensive institutional services. Second, the absence of community-based services had been well-documented by the Mental Health Working Group. Thus, the essential facts of the situation could scarcely be denied by key decision makers. Third, the cleavage issue could be directly linked to human suffering which was felt by the organizers and others to be unnecessary, unjust, and critically important to the lives of those involved. This aspect of the issue was essential to winning the support of not only potential constituents of the Coalition but also liberal elites, mass media, and the general public. Fourth, the issue was broad enough to accommodate the diverse interests of different Coalition members, from self help groups to professional associations. Each member could focus on selected aspects of the problem without necessarily coming into conflict with other members. Finally, the cleavage issue led almost immediately to the question of how such a situation could be understood and, hopefully, changed for the better. In other words, it led to ideology.

Ideology

Resource mobilization theory attaches critical importance to the role of ideology in shaping social relations, especially as it relates to mobilization of individual participants in social movements (Ferree & Miller, 1985). Ideology is defined as "a flexible structure of beliefs about the nature of social relationships, one's position in the social structure, and the causes and consequences of social action" (p. 42). Dominant ideologies, by definition widely shared, serve to explain and justify an unequal distribution of resources. They legitimate sociopolitical systems in which some individuals have much while others have little. This is a more subtle form of social control than coercion but effective nonetheless because it permits dominant groups to present themselves as benign rather than exploitive.

In Western society, dominant ideologies reflect the general tendency of people to overemphasize personal disposition and free will as opposed to situational factors in explaining behavior. They attribute social outcomes to personal ability or individual effort, both of which are defined as "good" characteristics, thereby imputing moral worth to those who succeed and even blaming the victims of oppression for their suffering (Kidder & Fine, 1986; Ryan, 1971). By doing so, dominant ideologies discourage challenges to the system by nondominant groups, for even those who experience objective deprivation will not view it as a grievance if they adopt an explanation that attributes the situation to their own failings.

In Manitoba, as elsewhere, the dominant ideology surrounding the absence of comprehensive, community-based mental health services was intimately connected to a medical understanding of the causes and treatment of mental illness or disability. Simplified, the reasoning goes like this: Certain people are born with or develop weaknesses that cause them to become mentally ill; these people can sometimes be assessed and treated by a physician as outpatients but, if the illness is moderate to severe, they must be hospitalized. Once in the hospital, the mentally ill are dealt with by psychiatric specialists who cure or at least stabilize patients' conditions. They are then discharged to independently resume their lives until the next episode of illness.

The dominant ideology further argues that government, for its part, has a responsibility to provide funding for outpatient medical services and hospitals, which are otherwise organized and operated as if they were private services. However, hospitals especially are very expensive and require highly trained staff. Therefore, despite the best efforts of government, hospitals are always in short supply and must be located predominantly in urban areas where they can serve the most people and professionals are available. Individuals who choose to live in rural areas are necessarily obliged to travel farther for medical care than their city counterparts.

The essential features of this dominant ideology are fivefold. First, the cause of mental illness is deemed to be a stable, medical condition within the individual. Second, it is the responsibility of ill people to present themselves for treatment, adopt a patient role, and acknowledge their weaknesses. Third, only psychiatrists and, to a lesser extent, nonpsychiatric physicians are designated as expert helpers. Fourth, the responsibility of the health care system is largely confined to providing medical and hospital services for acute mental illness. Fifth, government allocates limited mental health resources in the most cost-effective manner possible, thereby fulfilling its mandate to act in the public interest.

This ideology provides a seemingly logical, benign explanation for the relative profusion of medical and institutional mental health services in Winnipeg and the extreme scarcity of community-based services throughout Manitoba. This pattern has always been presented as the inevitable outcome of rational, fair policy decisions by government based on the nature of mental illness and the realities of mental health service delivery. As long as the dominant ideology remained unchallenged, systematic change was a pipe dream. Community mental health programs would continue to compete among themselves for mere survival while 96 cents of every mental health dollar went to medical and institutional care.

The inevitable ideological struggle had actually begun in earnest within the Mental Health Working Group. In response to articulation of the dominant ideology by representatives of government and psychiatry, community representatives presented research showing that: (a) mental disability was heavily influenced by environmental factors such as stress and social support; (b) community-based mental health services were more cost-effective than institutional services for all but the most acutely disabled individuals; and (c) jurisdictions which years ago resembled Manitoba had systematically reoriented their mental health services, with good results. In addition, the inequity and human costs of the current mental health system were repeatedly emphasized as unavoidable value issues. At every opportunity, problems framed by the dominant ideology as private, individual troubles were deprivatized, deindividualized, and reframed as system deficiencies (Kidder & Fine, 1986). Eventually, this new (for Manitoba) community mental health ideology was heavily emphasized in the final report of the Working Group.

Beginning with the initial organizational meeting of the Coalition, the dominant ideology was attacked as the conceptual foundation of serious problems commonly experienced by potential members. Increasingly, they shifted from perceiving their organizations in particular and the mentally disabled in general as unworthy beggars for more resources to perceiving themselves as oppressed by a system of vested interests. Over time, members came to understand who were the key actors and why mental health policy decisions were so often contrary to their interests. The organizers recognized that the ideological transformation necessary for coalition formation was already underway. However, a new ideology would be insufficient without organizational commitment from a constituency. That is to say, the next step was mobilization of heretofore unconnected organizations into a viable coalition.

Mobilization

As discussed previously, resource mobilization theory attributes the formation and mobilization of social movements to changes in resources, organization, and perceived opportunities for collective action. Each element is more or less important depending on the pre-movement situation (Jenkins, 1983). Where any element is below a critical threshold, its strengthening will have a disproportionate impact. In Manitoba, all three elements required intensive work.

Resources. Formation of the CCOMH was heavily dependent on the emergence of leadership, both individual and organizational. The author and the Executive Director of CMHA were well positioned to advocate for community-based mental health services. They brought valuable resources and an exceptional degree of commitment to this task. As an academic and community mental health specialist, the author had extensive professional knowledge of mental health services and could quickly tap into university information sources whenever they were needed. He also brought to the Coalition considerable prestige as a professor and unusual work schedule flexibility, an important practical asset. The Executive Director of CMHA had training and grass-roots experience in community development, a solid working knowledge of rural Canadian culture, and good people skills. Further, his employment thrust him into a natural leadership role among mental health organizations in the voluntary sector.

From an organizational perspective, CMHA had recently adopted development of community-based mental health services as a central aspect of its mission. It had strengthened its staff in keeping with this objective and was much better prepared than ever before to exercise leadership within a coalition. This was particularly fortunate, in that CMHA was generally acknowledged as having a legitimate advocacy role on behalf of mentally disabled persons. Therefore, its right to speak out was unassailable.

Organization. The second major contributor to the social movement under consideration was enhanced organization. Of course, this entailed the mechanics of coalition formation. In July, 1984, an initial letter was sent by CMHA to 23 organizations believed to support community-based mental health services. Organizations as opposed to individuals were targeted as prospective members to take advantage of existing membership networks. In addition, organizations wre viewed as potentially much more powerful agents for system reform than individuals. The letter described the nature and mandate of a proposed mental health coalition. It invited the recipient to attend an exploratory meeting in August at CMHA. All invitees responded favorably to the proposal and 14 actually attended the meeting, despite the attraction of summer holidays. Fundamental issues of organizational structure and functioning (discussed below) were tentatively resolved and terms of reference (Appendix A) were adopted. Thus, the Community Coalition On Mental Health was created. All but one of the original invitees eventually joined the Coalition.

Over the next six months, several additional members were recruited while a few dropped out as goals were clarified and translated into specific actions. This was an extremely fluid, unsettled period for the Coalition. New members needed orientation and altered the dynamics of meetings. New working relationships required an intensive investment of time and energy. New issues focused attention on differences in values and priorities. Consequently, organizational development was a long, complex, and arduous process. It demonstrated all too clearly why this ingredient of social movement formation had been so largely absent up to that point.

Incentives for prospective members was a key factor for success. From an organizational perspective, provision of adequate incentives is the primary economic exchange mechanism through which an association like CCOMH secures necessary resources such as a broad membership base, commitment to important objectives, active participation in specific tasks, and so forth (Knoke, 1986). The Coalition was able to offer immediate normative and affective incentives, and the hope of future material incentives. The normative incentives included a shared belief in certain global values and in the essential goodness of altruistic community service. These were critical to establishing trust among organizations which until recently had perceived themselves as competitors for very limited government funds. Affective incentives included socialization and a sense of belonging to an important social movement. Many members were independent agencies and associations that had existed for years in relative isolation from other like-minded organizations. They welcomed the social support and comraderie available through the Coalition. In addition, they felt safer advocating as part of a large coalition than as individual organizations. The hope of future material resources was related to possible reallocation of funds from institutional to community-based services. Rather than compete ever more fiercely among themselves for the same small pie, perhaps they could increase the pie itself. A secondary material benefit would be creation of a much more dynamic, exciting mental health system in which to work.

Opportunities for collective action. Resource mobilization theory argues that perception of opportunities for collective action is a necessary condition for the formation of a social movement. Opportunities may have existed previously but gone unrecognized or they may emerge through changing conditions. One gradually changing condition and two specific events provided new opportunities for collective action for the Coalition. Concerning the former, pressures for reform of health care spending in Manitoba had intensified significantly in the past several years. The health budget was increasing at a rate far exceeding inflation, overall government expenditures, and additional government revenues. Already accounting for over one-third of total spending, health expenditures were projected to all but bankrupt the province by the year 2000 unless something dramatic was done to curtail them. Consequently, the Department of Health came under considerable pressure from within government to reorient its spending toward cost-effective, community-based health care. The Coalition, armed with research showing the relative cost-effectiveness of community mental health services, perceived this issue as an emerging opportunity to attract support for its cause and bring further pressure to bear on the Department.

Turning to specific events, the galvanizing effect of the Mental Health Working Group (1983) report on organizations favoring community mental health has already been described. It focused attention on longstanding grievances as never before, illuminated future directions, and became a symbol for reform. The report's analysis of mental health expenditures provided an undeniable benchmark against which succeeding budgets could be measured. Importantly, the process leading to its publication demonstrated the power of a determined, well-organized coalition. The second specific event which constituted an opportunity for collective action was the resignation of the Head of Psychiatry who had been such a prominent advisor to government on mental health policy. A prolonged, hotly contested race to replace him ensued, involving several potential successors. Although his resignation was unrelated to government decisions, it substantially, if temporarily, weakened the ability of the psychiatric community to resist reform. This vacuum allowed the Coalition to play a more prominent role in development of new mental health policies than would have been possible otherwise.

In summary, mobilization of the Coalition was accomplished through strengthened resources, organization, and opportunities for collective action. Most of these improvements resulted from deliberate, planned activity by the organizers. However, some improvements were tied to changes beyond our control in the wider community. Still, these fortuitous circumstances had to be recognized and exploited. Careful preparation and hard work made this possible.

STRUCTURE AND DECISION MAKING

Proponents of resource mobilization theory have engaged in a lively debate concerning the most appropriate organizational structure for SMOs. The alternatives range from a decentralized, informal structure to a centralized, formal structure. A broad shift in SMOs over the past two centuries from the former to the latter has been linked to the rise of urbanization, industrial capitalism, liberal democracy, mass media, and the modern state (Jenkins, 1983). Different types of structures appear to have consistent effects on the movements which adopt them. Moreover, once set, structures are relatively immutable. Thus, the initial selection of an organizational structure can have far reaching consequences.

There is growing consensus that neither decentralized nor centralized structures are uniformly superior. Instead, each is advantageous for some purpose and not for others. Therefore, each tends to be adopted by different types of movements. A decentralized structure maximizes direct communal participation and consensual decision making. It is most effective in mobilizing large numbers of individuals for personal change and avoiding the dangers of oligarchy and co-optation by institutions. It also allows for diverse ideologies and interests. A decentralized structure is often deliberately chosen to model ideals or values held by grass-roots participants. In contrast, a centralized structure maximizes technical expertise and coordination necessary for strategic efforts toward institutional change. It also maximizes consistency of purpose and the probability of coopting institutional resources such as the mass media or external funding. Emerging SMOs that combine incongruent values or goals must confront difficult choices regarding their organizational structure, which can lead to major internal strains as some goals are given priority over others.

Context played a major role in determining the Coalition's structure and decision making process. CCOMH was formed in part due to frustration with a centralized, bureaucratic Department of Health, which was perceived as insensitive and autocratic. This was to be avoided. Further, many CCOMH members were relatively small, grass-roots organizations with minimal administrative hierarchy. Therefore, they were used to operating within a decentralized structure. Finally, the overtly political nature of the Coalition caused apprehension on the part of some members. They felt vulnerable to possible government retaliation and wanted direct input into Coalition decisions that might put them at risk.

For all these reasons, CCOMH chose a decentralized, informal structure in which decisions were based on consensus achieved through face-to-face discussion. Bureaucracy was created only to the minimum necessary for organizational functioning. Initially, there were only two officers (Chair and Vice-Chair) with no fixed terms, no formal Executive Committee, no constitution, and no bylaws. Issues were discussed at large monthly meetings and decisions implemented by the officers with ad hoc assistance as needed.

The above structure worked well for approximately six months, during which time the Coalition was absorbed with internal tasks related to organizational growth and fostering group solidarity. New members were added, working relationships formed, and strategy developed. Increasing trust in the leadership that naturally emerged over time permitted members to feel less apprehensive about the Coalition in general and delegating authority in particular.

Once the work of this initial period had been completed, however, attention turned to implementation of strategic plans. This was a qualitatively different task, for which a highly decentralized structure was less well suited. Delaying action until after the next monthly meeting often was either impossible or ineffective. In addition, membership had increased to over 30 organizations. Even if only two-thirds attended any given meeting, discussion of issues could be very extended. Lastly, the sheer quantity of Coalition work increased dramatically, placing an unreasonable burden on the two officers.

Therefore, an Executive Committee was formally constituted to act between general meetings. However, even then it was understood that the Committee would be very cautious concerning actions that might be controversial or call attention to any individual member. No further centralization of authority has occurred in the succeeding three years. The only additional formalization of operating procedures has been adoption of fixed terms for officers and the Executive Committee. Thus, the Coalition has remained a decentralized, informal, grass-roots organization.

The deliberate choices described above have had predictable consequences, good and bad. On the positive side, members have a definite sense of ownership and feel free to participate as actively as they wish. They appreciate the democratic nature of decision making and trust the Coalition's collective judgement. Those who participate regularly have become well informed concerning mental health issues and have advanced their interests within the Coalition. On the negative side, there have been costs in terms of reduced strategic effectiveness and economic marginality. Decisions have often been arrived at slowly and have reflected the "least common denominator" principle, whereby any significant dissension (usually in a conservative direction) is sufficient to block action. Further, like most decentralized organizations, the Coalition chose to finance itself entirely from internal contributions so as to retain its independence. Given tight member budgets, this has precluded even part-time staff support and placed the demanding task of organizational maintenance on volunteers. As a result, maintenance has been a continuing problem. The Coalition is currently discussing this situation with a view toward securing some external assistance without compromising its fundamental nature as a voluntary, grass-roots organization. In the long run, it will also have to examine the relationship between organizational structure and strategic effectiveness, especially as the former detracts from its ability to respond to emerging challenges and opportunities.

STRATEGIES AND TACTICS

As discussed previously, resource mobilization theory views the primary purpose of SMOs as the achievement of greater social power. Success in this regard is defined in terms of changes in relevant public policies, alteration of decision making elites, and changes in the distribution of socially valued goods or all of these. In the present context, these goals would translate into greater emphasis in provincial mental health policy on community-based services, inclusion of Coalition representatives or supporters in government decision making processes, and reallocation of mental health resources from institutional to community programs.

Concerning factors related to the outcomes of social movements, resource mobilization theory takes an open system approach whereby outcomes are shaped not only by SMO strategic choices but by the larger political environment. Very few, if any, SMOs have the capacity to force change entirely from outside the normal decision making structure. Therefore, perhaps the most critical determinant of outcomes is the degree to which an SMO can forge alliances with powerful, preexisting institutions and interest groups (Jenkins, 1983). Institutions and interest groups are likely to form such alliances if they share the SMO's normative beliefs or perceive it as a means of furthering their own ends. Alliances with powerful elites serve two important functions, namely to magnify the impact of SMO action and to shelter it from repression by the target group. This was certainly the case with the Coalition, as will be seen below.

The principle strategies employed by the Coalition are advocacy, public education, and applied research. These strategies and the tactics by which they have been implemented will be discussed next.

Advocacy

Four different constituencies have been addressed through advocacy. The most obvious but in some ways least important constituency is the Minister of Health and his senior officials. There is little hope of converting these individuals to the Coalition's viewpoint, since they are the main architects of the system requiring reform. Moreover, they are all approaching retirement and cannot be expected to alter their basic values or beliefs about the mentally disabled and appropriate treatment. However, it is vital to be seen by potential allies to be working cooperatively with the Department of Health. By attempting to do so and being frustrated, the Coalition gives allies license to exercise influence beyond the boundaries of the Department. For tactical reasons therefore, we request meetings with the Minister at least once each year and regularly correspond with him concering relevant issues, despite the generally fruitless outcome of these efforts.

The second constituency targeted for advocacy consists of government ministers in other departments who are receptive to the Coalition's position. Some are strong proponents of decentralized, community-based human services on philosophical grounds and view current mental health services as regressive. Other ministers are more concerned on pragmatic grounds with rising health care costs and recognize the need for a major shift in direction away from institutions. In either case, these ministers can influence government policy far more powerfully than the Coalition. We meet and correspond with them at every opportunity to provide information on cost-effective alternatives to the present system and ask for their support in Cabinet. These ministers have been our most helpful allies in pressuring government for change.

The third constituency includes both opposition parties in the provincial legislature. They are the Coalition's means of addressing government directly, publicly, and in a manner sure to gain coverage in the mass media. Especially at times when annual mental health spending estimates are debated in the legislature, the Coalition works intensively with the health critic of each party over a period of several weeks. We brief them thoroughly on current mental health issues and receive feedback on how they wish to approach the estimates debate. The Coalition then prepares background material and drafts a series of questions for each critic. This tactic has proved enormously valuable in calling the Minister of Health to account for unfulfilled commitments, as well as obtaining detailed information about mental health expenditures and future plans.

The fourth constituency with whom the Coalition advocates is actually a heterogeneous mix of community opinion makers such as individual legislators, private funders, and media representatives. Key individuals are identified and tactics developed on an issue-specific basis. While this type of advocacy often involves a great deal of work for relatively little short-term gain, we believe that the eventual payoff justifies its continuation. It helps establish our credibility with influential citizens and can produce unforseen benefits by creating a receptive climate in the community.

It should be readily apparent that advocacy by the Coalition is heavily oriented toward forging alliances with dominant elements of society. We view this task as equal in importance to articulating a coherent program of mental health reform. One is process, the other content. One without the other would be futile.

Public Education

In some sense, public education can be conceptualized as simply another type of advocacy. However, while both activities involve persuasion, public education by its nature is a less overtly political, more indirect, mass phenomenon. It presents different problems and requires specialized skills, perhaps the most important being an ability to work collaboratively with the mass media. CCOMH regards the general public as holding great potential for either benefit or harm to our objectives, depending on how mental health issues are framed. Moreover, the public is the final arbiter of mental health policy. The shift advocated by the Coalition cannot occur without substantial public understanding and support.

To mold public opinion, CCOMH works with print and electronic media to identify and develop newsworthy approaches to mental health issues. We are assisted by a volunteer media consultant familiar with both types. The media usually favor a personalized approach focused on the negative consequences of poor planning or inadequate services. To advance its public policy objectives, the Coalition respects this approach without crossing over into exploitation. For example, a recent television documentary chronicled in a sensitive manner the case of a young man in rural Manitoba who, due to a lack of community-based services, had to be institutionalized far from his family. The documentary went on to explore reasons for this situation and described the reforms necessary to prevent similar incidences in the future.

Occasionally, a special event provides particular opportunities for public education. One such event was the 1984 provincial election. The Coalition developed a "challenge ballot" which described seven key mental health issues and asked the respondent to agree or disagree with the positions taken. Each major political party and their individual candidates received a challenge ballot. Over a four week period, responses were tallied and relayed to the media, who exhibited keen interest in the results. The ballot proved an excellent vehicle for raising public awareness of mental health. It also forced each party to go on public record for the first time concerning its policies in this area.

Another, more frequent opportunity for public education involves public hearings on mental health related legislation. These are usually attended by the mass media, who highlight opposing positions in their coverage. Organizations can request to appear before the legislative committee considering a bill and present a brief. Although the time constraints on any speaker are often severe, the format tends to be quite open and flexible. Especially in cases in which controversial issues or major expenditures are at stake, public hearings are an excellent forum in which to educate the public through media exposure, all at relatively little cost. The Coalition takes advantage of these opportunities whenever they arise, as has occurred regarding the Mental Health Act, zoning regulations, extra billing, minimum wage legislation, and affirmative action for mentally disabled persons. Coalition participation in the legislative process has the secondary benefit of helping to build the political bridges necessary for effective advocacy.

Applied Research

In Western democracies, a SMO challenging the status quo ultimately must rely on persuasion more than other forms of power. Any attempt to use tactics regarded by society as illegitimate (e.g., coercion) is almost always counterproductive because it alienates potential supporters (Jenkins, 1983). In practical terms, this means that SMO must present an alternative to the status quo that is seen by influential allies as more desirable according to valid criteria. The alternative may be only an idea or vision of the future or it may already exist elsewhere in some form. Evidence of the latter can be extremely helpful in persuading potential allies, who often are not theoretically oriented, of the alternative's feasibility and actual benefits.

CCOMH has defined three aspects of mental health system reform as warranting priority for applied research. The first aspect involves determining how other jurisdictions in North America have successfully managed to make the transition from a seriously imbalanced, institutionally-dominated mental health system to a system in which institutional and community mental health services are roughly balanced. This issue goes to the heart of the Coalition's mission. The second aspect involves development of mental health services legislation that mandates a comprehensive range of care from minimal (e.g., supervised independent living) to maximal (e.g., continuous hospitalization) intensity. Such legislation is distinguishable from traditional mental health acts, which typically deal much more narrowly with regulations concerning involuntary hospitalization. The third aspect of reform being researched is the devolution of centralized system governance to regions. Regionalization of responsibility for planning and budgeting in particular is viewed as a necessary condition for fairness, equity, and accountability of mental health services.

In each of these areas, research has taken the form of an extensive, computer-assisted review of both published and unpublished literature. The Coalition identifies guidelines for and examples of progressive action, applies this intelligence to the Manitoba context, and disseminates selected findings to various constituencies in a format appropriate to their interests. For example, information on the relative cost-effectiveness of alternative approaches to service is condensed and directed at the Minister of Finance, whereas the general public is targeted for information regarding the impact of community care on neighborhoods. Thus, applied research is utilized to further the Coalition's objectives concerning advocacy and public education. Even though it is labour intensive, research must be an ongoing activity, since mental health system reform has only recently become the subject of systematic research and new knowledge is developing rapidly. Moreover, the persuasive power of CCOMH depends heavily on being better informed than its opponents.

EFFECTIVENESS AND FUTURE PROSPECTS

Since its inception, CCOMH has strongly emphasized the need for accountability by mental health decision makers, especially concerning the utilization of scarce resources. Therefore, it is only fair that the principle of accountability be applied to the Coalition itself, which uses very scarce budgetary and volunteer resources from members. This concluding section also examines some critical challenges facing the organization and, to whatever extent possible in an uncertain world, its future prospects.

Effectiveness

Earlier we stated that the fundamental goal of social movements, and by implication the SMOs that exercise leadership within them, is achievement of greater social power. Next, this goal was operationalized in terms of public policies, decision making elites, and socially valued goods. Before discussing the effectiveness of CCOMH on these criteria or dimensions, however, two general observations are warranted. First, the criteria listed above are all measures of Coalition outcome or impact, as opposed to process or functioning. Yet, the Coalition has accomplished much in the way of process, from educating members to giving them an increased sense of control over their lives. This effectiveness in process terms has been instrumental in achieving intended outcomes and must be clearly recognized. Second, the political process engaged by the Coalition is fundamentally so complex and convoluted as to make definitive conclusions impossible about CCOMH effectiveness in outcome terms. Just as the Coalition is both a product of and contributor to larger social forces, its effects are inextricably interwoven with those forces. This makes it extremely difficult to prove that Coalition activity caused or brought about any particular outcome. At best, some causal connection can be tentatively inferred from a temporal association between activity and outcome, in full awareness that additional causes were almost certainly at work. This limitation is not at all unique to the present context (Knoke, 1986).

Turning to the criterion of changing relevant public policies, the Coalition appeared to contribute importantly to government's adoption in principle of the policy framework recommended by the Mental Health Working Group. It can also take some credit for the absence of any significant backtracking from that framework despite pressure from medical and institutional interests to do so. Although since 1984 community mental health as a public policy for Manitoba has not always been well understood or implemented by the Department of Health, it is now more firmly entrenched and widely accepted than at any time in the past. The public debate largely centers around implementation issues, not the policy per se.

Concerning decision making elites, in 1985 the Minister of Health established a ten person Mental Health Advisory Committee (MHAC) spanning government and the community. Leaders of two Coalition members are among these 10 advisors, albeit as individuals rather than organizational representatives. Both leaders are also included in a five person Executive Committee. The MHAC has significantly broadened the scope of information and advice the Minister receives regarding important mental health issues. To date, he has accepted this advice far more often than not. Other evidence of change in decision making elites is acceptance of the Coalition as a legitimate mental health advocacy organization by influential government, media, and other opinion leaders. This is most apparent in the frequency of contacts between CCOMH and such individuals, with requests for contacts flowing both ways.

Regarding the distribution of socially valued goods, the Coalition has lobbied hard from the beginning for development of a five year plan which would reallocate resources necessary to create comprehensive, community-based mental health services. In the past several months, such a plan has been examined by the MHAC, and has now been recommended to the Minister. It would increase the proportion of mental health expenditures for community services from 3.9% to approximately 12.5%. If approved by the Minister and ultimately by Cabinet, the plan would entail the first substantial reallocation of mental health funds in Manitoba history. While the overall pattern of expenditures will require further reallocation to achieve balance, the symbolic and practical value of the present proposal would be enormous. The mere fact it is being seriously considered is a remarkable shift from just three years ago.

In conclusion, there is considerable evidence supporting the effectiveness of the Coalition on all three dimensions of social influence. What might have occurred with CCOMH cannot be determined, nor can the exact contribution of the Coalition to the events described above. However, the almost total lack of change prior to formation of the Coalition suggests that it has played a meaningful role in mental health system reform.

Critical Challenges

Notwithstanding the above accomplishments, the Coalition faces critical challenges in at least three major areas, namely strategic effectiveness, organizational maintenance, and leadership. These challenges are briefly discussed next.

Strategic effectiveness. Under structure and decision making, the Coalition's decentralized nature and heterogeneity were portrayed as limiting its strategic effectiveness by often delaying decisions or rendering them more conservative than necessary, in order to achieve consensus. This already important problem may assume additional significancce in the future as proposals for change increasingly involve alternatives to the traditional mental health services provided by some Coalition members. For example, how will CCOMH's decentralized structure cope with a recommendation for mandated rationalization and coordination of services by certain member agencies rather than by external (i.e., medical and institutional) caregivers, as has been the case up until now? Decision making could become even more difficult than before if member interests are perceived to be jeopardized. In another scenario, would the degree of decentralization characteristic of the Coalition today eventually limit the extent to which it can participate actively in decisions at an intermediate (e.g., programmatic) as opposed to macroscopic (e.g., strategic) level? If the answer is yes, a choice between further centralization and noninvolvement at that level would be necessary. The point is simply that strong decentralization may be less and less viable as decisions become more controversial within the Coalition or go beyond broad issues of values and strategies.

Organizational maintenance. As discussed before, the extensive activities necessary to maintain the Coalition (e.g., preparing mailings) have fallen on volunteers or, perhaps unfairly, on CMHA staff, with whom CCOMH works closely. The task is large and the pressure unrelenting. After the initial drive for members in 1984-1985, organizational maintenance took second place to more exciting pursuits. The cost of this inevitable letdown is now becoming apparent as representatives of member organization turn over. New representatives often do not share the same understanding and commitment to the Coalition of those they replaced. A major reorientation and renewal is needed, yet without paid staff support, this is very difficult to conduct while other demands remain undiminished. This problem must be addressed in the near future.

A related but more specific maintenance problem involves providing incentives to Coalition members that enhance rather than reduce ideological commitment. Ferree and Miller (1985) observed that heterogeneous SMOs often develop complex incentive systems to satisfy a diverse membership. However, to the extent that these incentives are only tangentially related to the organization's social influence objectives, they tend to attract members whose ideological commitment is questionable. They also divert resources away from strategic activities. An example would be frequent, purely social events. In the face of declining attendance at Coalition meetings, the challenge will be to identify incentives that solidify ideological commitment in new representatives and integrate them into organizational roles.

Leadership.   At least initially, social movement organizations are heavily dependent on individual leadership for energy and direction (Jenkins, 1983). Later, leadership may or may not be broadened or institutionalized, or both. The transition from a founding leader or leaders to whatever follows is a critical event for any SMO. At one extreme, it can be smooth and rejuvenating or, at the other extreme, traumatic and injurious. Leadership transition is a predictable, repeated test of an organization's viability and sense of purpose. Moreover, a prolonged search for a new leader can sharply reduce an organization's external orientation in favor of internal demands.

The first leadership transition for the Coalition occurred in April, 1986, approximately two and one-half years after its formation. The founding Chair indicated his intention to resign from that office to devote more time to his paid employment. A call for nominations brought no response. Concern was expressed by potential leaders that the workload of the Chair was far too heavy. Necessity being the mother of invention, the position was informally divided and, after considerable persuasion, co-Chairs were elected. One was a self help group representative, the other a municipal government personnel officer, and both were women. The former Chair agreed to remain on the Executive Committee to enhance continuity of leadership. Thus, the transition was successfully completed. However, a year later one co-Chair resigned, again citing work overload, and the leadership issue was reactivated. No replacement has yet been found. While adequate staff support could ease this problem, it will remain a sporadic but vital challenge for the Coalition. Stable, capable leadership is absolutely essential for long-term effectiveness. The realities of changing a major human service system place a premium on developing trusting relationships with allies, understanding historical complexities, and sheer persistence. Frequent, unplanned leadership transitions threaten satisfaction of all three requirements.

Future Prospects

The challenges discussed above are broadly applicable to decentralized, grass-roots, voluntary organizations. Although they still must be met, CCOMH can take some comfort in the fact that comparable SMOs have found workable solutions. Another encouraging factor is the nearly overwhelming social and economic forces driving continued deinstitutionalization of mental health services. This pressure creates both a need and an opportunity for an organization such as the Coalition. In a very real sense, if the Coalition didn't exist, it would have to be invented. It is very unlikely that organizations which support comprehensive, community mental health services in Manitoba will ever return to their pre-1984 state of isolated struggle. Ideological consciousness, political sophistication, and expectations for systemic reform have been raised too high for that to occur.

Paradoxically, the greatest danger to the Coalition may stem from either too little or too much success. Failure by government to meaningfully reallocate mental health resources in the near future would be extremely discouraging after three years of intensive effort. Conversely, aproval of the five year plan currently under review may be interpreted as the end of a campaign which, in fact, is only in its early stages. In either case, the Coalition could stop doing those very things that have brought it to prominence. Continuation of the present strategy of pursuing "small wins" (Weick, 1984) regarding circumscribed issues would appear to hold the greatest promise for strategic effectiveness and organizational endurance.

REFERENCES

Ferree, M., & Miller, F. (1985). Mobilization and meaning: Toward an integration of social psychological and resource perspectives on social movements. *Sociological Inquiry, 55*, 38-61.

Jenkins, J. C. (1983). Resource mobilization theory and the study of social movements. *Annual Review of Sociology, 9*, 527-553.

Kidder, L., & Fine, M. (1986). Making sense of injustice: Social explanations, social action, and the role of the social scientist. In E. Seidman and J. Rappaport (Eds.), *Redefining social problems*. New York: Plenum.

Kiesler, C. (1982). Mental hospitals and alternative care: Noninstitutionalization as a potential public policy for mental patients. *American Psychologist, 37*, 1323-1339.

Knoke, D. (1986). Associations and interest groups. *Annual Review of Sociology, 12*, 1-21.

Mental Health Working Group (1983). *Mental health services in Manitoba: A review and recommendations*. Government of Manitoba: Queen's Printer, 200 Vaughan Street, Winnipeg, Manitoba R3C 1T5.

Richman, A., & Harris, P. (1983). Mental hospital deinstitutionalization in Canada: A national perspective with some regional examples. *International Journal of Mental Health, 11*, 64-83.

Roch, D., Evans, R., & Pascoe, D. (1985). *Manitoba and medicare: 1971 to the present*. Government of Manitoba: Queen's Printer, 200 Vaughan Street, Winnipeg, Manitoba R3C 1T5.

Ryan, W. (1971). *Blaming the victim*. New York: Random House.

Weick, K. (1984). Small wins: Redefining the scale of social problems. *American Psychologist, 39*, 40-49.

APPENDIX A

Terms of Reference

Community Coalition On Mental Health

A coalition of supportive organizations to pursue the development of comprehensive, community-based mental health services in Manitoba.

Purpose

1.1 Lobby for implementation of the recommendations of the Mental Health Working Group Report (Pascoe Report).

1.2 Promote comprehensive, community-based mental health services consistent with the principles and policies recommended by the Mental Health Working Group Report.

Strategy

Establish a coalition of supportive organizations to:

2.1 Gather and organize relevant information.

2.2 Lobby government and other relevant organizations.

2.3 Engage in public education activities, particularly with regard to the mass media.

2.4 Engage in other actions deemed appropriate to achieve goals of coalition.

David Hallman

7
THE NESTLE BOYCOTT: THE SUCCESS OF A CITIZENS' COALITION IN SOCIAL INTERVENTION

INTRODUCTION

After seven years of perseverance, a disparate, informal, international network of citizens forced one of the world's largest multinational corporations to fundamentally change the way it operated in developing countries. Why did the campaign attract commitment from such a wide variety of supporters? How did the network evolve and what strategies were employed in relating to the corporation? What accounted for Nestle's final agreement to accede to the boycott demands?

The story of the Nestle Boycott and the answers to these questions provide an interesting example of a successful, large-scale, specifically-focused social intervention. Though the initial odds would have seemed overwhelmingly against the boycott's success, the leadership and supporters of the movement were able to draw upon a range of resources which the company eventually found too difficult to resist. The Nestle Boycott is a story of ordinary citizens acting on what they believed was a moral issue. In some significant ways, it is a novel story of social intervention. The social interventionists did not have a direct stake in the oppression and exploitation they opposed. Rather, they acted out of a sense of moral outrage to protect those unable to protect themselves (i.e., mothers and infants in developing countries). The leaders and supporters of the boycott organized and persevered until Nestle finally agreed to eliminate its aggressive promotion of infant formula in developing countries.

The whys behind this campaign provide some interesting reflections on social commitment. The hows of the campaign illustrate some effective strategies for social intervention.

A BRIEF HISTORY

Infant formula was developed in 1866 by Henri Nestle to save the life of a baby unable to tolerate other types of food (Nestle, 1977). Over the decades, as the formula was improved, it began to be seen as a viable alternative to breastmilk for mothers who either could not or chose not to breastfeed. Previously, infants of such mothers were provided with breastmilk by "wet nurses," women who nursed the children of others in addition to their own. By the early part of the twentieth century, commercial infant formula had been developed by a variety of companies and was marketed throughout Europe and North America.

Still not understood at the time was the "living nature" of breastmilk, which provides infants with immunities and antibodies providing protection against infections and disease and contributing to the development of their own immune systems. Such properties cannot be duplicated by artificial products. The medical community at that time received much of its information about infant formula from the companies promoting it, which in turn, used research results to extoll the product's virtues. Medical texts counselled student doctors and nurses to encourage women to use infant formula. Not only was it seen as of equal value to breastfeeding, but it was promoted as a way to free women from the "drudgery" of breastfeeding and to help them better maintain their figures after childbirth.

Research conducted in the early part of the century which was not company-sponsored, challenged claims made on behalf of formula. One major study in the Chicago area in the 1930s identified a pattern that was to be replicated many times over: infants bottlefed with formula were more likely to contract illnesses, particularly gastrointestinal infections, than were breastfed babies (Grulee, Sanford, & Herron, 1934). But the intense marketing of formula as the "modern way" to feed one's infant had such appeal that these cautionary notes received little attention.

By 1972, only 28% of American infants were nursed by their mothers by the age of one week, and 15% by the age of two months (Martinez, 1974). A marketing survey by Ross Laboratories in Canada indicated that by 1973, 35% of infants were breastfed during the first week of life; 17% by the third month, and six percent by the sixth month (American Academy of Pediatrics, 1978).

Though the use of formula continued to increase in industrialized countries, the rate of increase was not as significant in the '50s and '60s as it had been previously. The market was saturated, with the majority of mothers in Canada and the U.S. bottlefeeding. Serious questions as to whether formula was, in fact, as good as breastmilk were being raised and companies realized they would have to find markets in places other than industrialized countries, if dramatic growth in formula sales was to continue. Third World countries loomed as a vast, untapped market. Companies producing infant formula, Nestle chief amongst them, entered this new market with relish, using similar promotional tools to those they had used in industrialized countries. Mass media advertisements idealized the results of feeding formula to new-born infants. The health care delivery system was co-opted as part of their promotional chain. Attractive posters showing babies being bottlefed were given to hospitals and doctors to adorn their usually drab facilities. Free samples were given to hospitals, supposedly to relieve the pressure of having to bring new-born infants and their mothers together for breastfeeding. Instead, the babies were bottlefed, and free formula samples were given to mothers to take home. The insidiousness of the free sample as a form of promotion was that poor mothers naturally wanted to use this new product, seen as a symbol of western progress and affluence. Unfortunately, by the time the free sample was exhausted, the woman's own breastmilk had ceased, and she no longer had a choice. She had to bottlefeed.

In the three decades following the Second World War, breastfeeding rates in many developing countries dropped dramatically. In Singapore, women in low-income families who breastfed for at least three months decreased from 71% in 1951 to 42% in 1960; in Chile from 1957 to 1969, breastfeeding beyond two months fell from 95% to 20%; in the Philippines, breastfeeding in urban areas dropped from 64% to 23% between 1960 and 1974 (see Figure 1) (Berg, 1973).

The first signs of trouble were identified by health workers in the Third World who noticed a drop in the average age of malnourished children. While they had once seen a limited number of babies under the age of one year, the average age of those with malnutrition was falling to about nine months. Informal research pointed to the fact that the majority of these younger infants had been bottlefed rather than breastfed.

More systematic research was initiated, both on the rates of breastfeeding and bottlefeeding, and on the incidence of illness and death corresponding to each (see Figure 2) (Gerrard & Tan, 1978). Plank and Milanesi (1973) interviewed 1,712 rural Chilean mothers to see how feeding practices contributed to infant mortality. They con-

Figure 1

Extent of Breast Feeding in Selected Countries and Years, 1946-71

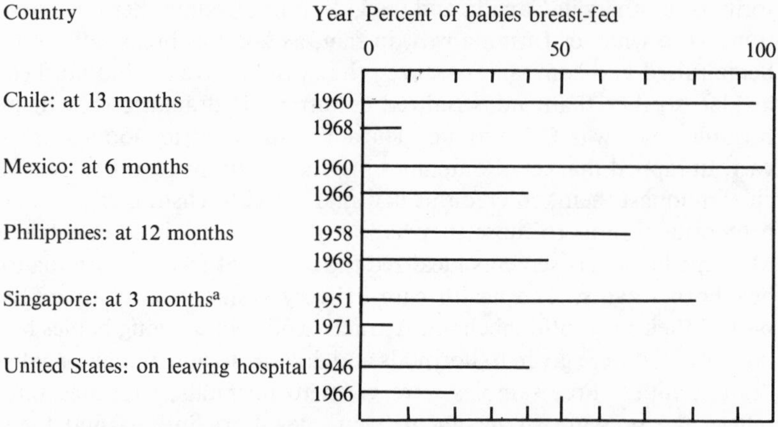

Country	Year	Percent of babies breast-fed

Sources: Diva M. Sanjur and others, "Infant Feeding and Weaning Practices in a Rural Pre-industrial Setting," *Acta Paediatrica Scandinavica*, Supplement 200 (1970), p. 15; Ma(ria) Linda Gabucan-Dulay, "Current Feeding Patterns as Observed among 1,000 Filipino Infants," *Philippine Journal of Pediatrics*, Vol. 19 (April 1970), p. 101; F.B. Mönckeberg, "The Effect on Malnutrition and Environment on Mental Development," *Proceedings of Western Hemisphere Nutrition Congress II, San Juan, Puerto Rico, August 1968* (Chicago: American Medical Association, 1969), pp. 216-20; Wong Hock Boon, *Breastfeeding in Singapore* (Singapore: J.L. Morison Son and Jones (F.E.) Pte., 1971); and Herman F. Meyer, "Breast Feeding in the United States," *Clinical Pediatrics*, Vol. 7 (December 1968), p. 709.

    a. Low socioeconomic class only.

    Note. From *The Nutrition Factor: Its role in national development* (p. 91) by A. Berg, 1973, Washington, D.C.: Brookings Institute.

cluded, "There were three times as many deaths among babies given bottles before the age of three months as among those who were wholly breastfed . . ." (p. 204).

    Puffer and Serrano (1973) studied 35,000 childhood deaths in 13 project sites across Latin America. Among infants dying of diarrheal disease at 28 days to five months, 51.7% were not breastfed as compared to 31.7% who were breastfed and not weaned. Among babies in the same age group who died of nutritional deficiency, 51.5% were not breastfed as compared to 34.1% who were breastfed and not weaned. The authors concluded: "This is important, indirect evidence of the protective value of breastfeeding" (p. 1).

    Several trends became obvious: the rates of breastfeeding in many developing countries were dropping dramatically: bottlefeeding

Figure 2

Life Expectancy Tables in Breast and Bottle Fed Indian Babies 1962

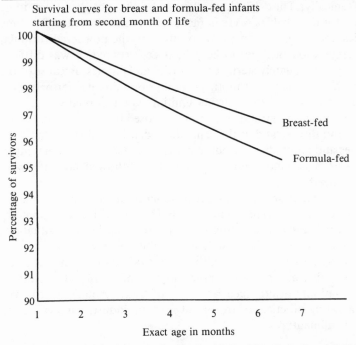

Survival curves for breast and formula-fed infants starting from second month of life

Note. From Hazards of formula feeding (p. 21) by J.W. Gerrard and L.K-T. Tan, January/February, 1978, *Keeping Abreast, Journal of Human Nurturing.*

rates were climbing just as rapidly, and the likelihood of an infant becoming sick or dying was about three times as great if the child had been bottlefed rather than breastfed. Why were the patterns of infant feeding changing so dramatically, and why did bottlefeeding place infants at a higher risk to infection and disease?

Reasons for the change in feeding practices were somewhat complex and related to a number of factors, including increased urbanization, a larger number of women in the industrialized work force, hospital practices of separating infants and mothers, etc. However, health workers consistently identified the intense and aggressive promotion of infant formula as a major factor in the change of feeding practices. The impression was being created that this was the modern way to feed one's infant. It was a popular theme in developing countries where people attempted to emulate what were perceived as western practices. Sophisticated promotion of infant formula led many mothers to believe that it was as good as or better than breastmilk. In fact, breastfeeding became stigmatized as a symbol of poverty, and associated with the old ways of doing things.

Tragically, Third World mothers, who thought they were doing the best for their babies, were in fact placing them at great risk. Many families had neither clean water to mix with the powdered formula, nor refrigeration facilities to keep it, once prepared. It was difficult for them to adequately sterilize the bottles and nipples. Because of the cost of the formula, poor mothers would often dilute it far below the intended proportion, thus further limiting its nutritional value.

Consequently, infants were being exposed to many sources of infection and disease and at the same time, deprived of the natural immunities and antibodies present in breastmilk. Gastro-intestinal infections were a common result. Malnutrition followed and, if severe enough, death.

Critics did not hold the infant-formula companies responsible for the poverty and economic conditions of Third World families, but objected to aggressive promotion of infant formula in those situations where it was virtually impossible to prepare it safely.

During the early 1970s, health workers raised these issues at international gatherings, resulting in the adoption of a series of resolutions by international health agencies. Most of these resolutions criticized the marketing practices of the infant-formula industry and called for their curtailment:

> Strong action should be taken to prevent:
> (a) advertising of commercial milk products on government premises, especially hospitals, health clinics and schools by the distribution and use of calendars, diaries, posters, and milk samples;
> (b) access of "commercial milk" nurses to government premises, especially hospital boards, health centres and schools;
> (c) acceptance of "free" milk samples. If, however, the need arises to supplement diets of malnourished children, these milks should be issued only in unlabelled containers (Pan American Health Organization, 1970, cited in Interfaith Center on Corporate Responsibility, 1979, p. 1).
>
> Noting the general decline in breastfeeding, related to social, cultural and environmental factors, including the mistaken idea caused by misleading sales promotion that breastfeeding is inferior to feeding with manufactured breastmilk substitutes . . . the World Health Organization

(WHO) urges member countries to review sales promotion activities on baby foods and to introduce appropriate remedial measures including advertisement codes and legislation where necessry (Proceedings of the 27th World Health Assembly, 1974, cited in Interfaith Center on Corporate Responsibility, 1979, p. 1).

. . . Because we are convinced that breastmilk is the best food for infants and that breastfeeding constitutes the more effective safeguard against malnutrition and infection in infants, particularly in disadvantaged communities . . . sales promotion activities of organizations marketing baby milks and feeding bottles that run counter to the general intent expressed in this document must be curtailed by every means available to the profession, including, where necessary and feasible, legislation to control unethical practices; dissemination of propaganda about artificial feeding and distribution of samples of artificial baby foods in maternity units should be banned immediately (International Pediatric Association, 1975, cited in Interfaith Center on Corporate Responsibility, 1979, pp. 1-2).

Unfortunately, these calls for change had little appreciable impact upon the infant-formula industry, aside from an increased consciousness of potential public relations problems. Companies began to formalize their marketing practices in policies which seemed to deny the existence of any real problem, described the industry's role in seemingly responsible terms, and in effect, exonerated and rationalized their current marketing activities.

In 1973, an article on the subject appeared in *The New Internationalist*, a British magazine sponsored by several charities, including Oxfam, and devoted to the discussion of issues related to the Third World. The article was highly critical of the infant-formula industry and cited Nestle, in particular, as engaging in aggressive promotional practices which contributed to the decline of breastfeeding (Geach, 1973). In 1974, a British development education agency, "War on Want," published a brochure about infant-formula promotion and entitled it *The baby killer* (Muller, 1974). The following year, a Swiss-German development organization reprinted the pamphlet in German, giving it the more assertive title *Nestle totet babys* (Nestle kills babies). That action appreciably raised the stakes in the issue, and Nestle took the group to court on grounds of libel. The court case resulted in considerable publicity, and the day before the judge was to hand down a sentence, Nestle dropped five of its six charges, retaining only that which claimed it was impossible to prove the company intentionally killed babies. The judge concluded in Nestle's favour on that specific charge, but fined the development action group only a nominal amount and recommended that the marketing practices of Nestle warranted serious review.

North American groups, particularly those related to churches, became increasingly aware of infant-formula promotion in the Third World during the mid-1970s. Medical missionaries working for the churches communicated back to their parent bodies the seriousness of the problem and encouraged them to become involved in attempts to get companies to change their marketing practices. As a result, numerous religious bodies sponsored shareholder resolutions at the annual general meetings of some of the American companies who promoted infant formula, calling upon them to change their aggressive marketing of infant formula by eliminating direct consumer promotion, improving the literature aimed at health professionals and mothers, and restricting the distribution of free samples of formula to mothers. A Catholic order even launched a civil suit against one of the companies (National Council of Churches, April, 1977).

At about this time, some community groups formed the Infant Formula Action Coalition (INFACT) to address the issue of infant-formula promotion. INFACT began in the United States and a Canadian counterpart was organized shortly thereafter. The coalition soon realized that shareholder resolutions addressed to American companies would not have any impact on Nestle, which was wholly Swiss-owned and the major promoter of infant formula in the Third World, with almost one-third of the entire market. It was decided to raise public awareness of Nestle's role by launching a consumer boycott of the many products they distribute in North America, including coffees (Nescafe, Taster's Choice), other drinks (Nestle's Quik, Nestea), and a wide variety of other food products. Thus, the Nestle Boycott was born in the summer of 1977.

The boycott quickly caught on and became an action strategy in which many people could become involved. Many major organizations, particularly national religious bodies in Canada and the United States, began endorsing the Nestle Boycott, thereby opening up channels for a wide dissemination of information, and the involvement of many citizens at the community level.

The U.S. Senate Sub-Committee on Health and Scientific Research, under the leadership of Senator Edward Kennedy, held hearings in May, 1978, at which testimonies were heard from Third World health professionals and critics, medical and marketing experts, and company representatives (National Council of Churches,

1978). The event turned into a major public relations disaster for Nestle when Kennedy responded with incredulity and ridicule to the claims of Dr. Oswaldo Ballarin, chairperson of Nestle's operations in Brazil, who said the campaign against the industry was spearheaded by "a worldwide church organization with the stated purpose of undermining the free enterprise system" (Nestle, 1983, p. 4).

Partly as a result of the increasing politicization of the issue and greater citizen awareness, international health organizations, including UNICEF and the World Health Organization (WHO), were encouraged to take a more aggressive posture on infant-formula marketing in the Third World. In the fall of 1979, the two organizations co-sponsored a major consultation among industry, industrialized and Third World countries, health experts, and, for the first time in the history of a UN organization, representatives of non-governmental organizations (NGOs) (i.e., the boycotting groups). The status accorded the NGOs was an explicit acknowledgement of the role they played in bringing the issue to international attention, of their international contacts for monitoring industry practice, and of the technical expertise their leadership had developed on the issue.

The consultation resulted in a series of recommendations, including some encouraging a drastic revision of infant-formula marketing practices by (a) eliminating direct consumer advertising and the use of company personnel and free samples to promote formula to mothers, and (b) ensuring that literature and labels identify the risks and hazards of improper formula feeding. From these recommendations, the World Health Organization developed drafts for an international code on which countries could model legislation to change marketing practices.

The process of developing a code became highly politicized when the industry lobbied governments, particularly of industrialized countries, to refuse to support the concept or specifics of the code. INFACT Canada and its network of supporting organizations played a key role in moving the Canadian government's position from one of opposition, to one of relatively enthusiastic support for the code. This was accomplished through letter-writing campaigns and contacts with politicians and senior civil servants who apparently became convinced of the code's importance and of Canadian political support for its adoption. The U.S. Republican administration remained intransigent in its opposition to the code, having been extensively lobbied by the American infant-formula industry. However, it was unable to convince other industrialized countries, including Canada, to join it.

The code was adopted after considerable discussion by a vote of 117 countries to one (the U.S.) at the assembly of the World Health

Organization in May, 1981 (World Health Organization, 1981). The U.S. administration's position gained a great deal of publicity and acted as a channel by which more people became aware of the problem.

Though Nestle tried unsuccessfully to get the draft of the code weakened, they realized they could no longer oppose it once it was adopted by such an overwhelming majority. They thus expressed support for the aims and principles of the code, anticipating that this action would undercut popular support for the boycott. They were surprised to find that the boycott continued as strongly as ever, with the boycotting groups' assertion that it would not end until Nestle could prove it was in fact implementing the code in its Third World operations. In the meantime, organizations supporting the boycott coordinated themselves under an umbrella organization called the International Nestle Boycott Committee (INBC). This group became the primary contact with Nestle, and included in its membership the major religious organizations, health groups, labour unions, women's and students' groups supporting the boycott in the United States and Canada. European groups joined the INBC in subsequent years.

The next two and a half years tested the boycotting organizations' commitment to the struggle. Nestle had changed some of its most blatant forms of promotion, but the more insidious ones, like free samples and promotion directed at new mothers, continued. Nestle began investing vast sums of money to fight the boycott. Full-time public-relations staff produced materials and engaged in public debates, presenting Nestle in the best possible light. They conveyed the image of a company deeply concerned for the welfare of mothers and infants in developing countries, and acting responsibly in the distribution and promotion of infant-formula products. Groups involved in the boycott constantly monitored Nestle's practices in the Third World with the assistance of Third World health and consumer groups and then fed the information back to the boycotting groups' constituencies. The documentation of violations of the WHO code was needed to maintain the credibility of those supporting the Nestle Boycott.

Nestle realized its public relations efforts were not sufficient to undermine support for the Nestle Boycott. Thus, in March, 1982, it announced revised instructions to its field personnel regarding their implementation of the international code in the Third World. The news media carried the story Nestle wanted: Nestle was complying with the international code and the boycott could be terminated.

The boycotting groups scrambled to get details on Nestle's announcement. Intensive analysis of Nestle documents revealed that, in fact, Nestle had not dramatically changed its practices, and its policy continued to include numerous violations of the WHO code. Several months of communication through networks of the boycotting groups were required to reverse the popular image that the problem had been solved. The constituencies of the boycotting groups and the public at large proved their commitment to the issue by continuing to boycott Nestle.

Realizing that the boycott would not evaporate as they had hoped, Nestle made further changes over the next 18 months. Rather than negotiating with the INBC, the company began speaking directly to senior church officials in the U.S. The strategy proved successful in building pressure within the churches to terminate their endorsement of the boycott. Aware of this strategy and of the changes Nestle had made both in policy and practice, the INBC decided to do an intensive overview of Nestle's policy and practice in relation to the international code. That analysis, conducted in the fall of 1983, resulted in the identification of four areas in which Nestle still failed to comply with the international code: (a) the distribution of free samples and supplies, (b) gifts to health professionals, (c) the content of literature aimed at mothers, and (d) the text and graphics on product labels. In December, 1983, the INBC told Nestle they expected signifant changes in these four areas, and informed the company that a major meeting of the boycotting groups and their Third World partners was planned for early February, 1984, in Mexico City. At that time, decisions about the future of the boycott would be made. The INBC encouraged Nestle to make significant changes before that meeting and held a press conference to release the substance of this communication to the media.

Nestle responded with a proposal to meet and discuss the remaining areas of disagreement. This was the first time Nestle had indicated a readiness to respond to the INBC's longstanding invitation for direct discussion. Presumably, Nestle concluded that its former strategies of dividing boycott supporters, making incremental policy changes, and using public-relations approaches, were not successful in dissipating the boycott. The company was frustrated by the boycott's persistence and was attracted to the possibility of ending it at the Mexico meeting.

Preliminary meetings between two senior representatives of each side were held in late December and early January to discuss the format and agenda for formal discussions. The formal discussions began at UNICEF headquarters in New York City on January 14, 1984. Over the next week, Nestle and INBC representatives met for over 50 hours, with UNICEF personnel acting as facilitators of the discussion. Nestle had originally suggested, and the INBC agreed, to have

UNICEF act as a facilitator. Nestle executives gambled that they could convince UNICEF no further changes in policy and practice were necessary for Nestle to comply with the code. If that had happened, the INBC would have been isolated without UNICEF support, making it much more difficult to continue the boycott and to maintain public support.

During the negotiations, UNICEF consistently verified the INBC's interpretation of the changes Nestle had to make in order to fully comply with the international code. Nestle's negotiators communicated regularly with their headquarters in Switzerland during these sessions.

Finally, on Friday, January 20, the last of the four issues was resolved and the INBC representatives indicated they would take to the Mexico meeting a recommendation to suspend the boycott.

A joint press conference was held the following week to announce this agreement (see Appendix B) (INBC & Nestle, 1984). From February 3-6, representatives from 25 different countries and most of the boycotting organizations met in Mexico City to review the agreement, identify ways of monitoring Nestle's compliance, and discuss strategies related to other infant-formula companies. The international conference agreed to recommend to its member groups that the boycott be suspended for six months while Nestle's practices were monitored to ensure compliance with the agreement (INBC & IBFAN, 1984).

Over the next six months, the INBC Steering Committee met regularly with Nestle to receive reports on its progress in changing its practices and policies to comply with the agreement. In late September, 1984, the INBC held another major meeting at which the monitoring data was reviewed, the results of the accountability meetings discussed, and the formal termination of the boycott decided. Mechanisms for continued contact with Nestle were formed to ensure ongoing compliance and to bring pressure on other infant-formula companies to comply with the international code.

As an overview of this history of the Nestle Boycott, Figure 3 graphically illustrates the varying intensity of activities during the years 1976-1984.

NESTLE BOYCOTTERS AS SOCIAL INTERVENTIONISTS

Ira Goldenberg (1978) provides criteria for measuring the degree to which change agents act as social interventionists.

Figure 3

Graphic Illustration of Intensity of Activity Related to the Nestle Boycott
1976-1984

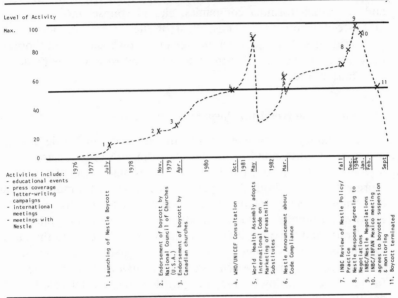

(1) Degree of Identification with the Setting's Underlying Goals, Assumptions & Intentions

Goldenberg maintains that change agents do not function as social interventionists when they identify with the goals, assumptions, or intentions of the organizations they criticize. One could assume that Nestle's basic goal as a corporation operating in a free enterprise system is to make a profit. Though many supporters of the Nestle Boycott did not reject the free enterpreise system, they did object to using infant formula as a source of considerable profit in the Third World. Many supporters of the boycott, having become increasingly aware of Third World development issues through the educational programs of their churches, were conscious of the ways in which corporations can exploit the resources and populations of Third World countries. They had come to understand that the social and economic needs of Third World countries require the co-operative involvement of international development agencies, host and foreign governments, and they were becoming increasingly sceptical of multinational corporations because of their sacrifice of local needs and long-term development for profit and short-term gain.

Those who became aware of the infant-formula problem found it inexcusable that corporations were prepared to deny the health-endangering aspects of their infant-formula promotion in order to protect a lucrative market. The boycott supporters felt health agencies and not infant-formula companies, should counsel mothers about infant-feeding practices. Thus, most of the boycott supporters experienced a fundamental clash between their own values and those of the corporations concerning the place of infant-formula companies in the Third World.

(2) Belief in the Need for Basic Systemic Change

Depending on how one analyzes the situation, the Nestle Boycott might either correspond to, or deviate from, this criterion for social intervention. On the one hand, a change in the marketing of a product representing only about three percent of the sales of a multinational corporation seems relatively insignificant, and hardly systemic. However, a number of factors made it much more than symbolic.

Nestle and the other infant-formula companies entered the Third World market with promotional strategies similar to those used in industrialized countries. When asked to abandon these practices in favour of a much lower company profile and a greater role for the health system in advising mothers on infant-feeding practices, Nestle was essentially being told to act counter to its goal of increased sales and profits.

The fact that pressure for this change was coming from loosely organized citizen groups was a source of considerable annoyance to Nestle and the other infant-formula companies. They were accustomed to making decisions about marketing strategies exclusively at the management or shareholder level, based on criteria about developing and exploiting markets. To be involved in a situation where they might have to accede to the wishes of people quite beyond this close network threatened both their independence and pride.

The infant-formula controversy was a significant one because of the precedent it could set for the marketing of other products (e.g., pharmaceuticals, tobacco, alcohol, herbicides and pesticides). All of these products were already cited as contributing to Third World health problems when marketed in a largely uncontrolled manner. The involvement of international health organizations, the development of marketing regulations or guidelines, and the monitoring of company practices by citizen groups were all antithetical to the way the corporation felt it should be able to function in a free enterprise system. It was this concern which in large part accounted for the U.S. administration's opposition to the international code as developed by UNICEF and the World Health Organization.

(3) Source of Agency

Goldenberg maintains that, if the change agent is hired by the setting which is to be the subject of the change, then that agent's independence and commitment to social intervention is questionable. Certainly in the case of the Nestle Boycott, those providing its leadership and support were independent of, and not controlled by the company. This was, of course, a great frustration for Nestle. At a later stage in the boycott, the company established a supposedly impartial commission to monitor its practices in the field and to report violations. The Nestle Infant Formula Audit Commission (NIFAC) was headed by former Senator Edmund Muskie and hence often referred to as the Muskie Commission. Precisely for the reasons raised by Goldenberg, the boycotting groups were sceptical of the operation of the Muskie Commission which was established with terms of reference and remuneration provided by the company it was supposed to critique.

(4) The Problem of Process

Golbenberg suggests that change agents do not truly function as social interventionists when their intention is to adapt the constituency to the existing setting, rather than to help it address the larger social forces in which its problems are imbedded. One can readily see that those who supported the Nestle boycott were not trying to help mothers learn to adapt to the promotion of the formula companies, but to challenge the existence of the promotion itself, and to get the companies to make significant changes.

(5) Belief in the Changeability of the System
Through Essentially Peaceful Means

A change agent who envisages violence and/or the total destruction of all existing institutional arrangements as the basic vehicle for systemic change is, according to Goldenberg, not functioning as a social interventionist, but as a social revolutionary. The leadership and supporters of the boycott never entertained and consistently renounced any suggestions of the use of violence as a means to force the company to make the changes they felt were necessary. Indeed, many of those from churches who supported the boycott would never have done so if they felt violence would be considered.

An anxious time occurred in 1982 when a fire broke out at a Stouffers hotel in New York State at which a meeting of Stouffers executives was being held. Stouffers hotels and restaurants were owned by Nestle. Since the hotels had been the object of demonstrations and boycott activities to publicize their connection to the Nestle corporation, there were initial suggestions that the fire might have been precipitated by a zealous boycotter. The leadership of the boycott immediately denied any connection to the fire and expressed revulsion at the suggestion that the fire might be connected to the boycott. It later became public that the fire had been set by a disgruntled former employee of the hotel.

BUILDING THE COALITION

(1) Who Were the Boycott Supports?

A number of dynamics can be identified which contributed to the success of the boycott coalition. Individuals and groups participating in the boycott represented a wide diversity of interests, and those most actively involved in it would not benefit directly if the boycott were to meet its goal (i.e., the elimination of aggresive marketing of infant formula in the Third World). This appears to be in conflict with a traditional assumption about social movements—that they are only effective when their members constitute a fairly homogeneous group directly affected by the problem.

In his commentary on social movement theories, Jenkins (1983) notes, "The middle class 'participation revolution' was rooted in the shift toward 'post-materialist' values emphasizing self-fulfillment that supported demands for direct participation in political decisions and moral concern for the plight of others. When elites challenged these values by manipulative acts and outright rejection, the middle class rallied around the movements" (p. 535).

This moral concern for the plight of others was a primary motivating factor for several of the groups which became active in the Nestle Boycott. Some of those involved had been working as volunteers or consultants in Third World countries and had seen first-hand the damage resulting from aggressive marketing of infant formula. The Nestle Boycott enabled them to work directly on this problem in the industrialized world, where pressure on the multinationals was likely to have more impact.

Religious denominations, which constituted by far the largest number of Canadian boycott supporters, represent an even more interesting example of resource mobilization. Members of the major religious denominations were not, of course, Third World inhabitants affected by the problem, nor, for the most part, had they had any direct experience in the Third World. They had, however, grown more sensitive not only to social and economic problems in the Third World, but to some of the economic and political dynamics contributing to them. For much of this century, Canadian church members looked on the Third World as a place of great poverty and malnutrition. The appropriate Christian response was one of charity—sending food, clothing, and other donations—particularly when disaster occurred. There was limited questioning of the root causes of poverty.

This began to change in the late '50s and '60s when missionaries and partner churches indigenous to the Third World began describing how development efforts were hampered by dynamics beyond their control. This information, combined with work by academics and other researchers, underlined the fact that the industrialized world might have more to do with Third World poverty than it cared to admit.

In Canada, the development and relief agencies of the Anglican, Catholic, Lutheran, Presbyterian, and United Churches combined their educational efforts in the early 1970s, in an annual program known as Ten Days for World Development. The Ten Days program aimed to increase public awareness of development issues. Their initial goals were "to focus attention on the realities of the present relationship between industrialized nations and economically developing nations, and to foster among Canadians an awareness of our responsibility towards our neighbours in the Third World" (Ten Days for World Development, 1973, p. 1). In subsequent years, the Ten Days message became increasingly more explicit:

> Poverty, hunger and disease are no longer necessary. The poor, the hungry and the diseased need no longer accept their condition with fatalism. Indeed, as they recognize that their condition is the consequence of greed—our overdevelopment at the cost of their underdevelopment—their response is an outraged demand for justice . . . . Our compassionate concern need no longer take the form of mere palliatives—soup lines and band-aids. Our compassionate concern may now become human solidarity with them in their struggle. The rules of the game, which prevent more equitable distribution and opportunity, can be changed when more people understand the rules of the game (Ten Days for World Development, 1974, p. 1).
> When people are hungry as a consequence of natural or man-made

catastrophe, we feed them. This is charity, and is right and good. But it is not justice. Justice will be accomplished when the obstacles to peoples feeding themselves are removed. Among the obstacles to be removed are some myths concerning food you and I carry around in our heads. Only when we understand why people starve in the midst of plenty, can we begin to do something about it (Ten Days for World Development, 1977, p. 1).

The Ten Days material draws heavily on the work of Frances Moore Lappe and Joseph Collins of the Institute for Food and Development Policy. They have explored how Third World hunger is often more related to the economic policies imposed on countries by trade agreements with industrialized countries, and to the practices of multinational corporations, than to intrinsic weaknesses in Third World countries' development policies (Lappe & Collins, 1977).

Since the early '70s, church people, particularly women's groups in most of the major Canadian religious denominations, have studied these materials and incorporated this perspective in their own thinking. There had, however, been few opportunities for them to follow through on this awareness and to engage in concrete action aimed at these problems (other than to make some changes in their own lifestyle to address the problem of over-consumption).

When the issue of infant-formula marketing gained greater prominence in the late 1970s, the churches were well-placed to respond. They recognized that multinational corporations can contribute significantly to the development problems of Third World countries. Here was a specific situation in which a variety of companies, one in particular, were identified as contributing to the malnutrition and death of infants in the Third World in order to increase their sales. Members of churches responded with outrage to information about infants dying from malnutrition because of the inability of their mothers to properly prepare the formula which companies encouraged them to buy. As we have seen, this moral indignation was supported by the accumulated understanding that multinationals have in many instances contributed to rather than alleviated development problems in the Third World. Thus, the churches had the conceptual framework in which to place the specific problem of Nestle's infant-formula marketing.

People in religions organizations were careful to clearly understand the specifics of the situation, for they found it hard to believe that a company aware of the problems it created, would continue to create them. Once they were satisfied with the reality of the problem created by aggressive marketing, Canadian churches became one of the boycott's strongest supporters.

Women constitute another group of Nestle Boycott supporters who merit special attention. Many women were involved in church networks and some had first-hand Third World experience, but certain particular dynamics account for their commitment to the issue. Many North American women identified with the pressures exerted on Third World women just prior to and subsequent to the birth of their children. In workshops and public meetings on the infant-formula controversy, women described how they themselves had been subjected to the often subtle and insidious pressure to bottlefeed. This pressure came in the form of copious literature and pamphlets from companies extolling the virtues and simplicity of infant formula, the availability of free formula samples, and oftentimes a lack of awareness among members of the health system about the advantages of breastfeeding over formula feeding. Women in all countries have traditionally been the victims of exploitation within the health system and this was no exception. North American women could thus identify closely with women in the Third World and were incensed that their problems were created by multinational companies run by male executives, and exacerbated by unaware medical professionals, also primarily male. Many women became committed to the boycott in a sense of solidarity with other women.

Women's organizations formally connected to the boycott movement included church networks (e.g., United Church Women, Anglican Church Women, Lutheran Church Women), local groups of the YWCA, the Canadian Nurses Association, and the Canadian Religious Conference which co-ordinates Roman Catholic women's religious orders.

Other women became involved as a result of their participation in the La Leche movement which is committed to helping mothers breastfeed because of the nutritional value and mother/child bonding it provides. La Leche members were incensed to learn that aggressive promotion of infant formula in the Third World was interfering with breastfeeding there.

(2) Initial Stages of the Coalition

The reasons behind the Nestle Boycott's development as a social movement and the commitment it garnered from its supporters are better explained by the traditional explanations of social movement development than the more recent resource mobilization theory. Gusfield (cited in Jenkins, 1983) said social movement development emphasizes "sudden increases in short-term grievances created by the 'structural strains' of rapid social change" (p. 530). The specific grievance in the Nestle situation was obviously the mass promotion of infant formula in Third World settings subsequent to the Second World War. The grievance explanation of social movement development seems to fit in this context because people began supporting the boycott only as they learned of the impact of infant-formula promotion in the Third World.

Resource mobilization theory, as Jenkins (1983) discusses it, attributes social movement development not so much to the existence of specific grievances as to "long-term changes in group resources, organization and opportunities for collective action" (p. 530). These factors were relatively constant among the organizations which supported the boycott, primarily the churches. No major identifiable change prompted their response to the problems of infant-formula marketing, though a growing consciousness of the role of multinational corporations in the Third World may have prepared the churches to engage in a more dramatic form of pressuring than they might have done at earlier times.

The creation of the Nestle boycott coalition involved a number of steps. Initially, the problem of infant-formula marketing in the Third World was only one of many issues addressed by churches and development-education groups. As its significance became more apparent, it was decided that it required more focused attention and increased resources. As a result, in the United States, the Infant Formula Action Coalition (INFACT) was created in the Newman Center, a Catholic Third World development organization based in Minneapolis. Members of the National Council of Churches in the United States, which already participated in a related group addressing corporate responsibilities, agreed to form a special infant-formula project as part of its Inter-Church Center on Corporate Responsibility.

In Canada, members of Catholic and Protestant churches, made aware of the issue through the Ten Days project, started exploring how they might work together to focus their action. A small group representing a variety of Catholic and Protestant denominations and several Third World development education centres came together in the winter of 1978-79. They shared information about the problem and the activities their specific groups might be prepared to do. The Nestle Boycott had already been initiated in the United States, and several of the major Protestant denominations in Canada were considering their endorsement at that time. In the end, this informal group of Canadian churches agreed to continue sharing information. As further information came in, contacts with the Nestle Corporation increased, and member groups of the coalition took further actions.

(3) Role of Institutions

Jenkins (1983) suggests, "the most distinctive contribution of resource mobilization theory has been to emphasize the significance of outside contributions and the co-option of institutional resources by contemporary social movements" (p. 533). The development of the coalition, particularly in Canada, represented an example of the utilization of existing institutional resources. Jenkins' suggestion that there is a distinction between the institutions being tapped and the source of the social movement is not true of the coalition, however, in which the churches or at least key individuals within the leadership of the churches, were in large part initiators of the social movement. Nevertheless, it is true that the effectiveness of the coalition was largely due to the resources provided by the churches. Key amongst these resources was the allotment of staff time to the Nestle issue. The United Church of Canada (the largest Protestant denomination in Canada) donated a very significant portion of one national staff member's time to the infant-formula controversy. As a result, background research could be compiled to substantiate the trend from breastfeeding to bottlefeeding and its impact on the health of Third World infants. Original research from a variety of medical journals and Third World sources was synthesized and duplicated as a resource to members of the coalition and to other groups wanting to learn more about the problem.

A number of the large religious organizations, after studying the materials collected, and listening to their personnel in the Third World, passed resolutions calling for significant changes in infant-formula marketing and endorsing the boycott of Nestle consumer products until that company, the largest in the Third World, eliminated its promotion. Church endorsements gave credibility to the issue and were a major factor in obtaining the agreement of other groups to seriously look at the issue and eventually, to endorse the boycott. Other groups which endorsed the boycott included medical associations like the Canadian Nurses Association, nutrition groups like the B.C. Dietitians Association, and youth organizations like the University of Toronto Students Administration Council. In the early stages, major groups like the churches gave Nestle an opportunity to present its side of the story before deciding to endorse the boycott. A five-hour meeting was held in April, 1979, between representatives of a variety of Canadian churches and the senior management of Nestle Canada. Despite the presence of a senior Nestle executive from Switzerland charged with handling the infant formula controversy, the Nestle executives were unable to respond to the churches' satisfaction, to data documenting the problems created by infant-formula marketing (Hallman, 1979).

(4) Expansion of the Coalition

Once several of these major organizations endorsed the boycott in Canada, the expansion of the coalition went in two directions. First, major educational efforts were undertaken to acquaint the organizations' members with the nature of the problem and reasons for the boycott. Staff and volunteers in the churches conducted workshops and participated in public meetings sponsored by local congregations. The meetings were often organized as debates, with a national staff member of the church presenting the church's concerns and reasons for supporting the boycott, and a senior executive from Nestle defending the company's record. While formal votes were not taken, it was apparent from the local congregations' support of the boycott that the majority of those who attended the meetings found the church's case more credible than Nestle's.

The second direction for expansion involved enlisting the support of other organizations and individuals. The core group of INFACT Canada, which included the major church denominations and some very active individuals, contacted both personally and by letter other organizations and individuals assumed to be sympathetic. INFACT was often invited to present a more detailed description of the issue to the executives or boards of these organizations. A particularly interesting example was that of the Toronto Board of Health and then the Toronto City Council which, after considerable debate and representations both from INFACT Canada and Nestle, voted to endorse the boycott.

Enlisting endorsers for the boycott became a high-profile mechanism for broadening awareness of the issue. When organizations were approached about it, they could not dismiss the information they received as a generalized educational effort, but had to vote on a motion committing their organization to the boycott. Because it meant opposing a major multinational corporation, organizations spent considerable time and energy familiarizing themselves with the issue before voting to endorse the boycott. Thus, educational efforts and the enlistment of endorsers spread awareness of the problem and generated increased pressure on Nestle.

The most effective means of attracting the support of individuals not connected with organizations was through the public media. As Jenkins (1983) notes, "Because mass media coverage is decisive in informing elites and mass publics about movement actions, as well as in forming the morale and self-image of movement activists, the mass media are important actors in political conflicts'' (p. 546). One particular journalist played an exceptional role in creating greater awareness of the boycott in Canada. At that time, Michele Landsberg wrote columns on women's issues, family concerns, and consumer/political issues in the Toronto Star, the largest daily circulation newspaper in Canada. She became aware of the infant-formula issue in 1979 and wrote her first column on it in August of that year (see Appendix A) (Landsberg, 1979). She received much of the documentation for her columns from key people in the churches and INFACT Canada, as well as from American boycott leaders. Nestle executives spent some time with her and tried lobbying her editor, but she proceeded with the column and numerous others over the next several years. Landsberg already had a strong and faithful readership and her columns no doubt contributed to the high level of awareness of the boycott in Toronto.[1]

Other sources of broad public exposure to the issue included Canadian national television and radio broadcasts and Macleans Magazine which ran several articles over the years of the boycott. The national news programs of the Canadian Broadcasting Corporation (CBC) and CTV carried stories in 1981, 1983, and 1984. The Fifth Estate, a CBC news documentary program, broadcast a story in 1983. National and local radio stations carried interviews about the boycott at various times, particularly in 1981 and 1984.

One measure of growing support for the boycott across the country was the initiation of local groups to co-ordinate educational efforts. Such groups developed in Toronto, St. Catharines, Kitchener-Waterloo, London, Winnipeg, Regina, Vancouver, and Victoria. While formal groups weren't created in St. John's, Nfld., Halifax, Montreal, or Edmonton, some individuals from those cities worked on educational efforts.

(5) Sustaining the Coalition with Information

The initial stage of gathering endorsements from organizations and spreading the news to their members took considerable energy during 1979-81. Some new organizations joined the boycott following this period, but energy was primarily directed at updating existing supporters and maintaining their commitment. Of central importance was the need for accurate information on the latest developments and the actual practices of Nestle in Third World countries. With its considerable resources for public relations and its occasional major media blitzes, Nestle conveyed the impression that it was progressing in its

compliance with the WHO code. Members of boycotting organizations were in constant need of information as to the accuracy of Nestle's claims. The United Church of Canada and INFACT Canada produced regular newsletters to keep supporters up to date (Hallman,
June, 1980, to October, 1984). Monitoring information became exceptionally important. INFACT U.S. sponsored the occasional field trip
for several of its staff to Southeast Asia, Africa, and Latin America
where they interviewed medical personnel, visited hospitals, and
documented ways in which Nestle was continuing to promote its formula in contravention of the international code.

Of even greater significance than the field trips for monitoring
Nestle's activities, was a wide network of Third World medical personnel, women's organizations, consumer and religious groups which
voluntarily provided information about Nestle's activities in their
regions. Many of these individuals and organizations could not formally boycott Nestle, as could groups in industrialized countries. A
number of them were involved in breastfeeding promotion campaigns
and thus had a wider mandate than fighting infant-formula promotion. As a result, these groups formed the International Baby Food
Action Network (IBFAN). IBFAN was conceived in a small meeting
of representatives from Third World organizations and boycotting
groups from North America and Europe, following the adoption of
the WHO code at the May, 1981 meeting of the World Health
Assembly in Geneva (see Figure 4). While IBFAN's co-ordinating activities were broader than those of the boycotting groups, their efforts
to promote breastfeeding would be significantly enhanced if the Nestle
Boycott were successful in eliminating the company's aggressive formula promotion. The boycotting groups, on the other hand, very
much needed the monitoring data which IBFAN member groups
could provide. These data were compiled regularly and published in a
newsletter which was circulated to the boycott-endorsing organizations on a regular basis, providing them with information to refute
Nestle's claims that it was no longer violating the code (IBFAN, 1980
to 1985). Organizations supporting the boycott often included this information in their newsletters or magazines to up-date their constituents about the status of the boycott campaign.

The mass media also used information compiled by the IBFAN
networks and resulting from field trips of INFACT staff. Michele
Landsberg wrote a full-page article on a trip by the national coordinator of INFACT Canada to several Latin American countries in
which evidence of Nestle's continuing promotion was documented.
She also used some of the monitoring information in her columns.
Such information was especially important to people who had been

Figure 4

Examples of IBFAN Member Groups
(International Baby Food Action Network)

International:	IOCU (International Organization of Consumers Unions)
U.S.:	INFACT U.S.
	ICCR (Interfaith Center on Corporate Responsibility
	—National Council of Churches)
Canada:	INFACT Canada
Europe:	Baby Food Action Network (Great Britain)
	GIFA (Switzerland)
Third World:	Consumers Guidance Society of India
	Malaysian Infant Feeding Action Network
	Housewives Association of Trinidad and Tobago
	CEFEMINA, Costa Rica
	Instituto Nacional de Nutricion, Mexico
	Family Life Association of Swaziland

boycotting Nestle products, but who were not sure where things stood. In addition, Landsberg's brief summaries of the reasons for the boycott succeeded in recruiting further supporters. Occasionally, INFACT and IBFAN sponsored their own press conferences to release new monitoring data, which was then picked up by the wire services and reproduced in various newspapers across Canada, the United States, and Europe.

(6) Sustaining the Coalition with Organizational Support

The coalition required a form of organization which would allow information to be circulated rapidly, would provide a point of contact for initiating dialogue with Nestle, and would enable the co-ordination of all boycott activities.

In the United States, the organizations leading the boycott were the INFACT U.S. grassroots coalition and the Inter-Church Center on Corporate Responsibility, a project of the National Council of Churches. In Canada, the primary leadership organizations were INFACT Canada and The United Church of Canada. Representatives of these groups met in New York in September, 1979, to plan a general meeting of organizations endorsing the boycott. This meeting, held in November, 1979, was attended by representatives from approximately 50 organizations. They shared information on the outcome of a recent WHO/UNICEF Consultation and discussed strategies for pressuring Nestle to adhere to the recently adopted international code. It was decided to formalize the network of boycott supporters as the International Nestle Boycott Committee (INBC) and to appoint a steering committee which would meet on a regular basis and act as the INBC's contact with Nestle.

The steering committee became the critical co-ordinating element for the entire boycott campaign. It was kept small, with about 10 core working members, including representatives from INFACT U.S., IC-CR, the major Canadian and American religious organizations involved in the boycott, labour unions, women's groups, and INFACT Canada. Members of the steering committee were accountable to two groups: first, to the organizations they represented, and second, to the general membership of the INBC (see Figure 5).

Groups represented on the steering committee often provided services in kind, including secretarial help, office supplies, and the travel costs of their representatives to the meetings. Throughout the duration of the campaign, the INBC had only a very modest budget to cover the costs of correspondence, steering committee meetings, and conference calls. Member organizations, including INFACT U.S., INFACT Canada, and individual churches, devoted more significant budgets to their own activities in support of the boycott.

The organizational structure of the boycott is similar to that described by Gerlach and Hine (cited in Jenkins, 1983), who argue:

> . . . decentralized movements, with a minimum division of labour and integrated by informal networks and an overarching ideology, are (most) effective. A segmented, decentralized structure maximizes mobilization by providing extensive inter-personal bonds that generate solidarity and reinforce ideological commitments. In addition, such a structure is highly adaptive, encouraging tactical experimentation, competition among sub-groups, and lessened vulnerability to suppression or co-option by authorities (p. 539).

Certainly in terms of maintaining the boycott coalition, the informal adaptive structure of the INBC and its steering committee was very effective. Member organizations were responsible for educating their own constituencies. This was important not ony because it allowed the INBC and its steering committee to focus attention on its contacts with Nestle and on co-ordinating the dissemination of information, but also because it did not infringe upon the perogative of member organizations to adopt the educational and action strategies most appropriate to their settings. For instance, as a grassroots organization, INFACT U.S. was often more aggressive in its boycotting activities than the churches. Each were free to pursue strategies most suited to their constituencies, thus maximizing their continued

Figure 5

Examples of INBC Member Groups
(International Nestle Boycott Committee)

Canada:	The Anglican Church of Canada
	The United Church of Canada
	INFACT Canada
U.S.:	National Council of Churches (ICCR)
	INFACT U.S.
	American Public Health Association
	labour, medical, women's groups
Europe:	Baby Food Action Network (Great Britain)
	A.G.B. (West Germany)
	GIFA (Switzerland)

commitment to the overall campaign.

For a campaign of the magnitude of the Nestle Boycott, the organizational structure was surprisingly informal. The International Nestle Boycott Committee (INBC) acted as the overall co-ordinator of the campaign and as negotiator with Nestle. Representatives of the INBC's member organizations met once or twice a year, with the small steering committee meeting more often. Church organizations generally had staff persons working on the issue, as did INFACT U.S. and INFACT Canada, but the INBC itself, on which all these organizations were represented, had no staff. The high priority given to regular communication through the networks proved sufficient to keep the organizations co-ordinated and committed to the agreed-upon strategies.

This is not to say that there were not times of tension and conflict within the coalition network. On one occasion, an INFACT U.S. strategy to mobilize more support within major North American communities was recommended as an overall strategy for all member groups. However, the more aggressive street tactics of INFACT U.S. did not sit well with some of the religious organizations. The strategy was rejected by INFACT Canada because the Canadian organization already employed an extensive network to increase support and because the INFACT U.S. tactic was seen as inappropriate to the Canadian ethos. As a result, INFACT U.S. proceeded with its approach in a selected number of U.S. cities with good results. U.S. religious organizations and the Canadian networks proceeded with approaches already proven effective within their own contexts.

Another source of tension was the co-ordination of the campaign at the international level. American boycott leaders had provided much of the groundwork for the boycott campaign. The American world view, however, is significantly different from that held by Canadians and even more different than that of Europeans and people in the Third World. At times, conflict arose between the approaches taken or recommended by the Americans and those considered appropriate by Canadians, Europeans or Third World representatives. One of the strengths of the informal structure of the boycott movement was that, without a strict authoritatian decision-making system, boycott solidarity was dependent upon co-operation and consensus-building. As a result, when conflict arose, members kept meeting until consensus was reached.

LEVELS OF SOCIAL INTERVENTION

Throughout the course of the Nestle Boycott many forms of social intervention were employed, including: citizen organization and advocacy; the lobbying of governments and Nestle; and involvement with international agencies such as the World Health Organization and UNICEF. The extent of these activities varied, but all were employed throughout the campaign (see Figure 6).

Social interventions were conducted at three levels: (a) at the community level by individual members of the churches and unions and member organizations of the INFACT groups, (b) at the national level by the leadership of those organizations, and (c) at the international level by the INBC and IBFAN.

Supporters at the community level were primarily involved in education and advocacy within their communities, but at strategic points in the campaign they corresponded with their governments, the Nestle Corporation, and international health agencies. The leadership of national organizations endorsing the boycott contacted Nestle on selected occasions as co-ordinated by the INBC. The INBC and IBFAN were most often in direct contact with governments, Nestle (culminating in the January, 1984 negotiations), and the WHO/UNICEF (see Figure 7).

(1) Citizen Education and Advocacy

There is little doubt that the boycott's success was primarily due to the wide-scale involvement of hundreds of thousands of citizens across Europe and North America. The discussions and negotiations between Nestle, governments, international health agencies, and the boycott leaders would have had limited impact if not supported by

Figure 6

Levels of Social Intervention

	Community Education & Advocacy	Lobbying of Governments	Lobbying of Nestle	Involvement with WHO & UNICEF
Individuals	Direct	Indirect	Indirect	Indirect
Community Groups	Direct	Indirect	Indirect	Indirect
Leadership of National Organizations	Indirect	Indirect	Direct	Indirect
International Leadership (INBC, IBFAN)	Indirect	Direct	Direct	Direct

Direct involvement: personal contact, meetings, phone calls, correspondence.
Indirect involvement: correspondence, donation of resources.

Figure 7

Symbolic Representation of the Direction and Intensity of Social Intervention

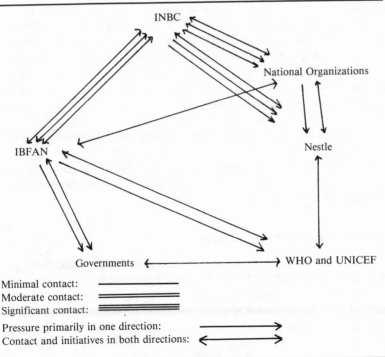

evidence of massive public interest and concern.

Many people learned about the infant-formula controversy through presentations at meetings of church organizations, women's groups, and university students' clubs. Others learned about it more incidentally through conversations with friends, magazine and newspaper articles, radio, or television programmes. All of these sources of education provided basic information about the issue and an analysis of the problem with suggestions for action.

Individuals could get involved in the campaign by boycotting Nestle products and spreading the word to others through word of mouth, leafletting at supermarkets, or speaking engagements. Individuals and organizations committed to boycotting Nestle products were often prepared to voice their concern to the company. Over the years, many people wrote to Nestle's head office in Switzerland and to their Canadian and U.S. headquarters to protest Nestle's marketing practices and to indicate that they would refuse to purchase Nestle products until those practices were changed. Occasionally people participated in marches organized by the INFACT Coalition, but letter-writing was the major activity beyond the boycott. At strategic junctures during the campaign, letter-writing was focused on specific demands to Nestle, governments, or international health agencies.

Individuals and groups participating in the boycott often solicited further endorsements for it. This usually involved educating organizations about the issue and encouraging them to pass resolutions endorsing the boycott. This was an effective means of education since organizations considering such a resolution would in turn educate their membership through their networks and newsletters. It also allowed those soliciting the organizations a considerable level of leadership and responsibility. Many assumed this responsibility with trepidation, not having had much experience in conflictual situations such as that involved in challenging a major multinational corporation. However, after receiving the support of a few organizations, they gained self-confidence.

(2) The Lobbying of Governments

In 1980, the Government of Canada indicated it would not support the adoption of the World Health Organization's draft of an international code providing guidelines for the marketing of infant formula. Using an argument already presented by the U.S. administration, the Canadian government said the code represented an infringement on the free enterprise system. The churches and the INFACT coalition in Canada were horrified to learn that their own government might not support the WHO code when the case for its necessity seemed so clear. They agreed to mobilize a large-scale letter-writing campaign to convince the federal Minister of Health and Welfare that Canadians were concerned about infant-formula marketing in Canada and the Third World, and wanted Canada to support the WHO code. All Canadian organizations which had endorsed the boycott were asked to encourage their members to contact the federal minister and to send copies of their correspondence to Members of Parliament.

Many groups and individuals also sent copies of their correspondence to the national offices of their organizations. It is apparent that the federal government and individual MPs received considerable correspondence about the issue, indicating substantial political support for the WHO code. By the time the World Health Assembly convened in May, 1981, Canada was one of the greatest supporters among industrialized nations for the adoption of a strong code. The federal minister herself spoke in favour of the code at the opening session of the World Health Assembly, noting the considerable Canadian support for its adoption.

(3) The Lobbying of Nestle

As support for the boycott continued to build, the individuals and groups became involved in specific action strategies, the boycott's leadership increasingly engaged in dialogue with Nestle's senior management. From early in the campaign, attempts had been made to convince Nestle of the destructive nature of their aggresive marketing of infant formula in the Third World. The early meetings between Nestle management and senior representatives of religious organizations contemplating endorsement of the boycott had been highly technical, with considerable conflict arising over the reliability of data and research. At those early stages, Nestle management defended the company's practices and indicated no significant likelihood of change.

When the International Nestle Boycott Committee (INBC) was formed, one of its mandates was to act as the primary source of contact with Nestle. The INBC steering committee immediately requested a meeting with Nestle, but the company's senior management refused from 1981 until late 1983 to even acknowledge the committee's existence. It is assumed that Nestle took this position because it suspected it would be more difficult to deal with the INBC steering committee, whose members were highly informed on the details of the issue, than with senior church officials who might not be well enough informed to refute Nestle's claims. In addition, dealing with the INBC would have indicated Nestle's tacit recognition of the widespread nature and credibility of the boycott, an acknowledgement they were not prepared to make.

Nestle would occasionally refer to the INBC in its press conferences when disputing information the INBC publicized from IBFAN monitoring data. They, nevertheless, continued to reject requests for direct meetings with the INBC steering committee. Nestle attempted to undercut support for the boycott by initiating meetings with U.S. national church leaders considered to be somewhat "softer" supporters of the boycott. Though some of these meetings were held, member organizations of the INBC generally maintained their commitment to leave negotiations with Nestle to the INBC. As a result, Nestle was not very successful in convincing organizations to suspend their support of the boycott.

The core leadership of the boycott and the senior Nestle management responsible for the infant-formula controversy came to know each other quite well through public debates and appearances on radio and television. Though Nestle recognized these INBC members as leaders of individual organizations, they continued to refuse to acknowledge them as part of the co-ordinated network of the INBC.

Nestle finally altered its position in the fall of 1983, after the INBC published an assessment of four remaining areas in which Nestle needed to make significant changes before a termination of the boycott would be considered. Why Nestle moved to acknowledge the INBC and to agree to direct discussions at this point is open to debate. A force-field analysis of Nestle's position at that juncture suggests reasons for continuing to avoid contact with the INBC as well as for agreeing to meet with the steering committee. Reasons for the former position included:

- a meeting with the INBC might have been perceived as a weakening of Nestle's resolve since the company had always maintained it would not meet with the INBC ("the activists").
- some weakening of support for the boycott was surfacing and the company might have been wise to hold out a little longer.

Reasons for agreeing to meet with the INBC included:

- the list of boycott demands had become more succinct after the INBC analysis and those four remaining areas might best have been dealt with in direct discussions.
- because of some erosion of support for the boycott among U.S. churches, the INBC steering committee might have been in a weaker position to withstand proposals from Nestle to end the boycott.
- if Nestle had presented what appeared to be reasonable proposals,

and the steering committee had rejected them, the company could perhaps have embarrassed the steering committee prior to the Mexico City conference, thereby undercutting its support.
- new management at the Nestle headquarters in Switzerland felt compelled to prove itself and settle the boycott once and for all.
- continuation of the boycott into its seventh year was further solidifying public relations damage to Nestle.

Thus, reasons for arranging direct discussions with the INBC steering committee outweighed the potential risks of such discussions.

The subsequent negotiations of January, 1984, could probably be most closely paralleled to labour/management negotiations. Proposals were presented by one side and differences of opinion were clarified in ensuing discussions. The two sides separated for private conversation, then reconvened to see whether any movement had occurred. The debate was highly technical and specific, with considerable discussion about wording and the interpretation of wording. The boycott leadership had to be exceptionally well-prepared for these discussions and familiar with all of the relevant documentation. The week of negotiations began with the identification of those areas most likely to be resolved, then progressed to the more difficult areas.

As mentioned earlier in this paper, Nestle and the INBC agreed to have UNICEF act as a facilitator for the discussions. UNICEF's significant political credibility among the general public meant their interpretation of Nestle's practices in relation to the code would carry significant weight. If the UNICEF personnel sided with Nestle's argument that the company was complying with the code, it would have been very difficult for the INBC to continue the boycott. On the other hand, if UNICEF sided with the INBC's interpretation, it would have been very difficult for the company to defend its position. Both sides had reason to feel nervous about UNICEF's position. On the one hand, UNICEF characteristically sided with the boycotting groups in maintaining a fairly strict interpretation of the code. On the other hand, both parties knew that UNICEF was under considerable political pressure particularly from the United States to play a less aggressive role in the infant-formula issue.

As it turned out, when asked for its interpretation of particular issues, UNICEF quite consistently adopted a strict interpretation of the code, supporting the INBC's position. In retrospect, it is quite possible that Nestle concluded they had made a significant miscalculation in requesting UNICEF's involvement. By the end of the week, Nestle had moved on all four issues to almost total agreement with the INBC's starting position.

This level of direct, and in some ways confrontational, negotiations between the INBC Steering Committee and Nestle senior management was a fitting emotional and strategic culmination to the boycott. It was a level of intervention very different from the grassroots involvement of citizens boycotting Nestle products. Both forms were necessary and complemented each other. Boycott leaders would not have had the political clout to enter into those negotiations if there had not been evidence of widespread consumer support for the boycott. Conversely, the boycott could only be resolved through high-level intensive discussions between the boycott leadership and senior management of the company. It is unlikely that the campaign would have been successful if these two levels of social intervention had not occurred.

A further level of social intervention warrants some comment. In the late 1970s, the boycotting organizations made a strategic decision concerning their involvement with the UNICEF/World Health Organization to develop an international code. The boycotting organizations began intensive discussions concerning the wisdom of becoming involved in this process. On the one hand, it was felt that increased grassroots support for the boycott and the resulting economic pressure on the company constituted the most successful strategy. Advocates of this strategy felt support for the UNICEF/WHO development of regulations could weaken the campaign efforts if it resulted in a political compromise between competing interests at the international level. On the other hand, if a strong set of regulations reflected the boycott demands for an end to all forms of infant-formula promotion, then the support of international health agencies would add immeasurable strength to the boycott. Such a code would make it much more difficult for the company to resist pressures for change, and the support of the WHO and UNICEF would encourage consumers to join the boycott. Governments would also be more likely to involve themselves in the regulation of infant-formula promotion if a model were provided by an international health agency like the World Health Organization.

The boycotting organizations decided to become involved in the UNICEF/WHO process, and campaign leaders from North America, Europe, and the Third World participated in the code's development from 1979 to 1981. The strength of the resulting WHO code is in part attributable to their work. Again, an intervention at a highly technical level was complemented and supported by the grassroots advocacy of ordinary citizens. It is likely that, without widespread consumer awareness of the issue, organizations like the WHO would not have felt the political strength to move as aggressively as they did in adopting a code as rigorous as that approved in May, 1981. In return, the boycott was considerably enhanced by the adoption of a code according to which Nestle's practices could be judged.

It is clear that the campaign may not have been successful if these three levels of social intervention had not been employed together. As mentioned earlier, the most basic and necessary characteristic of the movement was its broad-based citizen involvement. It is unlikely that the movement's leaders would have been successful on their own, but their direct lobbying of governments, international health agencies, and Nestle facilitated the boycott's resolution.

SOME EVALUATION COMMENTS ON THE NESTLE BOYCOTT

Many researchers have discussed the dynamics of social change and the measures for assessing its success. Watzlawick, Weakland, and Fisch (1974) have listed four steps of change: (a) a clear definition of the problem in concrete terms; (b) an investigation of previous attempts to resolve the problem; (c) a clear definition of the concrete change to be achieved; and (d) the formulation and implementation of a plan to produce this change.

It would be presumptuous to imply that the boycott leaders conducted an organized and systematic analysis reflecting these four steps. As the boycott movement developed, however, each of these tasks was addressed.

As malnutrition from improper formula-feeding became increasingly apparent, health workers in developing countries began to define the problem. Researchers analyzed the situation more systematically, and by the time the churches, health, and consumer groups became involved, the problem was defined in very concrete terms. This specificity was essential to the growth of the boycott movement. It is unlikely that vast numbers of people would have supported the boycott if the problem had been overly complicated or ambiguously described.

Since the boycott was a relatively drastic tactic to adopt, the leaders had to convince the organizations and individuals they approached that other means of change had been attempted or were unusable. International health agencies had pressured the formula companies to alter their aggressive promotion without success. Church groups in North America had pressured the American formula companies through shareholder resolutions and appearances at annual general meetings. The overall problem was still not addressed because Nestle, the industry leader both in terms of market share in the Third World and aggressiveness of promotion, was a wholly Swiss-owned company, inaccessible to North American shareholder pressure.

The ability to build large support for the boycott depended upon a clear specification of the desired change. Initially, the "boycott demands" were concretely identified as an end to: (a) mass media advertising of infant formula, (b) company representatives promoting formula to mothers, (c) the distribution of free samples to mothers, and (d) promotion within health institutions and to medical personnel. Once the International Code was adopted, the conditions for lifting the boycott were rephrased as "full compliance in policy and practice with the International Code."

Strategies for ending infant-formula promotion in the Third World developed over the course of the boycott movement. The boycott was initiated with the hope that it would gain sufficient support to impel Nestle to change. As time passed, it became apparent that more complex strategies involving a variety of related actions were needed (e.g., organizational endorsements, involvement with international health agencies, the development of a monitoring system, and direct negotiations with Nestle). The boycott leaders and supporters found it necessary to continually analyze the situation and to develop and refine strategies while remaining committed to the boycott and to their initial goal (i.e., to end formula promotion).

Jenkins (1983) has described measures of success for social movements including "the provision of tangible benefits that meet goals established by the movement organizations, and the formal acceptance of the movement organization by its main antagonist as a valid representative of a legitimate set of interests" (p. 543).

Nestle finally accepted the INBC as a valid representative of the boycott movement in November/December, 1983, when it indicated its willingness to meet directly with the INBC Steering Committee to attempt to resolve the remaining discrepancies between the International Code and Nestle's policy and practices. The final agreement between Nestle and the INBC listed the specific changes needed for Nestle's policies and practices to comply with the International Code. This agreement fulfilled the demands of the boycott.

Acceptance of the INBC as the legitimate representative of the boycotting groups led directly and quickly to the boycott's resolution. Within a month, Nestle and the INBC were sitting across the table from each other, discussing the International Code and company practice. After a week of intense negotiations, an agreement was achieved. After six months of monitoring Nestle's compliance with the agreement, the boycott was terminated.

Garner (1977) has categorized social movements according to their goals. He would classify the Nestle boycott as a "reform movement," where the aim is not a fundamental re-orientation in the relationships between societal groups, but "to manipulate or cajole the ruling class or state elites" (p. 6) to follow a specific objective. There were occasions when industry spokespersons questioned whether the boycott leaders had intentions greater than the specific boycott demands. During the 1978 U.S. Senate Health and Scientific Research Sub-committee hearings into the issue, a senior Nestle executive suggested that the boycott was actually inspired by an intention to overthrow the free enterprise system. This accusation was repeated in an article entitled "The Corporation Haters" in Fortune Magazine. Writer Herman Nickle (1980) (later named U.S. Ambassador to South Africa) labelled church people working on corporate responsibility issues as "Marxists marching under the banner of Christ" (p. 136).

The Nestle boycott may be accused of falling prey to some of the risks Garner (1977) describes for reform movements. For example, he says such collective action could "unwittingly and unintentionally contribute to the strengthening and stabilizing of a particular class system by modifying existing institutions or creating new ones that reduce conflict and lessen tensions built up by the system of inequality between classes" (p. 12). The boycott addressed one of the most obvious negative manifestations of multinationals marketing food products in developing countries. By publicizing one of the effects of aggressive infant-formula promotion (i.e., the malnutrition of Third World babies), the boycott succeeded in forcing a major change in the way Nestle and other large multinationals market infant-formula. There is a very real potential that this increased regulation of corporate marketing practices will have spinoff effects in other areas (e.g., the marketing of pharmaceuticals, herbicides, pesticides, tobacco, etc.). However, it is also conceivable that, with the reduction of the most blatant negative consequences of the presence of multinationals in developing countries, the pressure for more fundamental changes in the power relationship between corporations and the people of their host countries will dissipate.

One of the factors likely to determine the degree to which this occurs, is the nature of the commitment brought to the boycott by its various supporters. Earlier, we described the wide range of people who supported the boycott and the type of interests which brought them to the movement. Grayson and Grayson (1980) distinguish between the class base of a movement and its class interest base. The class interest base of the Nestle Boycott was the exploited women, infants, and families in developing countries who were persuaded by sophisticated marketing strategies to bottlefeed rather than breastfeed. The class base of those involved in the boycott was considerably broader, drawing largely on middle-class members of mainline religious denominations, professional health workers, students, etc. This latter group would be unlikely to reach a consensus about the justification of a more wide-ranging critique of the capitalist system and the right of private multinational corporations to be active in developing countries. Accordingly, Garner's concerns about the potential for such a reform movement to undermine the impetus for more fundamental change may have some relevance in this context.

A related risk of the boycott is the incentive it gives corporations to become more adept at handling their critics. Indeed, the Nestle Boycott is already used as a case study in business and marketing courses. Some of the senior Nestle personnel have also made themselves available as consultants to other corporations concerned about consumer movements. The danger is that such corporations will increasingly ignore the legitimate concerns represented by consumer protests and treat them simply as public relations problems.

The increased sophistication of multinational corporations will make it more difficult for citizens to challenge the policies and practices they view as unethical. However, if corporations learned from the Nestle Boycott, the consumer movement, religious organizations, and health networks probably learned more. Those lessons and skills will no doubt be called upon and generalized to a variety of related issues in the coming years.

NOTES

1. Information leaked to INFACT Canada in 1983 indicated Nestle had done market research in Toronto to identify consumer awareness of the boycott. According to the information received by INFACT, Nestle found that fully 25% of those interviewed knew about and could briefly explain the nature of the issue, and 10% of those interviewed actively boycotted Nestle products. This represents a very high level of public support for such an issue. Though INFACT never received documentation of this market research, it was quoted in public on a number of occasions and never denied by Nestle.

REFERENCES

American Academy of Pediatrics. (1978). Breast-feeding. *Pediatrics, 62*, 596.
Berg, A. (1973). *The nutrition factor: Its role in national development.*

Washington, D.C.: Brookings Institute.

Foman, S.J. (1974). *Infant nutrition* (2nd ed.). Philadelphia: W.B. Saunders.

Garner, R.A. (1977). *Social movements in America*. Chicago: Rand McNally.

Geach, H. (1973, August). The baby food tragedy. *The New Internationalist, 6*, 8-23.

Gerrard, J.W. & Tan, L. K.-T. (1978, January-February). Hazards of formula feeding. *Keeping Abreast, Journal of Human Nurturing,* 20-25.

Goldenberg, I. (1978). *Oppression and social intervention: The human condition and the problem of change*. Chicago: Nelson-Hall.

Grayson, J.P. & Grayson, L.M. (1980). Social movements. In R. Hagedorn (Ed.), *Sociology* (pp. 549-573). Toronto: Holt, Rinehart & Winston.

Grulee, C.G., Sanford, H.N., & Herron, P.H. (1934). Breast and artificial feeding. *Journal of the American Medical Association, 103*, 735.

Hallman, D. (1979, April 17). *Summary of meeting with executives of Nestle*. Toronto: The United Church of Canada.

Hallman, D. (1980, June, October, February; 1981, June, November; 1982, March, June; 1983, February, July, December; 1984, February, October). *Nestle boycott update*. Toronto: The United Church of Canada.

Infant Formula Action Coalition Canada. (1980-1985). *Quarterly newsletters*.

Interfaith Center on Corporate Responsibility. (1979). *What the international health agencies recommend about baby formula promotion*. New York: National Council of Churches.

International Baby Food Action Network. (1981-1985). *IBFAN news*. Geneva, Switzerland: IBFAN.

International Nestle Boycott Committee & International Baby Food Action Network. (1984, February). The international baby milk campaign: Strategies for action. Proceedings of the meeting of *the International Nestle Boycott Committee (INBC) and the International Baby Food Action Network (IBFAN)*, Mexico City.

International Nestle Boycott Committee & Nestle. (1984, January 24). *Joint statement of INBC and Nestle*. New York City.

Jenkins, J.C. (1983). Resource mobilization theory and the study of social movements. *American Review of Sociology, 9*, 527-553.

Lappe, F.M. & Collins, J. (1977). *Food first: Beyond the myth of scarcity*. Boston: Houghton-Mifflin.

Landsberg, M. (1979, August 18). A boycott in the name of babies. *The Toronto Star*, p. C-1.

Muller, M. (1974, March). *The baby killer*. London, England: War on Want.

National Council of Churches. (1977, April). The baby bottle lawsuit: The Sisters of the Precious Blood vs. Bristol-Myers Company. *The Corporate Examiner, Inter-Faith Center on Corporate Responsibility* (p. 3A-3D). New York: National Council of Churches.

National Council of Churches. (1978, November). Excerpts from Senate hearings on infant formula. *The Corporate Examiner, Inter-Faith Center on Corporate Responsibility* (p. 3D). New York: National Council of Churches.

Nestle. (1977). *Nestle Publications—new series no. 1*. Vevey, Switzerland:

Nestle S.A.—Economic Relations.

Nestle. (1983). *The dilemma of Third World nutrition—Nestle and the role of infant formula.* Vevey, Switzerland: Nestle S.A.

Nickle, H. (1980, June). The corporation haters. *Fortune Magazine,* 126-136.

Plank, S.J. & Milanesi, M.L. (1973). Infant feeding and infant mortality in rural Chile. *Bulletin WHO, 48,* 203-210.

Puffer, R.P. & Serrano, C.V. (1973). Patterns of mortality in childhood. *PanAmerican Health Organization, Scientific Publication No. 262.*

Ten Days for World Development Resource Kit. (1973). Prepared by the relief and development agencies of the Canadian Anglican, Lutheran, Presbyterian, Catholic, and United Churches.

Ten Days for World Development Resource Kit. (1974). Prepared by the relief and development agencies of the Canadian Anglican, Lutheran, Presbyterian, Catholic, and United Churches.

Ten Days for World Development Resource Kit. (1977). Prepared by the relief and development agencies of the Canadian Anglican, Lutheran, Presbyterian, Catholic, and United Churches.

Watzlawick, P., Weakland, J., & Fisch, R. (1974). *Change: Principles of problem formation and prolem resolution.* New York: W.W. Norton.

World Health Organization. (1981). *International code of marketing of breastmilk substitutes.* Geneva, Switzerland: World Health Organization.

APPENDIX A

A BOYCOTT IN THE NAME OF BABIES
Michele Landsberg

Picture the young, illiterate mother in teeming Singapore or rural Nigeria. She knows it will take her best efforts to keep her new baby alive. Above her bed in the maternity ward is a glossy poster of a fat baby, chuckling with its baby bottle and a tin of powdered formula.

Before the mother even begins to breast-feed her new baby, she is visited by a "milk nurse" dressed in crisp, authoritative whites. The "nurse" is an employee of the baby formula company, and she leaves a sample tin with the mother. Ah, the magic promise of this western elixir.

Back the mother goes to the village, where the stream that is the village water supply is also the village sewer. There is no fridge, and no way to sterilize the bottle. And there is no money: it would take 75 per cent of the family's income to keep on buying formula.

So she dilutes it more and more, stretching the powder with dirty river water. One tin, meant to last three days, lasts three weeks. When even that is gone she uses tea instead. She has no choice because her own breast milk dried up weeks ago.

The baby cries; he has diarrhea and begins to vomit. His belly is a swollen drum and his bones are etched sharply under his taut skin.

Then he dies, and is one of the 10 million Third World babies who, according to medical experts, succumb every year to "baby botle disease." If he had lived, he would have been retarded from infant malnutrition.

Horrible Scenario

This horrible little scenario is at the heart and core of the Nestle boycott. Nestle has 50 per cent of the Third World infant formula market, estimated at $1.5 billion annually. (Impressive as that may be, baby formula accounts for only 3 per cent of Nestle's sales.) Though its empire is flung across the globe from Guatemala to Bangkok, its ownership sits snugly out of reach in Switzerland . . . immune to North American laws, but not, it seems, to economic pressure.

The chorus of outrage began to mount a decade ago when leading medical and nutrition experts reported a stunning increase in babies damaged or dead through "bottled malnutrition."

Nestle and other smaller companies were aggressively marketing their product in every undeveloped nation of the world. "Milk nurses" penetrated even the Amazon jungle. Nestle wooed Third World doctors with fancy medical equipment, free travel to conventions, and loads of free samples. Posters, radio ads and billboards told naive mothers that formula feeding made "healthy, happy babies."

In Singapore, breast-feeding plunged from 71 per cent to 5 per cent. In Chile, bottle-fed babies had death rates two to three times higher than breast-fed babies. Here in Canada, where Nestle doesn't sell formula but others do, a 1962 study by two Canadian pediatricians showed that one-third of Canadian Indian baby deaths were due to bottle-feeding.

By last year, world support for the boycott was overwhelming. Just before the National Council of Churches voted to endorse the boycott, the distinguished Dr. Michael Latham, director of the program of international nutrition at Cornell University, rose to tell them: "I may sound emotional about this issue . . . I have frequently seen babies die unnecessarily because they were bottle fed . . ."

Frequent Violations

"I have no doubt," he said, "that Nestle is guilty."

Though Nestle's "milk nurses" are now called "medical representatives," promoting formula to doctors only, and though the company has vowed not to advertise to mothers, frequent and flagrant violations are reported.

Last year in the U.S., Senator Edward Kennedy chaired a Senate investigation into the scandal of those 10 million babies. Nestle argued that it was providing a clean, healthy product, a necessary service for working mothers. Experts showed that only 6 per cent of Third World mothers have to give up breast-feeding in order to work. And they argued that Nestle knowingly pushed its product at the world's poor, who can't possibly muster the literacy, cash or clean water to use the formula properly.

"We cannot have that responsibility, sir," a Nestle executive told the incredulous Senator Kennedy. When I phoned Nestle in Toronto and New York, no one was available to speak to me.

In Canada, the United Church is leading the Nestle boycott. Call David Hallman, the church's spokesman for International Year of the Child, at 925-5931 for more information.

Some of Nestle's products on the boycott list are: Nestle's CRUNCH, Quik, Taster's Choice, Nescafe, Nestea, Sunrise, Swiss Knight and Cherry Hill cheese, Libby's, Crosse and Blackwell, L'oreal and Lancome cosmetics, Keiller.

APPENDIX B

JOINT STATEMENT OF INBC AND NESTLE

The following statement was signed by Dr. Carl L. Angst, Executive Vice President of Nestlé, S.A. and William P. Thompson, Co-Stated Clerk of the Presbyterian Church, representing the International Nestlé Boycott Committee, in New York City, on January 24, 1984.

The International Nestlé Boycott Committee has decided to suspend its international boycott of Nestlé Company products.

Over the last decade a controversy has grown over the proper role of infant formula in the Third World, ways of marketing the products there, and the health hazards for infants resulting from improper use.

Much of this controversy has been directed at infant formula manufacturers, and in 1977 INFACT, supported by other organizations, initiated a boycott of the products of Nestlé, the world's largest manufacturer of infant formula.

Out of concern for the health of infants, the World Health Assembly in May, 1981 adopted the International Code of Marketing of Breast-milk Substitutes (WHO/UNICEF Code) which provides guidelines to industry, governments, health authorities and non-governmental organizations. Nestlé made a firm commitment to implement that code. Since that time there has been considerable pressure on all infant formula companies to fully comply with the Code, and much progress has been made.

INBC continued to express concern about differences it had with Nestlé's interpretation of some provisions of the Code. In December, 1983 INBC announced four areas of concern: educational materials, hazard warnings on labels, gifts to health professionals and free supplies to hospitals. Both Nestlé and INBC sought further guidance from WHO and UNICEF on these areas of the Code.

As a result of intensive discussions involving UNICEF, Nestlé further clarified its policies in these four areas of concern and INBC has recommended a suspension of the boycott.

Both parties praise UNICEF's assistance in clarifying provisions of the Code.

INBC commends Nestlé for taking the leadership role in industry's compliance with the International Code.

Nestlé recognizes and supports the commitment of INBC and its members to safeguard the children of the Third World from hazards related to the inappropriate marketing of infant formula.

Gail Czukar[1]

8

LAW AND ADVOCACY: A SOCIAL CHANGE STRATEGY WITH DISABLED PEOPLE

Most disabled persons have experienced the pattern of oppression and marginality described by Goldenberg (1978). Whether physically or mentally disabled, a person's freedom of movement is severely limited by prejudicial attitudes and a lack of resources and opportunities. As a class, disabled persons are treated as eminently expendable by governments, employers, and even human service providers, with the predictable result that the disabled see themselves as passive and dependent.

Fragmentation of the services and support systems available to disabled people reinforces feelings of isolation and the lack of a sense of community. The pattern of helplessness is so well established that many disabled persons interpret their marginal status as a personal deficiency even when the cause of disability is objectively beyond their control. The message that they are burdens on society has become so thoroughly internalized that collective action seems futile.

To reverse this pattern of discrimination and powerlessness, oppressed groups need access to information in usable form and to a mediating structure between them and the establishment (Berger & Newhouse, 1977). The structure described later in this chapter is the Advocacy Resource Centre for the Handicapped (ARCH). ARCH is a legal clinic which provides legal services and public education about legal issues to disabled persons across Ontario.

The use of law to achieve social change has had uneven results (Champagne & Nagel, 1983). One of the reasons cited for the failure of litigation and law reform strategies is that progressive changes in the law have not been communicated to the intended recipients (Champagne & Nagel, 1983). There are at least two ways in which this

231

can occur. When oppressed people do not control their own law reform strategies, but leave the decisions up to lawyers and other reformers, it is quite likely that the results will be inappropriate or irrelevant to people's real life needs. Secondly, even if disabled people form the board of an organization which engages in law reform, developments may not be promptly communicated to the majority of the disabled community. In either case, the syndrome of oppression is perpetuated. Specific measures must be taken to avoid this situation. If there is both control of the law reform strategies and efficient methods of conveying changes in the law to the intended beneficiaries so they can use revised laws to their advantage, at least two barriers to the effective use of law for social change will have been reduced.

To accomplish this, vision and leadership are required. Often disabled persons receive legal advice which is conservative, based on black-letter interpretations of the law. In contrast, advisers who see themselves as social interventionists will present radical, change-oriented information which leads to dynamic results. The values of the staff who provide the resource are thus critical to the ultimate success of any legal change effort. As Goldenberg (1978) points out:

> Social intervention and social change are ultimately questions of values—values and strategies and the relationship between the two (p. 17).

Of course, in any voluntary organization governed by a board of directors, emphasis on a staff value base which is independent of the board's value base is troublesome. This point will be elucidated more fully in the discussion of ARCH.

In this chapter, two examples of how law has been used as a vehicle for social change on behalf of disabled persons are described and analyzed. Issues of organizational structure and control, information flow, strategy, and values are highlighted. The focus is on the process by which the change has been achieved and on lessons learned from the experience.

A NOTE ABOUT LANGUAGE

Language and attitudes reinforce each other, and for this reason it is important that terms used to describe disabled persons are used with awareness and sensitivity. Many disabled persons today would prefer to call themselves "disabled" rather than "handicapped." One can have a disability but it need not be a handicap given appropriate societal attitudes and supports. On the other hand, this author has heard disabled people argue that the very fact that "handicap" is a socially created status means it can be removed, while a disability seems immutable. It is an indication of how quickly usages change that the organization described in this chapter is called the Advocacy Resource Centre for the Handicapped, and that much of ARCH's original documentation uses "handicap" rather than "disability." Where that is the case, "handicap" has been used in this chapter for historical accuracy.

Another term which causes problems is "consumer." As used throughout this chapter, "consumer" is synonymous with "disabled" or "handicapped" as a more neutral term. Thus, consumer groups are those controlled mainly or exclusively by disabled persons. The term "consumer" came originally from the notion that disabled people are consumers of services intended for their benefit. Now psychiatric ex-patient groups object to this term, preferring the term "victim" because "consumer" implies they could choose to receive services, when in fact most of their members were involuntarily committed. As this description would not be accurate for many of the other disability groups, the term "consumer" has been used here.

CHALLENGING THE CONTROL OF THE MEDICAL PROFESSION OVER MENTAL PATIENTS

In 1977, Ontario's health minister introduced amendments to the province's *Mental Health Act*, thus opening it for revision. A major study of the provincial mental health system was already underway, including examination of the civil rights of mentally ill persons by a legal task force, but the report was not due for release until 1979. Nevertheless, the minister promised to make interim amendments.

Major issues for psychiatric patients included the criteria and procedures by which people could be confined against their will, opportunities for review of involuntary commitment by an independent body, confidentiality of records, and informed consent to psychiatric treatment. In each of these areas, medical professionals dominated the decision-making. Patients could be involuntarily committed on the word of two physicians (neither of whom was required to be a psychiatrist) who said he or she suffered from a mental disorder and was a threat to his or her own or others' safety. A patient so committed could apply to a review board for a hearing, but there were few procedural protections. The Central Region Review Board, for example, was dominated by older, white, Anglo-Saxon, professional males. Needless to say, such a group did not at all reflect the cultural and socio-economic characteristics of the client population. In only one out of 250 review applications in 1976-77 was a physician's decision overturned.

No medical treatment may be lawfully performed without the patient's consent to the procedure at common law. For consent to be valid, it must be freely given by a mentally and legally competent person who has been adequately informed about the treatment and its side effects. The *Mental Health Act* (R.S.O. 1970, c. 269) gave physicians the power to determine their patient's competency. It was well documented that patients who refused treatment were more likely to be declared incompetent than compliant patients. Consent would then be sought from the incompetent person's next of kin, who were often the initiators of the person's hospitalization and may have caused the person's mental health problems in the first place.

There were no guidelines in law to prevent the record of a person's psychiatric hospitalization being divulged to employers, courts, family members, or other agencies. The doctor's or hospital's policy would prevail in this matter as in all others. Small wonder that psychiatric patients felt powerless to control their mental health treatment and their lives after discharge from hospital. The stigma of hospitalization would remain, leaving ex-patients with a sense of helplessness which continued to influence their ability to find decent housing or work and generally, to function in the community.

Input to the legislative amendment process was made by the Canadian Mental Health Association, Ontario Division, in the form of a brief and appearances before the provincial legislative committee holding hearings on the bill. The brief was developed after an extensive process of education, information-gathering, and discussion between local branches and the provincial board of the CMHA. The CMHA had not previously taken such a proactive role, nor such a strong civil rights stand on these issues. The change in approach arose from a social interventionist leader on the board and an activist lawyer on staff. As a student the lawyer had run a legal clinic in a large psychiatric hospital and there had become acquainted with the law, review boards, and an ex-patient self-help group. With his expertise, and the board's enlightened leadership, the CMHA's typically conservative, professional position was balanced by a more consumer-oriented approach.

In this instance, CMHA provided the mediating structure between the oppressed group (psychiatric patients) and the law-makers. This included encouraging consumer spokespeople and other concerned organizations to submit briefs and to participate in the hearings. The role played within the CMHA was less significant in terms of overall impact on the process than was this orchestration of input from many groups in the psychiatric patient and ex-patient community.

Those involved in the process saw themselves as social interventionists rather than as social technicians, reformers, or revolutionaries (Goldenberg, 1978). As described by Goldenberg, the social interventionist sees himself as helping oppressed persons acquire power, preferably through direct and collective involvement in the intervention process itself. He also expects change to involve challenging the target social system's values and power structure, thereby producing conflict.

All of these phenomena occurred in the *Mental Health Act* amendment process. Doctors clearly perceived the proposals put forward by the CMHA and patient groups as a threat to their power to make decisions and control treatment, and they fought back. The central theme of many debates was that psychiatric patients were too ill to know what they wanted or needed, so professionals had to tell them what was good for them. The notion that people who have emotional disorders can make choices and exercise rights was not accepted at the beginning of the change process. Some psychiatrists argued that by increasing patients' rights to legal recourse, treatment was becoming politicized and this destroyed treatment efforts by interfering with the all-important trust relationship between doctor and patient.

In the Act which was finally passed, committal criteria were considerably clarified and a dangerousness standard was adopted. The assessment period was reduced to five days from 30. Disclosure of records was regulated. Review procedures were greatly improved, although many of these sections were not proclaimed in force until six years later. These amendments to the original bill had been introduced at the committee hearings by the CMHA.

Not all the developments were positive, however. A new procedure was added whereby a physician who wanted to treat a patient against his or her will could apply to a review board for an order to do so. Under the old Act, neither a legally competent patient's refusal, nor that of a substitute decision-maker for an incompetent patient, could be overridden. Again, the process by which the involuntary treatment section was added is instructive. The provision had been proposed in the initial draft of the bill but had been removed during the hearings. It was only after submissions from the public had been completed that the section was reintroduced by politicians on the committee.

The involuntary treatment provision has been seriously contested by patients' rights groups and advocates since it was passed. It is particularly offensive that a competent patient's decision may be challenged. In a series of amendments to the *Mental Health Act* currently being considered by the Ontario legislature[2], a patient would be presumed competent to make treatment decisions until a review board hearing had been held to determine the patient's competency. The patient, while competent, would have the right to appoint a substitute decision-maker of his or her choosing. This person would make decisions on behalf of the patient only after a review board had determined that the patient was not competent to make treatment decisions. If the patient had not named a substitute, the review board would be bound to do so. That substitute decision-maker's determination would be binding.

Law in Canada

The changes made to the substance of the Act in 1978 were important because they increased patients' rights and laid the groundwork for further protections in light of the *Canadian Charter of Rights and Freedoms*. In order to appreciate the significance of the Charter and its importance for Canadians, it will be helpful to have an understanding of a few points of constitutional law in Canada. The *Charter of Rights and Freedoms* is the first constitutional declaration of individual rights in Canada since Confederation in 1867. Canada's constitution was brought home from Britain with the passage of the *Constitution Act* (1982) which incorporated the *British North America Act* (1867), several subsequent constitutional documents and the *Charter*. In the original *British North America Act* (1867), now known as the *Constitution Act* (1867), powers were divided between the federal and provincial governments and each level was granted exclusive jurisdiction to legislate in those areas. Matters pertaining to health, education, and civil rights, among others, came under the sole authority of provincial governments. Thus, the *Mental Health Act* of any province was not subject to any overriding federal law. The only justifiable issue under the pre-1982 constitution was whether the government which made the law had exceeded its jurisdiction according to the division of powers between the federal and provincial governments. The federal government held the residual power to legislate for peace, order, and good government, but this was never construed to include matters related to mental health. This has meant that mental health advocates could alter patients' rights by intense lobbying at the provincial level without worrying very much about federal law or policy.

Of course, the federal government had ways of influencing provincial policy, such as by attaching conditions to transfer payments and cost-sharing formulae in the provision of services. But it was not until the *Charter* that consistency of certain fundamental rights could be guaranteed across Canada. The *Charter* applies to all matters within the authority of Parliament (i.e., the federal government) and to the legislation and government of each province (Section 32(1)).

By section 52(1), the *Charter* is the supreme law of Canada and any law inconsistent with the *Charter* is of no force or effect. This includes provincial laws, provincial government policy and actions. There is a safety valve in section 1 which allows government to impose limits on individuals' rights if the limits are prescribed by law and demonstrably justified in a free and democratic society.

Some of the *Charter*'s provisions which are of particular importance for psychiatric patients' rights include:

Section 7. Everyone has the right to life, liberty and security of the person and the right not to be deprived thereof except in accordance with the principles of fundamental justice.

Section 9. Everyone has the right not to be arbitrarily detained or imprisoned.

Section 10. Everyone has the right on arrest or detention
   (a) to be informed promptly of the reasons therefor;
   (b) to retain and instruct counsel without delay and to be informed of that right; and
   (c) to have the validity of the detention determined by way of *habeas corpus* and to be released if the detention is not lawful.

Section 12. Everyone has the right not to be subjected to any cruel and unusual treatment or punishment.

Section 15. (1) Every individual is equal before and under the law and has the right to the equal protection and equal benefit of the law without discrimination and, in particular, without discrimination based on . . . mental or physical disability.

It should be noted that section 15(1) did not come into effect until April 17, 1985, three years after the *Charter* was proclaimed. The delay was to allow governments to bring their laws into compliance with the equality rights provision.

It has been against the background of the *Charter* that Ontario's *Mental Health Act* has come under scrutiny. The procedural protections passed in 1978, but never declared in force, were given effect in 1984 following a highly publicized case involving a woman whose refusal of ECT (electro-convulsive therapy, or shock treatment) was overridden by a review board. Although the patient's right to refuse treatment through a substitute decision-maker was not the legal point argued in that case, it was this aspect which attracted media and public attention. Members of the public were horrified to learn they could be subjected to a treatment as intrusive as ECT even if their loved ones had refused on their behalf. The government woke to its precarious Charter position and instituted procedural safeguards in the review process to lessen its vulnerability to a section 7 *Charter* challenge. However, these did not affect the consent and treatment issue, and that is why further amendments are being considered as part of a larger bill to bring all provincial statutes into line with section 15(1) of the *Charter*.

Conclusion

The process of change begun in 1978 involved consciousness-raising, mobilization of ex-patients and advocates, and legislative revision. An adult community mental health program was initiated in 1976 and existing ex-patient groups gained strength and credibility during the amendment process. These developments served to complement and reinforce the advances made in statutory reform.

Leadership and staff of the CMHA subsequently changed so that the association lost much of its momentum for law reform on behalf of ex-patients. Had there not been this slowing down, the CMHA might have been able to follow through on the process it initiated, and had the unproclaimed sections proclaimed sooner.

Within a couple of years after this effort, a new resource came on the scene, initiated by the same activist lawyer who had been involved in the mental health amendments. This was the Advocacy Resource Centre for the Handicapped.

THE ADVOCACY RESOURCE CENTRE FOR THE HANDICAPPED (ARCH)

ARCH provides legal services and public education about legal issues to disabled people across Ontario. ARCH's purpose is to assist in realizing the full social participation of the disabled community. Its goal is to ensure that the legal needs and concerns of people with mental and physical disabilities are addressed, thereby assisting in the process of complete social integration.

ARCH combines litigation and legislative reform with the legal education of disabled persons to ensure they can participate in the process of change. Its organizational structure is a key determinant of the ultimate success of ARCH's efforts. Through a representative board and committee structure, ARCH is accountable to consumers and voluntary organizations. Groups which wish to join ARCH are screened by a selection committee to determine their commitment to the involvement of consumers in their own organizations. Over 30 member groups have been accepted[3], each of which is entitled to two representatives on the board of directors, provided that one representative is a disabled person. There are also six members-at-large on the board. This ensures the board is controlled by disabled persons, and that there are direct links between consumer groups and ARCH.

Because the board is so large, it meets only five times a year. Committees meet as frequently as necessary, usually monthly or more often. Like the board of directors, their membership is more than 50% disabled persons. In addition to the usual administrative committees, such as executive, personnel, finance, and fundraising, there are consumer-controlled committees overseeing policy development, the legal education program, litigation, and communications. Further connections are maintained with consumers through groups such as the Employment Equity Coalition (to promote equality in employment of women, disabled persons, and other minority groups), the Coalition on Psychiatric Services, and the Social Assistance Review Board Study Group. ARCH is legal counsel to fifteen *ad hoc* or ongoing policy coalitions.

Recently, the organization faced the task of redefining its goals and objectives. When ARCH was formed in 1980, it defined objectives for the short, medium, and long term. The original goals were to provide direct legal services for handicapped people, legal education for member groups and the legal community, and improved access for handicapped people to legal resources within their communities. In the short term, legal services and educational activities were given priority. For the medium term, these basic activities were to be continued, "with a view to establishing ARCH as a credible legal resource" (ARCH, October, 1981) which would assume a leadership role within the legal profession on the rights and needs of disabled persons. In the long term, ARCH aimed to provide consultation and information to existing law firms and legal clinics in order to increase the legal community's ability to serve handicapped people. Supporting handicapped lawyers and facilitating the entry of handicapped persons into the legal profession were also seen as long-term objectives. Legal research and the establishment of legal precedents (i.e., test cases) were also long-term aims.

By mid-1985, these objectives had largely been accomplished, and new goals were needed. The process which evolved in setting litigation priorities illustrates how an oppressed group can begin to control its own social change strategies.

For the first five years, ARCH took every legal case involving disabled persons where no other appropriate legal assistance was available. The lack of access to legal services for disabled persons was well documented in a provincial study during this time (Abella, 1983). As ARCH's existence became known, and successful cases attracted media coverage, the demand for legal representation and information grew beyond the available resources. Even with an active legal education program, it soon became obvious that ARCH could not meet the demands for individual service with only three litigation lawyers. Staff members were setting priorities, out of necessity, on an *ad hoc* basis without board input. This situation was identified by the staff as a problem and a process to find a solution was set in motion.

Following the Abella study, the legal aid program at the provincial level developed a policy to improve access to legal services for the disabled by giving local legal clinics more support and resources to serve that population as part of their mandate to practise poverty law. The incomes of most disabled persons put them within the income guidelines laid down by the clinics. Those who could afford to hire their own lawyers were asked to do so. Part of the support package was a bolstering of ARCH's resources to enable it to provide information, legal expertise, and back-up to local clinics. As a consequence, ARCH staff expanded from seven to 12 in 1985, and a new structure was required. Three teams were formed: legal education, litigation, and support. The litigation team consisted of lawyers and support staff working on cases. One of the first tasks this team undertook was to recommend criteria and a process for selection of ARCH's litigation by the board. These criteria involved an increasing emphasis on test cases and precedent-setting litigation that would yield maximum pay-off for larger numbers of disabled persons with the fewest resources necessary.

If fewer cases were to be taken, choices had to be made with great care and as much foresight as possible. It was essential that the disabled community decide which issues required the most attention. If these decisions were left to the lawyers, scarce dollars and staff time might be directed to legally interesting cases which would have little impact on consumers' lives (Champagne & Nagel, 1983).

The board of directors appointed a litigation committee, consisting mainly of board members from the various member groups, to set priorities in substantive areas. Again, staff met and drew up an extensive list of options for the committee to consider. Staff rated the issues according to their own experience, but this did not result in a much-reduced selection. The committee had to take on the task of deciding which issues should be pursued, subject to the availability of suitable test cases, and which issues should be second (or lower) priority.

The process is still proceeding at this writing, with frequent heated debate at meetings. Staff lawyers offer their assessment of what legal strategies will produce desired social changes, and the consumers put forth their ideas. As Champagne and Nagel (1983) note, ". . . there is an amazing lack of knowledge about how law produces social change and about which laws will produce desired changes" (p. 204).

That may be so, but the values which guide both the choice of strategy and the process by which priorities are decided are crucial. Within ARCH, the value base is clear: disabled persons must make the decisions which determine the course of their lives. Empowerment of the consumer is an explicit value, and cases are guided by principles of equality, autonomy, and self-determination. These values must be followed by ARCH in its own organizational structure and processes, as well as in the courts and legislature by staff lawyers.

It would be naive to assume that a societal group as powerless as disabled persons could suddenly step up to the lectern and speak eloquently about its wants and needs. Some disabled persons have had more experience with empowerment than others and can provide leadership and support to those who believe all their decisions will be made for them by benevolent professionals or well-meaning family members. ARCH's function is to provide the information and advice disabled persons can use to further their own purposes.

ARCH is not a lobby group. Rather, it supplies its member groups with the information and knowledge they need to pursue their own political ends. It is also crucial that the disabled consumer, who is the intended beneficiary of changes in the law and policy, be informed about his or her new rights so a sense of progress can be imparted and lives improved.

For this reason, ARCH produces two publications. *ARCHtype* is a quarterly magazine-style publication which has articles of general interest on themes such as employment, independent living, and education. *ARCHalert* is produced ten times a year to keep member groups and others informed about developments in legislation and case law affecting disabled persons. *ARCHalert* also publicizes upcoming events so consumers can mobilize themselves to support or oppose initiatives at the critical political moment. This is especially important because it helps make the disabled community a visible, noisy, and politically identifiable group. Factionalism and in-fighting between various groups has traditionally allowed government to divide and conquer opposition to its policies and has helped feed the public's attitudes of paternalism toward the disabled.

ARCH must tread a fine line to avoid offending its funders and supporters. Its core funding comes from the Ontario Legal Aid Plan, and its primary identity is as a legal clinic which is part of the system of over 50 clinics for low-income Ontarians. Clinics have been criticized by the establishment legal profession for engaging in political and organizing activities instead of merely providing legal services to individuals who cannot afford lawyers privately. The tradition of individual advocacy, reinforced by strong historical emphasis on individual rights, is the dominant value of the legal community in Ontario. Lawyers are trained to remain separate from their clients' causes and lives. The governing body of lawyers in Ontario, the Law Society of Upper Canada, views the advocate as a hired gun, not a social reformer, and those who prompt clients to take action on issues in an organized, ideological fashion are frowned upon. Thus, it is acceptable to quietly act as an advocate for disabled persons, but one's professional integrity is questioned if one is seen picketing with the wheelies (chair-users) or making inspiring speeches to a crowd of angry blind people.

It is not only a concern for maintaining a healthy funding base which prevents ARCH's legal workers from joining the movement. Success in court, before legislative committees, and with government officials often depends on one's professional reputation and connections. Legal clinic staff are generally stigmatized, just as the clients are, and the leadership at ARCH has always worked hard to maintain the highest standards of professional excellence in order to preserve those back room advantages. The system's boundaries cannot be pushed too far, too fast by change-oriented lawyers without having counterproductive consequences for the client community.

There is also an internal structural reason for staff not being active in the movement (i.e., not becoming members of ARCH member groups). When ARCH was formed, this issue became a matter for board policy. It was considered that the historically antagonistic relations between consumer groups and voluntary agencies would force staff to take sides and would be a divisive factor within the organization. Thus, it was decided not to allow staff members to be active in any ARCH member organization.

While there is a lack of knowledge about which changes in the law will produce desired social effects, ARCH has achieved success by using a "total approach" (i.e., an issue is identified and defined as a priority by the disabled community, legal education is used to inform consumers of their rights and options, litigation or legislative revision or both are pursued, and finally, the results and implications are disseminated to the disabled community). ARCH cannot always take credit for bringing about changes, but being in the right place at the right time to inform consumers about developments or push politicians into action, can also be a valuable role. A simple example will show how this strategy worked to enhance civil rights and to create a new option for oppressed disabled persons.

Voting rights for mentally incompetent persons

Prior to 1980, every election statute in Canada contained some form of prohibition preventing people who were institutionalized or mentally incompetent from voting. Section 13 of the Ontario *Election Act* (R.S.O. 1980, c. 133 as amended) for example, stated:

> Persons who are prisoners in penal or reform institutions or who are patients in mental hospitals, or who have been transferred from mental hospitals to homes for special care as mentally incompetent, are disqualified from voting.

This issue had been identified by many consumer groups and agencies as a priority for change for some time, but little progress had been made. In 1982, when the *Canadian Charter of Rights and Freedoms* became law, disabled persons read section 3 with new hope. It states:

> Every citizen of Canada has the right to vote in an election of the House of Commons or of a legislative assembly and to be qualified for membership therein.

Section 15(1), quoted earlier, also promised to help eliminate the discriminatory voting laws in effect in Canada. However, because it was delayed in coming into force until April 17, 1985, it did not apply when this issue first arose. In addition, the limiting effect of section 1, also outlined earlier, was a potential barrier to a successful *Charter* challenge. If the government could demonstrate that it was reasonable not to allow people with mental disabilities to vote, the limits would be found legal. For this reason, it was important to have good facts for a test case.

Shortly before a federal election in 1984, a young man living in a large institution for mentally handicapped people contacted ARCH about his right to vote. Martyn Humm was keenly interested in politics, had followed the parties' leadership conventions on television, and held strong views on who should form the next government. He had just turned 18 and this was the first election in which he would be eligible to vote. Although he could not speak, he could communicate by means of a symbolics system. Since learning to communicate late in life, his intelligence had been assessed as normal.

However, as was the case for most residents of the centre, this man had been certified by a physician as incapable of managing his financial affairs when he was very young. The *Canada Elections Act* (R.S.C. 1970, c. 14 (1st Supp.) as amended) provides that ". . . every person restrained of his liberty of movement or deprived of the management of his property by reason of mental disease" does not have the right to vote.

Various government reports and interest groups had urged changes to the Act[4] without success. It was decided a test case, using the newly-acquired *Charter* right, would be initiated on the resident's behalf by ARCH.

An application was launched stating that the prohibition violated Humm's *Charter* right to vote, and that in any event, he did not suffer from a mental disease. Before the case got to court, the Chief Electoral Officer accepted the second argument and Humm was allowed to vote, as were any of his fellow residents who wished to do so. The Chief Electoral Officer also asked Parliament to amend the offending section.

The publicity surrounding the Martyn Humm case reinforced calls for an amendment of the provincial election law in Ontario. Late in 1984, after hearing representations from consumers, patient advocates, and ARCH, the Ontario government changed its law to allow everyone to vote, except inmates serving sentences in correctional institutions. In addition, changes were made to facilitate voting by disabled people. Persons who for medical reasons are physically incapable of attending a polling station can appoint a proxy. Every institution, retirement home, and home for the aged with 50 beds or more is required to have its own poll. The Deputy Returning Officer is required to go to the bedside of those residents who wish to vote but cannot get to the poll.

Less than a month after these changes became law, a meeting of all consumer groups and agencies interested in this development was held at ARCH to discuss and coordinate strategies for getting similar changes made in the federal and municipal voting laws. In this way, momentum was maintained.

When a provincial election was called for May 2, 1985, ARCH produced written materials for staff people in institutions for the mentally handicapped, informing them of changes in the law and encouraging them to provide information sessions for residents. A videotape was produced with members of the three major political parties stating their positions on issues of concern to institution residents. The issues and questions were identified by the President of People First, a group of mentally handicapped consumers and a member group of ARCH. In this way, political content was communicated to the residents in an unbiased manner, ensuring institution staff did not lay themselves open to criticism for attempting to influence residents' voting patterns.

Copies of this videotape were distributed to all 22 institutions in the province by the Ontario Ministry of Community and Social Services, along with written information suggesting local candidates be invited to view the tape with residents and to comment on local issues. Written information was also sent to 331 nursing homes throughout the province, informing residents of their new right to have special polls and assistance on voting day. This was done with the assistance of the Ministry of Health and the Chief Electoral Officer.

These educational activities had salutary effects beyond the immediate goal of helping people to vote for the first time. Links were made between the typically closed systems of the institutions and the outside world. The institutions had to look outside their walls for help in educating residents and making the event happen on election day. The political parties were required to answer questions on issues of direct concern to institutional residents, and to address them as a constituency. This forced certain politicians to educate themselves about the issues and to learn to talk in simple, straightforward language. From a legal standpoint, further inroads into the nebulous and troublesome concept of mental incompetency had also been made.

When the municipal elections of November, 1985, loomed on the horizon, discriminatory provisions remained in place to prevent mentally incompetent persons from voting because municipal elections are governed by a different statute than provincial elections. Amendments had been proposed, but they were part of a much larger bill to bring all provincial statutes into compliance with section 15 of the Charter. There was no hope that this bill would be passed in time for the elections. However, some behind-the-scenes lobbying resulted in the relevant sections being removed from the *Charter* amendments bill and passed independently. Having themselves set the precedent in the provincial voting law, the government really had no ground on which to refuse. In addition, the equality rights section of the *Charter* was now in force.

The federal law remains unchanged as of September, 1986. A White Paper on Election Law Reform (percursor to proposed legislation) was issued in June, 1986, and one of its recommendations is to give mentally disabled Canadians the right to vote. Because this is only one of hundreds of recommendations in a very comprehensive reform package, it remains to be seen how quickly this proposal will become law.

Conclusion

The extension of the right to vote to this previously disenfranchised population was accomplished through a combined strategy of lobbying, litigation, and education, supported by the *Charter of Rights and Freedoms*. A basic civil right was restored, and a significant number of disabled individuals were given an option they did not have before—to choose, or to decide not to choose, their elected representatives. Increased options and choices for people increase their personal power.

Disabled persons were directly involved in each of these activities—lobbying, litigation, and education—not merely as recipients, but as active participants and leaders. Education about the issues and constant communication between disabled individuals and ARCH staff was needed to keep the process moving and to make it meaningful. In this way, the sense of powerlessness was reduced, although there is always an aura of magic when the announcement of a much sought-after reform is made. Perhaps this, too, will dissipate as disabled persons come to expect their actions to have direct and positive consequences on the power structure.

Without the permanent organizational structure of ARCH, controlled by the oppressed group in co-operation with others, the voting rights issue could easily have been shunted aside after the federal election. Instead, change at all levels was pursued, and once the provincial law was amended, it was easier to have the municipal law altered. There are now two examples in Ontario, and one in Alberta,[5] to help push the federal government into action on its discriminatory law and practices. This focus and continuity result from the existence of a permanent structure with clear goals to assist the oppressed constituency in identifying and pursuing its objectives.

SUMMARY AND ANALYSIS

Two examples of the use of law to achieve social change have been presented: mental health legislation and voting rights. An organization which advocates for the rights of all disabled persons has been described as a mediating structure between an oppressed minority and the power structure. As used here, the term "mediating" does not imply a neutral role, but refers to the promotion of communication between the two sectors with the goal of advancing the position of the oppressed group.

These examples illuminate some important points about the use of law to achieve social change and about the empowerment of oppressed people. Champagne and Nagel (1983) point out that there is a highly dynamic interaction between social change and law and that the social and political climate within which this interaction occurs influences the outcome.

The social and political climate of Ontario in the late 1970s generally favoured the liberalization of laws governing psychiatric patients. The government, particularly key Ministry of Health officials, was committed to improving care and treatment in the mental health area and to investing some resources in the community for this purpose. Had the prevailing attitude been more hard-line, aimed at re-institutionalization or based on values of control or paternalism, it is less likely that the desired legislative change would have been achieved. Of course, citizen and patient groups such as On Our Own and the Canadian Mental Health Association had worked for some time to create this climate, but those efforts would have had little effect if the Minister of Health had been less sympathetic.

Similarly, the social and political climate of 1985 favoured voting rights for disabled citizens. The efforts initiated in the International Year of Disabled Persons in 1981, which included bringing disabled persons explicitly within the *Charter of Rights and Freedoms*, raised the consciousness and influenced the values of decision-makers. Disabled people themselves had gained visibility, and their consumer organizations had grown politically stronger over the period from 1980 to 1985.

At the same time, ARCH's legislative and court successes increased the real power of disabled people by enforcing their rights, but also by drawing media attention to the disabled movement. In turn, the higher political profile of disability groups enhanced ARCH's stature and power base. ARCH played an important role in working as professional equals with key bureaucrats on policy and legislative developments, while consumers focused on the political role. The result was a political climate of growing receptiveness to change.

ARCH's existence as an advocacy centre was also aided by a favourable political situation and supportive individuals in the legal aid hierarchy. No matter how valid the idea of an advocacy centre for disabled persons, it could not have come to fruition without that political and financial support. The acceptance of legal aid funding was an agonizing decision for the founding ARCH board because it was attached to conditions of direct legal service provision which seemed too restrictive for the goals which the board had chosen. At the same time, the need to get off the ground was great. As it turns out, the conditions have not been too restrictive, but they mean

ARCH must engage in alternate fund-raising in addition to all its other survival activities.

Further to the changing political climate, it is relevant that there was a change of government in Ontario in 1985. After 42 years of Progressive Conservative party rule, a minority Liberal government took charge. The New Democratic Party (NDP), traditionally most supportive of progressive policies for disabled citizens, had an important role to play in this change of government. As a minority government, the Liberals were forced to reach an agreement with the NDP on several important issues, or the NDP would have combined with the Conservatives to prevent the Liberals from taking power. Key NDP and Liberal politicians, such as the attorney-general, were well-known to disabled activists and their advocates. These personal connections, carefully groomed over the years, have paid off in gaining access to law-makers and the executive and administrative policy-making institutions. Without these like-minded allies, the struggle to create social change for disabled persons would certainly be at a less advanced stage today.

Champagne and Nagel (1983) highlight the need for policy-making institutions to work together if a law is to produce a significant impact on society. Interest groups play important roles in generating in decision-makers the norms and values necessary to obtain institutional support for social change policies. Although Ontario's mental health law had been changed by the legislature, it was not implemented because the Ministry of Health was not committed to the change. Enforcement of the procedural protections which were held in abeyance for six years entailed some financial commitment and a commitment of values to the importance of patients' rights. Neither of these was forthcoming until a court challenge drew attention to the issue and some intense lobbying was done by patient groups and their advocates. The sympathetic Minister of Health who had sent the amendments through the legislature left that portfolio the following year and there was not sufficient support within the bureaucracy to implement the changes.

The political power, resources, goals, and political popularity of an interest group affect its choice of forum and its lobbying behaviour (Champagne & Nagel, 1983, p. 209):

> Politically unpopular or financially weak groups . . . are greatly restricted in their ability to influence policy. They have little access to the Congress or the executive and must rely heavily on the courts. However, . . . the courts are unlikely to be effective in achieving social change without the support of other branches and levels of government.

Thus, the forum for the interest groups of the powerless is the most powerless forum.

Despite the obviously American emphasis of this analysis, the general principle holds true for the Canadian scene. Recognition of the limited effect of court success has led ARCH to use a combination of approaches and not to rely solely on litigation as a means of enforcing people's rights.

Six years ago, disabled people were not a politically powerful or popular group, nor did their resources or goals help them obtain access to all levels of policy-making institutions. With the use of legal education and political action, access has been gained to the legislatures and executive branches of government, and coherence of policy among the various policy-making institutions is beginning to take shape.

IMPLICATIONS FOR EMPOWERMENT

ARCH and the interventions it has employed have played significant roles in empowering disabled people. This has occurred both internally and externally. Within ARCH, the structure of the board and ARCH's early development were important empowering experiences. The presence of consumer groups and voluntary agencies on the same board was unique at the time ARCH was formed, as was the inclusion of mental and physical disability groups. Because the agencies did not want to be seen to publicly contradict consumers, the views of disabled board members were heard and given credibility. Having both mental and physical disability groups on the board helped to destigmatize the mental disability organizations. The majority of the non-disabled board members acted as facilitators, rather than as controllers, which encouraged consumers to express their opinions. The issues on which consumer groups had less influence were not policy matters, but management structure.

The relationship between staff and board is an important indicator of empowerment because, historically, voluntary agencies have been controlled by the staff. If consumer power is to be meaningful, board members must have real control over the definition of the organization's values and activities. ARCH staff did not decide who would be on its board. Rather, member groups appointed representatives of their choice to the board. With the exception of a few members at large, the staff did not know the board members until they attended their first meetings. Secondly, the long-range planning and priority-setting which took place during the first two years was the work of the board, not the staff. The staff responded to demands and opportunities as they came along, but the board directed it to involve itself in longer term projects and to finish what had been started.

There must be rewards in order for highly capable staff to accept a board's definition of goals and to invest maximum effort in the work of an organization. There are professional rewards, such as the opportunities to present papers at legal seminars and conferences, to publish papers, to be appointed to influential boards and committees, to argue high profile cases, and to be involved in quality litigation. Staff also gain personal satisfaction from seeing their work result in improvements to the law and people's lives.

From the beginning, ARCH made it a high priority to educate and provide resources to assist its member groups to carry out their own advocacy activities. Implementation of this objective has not always been perfect and there exists a healthy tension between some consumer members and non-disabled staff and board members at ARCH. Some consumer groups charge that ARCH is not fulfilling its mandate when it refuses requests of groups or individuals to take on political lobbying for particular purposes. Other groups and disabled individuals take ARCH to task for going too far and getting involved in issues which they believe should be exclusively handled by the consumer movement.

It is important to recognize that the tension does not merely result from personality differences or internal sources. ARCH needs to sustain itself in an often hostile environment and to resolve real differences among its member groups, and among staff, board members, and consumers of its services. There are frequently clashes of opinion as to how best to ensure ARCH's survival, and as to which actions will most benefit the disabled community. A position or strategy which benefits one group may harm another. One example is the potential conflict between advocates for learning disabled people, who want highly specialized and individualized programs, and developmentally handicapped persons' supporters whose goal is social and educational integration. These issues must be worked out among ARCH's members to allow consistent and well-reasoned action, while respecting the territory and integrity of each consumer group. There is little precedent for such dialogue and the learning process naturally produces conflict. ARCH's detractors can take advantage of these differences unless someone is looking after the survival issues as well.

The involvement of consumer members in important decision-making has increased over the years, but it cannot yet be said that consumers consciously and deliberately control all the processes and strategies of social change at ARCH, despite their majority status on the board. Strong and continuing efforts have been made to educate and train members of consumer groups in law, rights, and strategy so they may become more self-reliant and independent of the decisions of experts, even those experts who are ARCH staff members.

Another key element in increasing the power of the disability movement has been the building of a network of consumer groups that could act cohesively and pursue common advocacy goals. National and provincial cross-disability organizations (those which represent persons with any and all disabilities) have developed along with ARCH over the past five years. This has been a mutually supportive process, as outlined previously.

The fact that consumer groups can identify issues for legal change, develop appropriate strategies, and effectively campaign to achieve their goals indicates the increased empowerment of disabled persons. Cross-disability organizations are in an especially good position to evolve cohesive positions on issues of broad concern to all disabled persons and to pursue those positions through a variety of legislative, policy, and legal channels. They are invited by governments to consult early in the policy development process on policies affecting the disabled. In Ontario, PUSH (Persons United for Self Help) is consciously identifying test cases as one element in a larger political strategy.

There is no doubt that ARCH's educational and organizational activities have contributed to the increasing political power and sophistication of the disability movement. However, it is impossible to analyze in a cause-and-effect manner exactly how or when this has occurred. The relationships between ARCH and its member groups have not always been harmonious, but it appears growth and maturation have resulted on both sides. Tension and conflict have been healthy and productive parts of this process.

Attempting to predict the future is always a hazardous undertaking. It can safely be said the role of ARCH will change as consumer groups continue to gain power and political clout both within the ARCH organization and in the community. Direct legal service and legal education will likely continue to be ARCH's main activities, but the demands will grow more focused and more complex as disability groups become able to handle routine rights issues.

ARCH will have to remain flexible and responsive to change, or it will become an irrelevant fixture pursuing self-sustaining activities which have little impact on disabled persons' lives. The structural and process safeguards which have produced dynamic results for the first five years should prevent such a catastrophic turnaround.

Although there has always been an affirmative action hiring policy at ARCH to encourage disabled persons to become staff members, it is only recently that consumers can be counted among the lawyers as well as non-lawyer and support staff. This trend will likely continue as consumers' consciousness and desire for self-determination grow. However, non-disabled advocates have been welcomed by the disabled community on the basis of their ability to achieve results as long as their actions also contribute to de-stigmatization, de-mystification, and empowerment. There is no reason to expect this to change.

In the final analysis, an organization such as ARCH seems essential to continued progress towards the empowerment of disabled persons. As defined in the opening chapter of this book, increasing access to goods and services, altering consciousness, and organization and mobilization to achieve greater power are the priorities for change for the oppressed. ARCH and its member groups have not accepted the premises of the system that disabled people are second-class citizens who represent a burden instead of an asset. These assumptions have been and continue to be successfully challenged, resulting in second-order change. Disabled consumer groups and ARCH have been supporting each other to pursue these goals for over five years in Ontario, and the signs point toward a healthy and vital relationship in the future.

NOTES

1. Sincere thanks go to Mr. David Baker, Executive Director of ARCH, for his helpful and insightful comments on the first draft of this chapter. While his suggestions improved the final product immeasurably, any errors or omissions which remain are solely the author's responsibility.
2. As of September, 1986.
3. As of September, 1986.
4. Most notably, the report *Obstacles*, by the Special Committee on the Disabled and the Handicapped of the House of Commons, 1981 (the Year of Disabled Persons). Groups which submitted briefs to that committee and a later Committee on Equality Rights include the Canadian Association for Community Living (formerly the Canadian Association for the Mentally Retarded), the Canadian Mental Health Association, and many others.
5. The Alberta *Election Act* (R.S.A. 1980, c. E-2, sections 117 to 120) specifically addresses "treatment centre" voting and sets a code of procedure for in-patient electors. There is still a restriction, however, in that an elector must be "considered by an official of the treatment centre to be well enough to vote" (s. 120(2)).

REFERENCES

Abella, R.S. (1983). *Access to legal services by the disabled*. Toronto: Queen's Printer.

Advocacy Resource Centre for the Handicapped. (1981, October). *Statement of goals and objectives*. Toronto: ARCH.

Berger, P. & Newhouse, R.J. (1977). *Mediating structures: A form of empowerment*. Washington, D.C.: American Enterprise Institute.

Canadian Charter of Rights and Freedoms. Part I of the *Constitution Act, 1982*, being Schedule B of the *Canada Act 1982* (U.K.), 1982, c. 11.

Champagne, A. & Nagel, S. (1983). Law and Social Change. In E. Seidman (Ed.), *Handbook of social intervention*. Beverly Hills, CA: Sage.

Constitution Act, 1867 (U.K.), 30 & 31 Vict., c.3 (formerly *British North America Act, 1867*).

Constitution Act, 1982, being Schedule B of the *Canada Act 1982* (U.K.), 1982, c. 11.

Election Act, R.S.A. 1980, c. E-2 (Alberta).

Election Act, R.S.O. 1980, c. 133 as amended (Ontario).

Goldenberg, I.I. (1978). *Oppression and social intervention*. Chicago: Nelson-Hall.

House of Commons Special Committee on the Disabled and the Handicapped. (1980-81). *Obstacles*. Ottawa: Minister of Supply and Services Canada.

Mental Health Act, R.S.O. 1970, c. 269 as amended.

Mental Health Act, R.S.O. 1980, c. 262 as amended.

Patricia Hughes

9
THE MORGENTALER CASE:
LAW AS A POLITICAL TOOL

One of the most recent and well-known attempts to change the
social system by challenging the law is Dr. Henry Morgentaler's defiance of the criminal prohibition against abortion in Canada. Indeed,
it has been suggested that the first Morgentaler case (*Morgentaler v.
The Queen*, 1975) "furnishes material . . . for a case-study in the
dynamics of law-reform" and "when the social history of modern
times comes to be written, the name of Dr. Henry Morgentaler may
appear as the name not just of a person or of a judgment, but of a
development in social attitude" (Dickens, 1976, p. 229). It may be of
even greater validity to say the more recent efforts of Morgentaler to
repeal section 251 of the Criminal Code of Canada provide a prime illustration of the attractions and drawbacks of employing legal
mechanisms of social intervention.

In considering legal challenges to the law as reflected in Morgentaler's experience in Toronto, in particular, this chapter focuses on the
political nature of the legal challenge and the interrelationship between legal and political approaches. Thus, on the one hand, Morgentaler's activities have given the pro-choice movement a high public
profile; on the other hand, however, they have set the pro-choice
agenda in a specific direction.

Author's Note: The views expressed in this chapter are those of the author and do not
necessarily represent the views of the Ontario Government.

THE CONTEXT

The Purpose of Section 251[1]

Section 251 of the Criminal Code provides that anyone who uses any means "to procure a miscarriage" (that is, an abortion) for a woman and any pregnant woman who tries to obtain or obtains an abortion are guilty of an offence. The person who assists the woman is liable for imprisonment for life; the woman is liable for imprisonment for two years. However, the section goes on to set certain circumstances under which abortion is legal. A doctor who provides an abortion in an approved or accredited hospital is exempt from the prohibition against providing an abortion; the woman receiving the abortion is also exempt. The abortion must be approved by a therapeutic abortion committee (TAC) established by the hospital in which the abortion is performed; the only ground for approval provided for in Section 251 is that "the continuation of the pregnancy . . . would or would be likely to endanger (the woman's) life or health." The section does not define health. The woman has no opportunity to appear before the committee. A hospital is not required to establish a therapeutic abortion committee, nor, once established, is a committee required to approve any applications at all. For example, in 1984 Statistics Canada reported fewer than 30% of hospitals in Canada had TACs. Furthermore, 18% of hospitals with TACs performed no abortions during 1984 and, indeed, 15.6% of hospitals performed 74% of all abortions (cited in Pro-Choice News, p. 1).

The abortion law as established in the Criminal Code is the responsibility of the federal government, which is responsible for all criminal law. However, the provincial governments are responsible for enforcing criminal law and thus charges laid against persons under the Criminal Code are laid by the chief law officer of a province (such as the Attorney General in Ontario) who carries the case on behalf of the Crown. The provinces also have the power to accredit hospitals. Thus they can establish clinics, either in connection with an established hospital or as freestanding (that is, the clinic itself could be approved to conform to the requirements of section 251 of the Criminal Code). The extent to which provincial legislation can impose additional requirements on women seeking abortions is in doubt. The Saskatchewan Court of Appeal recently ruled in *Reference re Freedom of Informed Choice (Abortions) Act* that provincial legislation which would have defined "abortion" and "unborn child" more broadly than "contemplated by the Criminal Code," required a woman to obtain the consent of her husband or guardian before obtaining an abortion and to be told the risks of abortion (but not of pregnancy), and instituted a 48-hour delay after "informed consent," was unconstitutional because it invaded federal jurisdiction over criminal law ("the criminal law power"). This does not mean that TACs could not impose their own requirements, however.

Prior to 1969, abortion was illegal under any circumstances. In 1969, the Criminal Code of Canada was amended to allow women to have abortions under the circumstances set out above. Doctors had been performing abortions prior to 1969, however, on the understanding that the defence of necessity applied in Canada. That defence was accepted in England in the *Bourne* (1938) case in which Dr. Alec Bourne performed an abortion on a 14-year-old girl who became pregnant after being gang-raped. Bourne performed the operation openly in a hospital and without fee. The British court held that an abortion performed to preserve the mental health of the mother (liberally defined) was permissible. The trial judge made other comments, however, which are less comforting to persons concerned with extending access to abortion. He stated the law of England "has always held human life to be sacred, and the protection that the law gives to human life it extends also to the unborn child in the womb. The unborn child in the womb must not be destroyed unless the destruction of that child is for the purpose of perserving the yet more precious life of the mother." He cautioned that the case "does not touch the case of the professional abortionist." In the 1975 Morgentaler case, the Supreme Court of Canada clarified that the necessity defence was available with respect to section 251 offences, but gave it limited applicability.

In Canada prior to 1969, some hospitals defined their own regulations and, indeed, some " 'abortion review committees' were established in order to protect and review the decisions of individual physicians" (Long, 1985, p. 460). The Canadian Medical Association lobbied for a change in the law to protect doctors performing abortions under the *Bourne* (1938) rationale: "The changes to the law were not intended to grant to women the right to an abortion; they were merely passed in order to protect doctors from prosecution for performing abortions which were, in the physicians' judgment, necessary to save the lives or health of the women. The *ad hoc* system of 'abortion review committees' and regional regulations which varied from city to city and province to province were granted legitimacy by the 1969 Act . . . ." (Long, 1985, p. 461).

It is of significance to the current legal battles to remember that section 251 was passed to protect neither women nor foetuses, but to provide stability for the medical profession; it enabled the medical profession to give medical care when doctors believed it was required, without assuming legal liability.

Morgentaler and the Pro-Choice Movement

Morgentaler was active in attempting to change the pre-1969 law (Dickens, 1976, p. 230). In 1967, he presented a brief to the House of Commons Health and Welfare Committee investigating illegal abortions. After the change in the law, as President of the Humanist Association of Canada, he sought repeal of the new law. When that failed, he opened a clinic in Montréal, Québec, where he performed abortions. He was charged in 1970 with three counts of contravening section 251 of the Criminal Code and subsequently in 1973 with an additional 10 counts. At his first trial, he was acquitted by the jury. The Québec Court of Appeal overturned the jury verdict and convicted Morgentaler; he was sentenced by the trial judge to imprisonment for 18 months. That appellate court decision was upheld by the Supreme Court of Canada. Morgentaler was subsequently tried on a second count and again was acquitted by the jury. This time the Crown's appeal was unsuccessful. In 1976, the federal Minister of Justice ordered a new trial on the first charge and Morgentaler was once again acquitted. The Québec justice minister continued to prosecute, despite having stated he had "no intention of going after (Morgentaler). I don't want to humiliate him any more" (Dickens, 1976, p. 240).

Then, the Parti Québécois (PQ) won the 1976 Québec provincial election. The PQ was committed to taking Québec out of confederation and establishing it either as a completely separate country or, more likely, in some sort of sovereignty association with Canada. The PQ was also, especially in its early years, a social democratic party. For both these reasons, the situation changed for Morgentaler and for the state of choice in Québec. Morgentaler was released from prison, pending charges were dropped, and he was permitted to operate his clinic. Indeed, the Québec government established 15 other clinics under the provincial health care regime; there are also community health clinics in that province which provide abortions, along with other medical care. When the PQ were defeated by the Québec Liberals in 1985, there was some concern that money would be withdrawn from abortions and clinics closed. While it initially appeared the Liberals would not dismantle the clinic system or charge Morgentaler or any other doctors working in the non-government clinics with contravening section 251, recent events suggest access to abortion in Québec may be endangered. Although Québec's Attorney General, Herbert Marx, stated the independent clinics could continue to operate because "we find at this time there is no purpose in taking further prosecutions because . . . we haven't been able to find anybody guilty" (Walker, 1986, p. A13), a doctor has been charged with performing abortions in his clinic in 1982 after a private citizen laid a complaint (*Toronto Star*, July 9, 1986). In addition, doctors have been subjected to cuts in the amount the provincial health plan will pay for an abortion and, as a result, clinics have reduced the number of abortions they perform (*Globe and Mail*, July 25, 1986).

Morgentaler opened a clinic in Winnipeg, Manitoba, in May, 1983. Manitoba was chosen in part because it had (and has) an NDP government whose official position was (and continues to be) pro-choice. Nevertheless, in June, 1983, Morgentaler, Dr. Robert Scott, the director of the clinic, and six staff members were charged with conspiracy to perform abortions. Subsequently, these charges were changed to charges of actually performing abortions, preferable from the point of view of the accused because such charges bring certain fact situations into issue, making it easier to maintain a defence of necessity.

In 1982, Morgentaler announced he would open a clinic in Toronto, Ontario. Although Toronto had better (though not adequate) access to abortions than the rest of the province, and therefore some people argued a clinic should be opened elsewhere, such as in northern Ontario where abortions are more difficult to obtain, it was believed necessary to open the clinic where it would have wide support. Prior to opening the clinic, Morgentaler attempted to have it approved by the then Conservative Ontario Minister of Health so abortions could be performed there in accordance with the Criminal Code. However, approval was refused and finally Morgentaler opened it without approval on June 15, 1983.

Abortions were performed at the clinic, located on Harbord Street, above the Toronto Women's Bookstore, until it was raided in July, 1983, after two undercover police officers went into the clinic, ostensibly seeking an abortion for the female partner. Drs. Morgentaler, Scott and Smoling (the latter two, at least, having actually worked at the clinic) were charged with conspiracy to procure a miscarriage. Their lawyer, Morris Manning, attempted to have the charges dismissed on the ground that section 251 was contrary to the Canadian Charter of Rights and Freedoms as well as unconstitutional on the grounds it deals with health and therefore is a matter of provincial, not federal jurisdiction. The judge ruled section 251 was constitutional.

At a subsequent trial, the defence of necessity was put forward by Manning and the three doctors were acquitted by the jury. Manning had encouraged the jury to disregard the law if they believed it to be unfair and wrong. The Ontario Court of Appeal, in ordering a new trial, chastised Manning for this aspect of his address to the jury. The Court upheld the judge's finding on constitutionality, held that the jury had been wrong to disregard the law, and held further that the defence of necessity, relied on at trial, should not have gone to the jury. Argument on the appeal to the Supreme Court of Canada took place from October 7 to October 10, 1986.

After the acquittal, the clinic was re-opened and Morgentaler and Scott were again charged. As of this writing, Dr. Nikky Colodny is performing abortions in the clinic. It is constantly picketed by the anti-choice forces. Some of the picketers have been charged with trespassing and of them, a small number have been acquitted at their trials on the basis that their actions were for the purpose of preventing a crime (that is, the performing of abortions in the clinic). The Liberal Attorney General of Ontario has refused to charge any doctors again or to close the clinic until the case has been decided, despite the Court of Appeal decision. The Liberal government, elected in June, 1985, has made it clear that it does not favour clinics; however, Attorney General Ian Scott has suggested that a hospital in Toronto could be designated as a centre to which women outside Toronto could come for abortions and that the women could be granted assistance for travel costs (Walker, Sept. 27, 1986).

There is now a second clinic in Toronto, opened by Dr. Robert Scott, who previously performed operations at the Harbord Street clinic. As announced in *The Globe and Mail* on May 28, 1986, abortions were to be performed at the clinic beginning the first week of June, 1986. At the time of writing (late 1986), the Scott clinic is still performing operations. Attorney General Ian Scott (no relation, to my knowledge) stated, "if there is evidence that an offence was commited at the clinic, a charge will be laid."[2] *The Globe and Mail* reported the new clinic was being picketed by anti-choice people who had also been picketing the Harbord Street clinic and that "(t)he establishment of a new clinic is seen as a serious setback to their cause." During the doctors' strike in Ontario in the early summer of 1986, there were reports that "(s)triking physicians who are refusing to give women abortions in at least five Ontario hospitals are recommending that patients have abortions at Toronto's free-standing Morgentaler and Scott clinics" (Douglas, 1986, p. A10).

Although this chapter does not, and cannot, detail the involvement of the pro- and anti-choice forces in Canada, it is important to appreciate that both sides have engaged in education, political, and legal activities since the passage of the 1969 provisions:

Abortion rights became the rallying point of both the new feminist movement and of a grass-roots women's movement that abhorred the amorality of the 'just society' Prime Minister Trudeau's government was trying to create. Whether its members called themselves Protestants or Catholics or agnostics or Jews, the fledgling anti-abortion movement did not approve of casting aside laws that embodied Judeo-Christian values for laws that reflected a secular society. They wanted laws that embraced ideals rather than legislated realities. And neither the feminists nor the right to lifers thought it was right to leave the issue of abortion in the hands of experts (Collins, 1985, p. 20).

The pro-choice and the anti-abortion forces are reacting to the same law; but they are reacting to a different set of values perceived as inherent in that law. Pro-choice people are, of course, offended by the prohibition underlying the law; anti-abortion people respond negatively to the behaviours permitted by the law—abortion under some circumstances. Indeed, in practice there appear to be no firm rules about why or when abortions will be performed. Women needing abortions do not know how difficult it will be to get one, nor whether a hospital which performed them last week will perform them this week, nor what quotas hospitals will set. Those opposed to abortion believe abortions are performed for convenience and that the requirements set out in section 251 are being interpreted very loosely or even ignored by TACs which they believe "rubber stamp" abortion applications. Thus the law and the structure surrounding it are generally regarded as deficient. For feminists, the law is inconsistent with the advances women have made in other areas and represents a denial of autonomy and control; but for those who oppose the exemptions in the law, the law seems to depart from the fundamental principles upon which society as they see it is based—they react partly out of a confusion about new developments in the relationship between men and women and partly out of a fear that they have lost control over the direction of society, particularly in its treatment of the impaired and elderly (Clark et al., 1975).

Groups such as Alliance for Life, Campaign Life, and the Right to Life Association, on the one hand, and the Canadian Abortion Rights Action League, Ontario Coalition for Abortion Clinics, and the Manitoba Coalition for Reproductive Choice, on the other, have marched, lobbied, written letters, distributed pamphlets, raised money, supported the introduction of private members' bills in the House of Commons or provincial legislatures, and launched legal challenges. But while each side has experienced failures and victories, the debate now seems to have reached a stalemate. The law has remained what it was in 1969, despite the fact that it is being pushed at both ends. Politicians try to avoid it for the most part, although some, such as Iona Campagnolo in the 1984 federal election, have had the courage to proclaim their pro-choice sympathies, in the face of threats from and efforts by the anti-choice forces to defeat them. The courts have denied both groups their claims (challenges by representatives of both points of view have been rejected).

In all of this, it is probably correct to say, Morgentaler has attracted the greatest public attention. But it must be understood that, just as the pro- and anti-choice forces are acting and reacting against each other, Morgentaler's legal challenges comprise only one form of attack on section 251. It is not possible to appreciate the significance of the Morgentaler case without appreciating the nature of the other actors in the pro-choice movement and the relationship between them and Morgentaler.

The major pro-choice vehicle is the Canadian Abortion Rights Action League (CARAL) (previously the Canadian Association for Repeal of the Abortion Law) which has been active since the early 1970s. It has chapters across Canada and is an umbrella organization for many individual and organizational supporters of the pro-choice position. CARAL's stated purpose is "to ensure that no woman in Canada is denied access to safe legal abortion. Our aim is the repeal of all sections of the Criminal Code dealing with abortion, and the establishment of comprehensive contraceptive and abortion services, including appropriate counselling across Canada." Two other significant pro-choice actors are the Ontario Coalition for Abortion Clinics (OCAC), initiated in 1982 to support the establishment of clinics in the province, and the Manitoba-based Coalition for Reproductive Choice, formed in 1982 to educate the public on women's reproductive rights. All of these groups are controlled by women, although men may be active in the organization. All of them are special-purpose associations: in broad terms, their purpose is the attainment of reproductive choice for women. In practice, this has meant directing their energies toward the repeal of section 251 and/or the establishment of clinics.

In terms of the subject matter of this chapter, it is particularly significant that all these organizations have been forced to determine their relationship to the Morgentaler challenge to section 251 and, related to that, to establish a connection between the repeal of section 251 and the formation of the clinics. CARAL launched its own constitutional challenge to section 251; that challenge took second place to the constitutional attack which formed part of the defence for Morgentaler, Scott, and Smoling after they were charged with conspiracy in Ontario. At least some members of OCAC (and other pro-choice activists) favoured woman-directed health clinics, of which abortion would be only one function; but they put that goal aside in the face of the actual existence of the Morgentaler clinic. The Manitoba Coalition had its own agenda which it believed responded to the realities of Manitoba politics, but it had to support Morgentaler once he decided to open a clinic in that province (Collins, 1985, pp. 65-66). In one way or another, then, Morgentaler has determined the direction of the pro-choice movement—whether that is because he has taken the more dramatic initiative or has usurped indigenous activity depends upon where one sits in this whole picture.

PRO-CHOICE AS SOCIAL INTERVENTION

The Implications of the Debate

Abortion raises revolutionary notions about women and motherhood. While contraception involves making a decision about parenting, abortion involves a deliberate rejection of motherhood—at a certain time and under certain circumstances. It permits women to make a choice even at the point where the decision appears to have been imposed upon them. Thus, access to abortion in reality means access to a deliberate life.

The success of the pro-choice movement would constitute an acceptance by society and its decision-makers that women are capable of deliberate lives and are autonomous beings entitled to control their own reproductive activity. It would eliminate, at least in part, and symbolically in large part, the line between public and private activity which now cuts through women's lives. Women are required to be far more aware of the distinction between the two than are men: Women must choose or they must be prepared to organize their lives in a way not required of men. This is not to say that full access to abortion would end all public/private problems for women. Even when children are wanted and planned, women must still make decisions about how they are to spend their time in ways which men can avoid. For example, many young professional women today, having established themselves in careers, are now taking time away from them to have children and to be with those children for a period of a year or more. Many factors enter into these decisions, such as the type of career, income of the companion, where there is one; and ease of re-entry. But the right to make that initial decision about *when* to have children was crucial in permitting them to establish their lives. That does not mean all or even many such women have had abortions, of course; that is not the important issue: what is important is that under certain circumstances, their lives would be very different now had they required an abortion and been unable to obtain one. For other women, access to abortion can mean not bringing another child into an environment of dull, physically exhausting, and emotionally draining work in the factory, office, or restaurant, coupled with constant and expensive care for child after child. In other words,

> Whatever the outcome, the abortion issue slices into the heart of how this society makes (or refuses to make) decisions on social policy, how it views motherhood and child-bearing, how it views the individual's relationship first to family and then to society (Collins, 1985, p. xiii).

In this sense, the Canadian debate is not dissimilar to that in the United States:

> . . . all the previous rounds of the abortion debate in America were merely echoes of the issue as the nineteenth century defined it: a debate about the medical profession's right to make life-and-death decisions. In contrast, the most recent round of the debate is about something new. By bringing the issue of the moral status of the embryo to the fore, the new round focuses on the relative rights of women and embryos. Consequently, the abortion debate has become a debate about women's contrasting obligations to themselves and others. New technologies and the changing nature of work have opened up possibilities for women outside of the home undreamed of in the nineteenth century; together, these changes give women—for the first time in history—the option of deciding exactly how and when their family roles will fit into the larger context of their lives. In essence, therefore, this round of the abortion debate is so passionate and hard-fought *because it is a referendum on the place and meaning of motherhood.*
> . . . The abortion debate has become a debate among women, women with different values in the social world, different experiences of it, and different resources with which to cope with it. How the issue is framed, how people think about it, and, most importantly, where the passions come from are all related to the fact that the battlelines are increasingly drawn (and defended) by women. While on the surface it is the embryo's fate that seems to be at stake, the abortion debate is actually about the meanings of *women's* lives (Luker, 1984, pp. 193-194; emphasis in original).

And access to abortion can mean freedom from male dominance. Women who can make choices are more likely to establish themselves as economically separate from men (although how successfully depends, of course, on the opportunities available). It has been argued that men want to increase access to abortion because then they would not have to worry about getting women pregnant; it would relieve them of any sense of responsibility. Regardless of how true that may be, and no doubt it is true of some men, it is far more important that a woman who can make this particular choice about her life has said something extremely fundamental about herself as an autonomous being, autonomous not only in relation to the foetus, but also in relation to other people, particularly men. This autonomy (qualified in today's climate of contraceptive technology) means that women have the opportunity to make reasonable decisions about whether they have children and when they have children; and in doing so, they must take into account a variety of factors including their own needs, other family needs, the future of the foetus and so forth. Reproductive freedom is also a prerequisite to a fully developed female sexuality which is enjoyed for its own sake and not only in relation to (or in fear of) procreation.

But this description of the issue is phrased in terms of the pro-choice political agenda. It is complicated by the way in which the anti-choice proponents view the debate:

> A substantial portion of the anti-abortion movement believes it is a human-rights movement, as life-important and ground-breaking as the anti-slavery movement of the nineteenth century and the civil rights movement of the twentieth. It equates the endangered fetus with endangered old people and endangered handicapped people, all the dispossessed of the world (Collins, 1985, p. 216).

While this position may be supported by members of the pro-life groups, and indeed, was a central argument in Joe Borowski's challenge to the exculpatory provisions of section 251 (see below), it takes its most troublesome form when articulated by people who hold a wide range of feminist views, but are opposed to abortion. Although they view abortion as the first step on the "slippery slope" to a disregard of any and all human life, they also are opposed to nuclear weapons and in favour of more funding for child-care and single-support mothers (Collins, 1985, p. 198). But they part company with feminists on the abortion issue; in denying women this crucial reproductive right, they have aligned themselves with those whose politics is anti-feminist. Yet they have based their opposition on the fundamental basis of contemporary feminism, the life principle, which in feminism is manifested in rational reproduction of individuals and society. Generally speaking, the pro-choice movement does not distinguish between the traditional anti-choice proponents and the feminist anti-abortion adherents; that failure means, however, that pro-choice has not always appreciated the more sophisticated version of the anti-choice doctrine (Collins, 1985).

It is, however, true that for pro-choice activists, the political agenda is far broader than access to abortion; abortion is merely one aspect of reproductive freedom which in turn relates to women's place in the world and to women's rights to determine it. Such issues would indeed have a significant impact on society as a whole. For example, it has been suggested that the impact of *Roe v. Wade* (1973) in the United States may go far beyond the expectations or fears of either of the major protagonists and that its greatest implications may eventually lie in its "symbolic legitimization of biological manipulation or its fostering a new definition of life and death. Other more immediate effects might be the altered number of women in the labour market, changes in size and composition of families, reductions in population growth, and changes in the class and ethnic composition of society" (Feeley, 1978, p. 21). To some extent, that broader appreciation of the issue has been lost through the emphasis on the Morgentaler case.

The Legal Tools

The primary tools available to Morgentaler and all others charged under section 251 are two: the first is the constitutionality of the law; the second is the defence of necessity. Both these claims have been made in the Morgentaler cases and to date, both have been unsuccessful. Before analysing each of these defences, it is appropriate to detail the facts in the Quebec and Ontario cases.

In the first Morgentaler case, decided by the Supreme Court of Canada in 1975, Morgentaler had been charged with performing an illegal abortion on a woman who was in Canada from Sierra Leone on a student visa. She was 26 years old, unmarried, and in the words of Chief Justice Laskin, "without family or close friends in Canada, ineligible to take employment and also ineligible for Medicare benefits." To obtain an abortion through regular channels, she would have to pay for a surgeon, an anaesthetist and two or three days in hospital at $140 a day. She became "anxious, unable to eat or sleep properly, prone to vomiting and quite depressed" and her studies suffered. Morgentaler testified that he "considered that her determination to have an abortion might lead her to do something foolish." Morgentaler had previously been acquitted at a trial by jury. The verdict was set aside by the Quebec Court of Appeal; rather than sending the case back for a new trial, the Court of Appeal entered a conviction and sent the case back to the trial judge to pronounce sentence. There were several intervenors in the case, on both sides, emphasising that the case had significance for persons other than those actually involved in it as parties. The Supreme Court upheld the conviction.

The facts of the 1985 Ontario Court of Appeal decision were quite different. There was no specific abortion involved since Morgentaler, Smoling and Scott were charged with conspiracy. No facts at all were adduced with respect to any of the abortions performed at the clinic; however, voluminous evidence was presented by the defence on the inequitable state of the law, the lack of access, the consequences of delayed abortion, the relative safety of abortion and pregnancy, the relative safety of abortions performed in clinics and those performed in hospitals, and so forth. The doctors were acquitted at trial by the jury. The Ontario Court of Appeal (consisting of five judges, including the Chief Justice and the Associate Chief Justice, indicating the importance of the case) set aside the acquittal and ordered a new trial. That decision has been appealed by the doctors to the Supreme Court of Canada.

In both cases, the Courts stressed their role was not to determine the merits of the legislation, but only to rule on the legal merits of the case before them. In 1975, in the Supreme Court of Canada, Mr. Justice Dickson (now the Chief Justice of the Supreme Court) stated the Court:

> . . . has not been called upon to decide, or even to enter, the loud and continuous public debate on abortion which has been going on in this country . . . . The values we must accept for the purposes of this appeal are those expressed by Parliament which holds the view that the desire of a woman to be relieved of her pregnancy is not, of itself, justification for performing an abortion (p. 203).

In addition to citing these comments of Mr. Justice Dickson, the Ontario Court of Appeal stressed this point at the beginning, in the middle, and once again at the end of its judgment, declining the jurisdiction to consider "whether a woman should have a right to terminate her pregnancy and at what stage and subject to what safeguards" (p. 99) since these are policy considerations.

The courts have rejected the attack based on division of powers grounds. This challenge was based on arguments that section 251 did not meet the test for the criminal law power and was therefore outside the jurisdiction of the federal government to enact; nor is this matter within the provincial power to establish hospitals or regulate the medical profession.

The Canadian Bill of Rights was the focus of the challenge on rights' grounds in the first case and the Canadian Charter of Rights and Freedoms is the focus in the second; in both cases, the courts rejected this attack on the law. It should be noted that the Bill of Rights is not a constitutional document, although it is considered to be "quasi-constitutional." The courts can strike down a federal law which cannot be read as consistent with the guarantees under the Bill of Rights, but this power has been defined until very recently as quite circumscribed by the courts themselves (see the treatment of the Bill of Rights in *Singh v. Minister of Employment and Immigration*, 1985, in which the Supreme Court appears to have given new life to the Bill, compared to equality decisions in *Attorney General of Canada v. Lavelle*, 1974, and *Bliss v. Attorney General of Canada*, 1979, for example). In *Morgentaler v. The Queen* (1975), the Chief Justice stated that the status of the Bill of Rights as a "statutory instrument" is "a relevant consideration in determining how far the language of the Canadian Bill of Rights should be taken in assessing the quality of federal enactments which are challenged under (the Bill of Rights)." The Charter, on the other hand, has constitutional status; it permits the courts to strike down any law which is inconsistent with the rights guaranteed by the Charter. And the courts can assess the content of laws to some extent; in the *Reference re section 94(2) of the Motor Vehicle Act (B.C.)* (1985), the Supreme Court indicated that some form of substantive review is encompassed by section 7's guarantee of fundamental justice. It is acknowledged that the courts have greater power under the Charter to assess laws and to strike them down, but, as indicated by the *B.C. Reference* (1985), they still do not have the power to assess the wisdom of the legislation: that is the function of the legislature.

The major issues raised under the Bill of Rights were that women were denied procedural guarantees under section 2(e) because women cannot appear before TACs, are not given reasons for a denial, and have no right to appeal or review the decision; that the right to life, liberty, and security of the person guaranteed by section 1(a) encompasses a right to privacy which includes the right to abortion; and that women are denied equal access to abortions because of where they live or their income, an infringement of section 1(b), the equality provision. The majority of the Supreme Court did not deal with the constitutional or rights arguments; however, the Chief Justice (speaking also for Mr. Justices Spence and Judson), agreeing with the majority of the Court on these issues, explained in his dissent why section 251 was considered valid. Since section 251 does not take any rights away, the lack of counsel or a hearing does not constitute a contravention of section 2(e). The privacy argument was based on the decision by the United States Supreme Court in *Roe v. Wade* (1973) which prohibited state restrictions on abortion during the first trimester and permitted certain kinds of requirements subsequently commensurate with the stage of pregnancy and viability of the foetus. The different situation in Canada in 1975, with an exclusive federal criminal law power and no constitutionally entrenched bill of rights, did not permit this approach. Nor can the Court provide the desired remedy under the equality provision: "I do not regard s.1(b) of the Canadian Bill of Rights as charging the Courts with supervising the administrative efficiency of legislation or with evaluating the regional or national organization of its administration, in the absence of any touchstone in the legislation itself which would indicate a violation of s.1(b) . . ." (pp. 175-176). Furthermore, "(a)ny unevenness in the administration of the relieving provisions is for Parliament to correct and not for the Courts to monitor as being a denial of equality before the law and the protection of the law" (p. 176).

The Charter challenges were very similar—and so were the judicial responses. The Court of Appeal rejected arguments based on section 7 ("right to life, liberty and security of the person and the right not to be deprived thereof except in accordance with the principles of fundamental justice") and sections 15 and 28, the equality sections (as well as the other arguments based on Charter rights). Of particular significance is the Court's willingness to accept that section 7 protects some form of privacy right, but not one which extends to abortion:

> Some rights have their basis in common law or statute law. Some are so deeply rooted in our traditions and way of life as to be fundamental and could be classified as part of life, liberty and security of the person. The right to choose one's partner in marriage, and the decision whether or not to have children would fall in this category, as would the right to physical control of one's person, such as the right to clothe oneself, take medical advice and decide whether or not to act on this advice (p. 97).

> . . . (But) bearing in mind the statutory prohibition against abortion in Canada which has existed for over one hundred years, it could not be said that there is a right to procure an abortion so deeply rooted in our traditions and way of life as to be fundamental. A woman's only right to an abortion at the time the *Charter* came into force would accordingly appear to be that given to her by subsection (4) of s.251 (p. 98).

In rejecting the equality arguments under section 15, the Court appears to have been relying on The Chief Justice's analysis under the non-constitutional Bill of Rights: "on its face s.251 does not discriminate between individuals or groups" (p. 109). And even though "[t]he uneven administration of the section has caused [it] concern" p. 109, the Court was of the view that it is Parliament's responsibility to ensure the requirments of section 251 are administered equally, not the Court's. Of even greater concern, it adopts the view of Justice Ritchie in *Bliss v. Attorney General of Canada*[3] (1979):

> It is true that abortion, as a matter of biological fact, relates only to women. However, that fact does not make the section discriminatory on the basis of sex. It could not apply to men and the argument would be without any substance to say that the legislation is discriminatory or causes inequality before the law because it does not require men seeking an abortion to comply with s.251. As Ritchie, J., said in *Bliss* . . . :
>
> > Any inequality between the sexes in this area is not created by legislation but by nature (p. 111).

The Court believes abortion to be unlike other medical procedures and therefore it cannot be said that section 251 imposes special requirements on women with respect to a certain kind of medical procedure which it does not impose on men with respect to comparable procedures which affect only men (the basis of the equality challenge). Moreover, "whatever disparity or inefficiency there may be in carrying out the procedures required, they are not mandated by the law itself" (p. 112).

The other major defence is that of necessity.[4] Again, in the 1975 decision, the Chief Justice was of the view that the possibility that the young woman involved would do "something foolish" was a circumstance which justified putting the defence of necessity to the jury, particularly since "the woman was a friendless stranger in this country, adrift more or less in an unfamiliar urban locality"; his Lordship explicitly rejected the view of the Quebec Court of Appeal which defined the defence so it could apply only if it were *impossible* to obtain a lawful abortion under section 251. The majority took the more stringent view. Justice Pigeon stated there was nothing in the evidence showing "an urgent necessity for effecting the abortion in disregard of s. 251" and Mr. Justice Dickson took a similar position:

> On the authorities it is manifestly difficult to be categorical and state that there is a law of necessity, paramount over other laws, relieving obedience from the letter of the law. If it does exist it can go no further than to justify non-compliance in urgent situations of clear and imminent peril when compliance with the law is demonstrably impossible. No system of positive law can recognize

any principles which would entitle a person to violate the law because on his view the law conflicted with some higher social value (p. 209).

Both their Lordships mentioned that *Bourne* (1938) seems not to cover the "professional abortionist" and Mr. Justice Dickson also stated that since Morgentaler had made no attempt to bring himself within the requirement of section 251, the defence of necessity was not open to him.

The Ontario Court of Appeal similarly rejected the availability of the defence and held that the trial judge had erred in sending the defence to the jury:

> . . . we think that the defence of necessity was misconceived. As has previously been noted, before a defence of necessity is available, the conduct of the accused must be truly involuntary in the sense ascribed that term in the precedents cited. There was nothing involuntary in the agreement (to open the clinic) entered into in this case by the respondents.

> . . . there must be evidence that compliance with the law was demonstrably impossible, and that there was no legal way out (p. 137).

> . . . The defence of necessity recognizes that the law must be followed, but there are certain factual situations which arise which may excuse a person for failure to comply with the law. It is not the law which can create an emergency giving rise to a defence of necessity, but it is the facts of a given situation which may do so (p. 138).

The likelihood of success does not seem much better at the Supreme Court. Given the strict interpretation generally accorded the defence of necessity, the only way in which it could be successful is if the Supreme Court is prepared to re-examine the scope of the defence. This is unlikely in light of the Court's 1984 decision in *Perka, et al. v. Her Majesty the Queen*, in which five members of the Court considered the application of the defence of necessity where illegal drugs were found on a ship which had sought refuge along the Canadian shoreline. In that case, Mr. Justice Dickson (as he then was), for the majority, stated, "(a)t a minimum the situation must be so emergent and the peril must be so pressing that normal human instincts cry out for action and make a counsel of patience unreasonable" and that further, "compliance with the law (must) be 'demonstrably impossible' " (p. 251). There must be no reasonable legal alternative to the impugned action. Although Madame Justice Wilson was prepared to countenance a broader application of the defence, she nevertheless excluded "conduct attempted to be justified on the ground of an ethical duty internal to the conscience of the accused as well as conduct sought to be justified on the basis of a perceived maximization of social utility resulting from it" (p. 279). It does not appear that either view of the nature of the defence applies on the facts of the Morgentaler case. Even if the Court were prepared to adopt the more liberal view taken by Chief Justice Laskin in the 1975 case, the defence is much more difficult to apply to conspiracy charges than to charges based on performing specific abortions. On a charge of conspiracy, the "necessity" for opening the clinic must be related to the current situation facing women: inadequate access to abortion. That evidence was fully canvassed at the trial. But that evidence does not readily satisfy even a liberal defence of necessity test.

The constitutional arguments may be more successful at the Supreme Court. A brief analysis of the Court of Appeal's conclusions indicate there may be some room for change here. The analysis under section 7 was, with respect, indicative of a crucial misunderstanding of the nature of Charter rights. In *Big M Drug Mart* (1985) and *Therens* (1985), the Supreme Court of Canada explicitly rejected a "frozen rights" interpretation of the Charter which would limit rights to those existing at the time the Charter came into effect. Thus the question is not that asked by the Court of Appeal, "Did women have a right to abortion before the Charter came into force?" but rather, "Do women have a right to abortion under the Charter, regardless of any right or lack thereof prior to April 17, 1982, or April 17, 1985?" (p. 103). That question must be answered within the confines of the Charter (although there is no doubt that the culture of society will be relevant). Neither the trial judge nor the Court of Appeal appeared to take into account that the Charter potentially changed the status of some "rights" as they existed prior to its coming into force.

In addition, since the Court of Appeal's decision in *Morgentaler* (1985), the Supreme Court has held that there is some form of substantive review allowed under section 7 of the Charter. The scope of the review remains undefined; however, in the *B.C. Reference* (1985), Mr. Justice Lamer was critical of attempts to distinguish between procedural and substantive due process and stated that the courts had the jurisdiction to engage in substantive review of legislation. The Court of Appeal did, in fact, recognize that under certain circumstances the courts could probably review the content of legislation, and not only procedural safeguards. However, the very limited nature of that exercise, as seen by the Court of Appeal, appears to be at odds with the scope hinted at in the *B.C. Reference* (1985). The Court of Appeal said:

We have concluded that in applying the principles of fundamental justice the court is not limited to procedural review but may also review the substance of legislation . . . (however,) it is sufficient to say at this juncture that such substantive review should take place only in exceptional cases where there has been a marked departure from the norm of civil or criminal liability resulting in the infringement of liberty or in some other injustice (p. 103).

The Court of Appeal concluded that section 251 does not contain "any exceptional provisions which would require this court to subject it to a substantive review" (p. 103). While the Supreme Court did not seem to be restricting its applicability to such cases, it could be argued that the *B.C. Reference* (1985) did in fact deal with such a "marked departure from the norm of . . . liability" since it involved potential imprisonment of drivers driving when their licences were suspended, even if they did not know about the suspension. Furthermore, the Court refused to consider whether procedural due process requirements had been met because no specific decision of a TAC was being impugned. It is not clear that a specific decision is required for the courts to consider this issue. The court could ask, "If all the safeguards required by section 251 were met, would they satisfy the requirements of section 7 of the Charter?" It must be noted that section 7 applies only when legislation has violated "life, liberty or security of the person." It is necessary to bring inadequate access to abortion within one of those three, and in order to do so, the Supreme Court must be ready to extend the qualified right of privacy discerned by the Court of Appeal within section 7.

With respect to section 15 or equality arguments, the Supreme Court is likely to be more willing than the Court of Appeal to look at the effect of legislation and to recognize that the *Bliss v. Attorney General of Canada* (1979) approach is not appropriate. However, access to abortion is not an easy case with which to ask the Court to develop interpretations of section 15, and the Court may prefer to avoid the issue by labelling such an analysis as assessing the "wisdom" of the legislation and thus outside its jurisdiction.

In summary, the restrictions of the defence of necessity make it an unlikely source of successful challenge to section 251. The constitutional arguments may be successful, but will require the Supreme Court to apply substantive due process in a broad way or to apply section 15 to cases of disproportionate impact (in this case, the argument is that the law has a greater impact on women than on men). Put simply, the argument presented to the Court on the pro-choice side is that section 7 guarantees control over one's private life, including the right of a woman to decide whether to have an abortion. Furthermore, the current law contravenes section 15 because it does not ensure equal access to abortion by women. Federal and provincial government counsel argue that the current law balances the interests of women and of foetuses.

More broadly, those who advocate the legal approach have to grapple with a fundamental question: "Is the judiciary equipped to make decisions about social and ethical issues?" That the courts deal with social values and are influenced by them in almost all cases is not denied (even the most routine cases likely involve assumptions about the relationship between the state and the individual or about the nature of law between private individuals). One must deal with that, but that reality does not mean the resolution of social issues is best accomplished in the courts. Granted, the Charter has encouraged the view that all sorts of basic social concerns should be thrust into the lap of the judiciary, and no doubt the Charter will enlarge the courts' scope in that regard. However, the Supreme Court has expressed itself most reluctant to rule on the wisdom of policy; it professes itself content to leave that function to the legislature. Yet Charter challenges will very often involve the courts in mediating competing social values and even rather extensive world views. We must carefully consider whether that step across the courtroom portal is really to our avantage. Is it possible to raise the kinds of issues that need to be raised if they must be contained within and restrained by legal requirements? The law is almost by nature conservative; should we realistically expect it to give us radical solutions? It should be noted, however, that some members of the Supreme Court were reported as showing particular interest in the argument that the law is unconstitutional because it applies unequally (Walker, October 11, 1986).

The Law as a Political Tool

This review of the two Morgentaler cases and the conclusion that the defendants in the current case may be subject to a second trial may seem a short (negative) answer to the question, will the legal approach work? But such a surface analysis of the "success" of the Morgentaler case ignores the not-so-hidden agenda involved in the legal challenges. The agenda is the expectation that juries will continue to acquit doctors charged with performing abortions (or with conspiracy to do so) and that in the face of continued jury acquittals—that is, faced with mounting evidence that the law cannot be enforced—the Parliament of Canada will be forced to repeal section 251. To date, four juries have acquitted Morgentaler, three in Quebec in the early 1970s and one in Ontario in 1984 (the latter also acquitting Drs. Scott and Smoling). Four acquittals have not been enough to force the legislators into action. However, there may be an opportunity for further jury acquittals if the Supreme Court orders another trial for Morgentaler, Scott, and Smoling.[5] Furthermore, both Colodny, operating out of the Harbord Street clinic and Scott, in relation to his own clinic, are facing charges, pending the outcome of the Supreme Court of Canada case. And if the Ontario Attorney General charges Scott in relation to his own clinic, there will be yet another one. In addition, the Manitoba charges are pending. It is this course of events which is, in fact, central to the civil disobedience. It may be that the most successful way of ensuring the law is unenforceable is to increase the burden on the legal system beyond bearable amounts. The possibility of "mass" civil disobedience by doctors performing abortions outside section 251, thus increasing the burden on the legal system, was discussed at the 1986 CARAL Annual Meeting. The police would be faced with arresting doctor after doctor and clinic worker after worker, across the country. The attorney generals of each province would have to decide whether to press charges in all cases. And the courts would be tied up trying all the cases. Such an approach asks a great deal of all the persons willing to risk prosecution. But it forces those responsible for enforcing the law to decide whether the resources being applied to this one issue can be justified.

In assessing all of this, there are two questions to be considered. The first is whether law is of such a nature that legal methods of achieving social reform make sense at all: that is, can they be successful and if so, at what cost? Even a successful legal challenge may have dubious consequences for the winners. The second question is perhaps specific to the Morgentaler challenge: What impact has it had on the pro-choice movement and what is the nature of that impact? There are aspects of this whole affair which should be prompting the members of the pro-choice forces to consider carefully how Morgentaler has shaped the pro-choice movement and the actions of its supporters.

The first question draws on general considerations about law and its relationship to the political sphere. A common view of law is that it represents societal consensus and operates outside or above private interest. But the reality is quite different: "Law is made by men, particular men representing special interests, who have the power to translate their interests into public policy. In opposition to the pluralistic conception of politics, law does not represent the compromise of the diverse interests in society, but supports some interests at the expense of others" (Quinney, 1978, p. 40). It is important to understand, however, that law may not be the result of a deliberate conspiracy, but rather a reflection of the dominant (in the sense of belonging to those with the power to make laws) norms and interests of a country. It is therefore only when another group can acquire sufficient force to confront the law, that the content of the law becomes the subject of conscious analysis. Otherwise, it is more or less obeyed and its source and repercussions are rarely considered. In this case, section 251 is at odds with other societal developments; but the intensity of the struggle to change it, and the determination of the decision-makers not to change it, indicates how deeply-rooted are the norms it reflects.

Thus, control of the law is a form of power, that is, "more a partisan weapon in than a transcendent resolver of social conflicts" (Turk, 1978, p. 214). The aim of the Morgentaler approach is to dismantle the weapon: to render it of no utility because unenforceable. Confronting the law head-on does not work because the weapon has been defined in a certain way—the defence of necessity is less likely to be successful against conspiracy charges, and this is a difficult case in which to establish creative interpretations of the Charter of Rights and Freedoms, the only real defences available. Therefore, it is necessary to use the law against itself: that is, to obtain jury acquittals in defiance of the law. It is only in this way, that Morgentaler *et al* are not imprisoned, figuratively and literally, by their own choice of weapons. Success cannot ultimately be realised through the legal system but only through the broader, rule-making political system. The legal system thus serves as a conduit to the political system. Through the jury, the community, not merely both sides in the debate, speak to the legislators. The significance of the jury acquittal in defiance of the law—the way in which it might change the perception and control of the law (or return the jury to its original function) was not missed by the Ontario Court of Appeal, a point returned to below.

But the power of law is such that where legal mechanisms are available, they must be taken because:

> Conflicting or potentially conflicting parties cannot risk the possible costs of not having the law—or at least some law—on their side. When legal resources are not available or are negligible, parties are forced or able to rely upon nonlegal power to deal with the problematics of social interaction; law is irrelevant except perhaps in the loose sense of a generally recognized right of self-help for aggrieved parties able to assert it . . . . As law becomes available, it becomes relevant as a contingency which must be met. It then becomes necessary to act so as to gain or increase control of legal resources, if only to neutralize them as weaponry an opponent might employ (Turk, 1978, pp. 222-223).

However, "to the extent that law produces illusory instead of real conflict resolutions, it not only aggravates existing conflicts but also makes future conflict more likely, and likely to be worse" (Turk, 1978, p. 226). This is perhaps particularly true when law has been used to bring about social changes. There remains a large segment of the public for whom the changes are imposed and maintained with their society's resources. Those who "lose" the Morgentaler case will not accept defeat. They will continue the battle through other mechanisms. In addition, however, there is the danger of violent tactics. In this regard, for example, one might note the increase in violence on the part of anti-choice people in the United States. There have been bombings of clinics, as well as arson attacks. In addition, staff, doctors, and patients are harrassed at both the clinics and home. The exercise of legal rights has become a test of courage. In Canada, there has been harrassment of Dr. Colodny and other staff members at the Harbord Street clinic. Women have required escorts to protect them from the taunts (or worse) of the anti-choice picketers. Patients leaving the clinic have been harrassed, it has been claimed, by police seeking information about the clinic's operations. A man lunged at Morgentaler with garden shears when he opened the clinic. Dr. Scott was physically assaulted. An arsonist who chose the clinic as one of his targets, instead burned the women's bookstore which was the original tenant of 85 Harbord. Although no connection between him and the anti-choice movement was established, the "mood" established by the ferocity of the anti-choice proponents may make such "free-lance" actions seem legitimated by their focus on pro-choice targets. Legal success by the pro-choice movement may anger the opposition into violent reaction and, indeed, the issue may have to be fought and refought in the courts, as has occurred in the United States. The anti-choice movement may also use other tactics, such as fighting to exclude abortions from coverage under provincial health schemes. However, these may only be immediate reactions which disappear over time; in some sense, the losers' "last gasp," albeit a loud one. It has been suggested, for example, that immediately after the decision of the Supreme Court of the United States in *Brown v. Board of Education* (1954), which declared racial segregation in schools to be unconstitutional, racial tension increased, but that within ten years, segregation was no longer a significant issue (Champagne and Nagel, 1983). It should be noted, however, that the effect of the "last gasp" might well be influenced by the degree to which the losers reflect public opinion. In the case of abortion, the pro-choice position is supported by the majority of the public, although only about 45% favour clinics (Adams, Dasko, & Corbeil, 1986). Support for women's right to abortion varies from about 53% to over 70%, depending on the question, and has done so for several years. Nevertheless, the anti-choice proponents are well-organized, well-funded, and determined. And in the United States, although they are in a minority, they have been able to continue the battle for nearly 15 years after the Supreme Court determined there was a (qualified) constitutional right to abortion (although there the support of the fundamentalist "new right" must be considered an important factor in more recent years).

There should be no delusion that the courts can finally settle issues which have wide social ramifications. The judiciary is only one decision-making entity. Its decisions rarely have independent impact. Rather, as Champagne and Nagel (1983) point out, the way in which political institutions respond to court decisions may determine the effect the decision may have. Thus *Brown v. Board of Education* (1954) did not really have a major impact until the executive branch, under former President Lyndon Johnson, was prepared to enforce desegregation as a choice, and not merely as a response to extreme examples of failure to obey the law. The political branches in Canada have nowhere—except in Québec, where the political actors defied the law, rather than enforced it—shown any willingness to promote pro-choice positions. The NDP Manitoba government might be willing to enforce a decision which gives women a right to abortion. Other governments would probably not interfere with such a decision, but they might not actively promote the values inherent in such a decision (by establishing their own clinics, for example). And the anti-choice forces would exert much pressure on Parliament and the provincial legislatures to diminish the right. Apparently, the anti-choice groups have convinced some members of Parliament to join an all-party "right to life" committee which will support efforts to detract from whatever rights women do gain. It may be of some significance, on the other hand, that when a new system designed to increase the chances of a specified number of private members' bills coming to a vote was recently implemented in Parliament, one proposed anti-abortion bill was rejected by the committee choosing the lucky bills. One reason for doing so was that little debate is permitted on such bills; it was felt an issue such as abortion required a full debate, and that would result only in the case of a government bill.

Changes in the law do not end the issue; but they could shift the ground upon which the debate is fought. As Champagne and Nagel (1983, p. 195) suggest, "Rather than having a direct impact on society, a court decision might place an issue on the political agenda, forcing other policymaking institutions to consider and deal with an issue they probably prefer to ignore." It is of advantage to fight from the strength of having the law on your side, but that does not mean the fight does not have to be fought.

It is the use of law as a political tool that is significant, not law as an end in itself. The nature of the Morgentaler case was political from the beginning. As Dickens (1976) has said, "In contesting the apparent meaning of the terms of the law under conscientious compulsions, (Morgentaler) adopted a political posture, and conditioned a political response" (p. 242). And it is from that perspective that the case must be assessed.

Assessment of the Morgentaler Case

The Morgentaler cases (and the abortion debate as a whole) have produced certain changes in the judicial system quite apart from any impact on the abortion law. The course of the Morgentaler challenge has also had serious ramifications for the pro-choice movement.

The first Morgentaler case had the effect of changing the Criminal Code to prevent appellate courts from substituting convictions for jury acquittals. The Supreme Court held that the scope of the then section 613(4)(b) of the Criminal Code was broad enough to permit an appellate court to substitute a conviction for a jury acquittal, rather than send the case back for a new trial. But it is clear they were not happy with that result. The Chief Justice stated, "It must be an unusual case, indeed, in which an appellate court, which has not seen the witnesses, has not observed their demeanour and has not heard their evidence adduced before a jury, should essay to pass on its sufficiency" and substitute a conviction. Mr. Justice Pigeon considered the provision to be "a major departure from the traditional principles of English criminal law" and went on: "If I could see any room for doubt as to the meaning of the words used in the *Code*, such considerations would be of great weight but I fail to see how they could overcome what appears to be the clear literal meaning." Although he agreed this was "a power to be used with great circumspection," his Lordship thought *Morgentaler* (1974) was such a case. The Criminal Code was subsequently amended to remove the power of the appellate court to substitute a conviction for a jury acquittal.

A second development arose, not out of the Morgentaler case itself, but out of a legal challenge from the opposition. In *Minister of Justice of Canada v. Borowski* (1981), the Supreme Court of Canada granted standing to Borowski to challenge the exculpatory provisions of section 251 under the Bill of Rights, and in so doing, considerably broadened the rules for standing. As long as a person can show a genuine interest as a citizen in the validity of the legislation, and there is no other reasonable and effective way to bring the matter before the court, he or she may be granted standing. The Chief Justice, Lamer J. concurring, would have denied Borowski standing because he had "failed to establish a judicially cognizable interest in the matter [raised]" there were better plaintiffs (the majority's view that none of the suggested potential plaintiffs—doctors or male companions of the women seeking abortions, for example—were in fact likely to challenge the legislation is probably the correct one), and the issue was too abstract. Furthermore, the Chief Justice was obviously concerned about bringing political questions into the courtroom: "Even accepting, as is probable, that if standing was accorded to the plaintiff, other persons with an opposite point of view might seek to intervene and would be allowed to do so, the result would be to set up a battle between parties who do not have a direct interest, to wage it in a judicial arena."

But one of the most significant issues is the role of the jury. Defence counsel put it squarely to the jury that they could acquit if they did not like the law. The Court of Appeal's anger at that approach permeated their judgement: "Underlying the whole address was a powerful plea to acquit the accused because the law was bad law. Defence counsel urged that it was the right of the jury . . . to consider that law and decide that it should not be followed and applied." The members of the Court of Appeal believed that the trial judge obviously considered the defence address a "serious misstatement of the law" and they themselves considered it "of such gravity as to place the whole trial in jeopardy":

> Defence counsel was wrong in urging the jury that they had the right to decide whether to apply the law the trial judge instructed them was applicable. The defence submission was a direct attack on the role and authority of the trial judge and a serious misstatement to the jury as to its duty and right in carrying out its oath.
>
> . . . The jury has no right to do what they like according to their view of the law or what they think the law should be (p. 142).
>
> . . . The submission of defence counsel was a forceful plea to the jury to nullify a law passed by Parliament. The jury was told to exercise a right that the jury did not have, to determine not to apply that law in the face of the instructions given by the trial judge. In effect, this was a statement to the jury that they were the final arbiters of the law to be applied in deciding the guilt or innocence of the accused (p. 143).

These comments by the Court attack the heart of the Morgentaler stragegy: the use of the jury to signal the community's perceived injustice of the law to Parliament. The jury is the major factor in the legal challenge; the Court of Appeal's emphatic rejection of the jury's decision may undermine the greatest strength of the challenge—and it puts the nature of the legal forum itself under examination.

The jury plays an important role in showing when laws are outmoded. For example, when people were subject to the death penalty for minor thefts, juries refused to convict. It has been suggested that "the perjured jury that acquits the oppressed defendant has an honourable history in the common law tradition" (Dickens, 1976, p. 254, fn. omitted). This approach to the legal system is consistent with using the system in a political way: the jury is passing a message to the politicians (legislators) who are responsible for repealing and amending laws. With respect to the 1975 case, Dickens (1976, p. 254, fn. 140) notes, "The triple refusal of juries to convict Dr. Morgentaler when he faced life imprisonment, for aborting an unmarried student and a grade 12 schoolgirl who sought him out, speaks in historic tones as to the punishment, and perhaps the very existence, of the crime." Initially, the jury brought the "evidence" to trials, a function gradually taken over by the parties and their counsel. The jury still brings to the trial a knowledge of local or community realities, conditions, or events and although over time the jury's role may have changed to accommodate the production of evidence by the parties, rather than acquired through their own efforts, "Jurors have never been required to abandon their understanding of communal ways and circumstances . . . and may impartially resort to this understanding to find that a specific incident represents an emergency, whose solution comes within the social sense of necessity" (Dickens, 1976, p. 258). The jury's knowledge of the actual degree of access of abortion in Montreal (and now one might say in Toronto, and elsewhere in Ontario), rather than that concomitant with the law, meant they believed the Morgentaler clinic was necessary. The jury introduces, it might be said, the concept of "justice" rather than "legality" into the proceedings. Those who are trained in the law are responsible for the latter; citizens are responsible for the former. Thus Dickens (1976, p. 252) suggests, "Members of the public are increasingly coming to see justice as a social concept which they can identify in operation and whose presence they can evaluate." It must be recalled that Dickens' comments are made in the context of the Quebec Court of Appeal's substitution of conviction of a jury acquittal. But in both cases, the court's response has been to emphasize the legal or judicial aspects of the case—the role of the expert legal mind rather than the sentiment of the community.

A hard political lesson has been learned from the interrelationship between the clinic and the political actors in Manitoba. The Manitoba clinic has forced many members of the pro-choice movement to grow up politically, disillusioned by the New Democrat Manitoba government. Although the NDP have an official pro-choice position and the Manitoba Attorney General, Roland Penner, is personally pro-choice, that government refused to give the clinic permission to operate. Rather, the police raided the clinic not once but twice. The state, even when governed by "friends" of pro-choice, was not prepared to throw its weight behind the realization of the pro-choice position. The NDP were not prepared to follow the example of the PQ (and for the most part to date, the Liberals) in Quebec. For not a few women, that was a betrayal. It demonstrates that the political avenue, too, is closed, at least in part because governments can hide behind the shift of the issue into the legal forum.

The value of the Morgentaler (*et al*) trials to the broader issue of social change is not clearly positive. Mention has already been made of the accommodations made by other activist organisations to Morgentaler's decision to take the clinic path. There are other problems as well.

The pro-choice movement as a whole is attempting to change society, in part through on-going low-level activity and in part through dramatic activity. As one element in the women's movement, the pro-choice movement reflects many of the same assumptions and premises upon which the broader movement is based. For example, one assumption is that women should have the opportunity to participate fully in society, in the family and in the workforce, and should not have to choose between the two. Another premise is that women are autonomous individuals, not extensions of their male relatives. Access to abortion is crucial (although not sufficient) to realizing these assumptions. While contraception has been instrumental in freeing women to some extent from their reproductive roles, contraception as it currently exists is not perfect; it is either unsafe or not totally effective. The pro-choice movement, by itself and as an element in the broader women's movement, challenges current social arrangements; its members have intervened in the current system, intentionally attempting to disrupt it. Since abortion represents symbolically and influences in practice the freedom of women to participate in society, both as mothers and as workers outside the home, attempts to establish it as a question of choice are directed at the basic elements of patriarchal society. The success of the pro-choice movement in its broadest sense, in the long-run promises or threatens the substitution of woman-directed values for male-directed values. At least, the repeal of sections 251 and 252 of the Criminal Code and the realization of reproductive choice or freedom would represent a recognition that women's concerns must be considered in structuring society. It is somewhat ironic, therefore, that so much of the public face of the debate is male.

The fact that the pro-choice movement has been considerably determined by a man has raised some problems. And, of course, the Morgentaler case has been almost entirely a male affair, except for the women obtaining abortions (particularly one who was in the middle of an abortion when the police raided the Toronto clinic) and the clinic staff who were charged in Manitoba—and, ironically, the crown counsel representing the Ontario government at the Court of Appeal and the Supreme Court of Canada. Certainly the simple participation of women does not guarantee a pro-choice result or viewpoint. Women are very active in the anti-choice movement and it should not be forgotten that one of the anti-choice members of the United States Supreme Court is the lone women jurist, Justice Sandra Day O'Connor.

More specifically, women have delegated their decision-making power to experts—lawyers and doctors—and almost entirely to men. One commentator sitting through the Toronto trial wrote, after listening to one of the defence's medical expert witnesses state that "he doesn't like the word 'demand' ":

> He believes he should be an equal partner in the decision. And, suddenly, something that should have been obvious clicks. Which is that this constitutional challenge is not about a woman's right to abortion, or a woman's right to choose, but about a woman's right to choose *in co-operation with* her doctor . . . . Because this challenge is mounted on behalf of three doctors charged with illegally conspiring to procure abortions, its real aim is to achieve a breakthrough for doctors' rights—a doctor's right to perform an operation that *he* (sometimes she) thinks is the right decision (Collins, 1985, pp. 99-100; emphasis in original).

Indeed, the movement has been criticized for accepting that abortions must be performed by doctors, when there has been a drive toward taking other reproductive aspects of women's lives out of the hands of the medical profession and into the hands of women themselves (McDonnell, 1984, p. 125).

Thoughts on the Future of the Movement

Four vital issues arise out of this analysis of the Morgentaler case:

1. What possible future strategies for pro-choice are there?
2. What should be the role of men in pro-choice?
3. How does access to abortion fit into a reproductive rights framework?
4. What is the ultimate goal?

It is important that these issues be deliberately addressed by the members of the pro-choice movement. All of them are relevant, regardless of the outcome of the Morgentaler case, because abortion rights remain at bottom a political issue. If the Supreme Court upholds the acquittals on the defence of necessity, the law will remain in effect unless and until it is repealed by Parliament. If the Court strikes down section 251 on constitutional grounds under the Charter, the law will be of no further effect, at least to the extent that it is inconsistent with the Charter, but Parliament could enact an anti-abortion law responding to the Court's concerns. Should it do so, it will be besieged by lobbyists from both sides. If the Supreme Court orders a new trial, the Attorney General will have to make a decision about whether to pursue the matter or drop the charges—and that will be in large part a political decision. Morgentaler, Scott, and Smoling will have no choice. They cannot opt out of the legal process at will. Pro-choice proponents have a technical choice, but will be constrained by their conduct to date; they will have to (and will want to) support the doctors, but such support will not be sufficient. In other words, the movement must continue to analyse this matter politically and be prepared to engage in political action regardless of the outcome of the legal case. At best, the case is a preliminary step.

As already mentioned, the possibility of a "mass" challenge to the law was raised at the 1986 CARAL Annual Meeting. As envisioned by Morgentaler, this action seems to involve 10 to 15 doctors working in Morgentaler clinics across the country. Apart from the difficulty in finding a sufficient number of doctors (perhaps not insurmountable), this particular approach would continue to tie the pro-choice movement to profit clinics dealing solely with abortion and dominated by doctors. It should be stated that many, if not all, of the doctors who would be willing to engage in such an action, would be very much motivated by the desire to repeal section 251 and to eliminate the obstacles facing women seeking abortions across Canada. Nevertheless, it would be preferable if these clinics, or some large proportion of them, were women-centred clinics dealing with reproductive matters in a broader sense. That would take the pro-choice movement in a slightly different, but significant, direction. This alternative is raised in full knowledge that women-centred clinics were established in Québec after the Morgentaler clinic had been recognized and in conjunction with government and private abortion clinics; that is to say, the failure to establish women-directed clinics now does not mean they would not be established later. (It should also be remembered that the situation in Québec is currently somewhat tenuous.) Nevertheless, if the fact of male domination of this issue means anything, and a series of clinics is opened in defiance of the law, then women must be involved in the forefront of the very specific and fundamental activity of defining the nature of the clinics.

Alternatively, the movement could limit legal action to that already in progress and necessary to respond to legal action from the anti-choice groups, and could expand political action. Political action would include lobbying, as is already done, increasing the number of speakers and co-ordinating them across the country, developing specific themes referred to below, and perhaps running candidates in elections as a form of raising public consciousness, education, and attempting to force other candidates to confront the issue. Again, this approach requires resources, as well as an extremely active and knowledgeable membership.

Regardless of which approach is followed (and, of course, the above do not exhaust the possibilities), the movement must consider the role of men. This chapter has been critical of the highly public male presence with respect to the legal case. It is not clear that this could have been avoided, both because of institutional reasons (law is a male institution) and for reasons specific to this case (Morgentaler's personality, for example); even so, the movement needs to assess this reality and decide whether it is acceptable to it for the future. Pro-choice proponents will have to come to terms with many questions:

How can something so much at the heart of women's lives be directed by men?

How have women allowed this?

Is it merely a reflection of the general patriarchal system?

Or is an issue which so directly confronts the male-dominated system one which women alone can control?

Is there any chance of success if men are excluded?

Is male involvement, in very influential ways, the price of any chance for success?

Perhaps, indeed, we are forced to admit that by permitting some male involvement, women can diminish the threat the abortion challenge seems to pose to those with the power to make decisions. But, on the other hand, can we expect men to understand the importance of reproductive freedom in women's lives? Some men are able to transcend the biological imperatives of their own bodies in order to understand those of women. But we would be naive if we thought the Court of Appeal, male-dominated in structure and ideology, could do so. And they have not done so. They have insisted on treating women as a species apart. They want to continue a world made in their image.

Men are involved in the pro-choice movement at the grass-roots level. It is not this involvement which poses the difficulty. It is legitimate—and even desirable—to have male allies as long as they do not determine what women do or how we do it. If pro-choice supporters expect to influence Parliament, they must not be seen to be exclusionary. But more extensive involvement will have to be determined, not out of some accidental development, but consciously. In order to do so, a more basic question needs to be addressed: Why are abortion rights so important?

It is not simply access to abortion which is at stake here; it is not only more easily attainable abortions, abortions in clinics (especially if they are profit-motivated clinics), the desire not to travel to obtain an abortion, or even the right not to have to be approved by a TAC. All those matters are important, but the right to abortion carries more significant ramifications than any of those particular concerns. Yet, it is seen as significant only when it is aligned with other related issues and they are seen as aligned with a comprehensive theory about women's reproductive rights. It is possible to understand the right to deny parenthood only when the right to claim parenthood is understood. While for some (or many) women the right to decide when *not* to be pregnant is crucial, for other women the right to *be* pregnant is operative. For example, it is as important that women not be sterilized against their will (or pressured to be sterilized, perhaps in exchange for an abortion) as it is that women have access to abortion. And it is important to understand that such pressure is imposed primarily on women living in poverty.

It is useful to compare the pro-choice movement with the woman suffrage movement. The vote has an important symbolic value, more important than any individual vote in practice. And, like abortion, female suffrage raised fears that women would no longer be satisfied with domesticity. The vote is an admission that women have a political character, are "citizens" in the old sense of that word. Similarly, a right to abortion is an admission that women are not to be dominated by pregnancy or domesticity. It is an acknowledgement that women are entitled to an "examined life," a life the male philosophers would have us believe is the only life worth living. Yet, despite the great efforts exerted to obtain it, merely possessing the right to vote is not enough: it has rarely been realized in the fullest sense, used in a coherent way to substantive effect by women. Similarly, if abortion is interpreted as a concrete individual right, supporters may believe the goal will be reached the day section 251 is struck down or repealed.

But the repeal of section 251 (and section 252) will not be enough, not only because the anti-choice forces will continue to fight, but also because repeal is not in itself an end goal. It is at best an intermediate step; one to celebrate, but also one on which to build. If that is so, we must know the answer to another question: an intermediate step to what? That is where we have problems. It is not at all clear that we know what we are seeking in the long term. Until we do, we cannot involve men in a deliberate way. This may be a strange and unfair thing to say since it does seem that the majority of women (that is, the majority who seek change) want to involve men more in domestic life, in parenting, as well as in household tasks. We require institutional changes which acknowledge the importance of children in conjunction with the right of women to live lives not wholly involved with children; but we also believe changes in the family are necessary (although even that assumes the continuance of the family basically in its current form). Yet if we involve men now, our experience suggests we will lose whatever control we have over the development of the future, over the reorganization of society and over our own lives.

CARAL does concern itself with other reproductive issues. In its Summer 1986 issue of *Pro-Choice News*, for example, there is an article on the relationship between birth control clinics and sex education in schools and a decline in the rate of teenage pregnancy. Primarily though, CARAL addresses itself to abortion. Of course, CARAL has a specific purpose and it must concentrate on that purpose. However, as was pointed out by Anne Collins in *The Big Evasion* (1985), the anti-choice forces are clothing their appeal in the cloak of vulnerability and disadvantage, linking the foetus with the handicapped and the elderly. Pro-choice needs to wrap abortion in a framework based on reproductive freedom—and then go further to place that in a feminist world view: What will it mean for *all* women to have reproductive options? That means, for instance, safer birth control, child care in factories, higher deductions, or credits for child care. This message must be taken to communities which until now have been only lightly brushed: working class women and immigrant women have often been on the fringes of the women's movement in general, not only with respect to abortion.

The women's movement has failed to integrate or to provide a general reference point for the discrete issues which different segments of the movement have, and are pursuing. A few years ago, the

Feminist Party of Canada appeared to offer that reference point. It could have provided the linking necessary to bring women together on particular issues and to provide the necessary extended support groups for such an endeavour. Dealing with a specific matter in isolation may result in its not being fully understood, nor its interrelationship with other issues being understood. This leads to the conscious development of coalitions between and among already existing groups committed to women's rights. If the mass civil disobedience approach were followed (to give one example of the particular relevance of coalition-building), the groups would provide support for the staff of the clinics. Individual groups could assume responsibility for a particular person charged (or threatened with charges).

There are related external events which must be considered and which cannot be controlled by pro-choice. For example, opposition to home births, birthing centres, and midwives by the medical profession (or medical establishment) in Ontario may dissipate as doctors search for ways to circumvent the ban on extra-billing. Since the Ontario doctors' strike, doctors have talked about redefining the work covered by the Ontario Hospital Insurance Plan (OHIP) so that while they may not be able to extra bill for work covered by OHIP, they will do more work that is not covered by the plan. Treatment related to reproduction, if still covered by OHIP, may attract less attention from doctors. (I merely raise here the effect that may have on how seriously reproductive matters will then be perceived.)

Although it is only possible to raise such possibilities here, what is clear is that this all relates to *political* activity, albeit sometimes in conjunction with legal action. In other words, too many resources devoted to the legal approach may have a negative impact, for ultimately, this issue must be decided in the political forum.

The role of the oppressed in the cessation of their oppression is, of course, a highly salient political question: Who defines the debate or, more specifically, who has the power or capacity to define it? It is understandable that women should seize on whatever vehicle may be available to eliminate restrictions on abortion (and the Morgentaler vehicle may well be a successful one); but as long as they continue to sit in the back seat, they are at the mercy of the driver. Should the driver change direction, women will have to go with him or abandon the journey. The legal case has become the predominant vehicle; and women are not driving it. They are being taken to the destination (even if they are paying for it). In other words, to continue this somewhat trite analogy, women have to capture the steering wheel. Furthermore, although the practical and symbolic consequences of repealing the abortion laws would be considerable (as discussed earlier in this chapter), that would hardly end the matter. Alone, it is not sufficient, but must be appreciated in conjunction with improvements in the marketplace, new dynamics in the family, elimination of pornography and similar changes. The abdication by women of the dominant role in this particular matter has implications for the larger endeavour of undermining patriarchy. Individuals and groups must accomplish the end to their oppression through their own action. It cannot be done for them and it cannot be under the supervision of representatives of the oppressors (although it can be done with the assistance of some of them who are willing to subordinate their actions to the agenda determined by the oppressed group). The oppressed must develop links among various interests, reconcile contradictions, establish their own agenda and determine means and goals. That is to say, process is as significant as result. This chapter has raised some of the difficulties arising out of the Morgentaler case. Inherent in the discussion is the view that women have not maintained control—despite all the contributions of the long-time workers of the pro-choice movement.

As is usual, we are reluctant to criticize in case we appear ungrateful. We shy away from seeking new direction for fear of being abandoned. We are afraid to assert ourselves because that may hurt those who have helped us. These are all characteristics which have served patriarchy. It must be part of the overthrow of patriarchy that we discard the attitudinal and emotional baggage with which we have travelled through this patriarchy. (And in case anyone is in doubt, it is not suggested here that we replace these "virtues" by indifference to the cares and accomplishments of others—merely that we learn where nurturing, consideration and self-effacement are appropriate.) In sum, in remaking society, we remake ourselves—this is just as much political activity, just as equally a form of social intervention (for what is "social" as the sum of we who comprise society?), as is direct confrontation with the state.

CONCLUSION

The establishment of the Harbord Street clinic has had some extremely positive effects on the pro-choice movement. In particular, it has mobilized the movement and provided a concrete focus for its activities. Certainly the jury acquittal of Morgentaler, Scott, and Smoling imbued the pro-choice forces with great optimism. A simple challenge on constitutional grounds, which would not have required anyone to break the law, might not have had the same effect, although it may well have had the same (so far negative) result and would have been almost as costly from a financial point of view. However, the clinic has also mobilized the anti-choice forces who have picketed the clinic on a regular basis since it was established in 1983. They have established a "café" next door to the clinic in order to provide a continuous presence. They have shown they can organize marches and have the funds to bus people from outside Toronto. And they have shown their fanaticism.

But there are other elements to consider. The most salient fact about Morgentaler (and the other doctors) is that they have acted: that is hard to gainsay. It is hard to criticize even obliquely those people who have put their professions, their family stability, their privacy, their personal liberty on the line. That is not the issue. The issue is: Who controls the process? Legal processes tend to take on a life of their own, to develop an independent momentum, to establish a separate agenda—how much more is that the case when one does not control one's own lawsuit? It cannot be denied that Morgentaler's own personality has contributed to that reality, for despite his good intentions, he has not appeared willing to act within a framework of women-directed clinics dealing with a range of women's health issues, or to accommodate his own conduct to the plans of women-controlled pro-choice organizations.

The appeal of the Morgentaler case is that a direct challenge in the form of an illegal clinic was successful in Québec in a *de facto* rejection of the law; although the law has never been struck down, it has not been enforced. In practical terms then, women have a right to abortion in Québec, and they have that right in clinics. But it cannot be assumed these results will easily transfer to other provinces. The specific political reality of Québec under the PQ cannot be ignored. And while the Liberals have not yet made any significant and obvious move to change the situation which has been in effect for a decade, the right to abortion is vulnerable because it exists in direct contravention of the law, and it is not clear whether the government will "starve" the clinics financially in order to decrease the number of abortions performed outside the framework of section 251, or will encourage or reinforce private prosecutions. Clearly, the movement must continue its efforts on all fronts and it has always shown it understands the importance of maintaining a political presence.

The movement is tied to the Morgentaler challenge politically, financially, and emotionally. There is no question that the case has forced the issue into the open—again. But it has done so at considerable personal cost to the doctors and at some cost to the autonomy of the movement itself. Now the dilemma facing the members of the pro-choice movement is how to assert their autonomy when all across the country they have abdicated control of their own movement and strategy. The definition of the debate as described by Luker (1984) has been lost as the pro-choice proponents have allowed the movement to be defined by medical and legal experts. Even if those experts are successful in achieving their goals, the movement will be faced with the task of remoulding the abortion issue within a reproductive freedom framework and reclaiming for all women, and especially grass-roots women, the right to define that framework within their own world view.

NOTES

1. Section 252 of the Criminal Code, which prohibits supplying or procuring drugs or instruments to be used for abortions, is also a target of the pro-choice repeal efforts.
2. Drs. Scott, Colodny, and Morgentaler were in fact arrested on September 25, 1986; they returned to the clinics after the Attorney General obtained a stay of proceedings, with the result that the three will not be tried until after the Supreme Court of Canada has issued its decision in the case before it, involving Morgentaler, Scott, and Smolding (Delacourt & MacLeod, 1986).
3. In *Bliss* (1979), a woman who satisfied the eligibility period for regular unemployment insurance benefits was denied them because she was pregnant and therefore was entitled only for pregnancy benefits, the eligibility period for which she did not satisfy. The Supreme Court of Canada rejected her argument that the Unemployment Insurance Act discriminated on the basis of sex. The Act was subsequently amended to remove the discrepancy and the Canadian Human Rights Act was also amended to treat discrimination on the basis of pregnancy as discrimination on the basis of sex.
4. A further defence was raised in the first case: section 45 of the Criminal Code. Section 45 protects persons performing surgical operations if they are for the benefit of the person, performed with reasonable skill and care, and it is reasonable to perform them, considering the health of the person and the circumstances of the case. The majority of the Supreme Court in the 1975 case held that section 45 was not available because of the provisions of subsection 251(4). However, the Chief Justice, dissenting, concluded that section 45 would have been available to a physician who had performed an abortion under the predecessor abortion provision which made abortion illegal under any circumstances and that since section 251 does not contain a provision similar to section 45, under certain conditions (met in the Morgentaler case), it would be reasonable to put a section 45 defence to the jury. Section 45 was not raised in the Ontario case.
5. Should a new trial be ordered and the doctors again be acquitted, it is at

least questionable whether the Ontario Attorney General would be prepared to launch another appeal.

REFERENCES

Adams, M., Dasko, D., & Corbeil, Y. (1985, June 15). Abortion debate: Slim majority of Canadians favors free choice, poll finds. *Globe and Mail*, p. A1.

Champagne, A., & Nagel, S.S. (1983). Law and social change. In E. Seidman (Ed.), *Handbook on social intervention* (pp. 187-211). Beverly Hills: Sage.

Clark, S.D., Grayson, J.P., & Grayson, L.M. *Prophecy and protest: Social movements in twentieth-century Canada*. Toronto: Gage.

Collins, A. (1985). *The big evasion: Abortion, the issue that won't go away*. Toronto: Lester & Orpen Dennys.

Dickens, B.M. (1976). The *Morgentaler* case: Criminal process and abortion law. *Osgoode Hall Law Journal, 14*, 229.

Delacourt, S., & MacLeod, R. (1986, September 25). Miffed at timing of abortion charges, Scott blocks trials until top court rules. *Globe and Mail*, p. A1.

Douglas, J. (1986, June 23). Striking MDs send patients to Morgentaler, Scott clinics. *Globe and Mail*, p. A10.

Feeley, M.M. (1978). The concept of laws in social science: A critique and notes on an expanded view. In C. Reasons & R. Rich (Eds.), *The sociology of law: A conflict perspective*. Toronto: Butterworths.

Long, L. (1985). The abortion issue: An overview. *Alberta Law Review, 23*, 453.

Luker, K. (1984). *Abortion and the politics of motherhood*. London, England: University of California Press.

McDonnell, K. (1984). *Not an easy choice: A feminist re-examines abortion*. Toronto: Women's Press.

Quinney, R. (1978). The ideology of law: Notes for a radical alternative to legal oppression. In C. Reason & R. Rich (Eds.), *The sociology of law: A conflict perspective*. Toronto: Butterworths.

Turk, A.T. (1978). Law as a weapon in social conflict. In C. Reason & R. Rich (Eds.), *The Sociology of law: A conflict perspective*. Toronto: Butterworths.

Walker, W. (1986, May 31). Provinces powerless to enforce laws on abortion, Quebec legal chief says. *Toronto Star*, p. A13.

Walker, W. (1986, September 27). Toronto hospital could be abortion centre, Scott says. *Toronto Star*, p. A1.

Walker, W. (1986, October 11). Abortion gets its day in (high) court. *Toronto Star*, p. B4.

Abortion charge first in Quebec since 1970s. (1986, July 9). *Toronto Star*.

Funds curbing Quebec abortions. (1986, July 25). *Globe and Mail*.

Pro-Choice News (1986, Summer).

CASES

Attorney General of Canada v. *Lavelle*, [1974] S.C.R. 1349.
Big M Drug Mart, R. v., [1985] 1 S.C.R. 295.
Bliss v. *Attorney General of Canada*, [1979] 1 S.C.R. 183.
Bourne. Rex v. (1938), 3 All E.R. 615.
Brown v. *Board of Education*, 347 U.S. 483 (1954).
Freedom of Informed Choice (Abortions) Act, Reference re (1985), 25 D.L.R.
   (4th) 751 (Sask, C.A.).
Minister of Justice v. *Borowski* (1981), 130 D.L.R. (3d) 588 (S.C.C.).
Morgentaler, R. v. (1974), 47 D.L.R. (3d) 211 (Que. C.A.).
Morgentaler v. *The Queen* (1975), 53 D.L.R. (3d) 161 (S.C.C.).
Morgentaler, R. v. (1985), 11 O.A.C. 81 (C.A.).
Operation Dismantle v. *The Queen*, [1985] 1 S.C.R. 441.
Perka, et al. v. *Her Majesty the Queen*, [1984] 2 S.C.R. 232.
Section 94(2) Motor Vehicle Act (B.C.), Reference re (1985), 53 N.R. 266
   (S.C.C.).
Roe v. *Wade*, 410 U.S. 113 (1973).
Singh v. *Minister of Employment and Immigration*, [1985] 1 S.C.R. 177.
Therens, R. v., [1985] 1 S.C.R. 613.

Françoise Boudreau

10
THE VICISSITUDES OF PSYCHIATRIC INTERVENTION IN QUEBEC— FROM THE INSTITUTIONAL TO THE ECOLOGICAL MODEL

INTRODUCTION: A PROMISE TO FULFILL

Québec, July, 1986. The mental health scene is bubbling with activity. All concerned parties and parties who feel concerned are busy at the drawing board. The milieu is permeated with a feeling of eagerness, imminence, and urgency prompted by the conviction, or should we say the hope mixed with determination, that finally there will be in Québec a "true-to-form" mental health policy.

This is felt and understood as crucial: a unified and unifying, comprehensive, rational and consistent, just and politically powerful mental health policy, which will mark the beginning of a "new era" to follow the "old new era" of unprepared deinstitutionalization, and which will, it is hoped, put an end to the nightmarish headlines found with assiduity in the daily newspapers. Promised by Minister of Social Affairs Pierre-Marc Johnson in 1983 for no later than 1985, kept on the agenda by successive ministers, the promise has survived the demise of its Parti Québécois originators. Now, July 10, 1986, a communiqué from the newly elected Liberal government under the leadership of Robert Bourassa, confirms the project is indeed a priority: "the Minister of Health and Social Services (until recently called the Minister of Social Affairs), Madame Thérèse Lavoie-Roux," says the communiqué, "has reached her decision concerning the composition and mandate of the 'mental health policy work group' which she has recently created." *La machine est en marche*, as they say in Québec.

What is aimed for: a policy for the Québécois designed by the Québécois. The work of democracy and popular consultation. The new motto? In mental health, *everyone* should and can contribute—and this motto inspires all hopeful policy influencers, each in their own way.

The official message is clear, sent directly by the ministry of health and social services: *Mental Health: It Is for All of Us to Decide* (1985) says the title of its latest working document drawn for public discussion and feedback. The process of "intellectual cogitation" as the first step in policy design is on. Since 1983 it has given birth to a flurry of documents, personal testimonies, research studies, discussion papers, journal articles, and extensive and highly sophisticated *Avis* from Québec's *Comité de la Santé Mentale*, an advisory committee to the ministry. Public forums, conferences, commissions, and sub-commissions were also organized, totalling all in all, hundreds of recommendations aiming for the betterment of mental health and the humanization of psychiatric-mental health intervention in the province of Québec.

Cries for political intervention are loud and clear, for the recent years have also had their share of highly publicized scandals. Psychiatric hospitals, yesterday's asylums, were regularly making the headlines facing allegations of violence, drug trafficking, sexual abuse, and prostitution, as was the case of the Rivière des Prairies Hospital in 1985. Reports showed them torn by internal squabbles and accusations of professional incompetence; their direction was brought under "tutelle"—as with the Hôpital Louis-H. Lafontaine, in 1984, or again, they were shown to be essentially carceral, punishing, and violent to use the terms of the 1984 study commissioned by the Direction of the Centre Hospitalier Robert Giffard on the conditions of violence and sexual intimacy within its walls. "Measures of punishment and control, said the report, are disguised as therapy" (Jacob & Dumais, 1984, p. 5). Adorned with slashing declarations that a lot has been said and done since 1960 but nothing has really changed (Beausoleil & Godin, 1983), that "if psychiatry is sick, mental health is no better" (Roberts, 1985, p. 23) and more generally, that the mental health of the Québécois is in worse shape than ever before (Plante, 1984; Lamontagne, 1985), this state of turmoil contributed to further arouse individual and collective consciences, heightening the demand for change and intensifying pressures on government for the immediate fulfillment of its promise. The Québec psychiatric system along with the principles and golden words of the two previous decades—deinstitutionalization, normalization and social reinsertion—were put on trial.

A self appointed sub-commission on social reinsertion officialized this process. This sub-commission was led by Madame Thérèse

Lavoie-Roux—then member of the Liberal opposition, and held its public hearings in August, 1985, a few weeks prior to the elections which won her the title of minister of social affairs. Testimonies came from private citizens, former patients, and their families, and from the more politicized psychiatrized; they came from fed-up neighbours and citizen committees, from professionals involved as care-givers or service givers or support givers—the label reflecting their ideology; they came from voluntary associations such as the CMHA, from self-help groups and associations of alternative groups who spoke of their personal beliefs and experiences; they came from associations of "reception centres" or *centres d'acceuils* who were asking for more subsidies, from directors of institutions in the process of being "dehospitalized"; they came from unionized employees of those same institutions who held that "deinstitutionalization of patients must also mean deinstitutionalization, retraining and relocation of staff in jobs of equal status and income" (Marshall, 1982, p. 155). From all parties concerned, the call was for a coherent, rational, unified mental health policy. The belief, or perhaps the illusion, is that it can be done—and that there lies the solution! The new target? The year 1987.

The mood is thus for a reform, a reform inspired by a specific conception of wisdom—not the wisdom of incrementally adding ever so new, and ever so many programs and areas of intervention as designed and approved by government and "specialists above," not the wisdom of "illusory adaptations" (Appollon, 1986, p. 104) which would perpetuate the status quo, but the wisdom of a coherent and global policy thought *by* and *with* all the people involved. This policy in which all put their hopes and faith is to be a collective enterprise aiming at a total reconceptualization of the psychiatric-mental health field. The model favoured? With apparent consensus, they call it the ecological model, a model which would make psychiatric-mental health intervention the project of a whole society.

PURPOSE

The purpose of this chapter is to understand this most recent call for psychiatric reform in Québec with its taken-for-granted truths and conception of reality as well as the particular language in which it is conceived and formulated. This will be done, first, by examining the changing forces which in the past 25 years have penetrated and invaded, molded, steered, and stirred the province's system for the delivery of psychiatric care. We will outline here the particular "psycho-political" (Greenblatt, 1978) scenario which has brought about the successive transformation of the system for the management and delivery of psychiatric care from what was an *asylum system* aimed at craziness whose official purpose was, up until the early 1960s, to provide *custodial care* to a population of *inmates*. This later became known as a *psychiatric system* aimed at mental illness whose official purpose was to provide *medical care* to a population of *patients*, and was subsequently legislated as an integrated component of a global *Health and Welfare system*. This integrative move known as the Castonguay reform of the 1970s promised *comprehensive and holistic services* to a population of *clients*. Finally, we will examine the system's latest movement toward the formulation of the new ecological approach interested in the *social health* of *all of Québec's population* and focusing on the bio-psycho-culturo-social dimensions of psychiatric-mental health intervention.

After looking at the key threshold points which have propelled these changes since 1960, we will examine today's call for a "true-to-form mental health policy" and the premises upon which it is built as part of a more global "mindscape" concerning the role of the state, of individual and collective responsibility in policy making and social intervention. In other words, we will examine today's hopes and formulations as part of the "spirit of the times" that is, as part of a particular sociopolitical *zeitgeist* characteristic of the sociopolitical milieu of the moment in the western world—for such a milieu essentially determines and constrains the selection and formulation of social problems and their solutions (Seidman, 1983).

TWO RECENT THRESHOLDS OF CHANGE

The recent history of psychiatric intervention in Québec is a history in several episodes, each one begun with crisis and turmoil. In *Beyond the Stable State*, Donald A. Schon (1971) notes that because of its self preserving nature, a social system is unlikely to undertake its own change of state referred to, by Watzlawick (1974) as second-order change. Because of this dynamic conservatism, defined as "the property of a system to fight to remain the same," transformation from one structural, technological, and conceptual configuration to another becomes a kind of war. A system's *structural* configuration refers to relationships of control and interaction among the system's constituting units, be they called people or interest groups, territory, or resources. Its *technological* configuration refers to the tools, techniques, and productive processes which extend the human capabilities of the system and are used in accomplishing the system's purposes. Its *conceptual* configuration or theory refers to the system of ideas, values, and ideologies which provide definitions of the situation, goals, justifications, and models for action. These three dimensions of a system are interdependent and built upon one another. Hence, one cannot be changed without inducing change in the others. Moreover, because of this basic self-defense mechanism, action upon the system at any of these levels may have little perceptible effect until it reaches a critical threshold. At this point it is possible to break the old dynamic conservatism and precipitate a change of state.

One cannot understand today's particular mood and call for a "new, new era" without examining the two recent thresholds of change which have made the psychiatric system in Québec what it is today. These we have called, the Québec Psychiatric Revolution of the early 1960s, and the Québec Psychiatric Crisis of the early 1970s (Boudreau, 1984).

INSURGENCE AND INVASION:
THE LANGUAGE OF POWER AND CONFLICT

According to Schon (1971), disruption-provoking energy leading to a change of state may take two forms: *"insurgence* and *invasion* which make the history of significant innovations a history of guerilla movements from within and invasions from without"* (p. 55). Schon's rather colourful language is in our case, particularly appropriate. Without in any way putting in doubt the personal dedication and the humanitarian convictions of each individual involved, the Québec Psychiatric revolution can be understood as the result of an insurgence on the part of young modern psychiatrists from within the church dominated asylum system in order to carve themselves a place in a system which they felt legitimately belonged to them and which yet, as it stood, had little room for them and even less for upward mobility and professional dominance. The second threshold point triggering the Québec Psychiatric crisis can be understood in terms of a gradual invasion of the psychiatric system by a new elite of government technocrats, professional rationalizators, and social engineers who wished to impose, in the name of the state and of the collectively, their own conception of effectiveness, rationality, and system management. Insurgence and invasion, says Donald Schon, employ the language of power. More specifically, they employ the language of conflict between interest groups who, through the interplay of interest and commitment, are pushing their own theory of the system and manoeuvering within their respective power budgets (Long, 1962) in their bids for dominance and thus for the ability to implement their own plans for action, their own "solutions" to the identified social problems. For indeed, as Schon (1971) writes, "ideas are vehicles through which persons and agencies gain power. When individuals push or ride ideas, they also seek to establish their own dominance" (p. 18). However, far from labelling as villainous, machiavellian, or power hungry the individuals involved, we see in them the conviction of vanguards, crusaders, and missionaries. In those who ardently resist the changes and defend the status quo, we recognize, not stupidity and selfishness, but the conviction of warriors defending their territory with the certainty that there is a direct relation between the best interests of the public and their own best interests. Those who find themselves threatened by new definitions of the situation and potentially powerful policy making ideas typically experience an intolerable state of anxiety and therefore defensiveness, as the past which they have built and the present which provides them with status, rights, privileges, meaning, and even personal identity, is criticized, questioned, and said to be outdated.

THE ASYLUM SYSTEM
AND THE MONOPOLY OF THE CHURCH

"Whatever you do to the least of these, that you do unto me" (Luke VI:31).

This principle, which for more than 100 years was to guide employees at the Hôpital St-Michel Archange, did not prevent two attendants from killing a patient because he had refused to wash a floor—in 1948. This was only one of the contradictions of the asylum system which served Québec's francophone and Catholic population until the early 1960s. Owned and operated by religious communities, this system was comprised of two so-called "active institutions"—l'hôpital St-Jean-de-Dieu and l'hôpital St-Michel Archange, to which were affiliated, exclusively for storage purposes, more than half a dozen satellite institutions situated in remote areas of the province. As with all such asylums, chronic overcrowding and understaffing, insufficient sanitary facilities, lack of personal attention and care, punitive attitudes, indefinite stays, dictatorial and autocratic management were the rule. The entire Catholic, public network provided by 1961, 87.3% of the province's 22,694 psychiatric beds.

The monopoly of the religious community over the public asylum system rested above all, on the theory that craziness is either a gift from God to test his faithful or the instrument of his anger to punish the sinners. The nuns, in their unlimited devotion, were seen as the best qualified to take care of these "suffering limbs of the body of Christ and lead their Souls to Heaven."

The religious community's power base was also nourished by the long tradition of paternalistic intervention by the church in all human services: education, health, and welfare. As long as the normality of it remained unquestioned, and as long as Premier Maurice Duplessis' "laissez faire" in the area of human services prevailed, the system was at peace. No competition, no outside control. The fact that these communities possessed enormous capital in this area and provided a large cohort of devoted, unpaid personnel was for more than a century very convincing.

THE OLD AND THE NEW—THE OPPOSING CAMPS

Toward the end of the 1950s, however, psychiatrists did not constitute a homogeneous group. Members of the traditional "petite bourgeoisie," the traditionalists, as we call them, did not question the church dominance. They had assimilated and contributed to the prevailing definition of the situation. "Common sense," writes Dr. Dumas (1961), "serenity, compassion, objectivity and unpretentiousness before the difficult facts are the only qualities necessary for psychiatrists to assume their noble mission" (p. 429).

The first sign of the impending shift in the balance of power came with the massive arrival of young psychiatrists, modernists as we shall call them, into this system where psychiatry as a "science serving God and the Church" had little resemblance to what they had learned in the American and European schools of medicine. From 15 in 1950, the number of psychiatrists in Québec suddenly increased to 170 by 1962. A confrontation between the old guard and this new generation of psychiatrists was imminent.

INVASION: THE CRISIS PROVOKING MOVES

The publication on August 21, 1961, of *Les Fous Crient au Secours* was the first crisis-provoking move in the Québec Psychiatric Revolution. This personal testimony of Jean-Charles Pagé describes à la Clifford Beers (1948) the horrors of his stay at St-Jean-de-Dieu: "Would hospitals for dogs have more respect for their patients than St-Jean-de-Dieu has for its humans?" (Pagé, 1961, p. 79). "The pa-

TABLE 1

Characteristics of Theories in Dominance in the Québec Psychiatric System

Characteristics of Theories	Phase I (– 1960)	Phase II (1961-1970)	Phase III (1970 +)	? Phase IV (1985 +) ?
1. System	"Asylum" system	"Psychiatric" system	Global "health and welfare" system	"Society" as a whole
2. Promoters	Religious orders —old professional bourgeoisie	Young psychiatrists—new professional bourgeoisie	The state, social planners and "bureaucratic rationalizers"	Various groups with a variety of interests: alternative groups, voluntary associations, citizens' committees, psychiatrized, ecologists, administrators, government bodies
3. Dominant theme	*Craziness* cannot be cured	*Mental illness* is an illness like any other	*Mental health* is a right for everyone	*Social health* is an individual and collective responsibility
4. Official goal	Salvation in heaven	Treatment and social reinsertion	Fulfillment of harmonious physical and mental self-growth	Harmonious adaptation of individual to environment
5. Ideological source	Credo of Catholic church	The Bédard, Lazure, and Roberts report (1962)	The Castonguay-Nepveu report (1970)	The Lalonde Report (enriched) & *Objectif: Santé*
6. Representation of the situation and responsibility	Religious orders are the most devoted and thus the most competent providers of care and managers of the system	Confidence in experts—mental illness is the responsibility of professionals	Belief in the managerial logic of the state being legitimately responsible for the collective well-being	Belief in individual potential, mutual help, and solidarity
7. Model for action	Custodial, institutional model	Medical curative model; individualized psychiatric care and deinstitutionalization	Integrated holistic model; public health care	Ecological model (bio-psycho-culturo-social model)

8. Logic	Feudalistic	Liberalistic	Social-democratic	Unique blend of individualism and collectivism
9. Target of intervention	The insane	The mentally ill patient	The client, beneficiary, consumer of services	The entire Québec population

tients are slaves under the nuns' whip . . . . They cry for help. In the name of justice we cannot close our ears" (Pagé, 1961, p. 114). Pagé's testimony acted as a propellor for Dr. Camille Laurin's call, at the end of the book, for a radical change of the system. "The true solution," writes the young modernist, "resides in the creation of a new system which would return to the patient his dignity *and* the chance to be treated as he should be" (Pagé, 1961, p. 156).

"The strategy of change is as important as the change itself" (Selznick, 1957, p. 27). For Donald Schon (1971), what precipitates a shift in powerful ideas is characteristically a disruptive event or sequence of events which set up a demand for new ideas. "Crisis in the system permits or compels new ideas to come to public notice and to begin their progress toward public awareness, currency and acceptance" (p. 131). However, this passage of ideas from free areas to the mainstream and to dominance is not automatic. Vanguards move ideas to public awareness, supplying the energy necessary to raise them over the threshold of public consciousness.

The sequence of events which followed Camille Laurin's bombshell and this first public exposé of a divergent definition of the situation and of a new, competing theory, illustrates well the crusade and warlike process of change. For indeed, the cry for help was immediately echoed in all Québec newspapers, under shocking headlines: "In Their Snake Pit, the Crazy Cry for Help", (*Le Petit Journal*, August 28, 1961); "Our System is 65 Years Behind" (*La Presse*, August 30, 1961); "It's Time for Us to Feel Guilty" (*La Presse*, September 29, 1961).

As Milton Greenblatt (1978) notes: "Probably the greatest asset of the mentally ill (. . .) is an aroused citizenry" (p. 30). Newspapers were flooded with feature articles, documentaries, editorials, and personal letters; some decrying the system and arraigning the religious communities, others professing their intense fervour and their faith in the system. They resulted in a strong public demand for new ideas which would resolve the disturbing situation these modern-psychiatrists had unleashed, and at the same time, a movement of resistance and negation whereby "a dynamic conservative system, once threatened, will attempt to protect itself against ideas which cannot be brought to the public without disruptive consequences'' (Schon, 1971, p. 129).

The *anciens* were holding on tight. In an article entitled "Concerning an Unjustified Campaign Against our Psychiatric Hospitals," Dr. Paul Dumas (1961), director of *L'Union Médicale*, professed with slicing verve that there existed no emergency in Québec psychiatry and that the real scandal existed only in the minds of these "young Machiavellian doctors" who, "instead of washing dirty clothes in public with their juvenile impulsiveness, their uncompromising and aggressive attitudes, should have discussed their problems with their seniors in small committees, within their families, in the smoking rooms of hospital canteens . . . . These young doctors," he adds, "have departed from a fundamental principle of medical deontology; that is, the duty of respect, justice and charity that all doctors must observe towards colleagues" (Dumas, 1961, p. 1396).

More negation led to more diffusion of competing ideas, to greater public awareness and pressure for solutions. Government response was quick. Within a few weeks all daily newspapers carried the front page headline: "Québec Decides: Inquiry on Psychiatric Institutions" (*Le Devoir*, September 9, 1961). A team of three "modern" psychiatrists had been appointed to investigate the situation. A few months later, the Bédard, Lazure, and Roberts' Commission handed in its report and recommendations, pressing for radical change: "half measures are no longer sufficient" (Bédard, Lazure, & Roberts, 1962, p. 142). They severely questioned the ability of nuns to cure and return patients to society when their main dedication was to a life of chastity, poverty, and obedience, away from the outside world, and when their main therapeutic tools or technologies of intervention were "prayer, religious sacraments, the use of understanding, good words, promises of rewards, constraints, firmness, menaces, punishments and sanctions" (Bédard, Lazure, & Roberts, 1962, p. 21). "Mental illness" was proclaimed "an illness like any other" to be managed, cared for, and cured by doctors; the technological revolution of the 1950s in the area of psychoparmacology and psychotherapy as well as what was called the Freudian enlightenment provided legitimacy for the psychiatrists' claim of ownership over the field of medical expertise.

The Bédard Report (Bédard, Lazure, & Roberts, 1961) was convincing: "These men of science surely deserve the trust of the public and the authorities for their professional qualifications and the services they have rendered," declared Jean Marchand to *La Presse* (May 15, 1962).

THE QUIET REVOLUTION
AND THE PSYCHIATRIC REVOLUTION

The psychiatric revolution must also be understood as part of a more global insurgence on the part of proponents of catching-up in Québec society as a whole. The death in 1959 of Québec's champion of conservatism, Premier Maurice Duplessis, and the subsequent accession of the Liberal "team of thunder" with their slogan, "things must change," had opened the way. The eagerness of the new Liberal Government became a key source of power for the psychiatric insurgents at all stages of the battle: The Liberals chose three modern psychiatrists to conduct the inquiry and almost immediately implemented the Bédard Report's first recommendation, creating a Psychiatric Services Directorate (P.S.D.) within the ministry of health on June 2, 1962, and giving it full administrative and financial power to implement the commission's recommendations. In creating the P.S.D., which was to be headed by Bédard himself, the Québec Government officially crystallized the psychiatrists' position of dominance over the delivery of psychiatric services. Furthermore, in delegating the management of the system to these "experts" hired by the Government and working within the ministry of health, the Lesage team also served its own overall political plan of greater state involvement in the delivery of human services. The interests of psychiatrists and government overlapped and the modernists had officially received the Government's benediction to proceed—along with a $5 million dollar increase in the relevant budget. After this, adds Schon (1971), "the ideas become an integral part of the conceptual dimension of the social system and appear, in retrospect, obvious" (p. 128).

THE GOLDEN AGE
AND ITS UNEXPECTED CONSEQUENCES

Propelled by the pioneering spirit of the modernists under the leadership of the new Psychiatric Services Directorate, Québec psychiatry soon became an object of praise: "The rapid expansion of Québec psychiatry is cited as an example" announced *Le Droit* (January 11, 1966); "Québec is increasingly leading in psychiatry and scores points on the international scene" announced *La Presse* (June 23, 1967). In 1970, the Castonguay Report on Health and Social Welfare wrote: "In truly psychiatric institutions, the recent period has witnessed accelerated progress . . . the psychiatric services without doubt constitute one of the most dynamic directorates within the Department of Health" (1971, 6 (Tome I), p. 99).

Change, however, is not without its "unintended and unanticipated consequences" (Merton, 1936). As a group in dominance proceeds (with more or less resistance) to transform the discredited system, it tones down by the same process the crisis situation which has brought it to power. Ironically, some of the seeds of the psychiatric system's later destruction also constituted an inherent and essential part of its creation. The migration into the system of other types of "experts" (psychologists, social workers, work therapists, and others) who brought their own baggage of theory, technologies of intervention, and claims to a territory of expertise, was indeed a necessary condition for the successful transformation of the relatively closed asylum system into a truly open, diversified, and effective psychiatric system.

With this rapid broadening of the system's structural, technological, and conceptual boundaries, mental *illness* was becoming too narrow a concept; a demedicalized all-encompassing mental *health* concept was acquiring greater currency. "Community psychiatry" soon became "community mental health." Known as inmates during the asylum phase and patients during the early years of the psychiatric phase, the consumers of mental health services were rapidly being referred to as clients. The organized simplicity of the asylum system had given way to unorganized complexity.

This process, which seriously put in question the dominance of psychiatrists over a system where no one group could claim exclusive mastery, simultaneously increased the demand for "decomplexification," rationalization, and coordination. The way was paved for a new type of expert who offered the "technological skills" of social planning and system management. Their invasion of the entire health and welfare system signified for Québec psychiatry a new period of second order change and the beginnings of the Québec psychiatric crisis.

NEW TECHNOLOGY, NEW THEORY, NEW BIDS FOR POWER

Coming from a variety of backgrounds in management skills, public relations, social, political, and economic sciences; professing a common theory of rationalization, quasi industrial effectiveness, and democratic participation; promoting the belief in greater state responsibility and involvement in human services; they rapidly found their way as upper-level civil servants, advisors to the government, consultants, and members of commissions of inquiry, such as the Commission of Inquiry on Health and Social Welfare headed in 1966 by a highly respected actuary, Claude Castonguay. By the end of the 1960s the Québec government had become one of the largest employers of this new brand of experts. The April, 1970, election which brought the Bourassa government to power constituted a real invasion of the upper-level government positions by this technocratic elite, a decisive victory over the "traditional" liberal professions. This was particularly true for Claude Castonguay who was immediately handed the health, family, and welfare portfolios.

It was seen earlier that one of the tactics of groups seeking dominance for their ideas is to pinpoint and highlight the many inadequacies and contradictions of the existing realities, thereby provoking a popular demand for a new model of action. In its July, 1967, report on health insurance, the Castonguay Commission had observed the interdependence of the different sectors of the health field and noted the flagrant "lack of co-ordination and balance among these various sectors" (Castonguay-Nepveu, 1967, *1*, p. 114). In its volume on health, in 1970, the commission concluded even more forcibly that "the shortcomings of Québec's health system are due to the absence of a true system of care distribution" (Castonguay-Nepveu, 1970, *4* (Tome I), p. 88). It further emphasized the full responsibility of the government as a representative of the collectivity:

> . . . the state must intervene progressively in the field of public health and health insurance. The maintenance of a people's health more and more is recognized as a collective responsibility. This is not surprising since it must be admitted that without various vigorous state actions the right to health would remain a purely theoretical notion, without any real content (Castonguay-Nepveu, *4* (Tome I), p. 30).

The shift in emphasis from illness to health, from individual care to public health care, from health as a privilege to health as a right, from illness as the care-giver's responsibility toward his or her patients to health as the responsibility of the government toward the collectivity, constituted the underlying premise of the theory. Calling for vigorous state involvement as the singular prerequisite to the attainment of these new goals was another way for the technocratic elite to acquire policy-making dominance.

From critic of the system and "political warrior," (Curran & Demone, 1974, p. 338), Castonguay had become the official manager, legislator, and implementor of his own reform. The master word was *integration*. The master piece was Bill 65 which completely rearticulated the system for the management and delivery of health and social services into clearly defined, identifiable, and therefore controllable units referred to as the *Centre Local de Services Communautaires* (CLSC); the *Centre Hospitalier* (CH), the *Centre d'Accueil;* (CA); the *Centre de Services Sociaux* (CSS); and a regional administrative unit, the *Centre Régional de Santé et de Services Sociaux* (CRSS). Exchanges of service between service centres and lines of accountability were to be clearly contracted, and therefore, it was hoped, predictable—all in the name of greater rationalization. In other words Bill 65 was an attempt on the part of a new government to select, organize, focus, and filter the forces in the field of health and welfare intervention—now to be referred to as the field of *social affairs*. And, since mental illness was an illness like any other, there was no room in this integrated field for a psychiatric care delivery system as a distinct entity.

THE QUEBEC PSYCHIATRIC CRISIS: ITS MANIFESTATIONS

A week after the adoption of Bill 65, Dr. Dominique Bédard, by now described as "a man of action strangled, jugulated, who has lost faith in the government" (*La Presse*, January 30, 1970), resigned his position as director of the P.S.D. His resignation created a "real commotion in the world of Québec psychiatry" (*La Presse*, January 21, 1971). Crisis, writes Schon (1971), comes about naturally as the situations around which a now taken for granted reality was originally created, shift out from under them. Indeed, the rules of the game had suddenly changed. Psychiatrists had lost their exclusive, personal link with the government and their official grip on the system. Flight appears to be one dynamic conservative response of groups or individuals to the invasion of their domains. The new health insurance plan provided psychiatrists with the "way out." The media became the witness of a "massive exodus" of psychiatrists from rural areas to the city, from institutions to private practices, from the province altogether: "psychiatric hospitals soon to be without psychiatrists" (*La Presse*, March 17, 1971); "psychiatrists abandon large hospitals and psychiatric units" (*La Presse*, May 26, 1971); "alarming situation" (*La Presse*, May 21, 1971); "catastrophic" (*La Presse*, September 9, 1971). "Psychiatry is drowned," declared Dr. Naiman representing the Québec Psychiatric Association (*Journal des débats*, 1971, p. B-5347). In their dynamic conservative fight to remain the same, psychiatrists were demanding "a psychiatric presence" within the government. But the rules had changed; no longer were psychiatrists—and physicians at that—automatically recognized as the legitimate managers of their services. They saw themselves pushed into the position of "supplier." Tactics and cries for help which proved so successful in the early 1960s were ineffective. Those who then had proclaimed that "mental illness is an illness like any other" changed their discourse. They were now arguing, "the same way Québec is not a province like the others within Confederation, psychiatry is not a discipline like the others within medical disciplines"—to use Dr. Camille Laurin's own words (*Journal des débats*, 1971, p.B-5350) to the National Assembly shortly after Bill 65 was tabled. To no avail, integration had been legislated. But integration, for the psychiatric reformers of the '60s, was synonymous with dissolution, disintegration, and loss of control over the system's destiny.

THE CASTONGUAY REFORM: INTEGRATION OR DISINTEGRATION?

In the name of progress and managerial logic, inspired by the language of cybernetics and systems thinking, a politically powerful group of social engineers had concocted and legislated a "reform" which, as sociologist Marc Renaud (1984) aptly puts it: "extended their power over the organization of health and welfare services by placing suppliers—professionals, institutions and others—under the control of administrative councils, regional councils and above all, governmental bureaucracies" (p. 175). For Québec's psychiatrists, the reform as they experienced it in the following years was synonymous with neither progress nor logic. They saw the network of psychiatric services becoming an officially undifferentiated and largely devalued part of an ill-fitted patchwork which pulled together an old health and welfare system struggling for survival and a new one experiencing a very difficult and laborious birth. Their analyses of the situation after two, four, and six years of imposed integration, consistently speak of a *"période creuse"* or a *"retour arrière,"* of a *"cul de sac,"* *"stagnation,"* *"rétrogradation,"* *"effondrement,"* *"désorganization,"* *"désaffectation,"* *"déclin,"* *"malaise profond,"* and even a *"grande noirceur"*—all epithets which need no translation. More specifically, they denounce the pervasiveness of segregationist attitudes toward mental patients, psychiatrists, and psychiatry which occurs in spite of so-called integration; they condemn the abusive recourse to the "asylums" as garbage pails for those whom nobody wants—all this despite the general move toward deinstitutionalization started by the Bédard reform. They decry the absence of alternative services, the lack of continuity of care and adequate support in the community, and the flagrant disinterest for mental health exhibited by the Local Community Service Centers—the invention of Bill 65 whose responsibility was to provide front line, multidisciplinary health and social services to local populations. They speak of hospitals without psychiatrists, of multidisciplinary teams torn by quarrels over leadership, of hospital emergency wards breaking at the seams and unprepared for psychiatric urgencies; of general hospitals who refuse psychiatric patients; of patients taken by ambulance from hospital to hospital like ping pong balls because nobody wants them. Their lists of problems include as well the persistence of unserviced regions, of insufficient resources, of funds diverted from psychiatry . . . .

They attribute these gaps in the system to the total absence of psychiatric leadership within the ministry and to the lack of any specific and coherent governmental policy in the field of psychiatry and mental health.

NOVEMBER 16, 1976: A PSYCHIATRIC PRESENCE AT THE GOVERNMENT

November 16, 1976, came to the rescue, or so it seemed. The election of the Parti Québécois (P.Q.) government and the appointment of Dr. Denis Lazure, one of the principal authors of the Bédard Report (Bédard, Lazure, & Roberts, 1962), to the position of minister of social affairs brought an unexpected psychiatric presence to the government. Yet, the Bédard years were definitely *dépassées*. The new psychiatrist minister, or was it minister psychiatrist, who called himself "the psychiatric conscience within the ministry," quickly introduced new regional psychiatric structures called the *commissions administratives psychiatriques* and a central psychiatric committee whose official purpose as regional and central advisory bodies was to ensure at all levels the "coordination of a network of psychiatric services integrated to the more global health and welfare system" (Lazure, 1972, p. 2). Integration was thus accepted, but a new language was proposed by the psychiatric committee: the move toward a *système psychiatrique parallel-intégré*—for a combination of the Bédard reform and the Castonguay reform, the old and the new—with little regard for the complex gymnastics such contradictory epithets as parallel and integrated would impose on the human mind.

The committee's first document entitled (Comité de la psychiatrie du Québec, 1979): *Situation de la Psychiatrie au Québec: Lacunes et*

Perspectives D'organisation, was seen by "other professionals" in the field as an attempt on the part of psychiatrists to defend their corporate interests by favouring a return to the medical conceptions of mental health. The situation was explosive. What the minister had created were more administrative structures in psychiatry; what these "other professionals" wanted were structures in mental health. Old quarrels over definitions and unresolved issues over leadership were again brought to the forefront: Is psychiatry a specialized branch of mental health or is it mental health which comes under the realm of expertise and thus the leadership of the psychiatrists?

"As if there were only psychiatrists" was the angry response of the Unionized Professionals of Social Affairs—psychologists, social workers, nurses, and work therapists no longer content with being referred to as "other professionals." It was also the response of organized groups of patients—now referred to as the "psychiatrized."

The message sent to the ministry was clear: a return to the social democratic principles of the Castonguay-Nepveu Report (1967-1972); an end to the monopolistic tendencies of the psychiatrists; an end to "medical tutelage" and hospital centred services. The Québec Psychological Association further announced that health professionals were autonomous and need not obey the directives of psychiatrists in their own evaluation of the appropriateness of an intervention. It advocated the patients' right to consult professionals of their choice without the preliminary recourse to psychiatrists as required by the health insurance plan. The plan, it was felt, contradicted the very notion of the demedicalization of the problems of living promoted in the Castonguay reform. Patients, they said, did not need the stigma associated with a psychiatric diagnosis. And what to do when there are no psychiatrists in a clinic or region?

This apparent lack of psychiatrists became a key issue. For the Association of Psychiatrists, not enough are trained, the Québec Government must remove its quotas on medical schools. For others it is because most of the province's 750-plus psychiatrists are too comfortable in private practices and are established according to their own "*caprice*" (FPSCQ-CSN 1981) and not according to "need." Coercion is presented as a possibility while confrontations multiply; strikes and resignations break any appearance of harmony within multidisciplinary teams, clinics, and psychiatric units in hospitals. Discussions are long and time consuming—hours, days, months pass. Clinics who lose their psychiatrists are forced to close, others boldly announce they have become "psychological clinics" or "clinics of mental health." Technocrats in the government find the experience illegal but "interesting." The psychiatrist-tourist who simply comes in at regular intervals to sign forms and collect dues is no longer an acceptable part of the routine.

Meanwhile, the psychiatrized, refusing the role of victim-who-cries-for-help, have their own demands: a review of legislation for the protection of their rights: the right to refuse treatment, the right to their illness and the right to health; the right to be considered full fledged citizens; the right to their opinions and to their differences; the right to proper support structures and "alternatives" to "the abuses and barbaric practices" of psychiatry (*La Presse*, September 15, 1980); the right to minimum salary in occupational therapy; to see their files and to seek justice in front of the courts; to have a say in their daily schedules in the hospitals; to the suppression of all censure; to their own sexuality, contraception, abortion, pregnancy (Autopsy, September, 1980). They demand a government inquiry into the injustices done each day to psychiatrized citizens.

Amidst the flow of disagreements, interprofessional conflicts and shows of dissatisfaction, the main stakeholders involved as administrators, service givers, or recipients at least agree on the need for a specific, unified, cohesive mental health policy; a master plan which would reconcile the bio-psycho-social differences, prevent further disintegration of the system, rationalize and plan the already routinized program of deinstitutionalization from which no strategic retreat seems possible, and guarantee good quality services to the system's beneficiaries.

What everyone demands is a return to the original principles of communalism and to the social democratic spirit of the reform conceived 13 years earlier. What they refuse is a perpetuation of the way these principles have been applied. The call is for a reform of the reform. Most representative of this frame of mind is the *Mémoire Beausoleil-Godin* (Beausoleil & Godin, 1983) presented in 1983 to the Honourable Pierre-Marc Johnson, minister of social affairs. Written by a former director of one of Québec's two largest psychiatric hospitals, Léo-Paul Beausoleil, and by Michel Godin, a consultant on the Castonguay commission who for some time had also acted as an upper-level civil servant within the ministry of social affairs, the document provocatively articulated feelings surrounding the issue and brought new ingredients into the discussion. Their judgement is severe: "The last fifteen years have adequately shown that we are virtually at the same point nowadays as we were then" (Beausoleil & Godin, 1983, p. 141).

The proposed solution, which they acknowledge will require "a lot of courage," was to deprofessionalize the field, vulgarize expertise, and call upon natural helpers. They urge the state to recognize an individual's right to control his or her illness and problems of *mal-vie*. They call on professionals to share their knowledge with the general public "so that the population, individuals, community resources, alternatives or others can acquire the means to solve their own problems (. . .) in their own environment" (Beausoleil & Godin, 1983, p. 14). Hospitalization is not excluded from their vision of things, yet they emphasize that the curative model should not prevail over the preventative, nor should professional expertise prevail over individual and collective potential; the institution must not prevail over the natural living milieu; mental illness should not prevail over mental health. The existing situation, they conclude, "prevents all social partners from meeting the challenges they are faced with" (p. 122).

THE PROMISE:
A SEPARATE, DISTINCT MENTAL HEALTH POLICY

Every psycho-political drama moves toward a certain resolution which will then be the cause of new frictions, anxieties, and denunciation. This is the natural, dialectical reality of the historical process. The solution to the problems which divided the psychiatric-mental health services, the synthesis which was requested from the Québec government, became the object of a promise made in the spring of 1983 by Pierre-Marc Johnson, then minister of social affairs. This was after 13 years of so-called integration. It is in this promise of a distinct, unified, comprehensive, coherent, and rational mental health policy that all put their faith, and which reoriented their fighting energies toward the drawing board. For true to the social democratic idea, the policy was to be of the people, for the people, and by the people. Since there were so many stakeholders and interests involved, the official standpoint became: in mental health, everyone should and can contribute. From then on, the process of intellectual cogitation was on.

A preliminary reading of documents and testimonies drawn since then shows consistent agreement on some basic imperatives: greater accessibility, continuity, availability, deinstitutionalization, normalization, social reinsertion, diversification, complementarity, effectiveness, quality, investment in the community . . . . To these highly valued principles carried over from the 1960s are associated such concrete necessities as more crisis intervention units, aftercare programs, residential facilities, group homes, boarding homes and lodging houses, foster families, rehabilitation programs, sheltered workshops, work programs, self-help groups, and citizen advocacy programs. The consensus seems universal: the institutional model is *"bel et bien dépassé."*

The vision of things promoted by the Beausoleil and Godin report (1983) and which the Québec media soon called "a trifle utopian" (*Le Soleil*, March 19, 1983), is rearticulated, refined, and meshed with a bio-psycho-social conception of the individual, a conception which accounts for the multiplicity of social partners and stakeholders and is converted into what is now called an ecological model.

Presented as more enlightened than a model giving sole responsibility for so-called illnesses to professionals, and as more global than one focusing on a system's structure, integration, and management as a way to deal with a populations' health and welfare needs, it concerns society as a whole, and this is equated with justice and progress.

The ecological language soon found favourable ears within the ministry of social affairs (M.A.S.). This model, says the *Direction Générale de la Santé* (D.G.S.), is based on human values, the values of a society, the most fundamental of which is:

> . . . what I can do for the welfare of . . . my child, my parents . . . my friends, my neighbours . . . my fellow citizens (Ministère des affaires sociales (M.A.S., D.G.S., 1985, p. 3).

MENTAL HEALTH OR SOCIAL HEALTH?

In the very first pages of its consultation paper on the elements of a mental health policy, entitled *L'Intervention en Santé Mentale: Du Modèle Institutionel Vers le Modèle Ecologique*, the D.G.S. presents mental health as an ecological concept defined as "coping." It is no longer "the fulfillment of harmonious physical and mental self growth" as the Castonguay-Nepveu Report (1970, p. 13) liked to call it. It is now "the result of a dynamic process of adaptation of the individual (as a bio-psycho-social entity) to his environment or milieu, in a process of growth and self-actualization" (M.A.S., D.G.S., 1985, p. 4).

Objectif: Santé, a 1984 report of the *Conseil des Affaires Sociales et de la Famille* explains that the ecological approach, as inspired from Lalonde's *New Perspective on Health* (1974), is based on the firm conviction that a natural and instinctive autonomy, a power of regeneration, exists in all human beings. "Individual responsibility is inherent to human nature" (p. 22), says the 1984 report, a decade after its predecessor. The new version, however, attempts to cut short any accusation of "blaming the victim" as it elaborates what one might call a collectivized individualistic approach. *Objectif: Santé* goes so far as to call this unique blend of individualism and collectivism "*du Lalonde enrichi*"!

The role of the professional and of a mental health service system is thus, to provide support, to inspire, to inform, "to assist the person and his/her family in their strategy of adaptation to the milieu" and to adapt to their needs (M.A.S., D.G.S., 1985, p. 46). Specialists, according to the *Direction Générale de la Santé* within the MAS, cannot artificially create the social conditions conducive to the maintenance and reinstatement of mental health. "Each and every Québecer must contribute" (D.G.S., 1985, p. 4):

> Respect, dialogue and mutual help between Québecers are not only the best safeguards of one's mental health but the essential tools to counter suffering, solitude, the aches and the pains of living, and to help overcome the difficulties of life (1985, p. 4).

Information, public education, and awareness therefore become key words and high priorities for those who endorse this world view and speak of "taming the community" (Centre Régional de Santé et de Services Sociaux (CRSS)-Montérégie, 1985, p. 386), of breaking the wall of indifference and even rejection, of dispelling myths (Canadian Mental Health Association (CMHA), Québec, 1985, p. 462).

By 1985, the language of citizen advocates and self-help groups applied to all of society and had become the preferred language of policy-influencers within the ministry of health and social services. Under their pen, mutual help, love, and social solidarity risk becoming a government precept. Blaming the victim might then take on a more collective dimension and extend to blaming the quality of human relationships in an intolerant, rejecting society which denies its responsibility.

In 1970, mental health had been proclaimed both a right for everyone and a government responsibility—nearly a political promise. Now, mental health, equated with social health, is deemed the personal and collective responsibility of the entire Québec population. This is the discovery of the '80s, the new politically powerful theory taken as a self-evident truth.

THE ECOLOGICAL MODEL AND THE 1980s MINDSCAPE

At this point in time it is highly important to ask ourselves why the ecological model so rapidly won the apparent consensus of such a broad variety of stakeholders in the Québec psychiatric-mental health system, from the grassroot to the upper echelons of government bureaucracies. We speak of an *apparent consensus*, for we are dealing here at the level of grand and general principles. As noted above, the actual conversion of these principles into the particularities of a real and realistic mental health policy is another ball game.

Nevertheless, the seemingly irresistible attraction of policy influencers in Québec to the ecological language of the early 1980s is a very interesting phenomenon. It must be understood as part of the new global "mindscape" of the time concerning the role of the state, of individual, professional, and collective responsibility in policy making and social intervention.

Richard F. Elmore (1983) speaks of the fundamental exhaustion of resources, knowledge, and authority brought about by past social policy. The big mistake of the past has been to raise expectations beyond the realizable, based on a blind belief in government. Indeed "health and well-being for everyone" was effectively presented as a government promise in the early years of the Castonguay reform. Elmore clearly saw that up until now, intervention has been thought of as the deliberate, rational use of central authority to alter the structure of political, social, and economic relationships. The government-designed-and-imposed "integration" of the health and welfare service delivery systems in Québec grew out of this belief and essential optimism—to paraphrase Elmore (1983, p. 213)—in central government's ability to know what causes health and social problems, to translate that knowledge into binding prescriptions, and to use beneficent coercion to implement these prescriptions. It was also believed that as long as a case could be made for intervention—by an appeal to data or political argument—government would provide the resources necessary to make intervention work. Elmore adds that the story of social policy over the past 15 to 20 years has proven these assumptions wrong on all counts, or at least sufficiently problematical to make them an unreliable basis for policy.

It is now clear to all that: (a) the resources which society is willing to allocate to social objectives are severely limited—aspirations must therefore be adjusted to resources; (b) the accumulation of scientific knowledge is not reliably related to the solution of social problems and to effective social intervention; and (c) government often lacks the knowledge, influence, and coercive power to make policies binding on private choices. This is coupled with the fact that governments and public organizations are increasingly identified as problems and impediments rather than solutions. Elmore (1983) calls these, respectively, the allocation, knowledge, and authority problems.

Since aspirations must be limited to "resources," the logical strategy to solve the first of these problems is to change our understanding of what resources are: to such intangibles as mutual help, brotherly love, dialogue, and social support within one's own natural milieu; which cost governments very little and are ideally unlimited in supply. The ecological model as defined in Québec does an admirable job of prestidigitation. In changing one's vision of things, limited resources become potentially limitless. It is also very handy that the burden of proof rests not with the language and its propagators, not with governments, but with the Québec population which is deemed individually and collectively responsible for its own mental health.

The adoption of the ecological language with its emphasis on deprofessionalization and the belief that in mental health everyone should and can contribute is also part of an ongoing trend affecting the socio-political milieu of most of the western world. This particular trend conveys a new view of knowledge and its role in policy making and effective social intervention. This shift in conception is brilliantly summarized by Elmore:

> In less than ten years, the terminology used to describe the relation-
> ship of knowledge to policy shifted from technical and cybernetic to
> geological and meteorological . . . . The earlier metaphors were
> calculatedly man-made; the later were drawn from natural forces
> (1983, p. 221).

The wholesale popularity of the ecological model as the new metaphor in psychiatric-mental health intervention is thus another example of the increasingly privileged belief in the powers of natural forces in the natural milieu. In this particular field more than any other, claims of professional "skills" and scientific knowledge have fallen into disarray. They are met with skepticism, cynicism, and at times real hostility. Faith is put in ordinary knowledge and in Weber's *Verstehen* or *intuitive understanding*. Lindblom and Cohen (1979) define "ordinary knowledge, skill and craft" as "ways of knowing that rely less on abstraction and precision than on close proximity to experience and simple rules of the thumb" (pp. 12-13). Ordinary knowledge, continues Elmore, is a term that captures the "common sense, casual empiricism (and) thoughtful speculation" used by most people, including scientists to make most routine judgements and decisions" (Elmore, 1983, p. 222). Given this belief that everyone's knowledge is equally valid or invalid, the privileged approach for dealing with social problem solving is social interaction. In Québec this privileged approach is evidenced not only in the basic premises of the ecological model, but also in the way the mental health policy is being elaborated through *popular consultation* (Bibeau, 1986).

Implicit in the notion of social interaction is a division of labor in the production and utilization of knowledge. Social scientists, legislators, administrators street-level bureaucrats, and citizens, each with some interest in problem-solving (or avoiding), each with a way of knowing and valuing that is influenced by social position, use various kinds of interaction to sort out the consequences of what they know (Elmore, 1983, p. 222).

Forums, public debate, a sub-commission on social reinsertion, presentation of briefs and counter briefs, discussion documents or working documents, and reports on various aspects of service delivery are some of the ways this social interaction as a democratic process has and is taking place in Québec. The goal: the formulation of a democratically designed mental health policy. The fact that it was promised in 1983 for 1985 and that in 1986 it is awaiting the recommendation of yet another commission of inquiry into the health system, however, shows the complexity of this process. "Pulled loose from its scientific moorings, knowledge is a particularly elastic and elusive thing" (Elmore, 1983, p. 223). "Knowing what is right" in order to to what is right is still seen as crucial, but since no one knows all of that for sure, since there is no one source of ultimate wisdom, going through the process of dealing with those who are judged to be knowledgeable (or at least continuously concerned) becomes even more crucial (Heclo, 1978, p. 103). That everyone should and can contribute in the formulation of the policy and in the provision of support for those who cannot cope is not an easy maxim, indeed.

A third characteristic of today's mindscape which may explain today's definition of reality in the field of psychiatric-mental health intervention and policy formulations is the recognition that while there is a desire for a government-blessed policy, "government in general and public organizations in particular are increasingly identified as problems and impediments rather than solutions" (Elmore, 1983, p. 227). Government authority is under attack. "Authority," says Elmore, "means but the power to command and the knowledge and skill to decide wisely; on both counts, government is in trouble" (1983, p. 227). The ecological model which puts primary emphasis on the "I" and the "We," on public education, collective conscience, and responsibility, is a quasi-instinctive response to this skeptical and pessimistic outlook concerning government knowledge, role, and ability. The call for privatization of state-administered organizations is yet another, associated in the social analyst's mind with the prevailing conservative or neo-conservative mood of the times. Once more, Elmore presents a very apt description of the process:

Just as the dominant conception of the relationship between knowledge and policy has shifted from a model based on central control to one based on a diffuse exchange of ideas, so too has the dominant conception of government authority shifted from a model that locates solutions at the center to one that locates solutions in the private and voluntary acts of individuals (1983, p. 227).

A serious problem, however, is that policy making which occurs through social interaction and popular consultation, inevitably searches for frictionless solutions as a necessary requirement for viability and performance. Frictionless solutions, however, given the belligerent nature of systems change (as seen earlier), are hard to come by and may be closer to wishful thinking than to plausible reality. Politically powerful ideas which put their trust in voluntary acts of individuals make a rather perilous wager on human nature. While the ecological approach's basic tenets appear to be reasonable, rational, and just, it may actually be very unreasonable, irrational, and unjust to expect everyone to live by them. While there may be consensus on the general principles, to transform these highly desirable abstractions into a unified, coherent, effective, and rational mental health policy and then into direct experience is a totally different challenge. To appeal to community solidarity, mutual help, voluntary action, and interpersonal support as a complement to mental health services is not new, but to make it the foundation of a grandiose vision of a mentally healthy society may very well be little more than an exercise in rhetoric or technocratic idealism. Or perhaps it will show itself to have been just another phase.

CONCLUSION

The loss of innocence which characterizes today's mindscape concerning resource allocation, knowledge, and authority has been responded to in the field of psychiatric-mental health in Québec with the formulation of an ecological model as a new way of acting, thinking, feeling, and policy making which contains many noble and attractive ideas. But it also contains a new kind of innocence.

Whether the actual official policy will be drafted in this kind of language is impossible to say at this time. The future cannot be predicted with exact accuracy. But, from the minister's July, 1986, instructions to focus on the "core issues surrounding the prevention of the most important mental problems, the treatment, readaptation, and support to give the persons with these problems," we can anticipate Québec's legislators will see this ecological model in the abstract as a beautiful source of inspiration, a highly admirable ethos indeed, ultimately destined to produce a moral impression on all stakeholders in the field, including the general population. In the concrete, however, they will see such a language can too easily camouflage the most urgent priorities: that of the "crazies" who we institutionalized as "inmates" for more than a century, who we "hospitalized" in the early '60s as "psychiatric patients," and "dehospitalized" soon afterward as deinstitutionalized "citizens" and who find themselves today nameless—for we refuse to call them "ill"—pseudo-integrated undesired undesirables of our society and its presumed-to-be normalizing communities.

In this context, where deinstitutionalization has shown itself to be a still unsubstantiated hypothesis which we had mistakenly taken for a self-evident, self-workable truth, the ecological model comes as a breath of fresh air. The challenge is to resist the temptation first identified by sociologist Ralph Dahrendorf (1959), whereby when a problem cannot be solved, we change the orientation, modify the content, and create new, greater, more noble objectives which absorb and minimize the initial objective. In order to avoid confronting the reality of dashed hopes, we change the conceptual framework, create hopes that are more fascinating, more attractive, but also more vague and abstract. We then seek universal approbation of these new hopes, which appear infinitely desirable and so obviously logical (Boudreau, 1986, p. 18).

The process of intellectual cogitation as a popular and generalized exercise toward the formulation of a unique, full-fledged mental health policy is building upon and attempting to correct the mistakes of a very fascinating and turbulent past. Seeking a consensual model upon which to drop anchor, it has already produced highly stimulating and challenging ideas—ideas which as we have seen are closely bound to the overall mindscape of the times. As analysts of this fascinating process, we can now only wait and see where it will lead us, in 1987, 1988, or perhaps 1990?

We must emphasize, however, that the process we have examined here is not unique to the Province of Québec. It has Québec's own flavour and tempo, but it is highly representative of the process whereby social problems are identified, solutions formulated (Seidman & Rappaport, 1986), and action undertaken—and this many times over—all in the name of progress and improved social intervention.

The Québec experience provides us with a vivid example of the drama of "psychopolitics" (Greenblatt, 1978), displaying the warlike, conflict-ridden process involved in creating and implementing second-order change. The big losers in the process, however, are too often those in whose name the various stakeholders have fought, and it is not yet clear that the way out is indeed to channel all fighting energies toward the formulation of a true-to-form, democratically-arrived-at, unique, and coherent mental health policy. With everyone's cooperation the strategy might prove fruitful, but expectations are very high and factionless solutions are in very short supply.

REFERENCES

Apollon, W. (1986). Pour une politique en santé mentale. *Santé Mentale au Québec, 11* (1), 75-104.

Autopsy. Association Québécoise des psychiatrisé(ées) et des sympathisant(es). (1980, September 10). Conférence de presse lors de sa création.

Beausoleil, L.P., & Godin, M. (1983, March). *Réflexion critique et prospective sur la santé mentale au Québec.* Brief presented to the Honourable Minister Pierre-Marc Johnson.

Bédard, D., Lazure, D., & Roberts, C. (1962). *Rapport de la Commission d'étude des hôpitaux psychiatriques.* Québec: Gouvernement du Québec.

Beers, C. (1948). *A mind that found itself.* Garden City, NY: Doubleday.

Bibeau, G. (1986). Le facteur humain en politique: Applications au domaine de la santé mentale. *Santé Mentale au Québec, 11* (1), 19-42.

Boudreau, F. (1984) De l'Asile à la santé mentale, Les soins psychiatriques: histoire et institutions, Montréal, Editions Saint-Martin, 274 p.

Boudreau, F. (1985). L'Eglise et la santé mentale: Vers un nouvel engagement? *Sociologie et Société, 17* (1), 93-109.

Boudreau, F. (1986) "De l'Asile à la santé mentale: le malade est-il mieux?", *Santé mentale au Canada, 34,* (1), 16-19

Canadian Mental Health Association, Québec Division. (1985, August 9). Brief presented to the Sous-commission des Affaires sociales, Assemblée Nationale, 5ᵉ session, 32ᵉ législature. *Journal des Débats,* S-CAS: 462.

Castonguay-Nepveu Report. (1967-72). *Report of the Commission of Inquiry on Health and Social Welfare* (Vol. IV, Tome II (the Health Plan, Part II)). Québec: Gouvernement du Québec.

Centre Régional de Santé et de Services Sociaux-Montérégie. (1985, August 9). Brief presented to the Sous-commission des Affaires sociales, Assemblée Nationale, 5ᵉ session, 32ᵉ législature. *Journal des Débats,* S-CAS: 386.

Comité de la psychiatrie du Québec. (1979, February). *Lacunes et perspectives d'avenir.* Ministère des Affaires Sociales.

Conseil des Affaires Sociales et de la Famille. (1984, August). *Objectif: Santé, rapport du comité d'étude sur la promotion de la santé.* Direction générale des publications gouvernementales.

Curran, W.J., & Demone, H.W. (1974). Implementing mental health planning recommendations into statutes: The legislative process in Massachusetts. In

W.H. Demone & D. Harsbarger (Eds.), *A handbook of human service organizations* (pp. 338-357). New York: Behavioral Publication.

Dahrendorf, R. (1959). *Class and class conflict in industrial society.* Stanford, CA: Stanford University Press.

Dumas, P. (1961, December). A propos d'une campagne injustifiée contre nos hopitaux psychiatriques. *L'Union Médicale,* 90, 396-397.

Elmore, R.F. (1983). Social policymaking as strategic intervention. In E. Seidman (Ed.), *Handbook of social intervention* (pp. 212-237). Beverly Hills: Sage.

Greenblatt, M. (1978). *Psychopolitics.* New York: Greene & Stration.

Heclo, H. (1978). Issue networks and the executive establishment. In A. King (Ed.), *The new political system.* Washington, DC: American Enterprise Institute.

Jacob & Dumais Inc. (1984). *Enquête du conseil d'administration de Robert Giffard sur l'institution.* Québec.

Lalonde, M. (1974). *A new perspective on the health of Canadians.* Ottawa: Information Canada.

Lamontagne, Y. (1985). *L'ampleur des maladies mentales au Québec.* Québec: Québec Science.

Lazure, D. (1977). La distribution des services psychiatriques au Québec. Allocation prononcée lors du colloque régional sur la santé mentale organizé par le CRSSS de la Côte Nord, Baie Comeau, le 18 mars 1977 (texte inédit).

Lindblom, C., & Cohen, D. (1979). *Usable knowledge: Social science and social problem solving.* New Haven, CT: Yale University Press.

Long, M. (1962). *Power and administration in the polity.* Chicago: Rand McNally & Co.

Marshall, J. (1982). *Madness—an indictment of the mental health care system in Ontario.* Based on the public inquiry commissioned by the Ontario Public Service Employees' Union, Toronto, Ontario.

Merton, R. (1936). The unanticipated consequences of purposive social action. *American Sociological Review, 1,* 894-904.

Ministère des Affaires Sociales, Direction générale de la santé (D.G.S.). (1985, January). *L'intervention en santé mentale: Du modèle institutionnel vers le modèle écologique.* Document de consultation sur les éléments d'une politique de santé mentale, Québec.

Pagé, J.C. (1961). *Les fous crient au secours, témoignage d'un ex-patient de St-Jean-de-Dieu.* Montréal: Les Editions du Jour.

Plante, M. (1984). Position du ministère des affaires sociales du Québec face aux alternatives en santé mentale. In *Les alternatives en santé mentale* (pp. 15-25). Collection NOEUD dirigée pas le GIFRIC. Montréal: Québec/Amérique.

Renaud, M. (1984). Québec: The adventures of a narcissistic state. In J. de Kervasdoné, J.R. Kimberly, & V.G. Rodwin (Eds.), *The end of an illusion: The future of health policy in Western industrialized nations.* Berkeley: University of California Press.

Roberts, C. (1985, May). Conference given to the AHQ (Association des

Hôpitaux du Québec. *Artère, 3* (4). A summary of papers delivered at the colloquium "De l'Espoir à la Réalité, March 14-15, 1985.

Schon, D. (1971). *Beyond the stable state.* New York: W.W. Norton & Co.

Seidman, E. (Ed.). (1983). *Handbook of social intervention.* Beverly Hills: Sage.

Selznick, P. (1957). *Leadership in administration.* Evanston, IL: Row Peterson.

Watzlawick, P., Weakland, J., & Fisch, R. (1974). *Change: Principles of problem formulation and problem resolution.* New York: W.W. Norton.

Part IV
COMMUNITY ECONOMIC DEVELOPMENT APPROACHES TO SOCIAL INTERVENTION

Michael Swack
and
Donald Mason

11
COMMUNITY ECONOMIC DEVELOPMENT AS A STRATEGY FOR SOCIAL INTERVENTION

INTRODUCTION

In this chapter we will introduce the concept of community economic development as a stategy for social intervention in poor communities. We will show how community economic development as a social intervention strategy differs from both traditional social welfare policies and traditional economic development policies. We believe that the strategy of community economic development is a much more effective long-term approach to addressing economic inequality in communities than either the traditional social welfare or economic development approaches.

Community economic development offers an effective and unique strategy for dealing with the problems of poor people, powerless people, and underdeveloped communities. As an intervention strategy in an underdeveloped community it does not seek to make the existing conditions in the community more bearable. Instead, community economic development seeks to change the structure of the community and build permanent institutions within a community. As a result, the community begins to play a more active role vis-à-vis the institutions outside the community, and the residents of the community become more active in the control of the community's resources.

Because community economic development seeks to change the

basic relationship between a community and the institutions that impact on the community, it is a strategy for social intervention markedly different from the traditional social welfare policies and economic development policies pursued by government.

The starting premise for community economic development is that communities that are poor and underdeveloped remain in that condition because they lack control over their own resources. What this premise implies and the implications of it will be more fully developed in this chapter.

THE COMMUNITY ECONOMIC DEVELOPMENT APPROACH

Introduction

Community economic development is premised upon an understanding of community similar to that of Sarason (1974) in that it seeks to create a network of relationships upon which members of a community can depend, as well as develop a real sense of participation in and control over issues involving the allocation of resources. It is a bottom-up approach to social change (Goldenberg, 1978) that relies upon the actions and skills of a community in its implementation.

Community economic development emphasizes and utilizes models of development which address issues of ownership and control of community resources. In addressing these issues, one quickly discovers that the traditional institutions which provide human and financial capital for development are inadequate to meet the needs of communities pursuing community economic development. For this reason, new approaches to capital formation, land ownership, and education become integral parts of the overall strategy.

As more and more communities undertake this strategy, financial institutions, educational institutions, and government will be forced to re-think their approach to development and provide programs and assistance to accommodate the demands of these communities. Thus, community economic development will have a long-range effect upon many of our existing social systems.

The CED Approach to Land and Housing

The community economic development approach to land and housing recognizes that housing stock is the largest single resource in many communities. As a major resource, how it is owned and who makes the decisions concerning its present and future use is of major importance to the long-range development of the community. A community's control or lack of control over this resource has a profound effect on its life as a distinct community.

The availability of housing and the condition of housing stock has always been a concern of urban planners. Traditionally, planners have approached the question of community revitalization by focusing on the elimination of slums (Jacobs, 1962; Hartman, 1975). This model of economic development has assumed that slums can only be revitalized by destroying them and relocating the community into newly planned housing units (Jacobs, 1962; 1984). Policy makers believed the problems with slums was solely the poor housing they contained. Remove the housing, they reasoned, and slums would no longer exist.

Jane Jacobs (1984) makes the point that those economic development planners who advocate this approach do not see the many complex factors that make up a community. Instead, they assume that deteriorated housing causes a community to become a slum. Jacobs argues that the factors which make a community economically vital are directly linked to the neighbourhood's internal economic vitality. In fact, it is her position that a community has already become a slum long before the housing stock begins to deteriorate. The development of new housing alone will not revitalize a community.

As Matthews (1983) states, "In contrast to the planners' criteria of economic viability, the residents of . . . communities used criteria of social vitality in judging their quality of life" (p. 8:149). The health of a community is much more complex than the outward appearance of the housing stock.

Nevertheless, urban planners for generations have been convinced that the elimination of slums alone would revitalize a community. This goal, they believed, can be accomplished by the destruction of the existing housing and the construction of new planned communities. The end result of this model is the construction of low-income housing projects such as Columbia Point in Boston, Massachusetts.

Columbia Point is a massive and monolithic low-income housing project built on an isolated point of land jutting out into the bay. It is separated from all other communities by a major interstate highway, as well as the bay. Many low-income residents who had been living in communities throughout the Boston area were moved to Columbia Point after the destruction of their communities by the construction of a highway system and other urban renewal projects.

Columbia Point quickly became a community of despair. Because of its massive size, its highrise housing, and its isolation, it became a community ruled and terrorized by gangs. The housing quickly deteriorated and those low-income families that could escape did so as soon as possible. Now, most of the housing is uninhabited, few residents remain, and it is a haven for drug addicts and drug dealers. There was a point during Columbia Point's history when the police were too afraid to even enter the complex to respond to calls for help. Now, Columbia Point stands as a decaying monument to a failed economic development approach for providing housing for poor people. Unfortunately, this model of economic development continues to be the dominant economic model used by policy makers at all levels of government.

This model assumes that forces from outside can somehow impose the creation of a "community" upon residents. It does not recognize that housing is a major community resource and if it is not constructively used by a community for its benefit, it can drain that community of its capital and its people.

The destruction of a community's housing stock by government policy makers is not the only threat that a community faces. The external forces of the market place can also result in the displacement of entire communities which is just as devastating to residents as is "slum clearance."

The major characteristic of the housing stock in an underdeveloped community is that it is generally owned not by the residents of the community, but by absentee landlords. This creates a situation wherein those from the community living in the housing have no voice in its use and development. Instead, they are tenants who do not exercise any control over a major community resource.

Since the owners of the property do not live in the community and therefore have no real interest in the community's affairs, decisions concerning the development of the housing stock occur without the community's interest being considered. Often the owners of the property make decisions concerning its use due to the pressures of the market place. Changing demographics around a particular community can begin to effect the value of property in that community. As property becomes more valuable, the owners of that property desire to capitalize on that increased value.

One of the most common effects of this situation can be seen in those communities that have experienced gentrification. Gentrification of a community's housing stock takes place when the owners of the property begin to sell or lease the property at prices too high for the residents of the community to afford. As a result of the higher prices, the existing residents are forced to move out and find more affordable housing. The property is then rented or sold to more affluent residents who have moved into the community from elsewhere. Over time the residents of poor communities can no longer afford to live in their community, are forced out, and generally move into another underdeveloped community. As the process of gentrification occurs in one poor community after another, the residents of those communities are pushed further and further away from those areas that are undergoing economic revitalization. Eventually, they end up in government created "communities" such as Columbia Point.

There are many reasons why the gentrification of a community's housing stock takes place. Speculation in land is probably the primary reason. As development occurs in surrounding communities, the value of the housing in all communities increases. Owners of this housing see this increase in value as an opportunity to make a profit and naturally do so. The speculation in real estate by absentee owners can quickly make a community's housing unaffordable. Communities can never prevent the gentrification of their housing stock as long as it is a resource outside of their control. A community economic development strategy pursues alternative methods of ownership to give communities control over this valuable resource. One of the more successful methods of ownership is the Community Land Trust (CLT).

Community Land Trusts

A Community Land Trust (CLT) is a non-profit community-owned corporation. The non-profit corporation is controlled by its members. They make all decisions concerning the use of property owned by the corporation. A Community Land Trust (CLT) can be as small as one building or as large as the specific community itself. In the case of the former, the residents of the building control its use; in the latter, all residents of the community control the use of its land.

Typically a CLT will own the land but not the improvements (building) on the land. The CLT will then lease the land (long term) to the owners of the building. In the case of multi-family buildings, the owner may be a cooperative composed of those people living in the building. The CLT owns the land, but the tenants, through a cooperative, own the building.

The concept of a Community Land Trust also works with single family residences. In this instance, a CLT buys both the buildings and the land. It then sells the buildings, but not the land, to local residents. The CLT then leases the land to the residents through 99-year term renewable leases. These leases permit the tenant to have all the benefits of home ownership, yet restrict the tenant's right to sell or transfer the lease at prices that reflect the speculative value of the property.

The CLT limits the resale value of the lease it negotiates with the tenant in such a way as to allow the tenant to receive a price upon sale or transfer of the property that reflects the value of any improvements made on the property and the inflation rate, yet does not allow the tenant to sell or transfer the unit for a price that is based upon the speculative appreciation of the property. This arrangement prevents the pressure to gentrify a community.

In addition to this protection from gentrification, the CLT will also have a provision in the long-term lease that will allow the CLT to maintain the property as housing for low- or moderate-income people. This provision requires that anyone wishing to purchase a lease from an existing tenant must become a member of the CLT and that priority for CLT property is given to those members with the greatest need.

By utilizing this manner of ownership, a community will begin to gain control over its housing resources and will be in the position to better protect itself against outside forces that attempt to drive up the value of land and thereby force residents from their homes.

Not only does outside ownership of a community's housing stock make it vulnerable to speculation, but it is also a major drain on the community's capital. Since most residents do not own their own homes, the money they pay for housing immediately leaves the community and cannot be used to reinvest in that community.

In economically healthy communities, the dollars earned by residents circulate throughout the community before leaving. The multiplier effect of money increases the wealth of communities. In underdeveloped communities, most of the dollars received by the residents never circulate, instead they almost immediately leave the community. This is called leakage. Leakage is a phenomenon seen at all levels of underdeveloped communities, whether at the local neighbourhood level or the national and regional level. Community economic development attempts to deal with the problem of leakage at all levels within a community. Since housing is a major community resource, as well as a major source of capital leakage, how a community gains control of this resource is extremely important.

When land and housing is controlled by a Community Land Trust, any money paid by the residents of the community to the CLT remains in the control of the community. Payments to the CLT can be used to pay the debt service on the property, or to provide the CLT with a surplus. This surplus can then be used by the CLT to purchase more housing or to re-invest in the community's economy in other ways. Even if the payments merely cover the CLT's debt service, the community is still purchasing equity and gaining control over its resources.

The Community Land Cooperative of Cincinnati (CLCC) in Cincinnati, Ohio, is an excellent illustration of the use of a CLT by a community to gain control over its housing resources.

CLCC was established in 1981 in a large community of low-income people, almost entirely black. The community was under pressure from surrounding communities that had already begun to exhibit signs of gentrification. The community had once been an upper-middle income community that had slowly become a slum community over many years. As a result of its earlier prosperity, many of the homes in the community were ideal for renovation and re-sell at higher rents to higher-income tenants.

CLCC started its land trust operations on a small scale. It first purchased a single-family home for the purpose of finding housing for a low-income family in desperate need. Financial assistance for the purchase was obtained from a local church. The transaction was done on the community land trust model and the building was leased back to the resident through a long term renewable lease. CLCC kept control over the land since it remained the property of the community land trust.

After this simple beginning, CLCC began an aggressive strategy of purchasing other buildings in the area and placing them in the land trust. After the first year of operations, CLCC had acquired a six-unit apartment house, a two-family house, and was in the process of acquiring two other buildings.

Since 1981, CLCC has continued to pursue this strategy and has had a significant impact on preventing the gentrification of the community. Other successful examples of the community land trust model have been detailed by the Institute For Community Economics in its book *The Community Land Trust Handbook*.

The CED Approach to Capital

The limited access to capital by a community can prevent it from undertaking a successful strategy to gain control over its resources, including its housing resources. There are many reasons why underdeveloped communities cannot access capital needed in the development process. One of the primary reasons is the reluctance on the part of traditional financial institutions to invest in underdeveloped communities because they are perceived to be too "risky."

At times the risk factor is a disguise for prejudice on the part of the financial institutions against the race of people living in the underdeveloped communities. Other times it is a reflection of the limited role which these financial institutions are willing to play in the development of new enterprises.

Community economic development practitioners have developed a strategy to address the problem of limited capital access for underdeveloped communities. It is also a strategy that reorganizes the institutional relationship between a financial institution and the community in which it invests.

As part of the overall community economic development strategy, the creation of Community Loan Funds plays an important role in the changing relationship between communities and the financial institutions which invest in them. What, then, are Community Loan Funds (CLFs) and how are they different from traditional financial institutions?

Community Loan Funds

CLFs are financial institutions that recognize that communities need access to capital to become fully developed economically. They also recognize that not only do underdeveloped communities need capital, but they also need technical assistance to ensure the projects they fund survive and prosper for the benefit of the community.

Generally, a CLF is a non-profit corporation that acquires capital from foundations and socially responsible investors for the sole purpose of reinvesting that capital in community economic development ventures. A CLF may acquire its capital from churches, individuals, or foundations that have a desire to participate in community economic development but lack the administrative capacity to service the loans that they wish to make. These investors loan the money to the CLF at a fixed rate of return. The CLF then loans the money to community economic development ventures such as community land trusts at an interest rate that reflects the investors' required return and the administrative costs to the CLF. In the area of housing finance, this permits the CLF to make loans for the acquisition of housing at an interest rate lower than that offered by traditional lending institutions.

Since a CLF is part of the overall community economic development strategy, it realizes that the loan to the community project is not where its role stops. Instead, the CLF continues to work with the community organization involved with the venture to provide technical assistance during the life of the loan. In this way, the traditional lender's "hands off" approach with its borrower is changed. The CLF becomes an integral part of the community's efforts to take control over its resources and is willing to assist the organization during difficult times. Nationwide, many Community Loan Funds have had a lower loan default rate than traditional financial institutions, notwithstanding the fact that they provide most of their capital to communities considered too risky for traditional lenders.

The creation of CLFs has occurred in many communities around the United States over the past decade. Usually, the CLF is created by interested community residents who realize that traditional financial institutions are unwilling or unable to meet their community's need for capital. Many already existing CLFs willingly provide technical assistance to these beginning organizations.

Most CLFs are designed to meet the capital needs of specific communities. Recently, interested residents in the State of New Hampshire created a CLF for the purpose of assisting housing cooperatives. While the New Hampshire Community Loan Fund provides capital to other community economic development projects, its primary goal is to assist tenants in the organizational and financial aspects of converting to cooperative ownership.

Since its creation in 1984, the New Hampshire Community Loan Fund has grown from a CLF with assets of $40,000 to over $1,000,000 by the end of 1986. It has also assisted in the creation and financing of New Hampshire's first co-operatively owned mobile home park. The tenants in this park were facing possible eviction due to a sale of the property. Many of the tenants lived on fixed incomes. Most had lived in the park for many years. The New Hampshire Community Loan Fund helped them form a cooperative and then loaned the cooperative enough money to purchase the park. The New Hampshire Community Loan Fund continues to provide technical assistance to the cooperative during its early formative years.

Community Loan Funds and Community Land Trusts working together provide many successful examples of communities gaining control over their housing resources.

Recently, the Institute for Community Economics (ICE), a nonprofit technical assistance organization in Massachusetts, illustrated how an aggressive approach to community economic development which utilizes community land trusts and community loan funds can successfully prevent gentrification in a low-income community.

A certain community within Trenton, New Jersey, that contained large populations of low-income and minority residents started to show signs of gentrification. It was clear that before long this community would no longer be affordable for low-income residents. Recognizing this trend, ICE quickly began to purchase property in the community from private landlords (utilizing its own community development loan fund) with the intent of turning over these properties to a local CLT owned and controlled by local residents.

During this process of purchasing buildings, ICE provided training and technical assistance to a local CLT in order to build the CLT's capacity to buy, develop, and manage property. As a result of the aggressive action by ICE, many low-income apartment buildings that would have become targets for developers' gentrification efforts have been placed in the control of the community.

ICE also has a loan fund that was created for the purpose of providing access to capital to communities that have traditionally been denied such access. The ICE loan fund makes loans to community-controlled organizations for the purpose of creating cooperatives and land trusts. It receives its funds from socially concerned investors who loan ICE money at low interest rates. ICE then loans the money to community organizations at interest rates that allow ICE to cover its administrative costs and provide the requested return on investment to the investor. ICE's intervention into the threatened low-income community in Trenton is an example of the way in which an alternative financial mechanism can be used to restructure institutions in a community.

The CED Approach to Business Development

Traditionally, the approach to business development in underdeveloped communities has relied upon the belief that these communities will benefit from the infusion of external capital. This external capital will invest in the community and the primary benefit to the community will be jobs to local residents.

This approach assumes several things. First, it assumes that capital, in and of itself, will provide needed development without regard to the question of ownership of capital. Second, it assumes that external capital will invest in the community in such a way as to influence the economy of the community. Finally, it assumes the capital will remain in the community long enough to become a permanent investment in the community.

The U.S. government's recent policy of Enterprise Zones is a manifestation of this approach to business development in underdeveloped communities. Enterprise Zones are specific areas usually located in extremely underdeveloped communities. They are special zones established to attract external capital into these areas through the use of generous tax incentives, lower minimum wage requirements, and government subsidies. While this is pursued by the U.S. government as a new policy for revitalizing the economies of underdeveloped areas, it is really nothing more than the contemporary use of the "Operation Bootstrap" model pursued for twenty years in Puerto Rico.

"Operation Bootstrap" was created by the Government of Puerto Rico and the United States for the purpose of undertaking wide-scale economic development of the island. The underlying assumption of the program was that Puerto Rico needed to industrialize its economy and to de-emphasize agriculture and land reform. The plan was to promote private rather than public investment.

This strategy was pursued by developing a comprehensive program of tax inducements to attract U.S. capital investment to the island. U.S. corporations were guaranteed abatement from taxes for periods ranging from 10 to 20 years, depending on the location of the plant.

The government of Puerto Rico aggressively pursued this economic development strategy and built highways and roads for the U.S. corporations that would link offices to plants, industrial centres to seaports, and mines to factories. It also granted loans and subsidies and rent-free space, and paid the cost of shipping machinery from the U.S. to Puerto Rico.

As a result of this economic development strategy, hundreds of textile mills located on the island. This drew thousands of Puerto Rican women who had previously worked at home in the needle trade to the factories sewing jeans and slacks for the New York market. They were paid 25 cents an hour and received few, if any, benefits and very little job protection.

For over 10 years the textile industry boomed in Puerto Rico and the U.S. corporations that had invested there received large returns on their investments. However, in the mid-1960s the factories began to move from Puerto Rico to the Dominican Republic because the wages there were even lower. As these corporations moved off the island, jobs were lost.

The textile industry was not the only industry attracted to Puerto Rico by the economic development strategy. Heavy industry began to move to the island. By 1970, U.S. corporations had more than 14 billion dollars invested in Puerto Rico. Ten percent of U.S. corporate profits around the world were taken from Puerto Rico and the rate of profit on the island was three to four times greater than the rate of profit in the U.S. The economic development plan for Puerto Rico seemed to be working. However, the facts do not seem to support that conclusion.

The industrialization strategy pursued by the government had a dramatic impact on the agricultural sector of the Puerto Rican economy. In 1950, at the beginning of the economic development plan, more than one-third of the island's workforce was employed in agriculture. During the next 20 years, the number of farm workers shrank by almost 70%. The decline of farm employment tended to overwhelm job creation in the 1950s. The addition of more than 30,000 new jobs in industry merely cushioned the loss of nearly 70,000 agricultural jobs. Those who for generations had worked in agriculture and supplied the food for Puerto Rico were leaving the rural areas and moving into the cities to seek work in factories.

Even with the increase in industrialization brought about by this economic development plan, the living conditions of the Puerto Rican people never approached that of Americans living in the U.S. By 1970, (Operation Bootstrap had been in effect for 20 years) 10% of all Puerto Rican families had a yearly income of $250; 35% of all families had a yearly income of less than $2000, and 70% of the population was eligible for food stamps. Infant mortality was 45 per thousand (as compared with 25 per thousand in the U.S.).

The plan emphasized the attraction of capital into Puerto Rico in the belief that this capital would benefit the people of Puerto Rico through the creation of jobs, tax revenues, and new industries. From 1950 to 1970, U.S. corporate investment in Puerto Rico increased from 15% of the island's GNP to 30%.

Clearly, large amounts of capital poured into Puerto Rico. However, the wealth created did not remain on the island. The jeans and slacks that were produced by Puerto Rican women in the textile industry were shipped for sale in the U.S. Oil refined in Puerto Rico was shipped to North America and drugs manufactured by the pharmaceutical industry were sold elsewhere.

During this same period of time, the Puerto Rican people began to import more and more goods from the United States. Between 1950 and 1970, imports from the U.S. rose from slightly more than $300 million to more than $1.9 billion. Puerto Rico quickly became the world's sixth largest purchaser of American goods, and its per capita purchases of U.S. goods were higher than anywhere else in the world. These imports continued to drain the island's capital and transfer it to the U.S.

After over 25 years of pursuing this economic development strategy, Puerto Rico's unemployment rate was nearly 24%. At the same time, the rate of labour force participation of islanders declined to 42%. The decline in employment occurred in all sectors of the economy. The companies that had been attracted to Puerto Rico by the low wages and tax exemptions began to leave and relocate in Asian and Latin American countries. Many left because the tax exemptions used to attract them to the island expired. Others left because labour costs were cheaper elsewhere. Overall, the economic development plan called "Operation Bootstrap" resulted in a Puerto Rican economy of dependency.

"Operation Bootstrap" illustrates why many of the assumptions of this economic development strategy are flawed. Even though external capital may come into a community, it remains under the control and direction of others. The community does not have any control or ownership interest in this capital. This capital may not be directed toward the creation of businesses that meet a need in the community.

External capital that is induced to locate in an underdeveloped community through tax benefits will generally look elsewhere once those benefits are exhausted. As regions compete with each other to provide tax inducements, capital will move to those regions that offer the greatest inducement. The move of many industries from the Northeast and Midwest to the South is an example of this kind of capital flight. External capital has no community loyalty.

While external capital generally does provide jobs to local residents of a community, the permanent nature of those jobs is always in doubt. Many of the jobs provided to local community residents are low-skill and low-paying jobs. External capital usually provides its own managers and skilled workers.

Finally, the reliance on external capital for development contributes to leakage in a community. As businesses make a profit, the profits are taken out of the community and used for development in other places. The experience of Puerto Rico demonstrates that external firms will ultimately expatriate their profits and any investment of those profits in the local community are generally short-lived.

The lack of community-owned and/or controlled businesses also accelerates capital leakage in other ways. As residents shop outside their communities for the goods and services they need, the money they spend leaves the community and does not recirculate. If one were to look at all goods and services purchased by a community over the period of one year, one would see that a substantial amount of capital flows directly outside of the community and provides no real benefit to the community. Generally, businesses attracted by tax inducements do not provide services and/or goods needed in the communities where they locate, but produce goods and services sold outside of the community.

Underdeveloped communities, whether local neighbourhoods or nations, are generally characterized by the fact that they export very few goods and import the majority of the goods needed for their community. A community economic development strategy for business development addresses this problem.

BUSINESS DEVELOPMENT AND THE CREATION
AND USES OF ALTERNATIVE FINANCIAL INSTITUTIONS

At its basic level, import substitution is a strategy that encourages communities to produce goods and services manufactured in the community or to purchase goods and services controlled by businesses owned by community residents. Import substitution is a complex remedy for an underdeveloped community since it must recognize that the technical development of a community's businesses might make true import substitution difficult, if not impossible. This does not mean that an import substitution strategy cannot be pursued by an underdeveloped community.

Many underdeveloped communities will continue to lack the resources to replace all of the goods and services they import with community controlled or directed businesses. However, certain goods and services that are presently provided by outside firms can be developed by the community itself if it directs its capital investment toward that end. The ultimate goal of an import substitution strategy for an underdeveloped community is not total substitution of all imports, but a balance between the importation of needed goods and services and the export of goods and services to other communities. For this reason, the development and encouragement of businesses is important in the overall community economic development strategy of a community. Business development is important not only because it assists import substitution, but because it is an integral part of a job creation strategy for a community.

The investment of capital in an underdeveloped community is usually limited for many reasons. Often capital is not invested in a community because financial institutions consider the community to be too great a risk. The basis for this decision can be nothing more than prejudice against the race of the community's population. The poverty of a community in and of itself can be considered by financial institutions as reason for not investing capital.

Communities in the process of developing are often stopped in that process by an inability to acquire capital for the development process. Small businesses owned by community residents need to expand to meet the needs of the residents over time. New businesses that service existing community businesses need capital to start. If these businesses cannot get needed capital they will either close or their owners will relocate in communities where financial institutions will invest. The development of a community can be slowly strangled by the inability of its residents to access capital.

A community economic development strategy looks at all of these factors and pursues a plan that seeks to restructure the relationships between certain institutions and the residents of a community. Community economic development recognizes that a community lacks control over its own resources and that the community can never begin to develop until it gains control over its resources. As discussed earlier, the problem of accessing capital for the continued development of the community is addressed by the creation of alternative financial institutions such as Community Loan Funds or Community Development Credit Unions. These community economic development institutions can be utilized by communities to assist in their import substitution strategies and to create businesses that are responsive to their needs.

A community economic development strategy approaches the problem of business development in a manner that encourages community directed businesses. This strategy recognizes that business development must take place in a way that benefits both the individuals undertaking the risks of a business and the needs of a community. In undertaking this strategy, communities can assist in the development of businesses by providing the business with customers for its services and products. Businesses that provide goods and services to a community that had previously been provided by businesses either outside of the community or controlled outside of the community should be encouraged and assisted by community organizations. As more businesses begin to become involved in this kind of import substitution, other businesses that serve their needs can begin to develop. The long-term benefits to the community will be a decrease in the leakage of capital from the community.

Many times businesses that will benefit a community cannot get started because they lack access to the necessary capital to start. Community Loan Funds can again play an important role in both providing capital and encouraging the development of businesses that assist the community in gaining control over its resources. There are many successful examples of Community Loan Funds playing this role.

In San Francisco, the Center for Southeast Asian Refugee Resettlement has, with the assistance of the Ford Foundation, created a Community Revolving Loan Fund whose goal is to assist recently arrived refugees develop businesses in their communities. The loan fund not only evaluates loan requests utilizing traditional financial criteria, but takes into account social criteria. Its goal is to encourage businesses that not only permit the individual refugee to obtain self-sufficiency, but which benefit the community as well.

The loan fund also provides technical assistance to businesses in order to assist them and to ensure they can be successful. Loan funds have been created around the country to assist many communities in the development of businesses that meet the goals of community economic development.

Community economic development as a strategy for social intervention in a community does not attempt to make existing institutions function in a better way for the community. Instead, the goal of a community economic development strategy is to change the institutions and create different institutions that are controlled by the community itself.

CED AND CO-OPERATIVE BUSINESS DEVELOPMENT

Community economic development practitioners recognize that the traditional method of organization for business development (i.e., corporate structures or small partnerships) might not meet the development needs of a community. The premise of community economic development is community control over resources.

Large businesses that develop and/or locate in a community may employ many community residents, but still remain controlled by stockholders or owners from outside the community. This outside ownership and control can prevent the residents of the community from benefitting in the success of a business and limit the control the community has over business decisions that affect the community. For these reasons, community economic development practitioners encourage and support the creation of cooperatively owned businesses.

Many low-income residents resist the concept of cooperative businesses primarily because they associate co-ops with small-scale consumer or food co-ops that cater to the needs of a small segment of the population. Many have seen the demise of food cooperatives in their communities due to lack of interest by the residents and the inability of the cooperative to supply the range of goods required by the community. A community economic development approach to cooperative business development takes as its model the Mondragon Cooperatives in the Basque region of Spain.

The cooperative experience in Mondragon has been extremely successful. Such a model can be an important component of a community economic development strategy in any community. However, like all community economic development strategies outlined in this chapter, this approach assumes the availability of individuals with the necessary technical skills to assist with the implementation of community economic development strategies.

The CED Approach to Education

All of the community economic development approaches described in this chapter require the active participation and assistance of knowledgeable individuals to assist communities during the development process. Many community loan funds recognize this need and provide technical assistance to communities during the development process. However, there are too many communities that require technical assistance and too few providers available to meet this need. The education of community economic development practitioners is critical to the success of community economic development as a long-range social intervention strategy.

A community economic development approach to education recognizes that one of the most valuable resources in a community is its people. Community economic development is an approach to social intervention that starts with people and provides them with the tools and knowledge to control the resources of their community. For this reason, a community economic development strategy approaches education as a function of providing technical skills and knowledge to people already working in a community and transferring those skills to community residents so that they can carry on the effort of development.

The economic systems that exist in today's world are complex. In order to understand the institutions that impact on a community within the economy as a whole, community economic development practitioners must become knowledgeable in areas such as financial management, organizational development, housing development, cooperatives, legal structures, project management, and business development. All of these skills can be acquired from traditional degree-granting programs in most business schools. However, the difference between a community economic development approach and the traditional approach is that the needs of the community are emphasized, rather than the private gain of the individual.

A community economic development approach to education transfers specific skills to members of a community for the sole purpose of developing those members' ability to transfer these skills *t* the needs of their community. An understanding of economic inst*' tions is an important element in the success of any comm*/ economic development strategy. However, a commitment to t*' ple of a community is the element that makes such a str* cessful. A community economic development approach to education provides this understanding to those with this commitment.

THE ROLE OF GOVERNMENT
IN COMMUNITY ECONOMIC DEVELOPMENT

Many of the examples of community economic development outlined in this chapter have been successful without the direct support of government. This is not to say that government cannot play an important role in assisting and encouraging community economic development as a strategy for underdeveloped communities.

Government, whether national or local in scope, can intervene in at least three ways to promote community economic development activities. It can pass laws and regulations that facilitate community economic development. In the area of Community Land Trusts, government could pass legislation specifically recognizing CLTs as special legal entities and exempting them from many of the laws that restrict agreements aimed at preventing speculative sale of property. At the present time, most CLTs have to operate under the general laws of non-profit corporations which are not necessarily appropriate, but are the only available legal entity.

Many of the vehicles used in a community economic development strategy, such as CLTs and Community Loan Funds, would benefit from regulations that would make them more acceptable to financial institutions chartered and regulated by governments. Since many of these concepts are new, access to capital from more traditional financial institutions would be made easier by regulations which exhibit government support for these new entities.

Government can also assist community economic development activities through favourable tax laws. Corporations and individuals could be encouraged to participate in projects with community development corporations through a system of tax credits awarded to those who participate in these ventures.

Finally, government can directly intervene through the creation of state controlled and financed entities that provide needed capital to community economic development ventures. The Massachusetts Community Development Finance Corporation is an example of this approach. The CDFC is a state created corporation which finances efforts by community development corporations to own or control real estate within their community. It also finances businesses undertaken by community organizations. This kind of direct intervention makes the government a partner in the community economic development effort.

CED AND TRADITIONAL SOCIAL WELFARE POLICY

The strategy of community economic development differs from traditional social welfare policies and traditional economic development policies in fundamental ways.

Traditional social welfare policies attempt to alleviate the suffering and pain experienced by those who are poor. In the modern welfare state this policy is translated into large transfers by the government to poor people. These transfers come in the form of housing subsidies, medical care, food subsidies and government-sponsored job creation. All of these programs certainly help the poor live more comfortable lives. Nevertheless, while these programs make the life of a poor community more bearable, they rarely transform a poor community into an economically healthy and independent community.

Traditional social welfare policies also raise serious questions of dependency. Recently, the American sociologist, Charles Murray, argued in his book *Losing Ground—American Social Policy From 1950-1980*, that the social welfare policies pursued by the United States government over the last 30 years did not help to eliminate poverty, but actually encouraged its continuation. While Murray's thesis has been successfully attacked by many scholars, his argument about the dependency nature of traditional social welfare policy continues to gain acceptance by many in policy-making positions. Even those who argue that the increase in poverty over the last decade is a result of less spending on social welfare programs rather than policy itself, do admit that dependency is a serious concern.

It is certainly understandable why traditional social welfare policy has been pursued by the majority of governments and institutions over the years. The poor need help immediately and cannot wait while government attempts to restructure society's institutions in such a way as to permit poor communities greater control over their resources. Of course, the more cynical explanation for government continuing to adhere to traditional social welfare policy is that those in control of the existing institutions have no desire to share power and resources with others.

It is also quite possible that government policy-makers desire to implement social welfare policies that lead to dependency. If people or communities are constantly dependent upon other institutions for their welfare and survival, they will be less willing to support policies that threaten those institutions upon which their welfare depends. In this way, social welfare policies become a method for controlling.

Piven and Cloward (1971) have convincingly argued that the

social welfare policies pursued by the United States have been designed and implemented for the purpose of controlling the poor. They also point out that these policies have been developed for the purpose of preventing major social upheavals during times of economic and social unrest. Many of the social welfare programs in existence in the U.S. today (unemployment insurance, social security, food stamps, Aid to Families for Dependent Children, Medicare) were instituted during either the depression or the civil rights movement of the early 1960s. The purpose of these social welfare programs was not to solve the structural problems that created poverty, but to pacify a segment of the population that was seeking major social change.

Community economic development recognizes that the poor and the oppressed have immediate needs that must be supplied in order for an individual to survive with any sort of dignity. Therefore, it does not underestimate the need for social welfare programs that provide the poor with a standard of living that allows them to live without fear and humiliation. However, community economic development also recognizes that the greatest dignity that an individual or community can achieve is control over his or her own life.

CONCLUSION

A community economic development strategy recognizes that communities have many resources and that these resources are not used to the benefit of the community. To gain control of these resources and to direct them for the benefit of the community is the ultimate goal of community economic development. It is a strategy that does not become successful overnight. Instead, it is a long-term strategy that attempts to restructure relationships between and among people, land, and capital.

Community economic development as a strategy for social intervention is not a quick fix. For this reason it usually does not appeal to those politicians who must look to re-election as their measure of success. In fact, such a short-term horizon has probably contributed to the acceptance of the traditional economic development and social welfare policies pursued by most governments. Community economic development is a long term strategy for social intervention that recognizes the reality of the existing relationships between an underdeveloped community and existing institutions. Its goal is to rearrange this relationship so that communities control more of their resources. Such a strategy will not be accomplished without resistance from those who have always believed that it is their right to direct and control the destiny of others.

The creation of alternative institutions to assist in the strategy of community economic development is a central component to its success. However, this component requires the education and training of committed people who are willing to work in their communities—whether in the United States or other countries—to facilitate a transfer of knowledge. The skills needed to successfully engage in community economic development must be developed by traditional and non-traditional educational institutions and then transferred to people. It is the people living in underdeveloped communities throughout the world who will ultimately implement this strategy, and its success will depend upon them, not upon traditional institutions or government. Community economic development is a strategy that starts from the bottom up.

REFERENCES

Goldenberg, I.I. (1978). *Oppression and social intervention*. Chicago: Nelson-Hall.

Hartman, C. (1975). *Housing and Social Policy*. Englewood Cliffs, N.J.: Prentice-Hall.

Jacobs, J. (1962). *The death and life of great American cities*. New York; Vintage Books.

Jacobs, J. (1984). *Cities and the wealth of nations*. New York: Vintage Books.

Matthews, R. (1983). *The creation of regional dependency*. Toronto: University of Toronto Press.

Piven, F.F. & Cloward, R. (1971). *Regulating the poor: The functions of public welfare*. New York: Vintage Books.

Sarason, S.B. (1974). *The psychological sense of community*. San Francisco: Jossey-Bass.

Christina Clamp

12
HISTORY AND STRUCTURE OF THE MONDRAGON SYSTEM OF WORKER COOPERATIVES

The Mondragon system is a highly complex federation of cooperatives bound together by much more than a formal contract of association. A cooperative is a democratic, voluntary association of people committed to economic self-help. Cooperatives serve a variety of purposes and are best known in North America in the form of consumer cooperatives, especially credit unions, and food and housing cooperatives. Though there are some worker cooperatives in the United States and Canada, none have been as successful as the Mondragon system. The system brings together more than 165 cooperatives with a common historical experience and cultural identity, and with similar social and economic goals. The Mondragon cooperatives are a heterogeneous collection of co-ops, affiliated with a cooperative bank, the *Caja Laboral Popular* (CLP), which serves all their major financial needs for long-term and short-term capital. It also provides technical assistance for the development of new co-ops and ongoing assistance to existing co-ops. As the following discussion illustrates, this system is an example of second-order change. The Basque cooperators successfully reframed a very oppressive social, economic, and political condition in the post-Civil-War period in Spain. While General Francisco Franco actively sought to destroy what remained of the economic infrastructure of the region, a group of Basque workers launched a prosperous cooperative movement.

This chapter begins with a discussion of the historical context in which the cooperatives developed. The basic structure of the cooperative system is outlined. It is this structure which ensures that ultimate authority will remain in the hands of the members.

HISTORICAL ORIGINS

The origin of what has come to be known as "the Mondragon Cooperative Experience" began in the Basque country of northern Spain in the post-Civil-War period. Despite its rugged terrain and relative isolation, Euskadi (the Basque name for the region) had a strong tradition of skilled tradesmen in shipbuilding and metalworking.

The cooperative movement began in 1956 with one firm, Ulgor, which was started with the help of a Catholic priest, Don José María Arizmendiarrieta. The priest was responsible for working with Catholic youth in the town of Mondragon, beginning in 1941. Many of the men of the town had fought in the Civil War on the side of the Republican forces. When the Basque country fell to the forces of General Franco in 1936, many of these men were killed, forced into exile, or went to jail. "The war brought with it, factions among the young people. Some fought with the nationalists; others with the Basque Socialists; others were with the Carlists. The unity of the town was broken by the war (Gutierrez & Whyte, 1975).

Mondragon was a very demoralized town with little hope for the future in 1941, when Don José María was appointed as the advisor to its young people through the Catholic Action movement. Catholic Action was a social movement which originated in Belgium. It was dedicated to social reform, guided by Christian social doctrine.

In those days, Mondragon was a company town whose name was synonymous with the *Union Cerrejera*. It was also a town with a strong socialist tradition. Alfonso Gorroñogiotia (personal communication, September 8, 1982), one of the founders of the first cooperative, described how he saw their situation:

> It was a totalitarian regime, dictatorial in the first postwar period . . . . Then there was no political action; there was no trade union activity. For Don José María, there was only the option of systematically forming a realistic cause, a cause with hope. One cannot live without hope, a horizon. And so, he introduced a simple problem. To these young men that could not focus on political or trade union activities, let's focus on the resolution of problems that always reoccur in the community.

The Mondragon cooperators were part of the Catholic Action movement which inspired a successful cooperative movement in Nova Scotia, Canada, a decade earlier.

Arizmendi had already shown the people of Mondragon that changes were possible. There was a successful effort to eradicate tuberculosis in the town; the initiation of a sports club, soccer field, and charity drives to help the poor; and the development of the Professional School and the League of Education and Culture. The latter was begun in 1948, and has played an important role in the development and overseeing of educational activities in the region. It is discussed more fully later in this chapter. The movement was based in Christian social doctrine:

> There emerged underground Catholic organizations at the forefront of the confused frontier of the spiritual and the temporal, the religious and the civil, and breathed new life into apostolic groups, such as: Catholic Action Youth (JAC), Catholic Action Youth Worker (JOAC), and the Brotherhood of Catholic Action (HOAC) . . . .
>
> In the decade of the forties, the people turned en masse to the Church. The Basque people are reputed to be a devout community. But the youth found in the Church, a way to channel their political options. A silence was imposed on the conventional organizations: trade unions, and political parties. This left only the possibilities of clandestine organizations, indifference, hedonism or violent struggle (Larrañaga, 1981, pp. 70-71).

The message which Don José María communicated to his young "actionists" was one of humanism, social justice, and democratic values. He believed the Church should use its resources to transform capitalism, to eliminate the exploitation of workers, and to return to them the economic resources produced by their labour. The Church gave their efforts legitimacy.

In Mondragon, there was only one technical school, that of the *Union Cerrejera*, which provided training for a limited number of sons of employees, plus 12 outsiders. When efforts to persuade the company to expand its enrollment failed, Don José María enlisted the support of the people to develop a technical school. Roughly 25% of the townspeople supported the project and the school opened in 1941 (Gutierrez & Whyte, 1975). From the technical school's first graduates, 11 were selected in 1947 to continue their studies at night through an extension program licensed by the Zaragoza School of Engineering. Within that group were the five founders of the cooperative movement. In 1952, they all took jobs as foremen or section heads in various firms.

The five founders worked at the *Union Cerrejera* where they sought to bring about changes in the work organization.

> Our first intention was not to create a cooperative enterprise but rather to transform the firm (we were in) into an organization in

which the workers would participate. In 1953 or '54—two or three years before there was the cooperative—when there was a capital expansion at the *Union Cerrejera*, we petitioned for 25% of that increase to be distributed amongst the workers . . . . (José María Ormaechea, personal communication, August 10, 1982).

The *Union Cerrejera* refused. When the five men realized that workers could not become shareholders in the firm, they decided it was impossible, in this case, to alter the structure of the capitalist firm. They left their jobs to organize their own firm.

The cooperative movement began with the purchase of a small firm in Vitoria which made small gas cookers. "We wanted to build a firm that conformed to the doctrine of the Church" (Gorroñogiotia, personal communication, September 8, 1982). Arizmendi did not want the cooperative movement to be doctrinaire or ideological. "It is experience, praxis in that one tries to be faithful to the undeniable exigencies of human values, where conscience takes precedence" (Larrañaga, 1981, p. 89).

The cooperative movement grew quickly from one co-op in 1956, to 31 in 1967; 64 in 1977; and 86 in 1982, in manufacturing alone. The consumer co-op and co-ops in agriculture, education, housing, and the service sector also developed and expanded. The system now employs more than 18,000 workers.

The goals of the cooperative movement were:

to fundamentally imbue consistent action in a vibrant process of assimilation and fostering of resources and methods for an accelerated and intense development that without a doubt will be social and economic in support of work and solidarity (Arizmendi-Arrieta, 1972, p. 65).

They were reflected in these rallying slogans:

1. Knowledge is power. (*Saber es poder.*)
2. Knowledge must be socialized for power to be democratic. (*Socializando el saber se democratiza el poder.*)
3. To create and not possess; to realize but not profit; to progress and not dominate. (*Crear y no poseer, actuar y no ganar, progresar y no dominar.*)
4. Better to become communities that are prosperous and just than personally wealthy in a poor community. (*Hacer comunidades evolucionadas, justas y rocas, mas que ricos en una comunidad pobre.*) (Retegui, 1979/1980, pp. 3-4.)

This commitment has translated into a movement that 25 years later remains characterized by mutual self-help, equality, and equity. Ormaechea (personal communication, 1982) maintains that "the principles have not been modified. The principles of solidarity, of efficiency have not changed. What has changed is the external form.'' He explains that the goals are usually implied rather than prescribed. This point was clarified in the example of the *Caja Laboral Popular*.

> I believe that when the *Caja Laboral Popular* was created, there was a moral and spiritual intent rather than a determined profile. Don José María launched ideas and upheld a belief in the work capacity and the beliefs of people, in criteria and ideas almost utopian. But there was no clear outline. Nowhere is it said that the bank is to create cooperatives. It is implied in the statutes which say "for the social, entrepreneurial, and economic wellbeing" (Ormaechea, personal communication, 1982).

The development of the cooperatives was facilitated by the strong support of the local community (both financial and in kind) and the sponsorship of the Catholic Church. While the cooperators were at times viewed with suspicion by the Franco government, both the local and national governments were generally neutral toward them:

> Franco viewed us, that is the Basque country, badly. It was a country that enraged him such that he denied its ability to develop its own national identity, language, customs, and politics. Therefore, we couldn't ignore the power of Franco. We weren't systematically enemies or opponents (but) we ignored Franco's presence and we worked in a different economy and a work distinct from that of Spain. Technically, we had good relations (Ormaechea, personal communication, 1982).

As cooperatives, Mondragon avoided any potential hostility. They also enjoyed certain tax advantages.

> In the scheme of possibilities, cooperation was a solution and Don José María broadened it. The Spanish cooperative law was very restrictive but he broadened it with the help of a legal advisor in Madrid (Ormaechea, personal communication, 1982).

The movement served to focus and transform the aspirations of the people into action in legitimate and constructive ways to rebuild Euskadi after the Spanish Civil War.

A MULTI-LEVEL SYSTEM

The Mondragon system has become a complex conglomerate of organizations (see Figure 1). There is a high degree of diversity in the cooperative experience of people within the group. Factors such as the size, age, and industry of a firm result in obvious differences. Less ob-

FIGURE 1

The Cooperative Complex

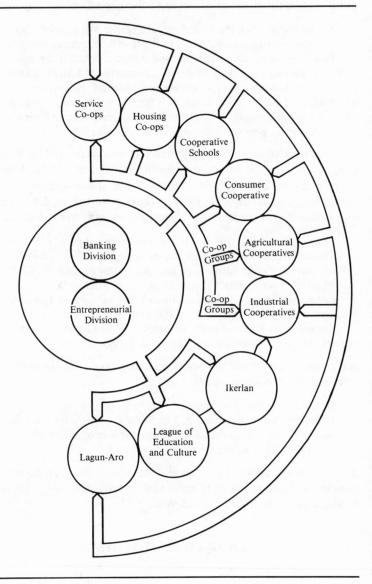

vious are factors related to the origin of the co-op (conversion or startup), the proximity to Mondragon, and the management style of the firm. Yet they all serve to create a richly diverse network of firms.

The Mondragon Group has four levels. This complex system enables the cooperatives to pool their resources of land, labour, and capital in a highly efficient manner. In so doing, the cooperatives experience a high degree of solidarity among themselves. At the superstructural level, there are four co-ops of co-ops: the *Caja Laboral Popular* (CLP); *Lagun-Aro*, the social security system; *Ikerlan*, a research and development firm; and the League of Education and Culture. These firms have a mixed governance structure with both institutional and individual members on the board.

Caja Laboral Popular

The bank, which was founded in 1959, plays a central role in many of the existing co-ops and in the promotion of new ones. Its role is critical to ensuring that the various cooperatives remain committed to the cooperative principles and maintain the same organizational and capital structure. All cooperatives associated with the CLP sign a contract of association which prescribes the cooperative model.

In those instances where there is an active cooperative group (the next level of the system which we will discuss), the bank generally serves a conventional banking function. Where co-ops lack the necessary size or resources on their own, the CLP plays a more extensive role, promoting and monitoring the firms.

The bank has three divisions (see Figure 2): the banking division (*Division Bancarial*), Entrepreneurial Division (*Division Empresarial*), and General Services (*Servicios Generales*). The bank-

FIGURE 2

Structure of the Caja Laboral Popular

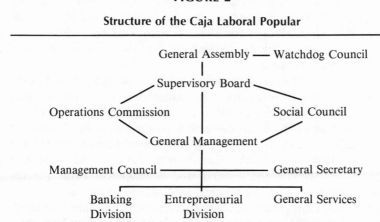

ing division channels local savings into the bank for investment in the cooperatives. It has more than 100 branch offices in the four Spanish Basque provinces and an office in Madrid. The CLP is the twenty-eighth largest bank in Spain and has five percent of all savings in Euskadi (*Caja Laboral Popular*, 1982). There were 892 people employed at the CLP as of 1980.

The Entrepreneurial Division serves as the technical assistance arm of the CLP. One of its principle functions is to create and promote new firms in the areas of manufacturing, agriculture, commerce, services, exportation, and high technology. Other functions are to provide advice and services in technical, economic, and social aspects; to monitor the performance of the cooperatives; and to provide intensive assistance to co-ops that are seen as high risks. The Entrepreneurial Division is responsible for protecting the bank's investments in the co-ops. Many of the people who work in this division have previous experience in the co-ops.

The third division, General Services, manages personnel, food services, buildings and equipment, and services and programs for individual worker members and the public. Assistance with urban planning and construction projects is provided to the co-ops and other institutions through the technical department.

The bank has had a tremendous amount of influence in the operation of the cooperatives and the development of new firms. This is partly a function of its financial role. Another facet of its power is the strong leadership of José María Ormaechea, the general manager of the bank, and one of the founders. The extent of his power is best described in his response to my question, "If it were possible to change the structure of the CLP, or of the cooperatives, how would you change them?" He replied: "I can't answer that because if I want to change something, I change it" (Ormaechea, personal communication, 1982). Ormaechea is considered a hard working and dedicated leader and is responsible for guiding much of the successful development of the cooperatives.

The bank is at times seen as the Vatican or the Ivory Tower of the cooperatives, but its role is likely to change given the extent to which controversy currently surrounds it. Ormaechea has begun to look for a successor and is likely to move to a position heading a proposed Cooperative Council (see Figure 3) which would consist of the top directors from the bank; *Lagun-Aro*; *Eroski*, the consumer cooperative; *Ikerlan*, the research and development firm; and the general directors of all the regional associations of cooperatives.[1] In addition, the CLP plans to decentralize its operations into four headquarters located in the provincial capitals of Bilbao, San Sebastian,

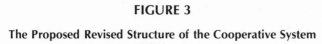

FIGURE 3

The Proposed Revised Structure of the Cooperative System

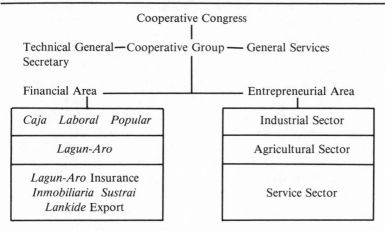

Vitoria, and Pamplona (Ormaechea, personal communication, 1982).

Lagun-Aro

Mondragon cooperators do not qualify for the national health care system because they are legally self-employed. In order to meet their social security needs, they had to develop their own insurance program. *Lagun-Aro* was part of the CLP from 1959 until 1967, when it became a mutual insurance firm. In 1973, it was officially recognized as a second-tier or superstructural co-op.

Lagun-Aro's services have grown markedly since the 1960s when it provided insurance coverage for disability, death, and retirement through an accord with the Autonomous Workers Mutual (*Mutualidad de Trabajadores Autonomos*), a plan available to self-employed workers throughout Spain. Today, *Lagun-Aro* is engaged in research on environmental and health hazards and absenteeism, in addition to tending to the social welfare needs of the associated cooperators. Pensions are still provided through the Autonomous Workers Mutual Insurance program.

The costs of the system are underwritten by individual payroll deductions and payments from the co-ops themselves. A co-op need not be affiliated with the CLP to be an associate of *Lagun-Aro*. *Lagun-Aro* employed 50 people as of 1980, to serve 18,216 cooperators, and a total of 46,505 beneficiaries.

Ikerlan

Ikerlan has the distinction of being the only research and development (R&D) centre in Euskadi. While many of the cooperatives, especially the larger ones, do their own research and development of new products and technological innovations, they have traditionally obtained licenses and patents from elsewhere. *Ikerlan* grew out of the Professional Technical School. The economic crisis of the mid-1970s prompted the group to consider the need for a separate R&D firm "to tackle technological development by means of picking up and developing technologies and their application to industrial products and production processes, in such a way that technological autonomy is gradually reached, thus allowing our industry to be more competitive in world markets" (*Ikerlan*, 1980, p. 1).

Rather than have each co-op rely on its own resources to meet all its R&D needs, *Ikerlan* was created in 1977 to reinforce and consolidate individual efforts. Ularco, which is one of the co-op groups; the CLP; and some of the smaller industrial co-ops, worked to establish *Ikerlan* as a superstructural co-op. As of 1980, there were 32 industrial co-op members and two institutional members; the CLP, and the League of Education and Culture. The initial investment for starting *Ikerlan* was largely financed by the CLP. The annual operating costs have been provided partly by the supporting cooperatives, by the CLP, and by self-financing through independent research for non-cooperative firms. The Basque government in 1982 assumed a major funding role in *Ikerlan* due to its singularity in the R&D field in Euskadi. In exchange, *Ikerlan* is expected to provide more support to non-cooperative firms in the region. The Basque government and the provincial government now send representatives to the meetings of the General Assembly of *Ikerlan* as informal participants.

The League of Education and Culture

The League of Education and Culture began in 1948 under the leadership of Don José María, as the legal overseer of the Professional School and other educational activities. It legally became a cooperative in 1964. As a second-tier cooperative, the League is governed by a membership of institutional supporters, parents and students, professionals, and League staff.

It is committed to the promotion and coordination of educational activities in Mondragon's municipal district, Alto Deva. It has three centres of higher learning: (a) J.M. Arizmendiarrieta *Eskola*

Politeknikoa, the professional school in Mondragon; (b) *Escuela de Estudios Empresariales* (ETEO), the business school in Onate; and, (c) *Irakasle Eskola*, the centre for language studies in Eskoriatza which trains professionals in the Basque language. In addition, it monitors 10 other educational centers: three nursery schools, three primary and middle schools, two senior and college preparatory schools, and two technical schools. The League does not monitor all the *ikastolas* (Basque language schools which have been promoted by the CLP). The League, which employed 57 people as of 1980, monitored 5,803 students, 234 teachers, and 188 classrooms.

The League played a dynamic role in the promotion of *Ikerlan* and *Alecoop*, an industrial co-op that integrates work and study for students of the Professional School. The League has a vital role to play in the continued development of the Basque language and culture, and in encouraging women to pursue technical programs of study.

THE COOPERATIVE GROUPS

In 1965, *Ularco*, the first cooperative group, was formed by four of the first cooperatives: *Ulgor, Arrasate, Copreci*, and *Ederlan*. It was established as a private association and regulated by a multilateral contract. Through such an association, the co-ops felt they could enjoy the benefits of shared resources without the problems of large-scale organizations. *Ularco* has served as the model for inter-cooperative solidarity. Today the *Ularco* group shares a common job-ranking system; the shared risks/benefits from their profits/losses; and sharing of services in such areas as personnel, marketing, new product development, economic and financial services.

The development of the cooperative groups has been a slow process. The fostering of intergroup solidarity is not always readily accepted by the co-ops. Currently, there are seven cooperative groups that are to some extent functioning on a geographic or district basis such as the *Ularco* group does. Efforts to develop cooperative groups by industrial sector have not been as effective. There are plans to develop 16 district cooperative groups.

The purpose of the group is to provide coordination rather than to direct the cooperatives. There is some controversy over the extent to which the cooperative groups should play an executive rather than staff role. The *Ularco* group has played an executive role when a cooperative is in financial trouble.

TABLE 1

CLP-Associated Cooperatives by Province (1982)

	Alava	Guipuzcoa	Navarra	Vizcaya	Total
Industrial	5	53	7	21	86
Forges and foundaries	–	4	1	2	7
Machine tools	1	18	–	6	25
Intermediate goods	2	16	5	7	30
Consumer durables	1	12	1	5	19
Construction	1	3	–	1	5
Agriculture/ Food Industry	–	2*	1	3	6
Consumer (over 50 stores in four provinces)		1			1
Schools (*Ikastolas*)	1	17	1	24	43
Services		4	2		6
Service co-ops		1	1		2
Community centres (or superstructural co-ops)		3			3
Total of Co-ops	7	86	14	49	156

Source: *Memoria* (1981). Caja Laboral Popular.

* One of these co-ops was scheduled to close at the end of 1982. The co-op had been converted from a privately owned firm three years earlier, but had not been able to overcome its financial problems through the reorganization.

The Cooperative Firms

In the Spanish Basque provinces, one finds co-ops dispersed through all four of the provinces, but they are especially concentrated in Guipuzcoa, the province of Mondragon (Table 1).

The cooperative movement began with an industrial cooperative, *Ulgor*, which produces consumer durables. The growth of industrial cooperatives has been at a rate of slightly more than three per year. The creation of jobs for the Basque working class has been a major objective of the cooperatives, with an emphasis on the traditional manufacturing sectors of metal and woodworking. These co-ops have been the heart of the system and have provided much of the capital for its development.

In recent years, the development of agricultural co-ops has taken on new importance. In the post-war period, there was a movement away from the family farm. Good work and educational opportunities

FIGURE 4

The Internal Organization of a Cooperative Firm

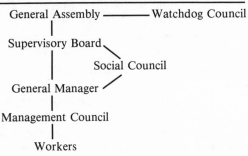

General Assembly ———— Watchdog Council

Supervisory Board

Social Council

General Manager

Management Council

Workers

existed for Basque youths. There is concern now that the Basque rely too heavily on imported foodstuffs. Much farmland was turned over to woodlots of a poor quality pine. The Mondragon group has made the development of local agriculture a priority. A department in the CLP's Entrepreneurial Division, with a staff of four, is devoted to both the development of new cooperatives in this area, and the support of existing agricultural firms.

THE COOPERATIVE ORGANIZATION

All the co-ops have the same basic formal organizational structure (see Figure 4). As the chart indicates, the co-ops have five managerial bodies in addition to the manager.

(1) The general assembly consists of all members of the cooperative. Cooperatives cannot have more than 10% of their workforce as non-member workers.[2] The general assembly meets once a year to examine and approve the financial statements of the previous year and the budget for the next year. It also elects the members of the supervisory board and the watchdog council for four-year, staggered, renewable terms. Voting is on a one-vote-per-person basis.

The general assembly has the right to veto decisions made by the supervisory board. Extraordinary sessions may be called by the supervisory board or by a petition of 20% of the members. The power of the general assembly is an important reciprocal check on the power of the leadership. This provides an effective forum for direct democracy, though less so in the larger cooperatives, which are hampered by the size of the firm. For this reason, the cooperatives have tried to limit firms to a maximum of 500 members.

(2) As the governing board of a firm, the supervisory board has a major role in the planning and oversight of the firm's operation. Depending on the size of the cooperative, the board will have between three and 12 members.

The composition of supervisory boards varies. Some firms have boards composed largely of blue-collar members, while others are mostly white-collar, technical, and administrative staff. The board is held accountable by four-year terms, but because they are renewable terms, they can result in some board members becoming, in a sense, institutionalized. In some instances, an additional problem arises when board members lack the necessary skills to be effective and/or lack clear understanding of the scope of their role as a board.

(3) The watchdog council, which usually consists of three members, is required by Spanish cooperative law (as are the general assembly and the supervisory board). The watchdog council's function is that of overseeing the conduct of the supervisory board and management in the operation of the firm. It may seek the advice of the CLP on specific problems. Neither members of the supervisory board nor the general manager can hold a seat on the watchdog council. This body is another important check in the governance system on the power of the leadership.

(4) The executive power rests in the management of the firm. The manager is hired on a four-year, renewable contract by the supervisory board. The manager is a member of the co-op, and attends the meetings of the supervisory board with a "voice but without a vote." Managers are accountable to the supervisory board in the performance of their duties. Yet, they may have a disproportionate advantage due to their superior expertise. This can serve to increase their authority relative to that of the board.

Another constraint can result when the managers are not expendable. When there is a shortage of qualified managers, as in 1982, the effect is to put pressure on boards to hold onto unpopular managers.

(5) The management council is composed of the top management of the firm. It advises both the general manager and the supervisory board. This group may include outside consultants who have been hired for their special expertise.

(6) Social councils exist only in the larger firms. The social council is intended to represent the concerns of workers when resolving issues related to social relations within the firm. Members of this body are elected by each department in the firm, on a one-person, one-vote basis, for a three-year term. The effectiveness of the social council varies from firm to firm. When management has demonstrated its

commitment by regular attendance and a willingness to address issues and inform workers on the firm's performance, the social council has a clear function. Effective social councils facilitate the flow of information and provide both workers and managers with a more complete understanding of one another's perspectives. They also serve to enhance the level of member participation in firms.

The day-to-day operation of the firm follows a conventional division of labour. Assembly lines have not been displaced by new work technologies although there have been a few experiments within the *Ularco* group. Workers have resisted the changes, and the recession has made management reluctant to invest in large experimental plant renovations.

The governance structure suggest a fairly comprehensive system of participation. Yet, it is a representative democracy. The effectiveness of these various governance bodies depends largely on the ability of the members and their representatives to effectively perform their roles. Older workers often have limited formal education. As one young worker observed, "Most workers do not understand how to read a budget, so they don't even try" (August, 1982). In interviews with managers, 62% expressed dissatisfaction with the level of participation which currently exists in the cooperatives. Some attributed the lack of participation to the reluctance of workers to devote their personal time to the cooperative; others attributed it to their lack of experience or the inadequacy of current structures.

COOPERATIVE CAPITAL

Economic democracy is ensured in the cooperatives through the system of compensation, the structure of capital, and the distribution of surplus earnings. This is an important feature of worker cooperatives as it relates directly to the issues of ownership and control of the firm.

The Compensation System

Workers in the Mondragon system are not paid wages. All members receive a portion of their anticipated share of the profits of the firm (the ratio between the highest and lowest paid was 1:3 from 1956 until 1983 when pressures on the system resulted in a change to a 1:4.5 ratio). Over the years there had been gradual inflation in the rankings, but the 1:3 ratio prevented inflation at the top of the rankings. Many of the co-ops had adopted the use of a labour compensation bonus for managers and other professional people, resulting in a de facto 1:4.5 ratio. The bonus enabled managers and other professionals to increase their earnings by 50% over what they would have received at a job rating of 3.0.

The labour compensation bonus was the only adjustment at the upper end of the scale. The mean to maximum displacement has gone from 2.4. times the mean index in 1960 to 1.79 times in 1982 (Caja Laboral Popular, July, 1982). The effect of this compensation system has been to pay workers at the lower end of the scale better than their cohorts in private industry. Managers, on the other hand, are paid far below their market value. In a 1980 study done by the bank, it was found that managers in the co-op group earn 72% of what they could earn in private industry in the region. Workers with an index of 1.3 in the co-ops were earning 103.9% of what they would earn in the same position in private firms. A second study found cooperative managers earn between 51% and 75% of what their colleagues in private industry earn (Caja Laboral Popular, July, 1982). By raising the differential, it is hoped the group will be able to compete more effectively for new managerial talent.

The inflation in indices occurred with the evaluation of work posts in the 1960s. Each new revision of the manual of valuation has resulted in a higher average index (Caja Laboral Popular, July, 1982). The decision to raise the differential in one sense merely formalized what had already existed through the system of compensation bonuses. In this instance, the cooperatives adapted to the demands of the market in order to assure better access to new management people and to be better able to retain existing managers.

This change does not address the problem of inflation. As a management consultant in the entrepreneurial division of the *Caja Laboral Popular* said:

> . . . to say 1:3 or 1:5 is nothing more than to say a number . . . . This is not just a question of 1:3 or 1:5. We are definitely discussing aspects of the structure in which there are already situations that exceed the 1:3. Nevertheless, the people recognize this . . . . This is not the way to resolve the management problem in the long run. The only way to ensure there will be committed managers is to provide them from within the cooperatives. We need to put much more emphasis on training people. In particular, we have to take the risk to invest in young people.

A staff member of *Ularco* agrees:

> The 1:3 ratio is a very serious problem which at this time everyone sees as insufficient . . . to eliminate the 1:3 is not a solution nor is

putting a limit of 4.5 or 1:5. Those who are talented and tempted to leave won't stay with a 1:4 ratio. This alleviates some tensions but it does not resolve much . . . . We have to recognize that we cannot compete in the market for professionals . . . We have to take people straight out of the university as they did with me. Once you are in, it changes you . . . .

The CLP staff which researched the change to a 1:5 ratio did not see it as a change in basic principles. The initial choice of a 1:3 ratio had been somewhat spontaneous and lacked a technical, social, or objective basis. The 1:3 ratio has served to limit development of sharp economic and status differences.

The cooperatives have adapted to address pragmatic concerns. What remains unclear is the long-term solution to the ideological commitment to solidarity and mutual compromise in the wage structure. The struggle between ideology and pragmatism is likely to remain.

The Structure of Cooperative Capital

Marx saw the relationship of labour to capital as the basic factor in the governance of work relations. It was the failure of people to obtain a modest reform in that relationship at the *Union Cerrejera* which led to the development of the cooperative movement in Euskadi. The CLP-affiliated cooperatives' capital structure is a social innovation which has overcome the limitations of the capital structure employed in many other worker cooperative ventures, worldwide.

The capital structure employed in earlier cooperative ventures has often led to the ultimate conversion of the cooperatives to private ownership or a hybrid structure with a mixture of wage labourers, worker-capitalists, and on occasion, capitalists. In the plywood cooperatives of the northwestern United States, workers' ownership shares have appreciated such that new workers cannot afford to buy the membership share of older worker members (Bernstein, 1980). This has led to the sale of some co-ops to private investors. The garbage collectors of San Francisco have resorted to hiring wage labourers rather than dilute the capital shares of their membership (Russell, Hochner, & Perry, 1977). The Mondragon cooperators have their own difficulties with capital structure, but the problems of these other co-ops have been avoided by the structure of social capital at Mondragon. The capital structure reflects the Spanish legal constraints and the concerns of the cooperators to provide a fair return to the workers, and working capital to meet the needs of the co-ops.

At Mondragon, the worker provides the capital investment and assumes the risks of profits and losses. Each worker makes a capital investment upon joining the cooperatives. Unlike the stockholder in a capitalist firm, this capital investment is not speculative. Capital is essential to all economic enterprise, but it need not take the form it has taken in the modern corporation. In the cooperatives, the capital contribution is treated as an investment and receives a limited return in the form of interest. That amounted to a six percent return in 1981. Members contribute three types of funds: (a) a nonrefundable initial membership fee (*retenido*), (b) an obligatory capital investment (*comanditario*) which varies from year to year, and (c) voluntary contributions (*voluntario*). The retained fees serve as the initial reserve fund of a new cooperative, and are a sinking fund for which members receive no interest. The voluntary and mandatory capital investments are the stock base (*aportaciones computables*). No member can own more than five percent of the voluntary and mandatory capital investment.

New members may pay their membership fees and mandatory capital investments through payroll deductions over a two-year period. The member cannot vote until these monies are paid. Mondragon has placed checks in the system's membership fee structure which ensure the cooperatives' commitment both to a central goal—job creation—and an open membership.

The Distribution of Profits

Members share in the profits and losses of the firm. The net profits are distributed between the reserve fund, the cooperative returns, and the social fund (see Figure 5). This profit distribution is governed by both Basque and Spanish cooperative laws. The reserve fund and the cooperative returns are the capital base of the firm. Along with the other capital assets (land, buildings, and equipment), they are the social capital of the firm. Social capital refers to those assets of the firm which are collectively owned rather than allocated to individual member accounts.

The reserve fund is the equivalent of "retained earnings." The cooperatives require a payment of 30% of the net profits until 50% of the social capital consists of reserve funds (retained earnings). Once that level is achieved the cooperative is required by law to allocate a minimum of 10% to the social works fund (Boletin Oficial del Pais Vasco, March 10, 1982). Fifteen percent of the net profits must be designated for the reserve fund each year, unless the amount in the fund is twice the social capital of a given fiscal year. The co-op then has the option of increasing the payment to the social works fund up to the 15% which would have gone to the reserve fund. In either case,

FIGURE 5

The Distribution of Net Profits

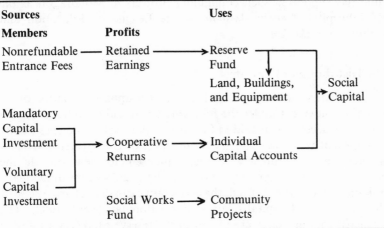

Sources		Uses
Members	**Profits**	
Nonrefundable Entrance Fees	Retained Earnings	Reserve Fund
		Land, Buildings, and Equipment
Mandatory Capital Investment	Cooperative Returns	Individual Capital Accounts
Voluntary Capital Investment		
	Social Works Fund	Community Projects

Social Capital

the co-op must allocate 15% of the net profit to one of these two funds.

The cooperative returns represent a maximum of 70% of the net profit. A cooperative can elect to retain all the surplus in the social and reserve funds, as the CLP did in 1981. According to Thomas and Logan (1982, p. 150), "In the majority of producer cooperatives, the pure surplus has been less than 43 percent of payroll costs from 1975 onwards: the allocation has therefore been 10 per cent to the social fund, 20 per cent to the reserves for job creation and contingencies, and 70 per cent for distribution to members' capital accounts." There are two ways in which the co-ops have chosen to deal with losses. In some co-ops experiencing losses, individual capital accounts and reserves were debited. Other co-ops have established a collective fund at the level of the cooperative group to cover such losses.

When co-ops opt to debit individual accounts, it can be especially hard on new workers who have not established reserves. Often they are still in the process of paying their obligatory contributions to capital when they must also take a cut in anticipated earnings to cover the previous year's losses. This has proven to be a problem especially since the worldwide recession in heavy manufacturing has affected a number of cooperatives.

Typically, 10% of the profits are designated to the social works fund. Spanish law requires a minimum of 10% but it can be higher (Reglamento de la ley general de cooperativas, 1974). These funds are to be used for the benefit of the community in projects of a cultural, professional, or educational nature. The funds may be directed to the community at large or the cooperators themselves. The social works fund has supported such community projects in Mondragon as the local hospital, *Centro Asistencial*; the League of Education and Culture; and *Ikerlan*.

The Distribution of Earnings

Individual earnings are paid to a worker upon termination of his or her employment under the following terms and conditions. An individual's account is repaid in full to a worker or to his or her family in the event of an involuntary termination of employment. When a worker leaves voluntarily to seek other employment outside the cooperatives, the cooperative may retain up to 20% of the individual's holdings. If a worker is fired, the cooperative can deduct up to 30% of their contributed capital (Caja Laboral Popular, April, 1982). The deducted capital shares are placed in the reserve fund (Caja Laboral Popular, July, 1976).

The supervisory board determines the amount to be deducted. It also determines the terms for repayment of a member's contributed capital. The board takes into consideration the financial circumstances of the cooperative and the member's family in determining the terms of repayment. Repayment must be within five years from the date of termination with interest. The interest rate is the basic rate of the Bank of Spain (Caja Laboral Popular, April, 1982).

Although the sanction for leaving the cooperatives seems severe, current and former white-collar employees in professional positions in the CLP, report that they are not generally invoked. Employees who leave are encouraged to return to work in the cooperatives in the future.

CONCLUSIONS

The structure of the cooperative system has become extremely complex since the first co-op was started in 1956. The cooperatives have embedded within their structure the means of maintaining, though not always perfectly, the cooperatives' goals. The broad goals of the cooperative movement—humanism, social justice, and democracy—continue to be adhered to, though the structure has changed over the past 28 years. The Spanish cooperative law which requires social investment in the community reinforces the preexisting commitment of the founders to community development. Yet the form of that development reflects an ongoing commitment to education; the Basque language and culture; improved health care, not only for themselves, but for the community as a whole; and continued expansion of the cooperatives to provide opportunities for new workers. The cooperatives could have utilized their social funds for the exclusive benefit of the cooperators. Instead the social investment has been in the broader community. This emphasis reflects a continued commitment to the original goals of the cooperators. There have been changes in the structure, yet they indicate a high degree of flexibility in the cooperatives, and a willingness to adapt to the needs of members and the environment, without severe goal displacement. These changes will be examined in more detail in the following chapter which examines some specific interventions in the cooperative system.

NOTES

1. See Caja Laboral Popular (August, 1982), especially pp. 77-92, for a discussion of this proposed change.
2. A previous restriction of five percent was raised to 10% in 1979. The change is reflected in the Caja Laboral Popular Estatutes para Cooperativas de Trabajo Asociado, 1976 and 1979.

REFERENCES

Arizmendi-Arrieta, J.M. (1972). La experiencia cooperativa de Mondragon. Documentos del Centro Nacional de Educacion Cooperativa. *Del Arco: 30 años de vida cooperativa.* Zaragoza, Spain: Centro Nacional de Educacion Cooperativa.

Bernstein, P. (1980). *Workplace democratization.* New Brunswick, NJ: Transaction.

Boletin Oficial del Pais Vasco. (1982, March 10). Ley 1/1982 de 11 Febrero sobre "cooperativas."

Caja Laboral Popular. (1982, August). Reflexiones para el cambio en torno a la "experiencia cooperativa." Mondragon: Internal report of the Caja Laboral Popular.

Caja Laboral Popular. (1982, July). Remuneracion de directivos en el grupo cooperativo asociado.

Caja Laboral Popular. (1982, April). Estatutos tipo para cooperativas de trabajo asociado.

Caja Laboral Popular. (1981). Memoria.

Caja Laboral Popular. (1976, July). Contrato de Asociacion para Cooperativas Industriales.

Guttierrez Johnson, A. & Whyte, W.F. (1975). Interview with Don José María Arizmendi. Caja Laboral Popular Library, Mondragon.

Ikerlan. (1980). Brochure.

Larranaga, J. (1981). *Don José María Arizmendi-arrieta y la experiencia cooperativa de Mondragon*. Mondragon: Caja Laboral Popular.

Reglamento de la ley general de cooperativas. (1974). Law 52, Article 42.3. Edita la Confederacion Española de Cooperativas.

Retegui, J. (1979/1980). Perfiles del desarrollo de la Escuela Profesional Politecnica y de Hezibidi Elkartea. *Trabajo y Union*, (December/January), 3-4.

Russell, R., Hochner, A., & Perry, S. (1977). San Francisco's "scavengers" run their own firm. *Working Papers*, (Summer), 32-35.

Thomas, H. & Logan, C. (1982). *Mondragon: An economic analysis*. London: George Allen & Unwin.

Christina Clamp

13
MANAGING COOPERATION AT MONDRAGON: PERSISTENCE AND CHANGE

Cooperatives seek to merge the reality of economic associations with a social vision based on the values of equality, equity, and mutual self-help. This distinguishes them from private corporations which have a different philosophical base. While ownership is separated from control in private corporations, members of cooperatives have control and ownership rights. This alters the practice of management with regard to the disclosure of financial information, the governance of the firm, the management of the firm's assets, and the management of members' aspirations for the firm (Craig, 1980).

Cooperatives rely on a division of labour, as do their counterparts in private enterprise. The key difference is the importance placed on social aspects. The Mondragon cooperatives have not become static over the years. Rather than allowing themselves to be changed by circumstances, the cooperators have sought to maintain a proactive posture. How effectively a co-op meets the social and economic demands of the organization depends largely on its leadership.

In this chapter, we will look at how well the Mondragon system has performed in specific social interventions. The chapter begins with an examination of the management of the cooperatives. Specific areas of social intervention in the recession of the 1970s and early 1980s are analyzed.

CHARACTERISTICS OF MANAGERS

Let us look more closely at who manages the cooperatives. The managers of Mondragon are generally between the ages of 30 and 55

371

and are mostly male. Very few women have entered the ranks of management. Compared to their parents, they are highly educated. Based on the findings of this study, the majority of managers have a background in engineering and have learned management skills through their work in the cooperatives. Fifty percent (n = 50) of the managers interviewed had a degree in engineering. The rest of those interviewed who had higher degrees were evenly divided between those with degrees in business management and those with degrees in arts and sciences (especially economics).

The managers in the Mondragon system acquire a diverse range of skills in their work. Most begin their career as technicians trained in engineering. Within a few years, they are often moved into management positions that require new skills which they learn on the job or through training opportunities.

Management as a Vocation

The experience of management in the cooperatives is a demanding one. This point is best illustrated by the following anecdote, which Alfonso Gorroñogoitia (personal communication, September 9, 1982) shared in an interview. "A manager recently resigned from a co-op with 230 members. And when he left, do you know what he said? 'I am prepared to have one love but not 230!' " Work in the co-ops for most managers is a vocation. Those who stick with it have set aside the opportunity for higher pay and status. Ormaechea agrees with this assessment. "No one wants to be a general manager today. It's more comfortable to occupy a secondary position. General managers are occupied with the problems of sales, purchases, finance, etc . . . . One must want to be a general manager, to have a vocation to be a manager" (personal communication, August 10, 1982).

Mondragon's managers stress that they are businessmen. Yet it is clear many managers have a strong ideological motive for working and staying in the cooperatives. This is an important strength of the managers in the Mondragon system. The general manager of the *Caja Laboral Popular*, José María Ormaechea, explained the importance of a cooperative ideology in management. "A person that only has technical and professional knowledge is of no use to a cooperative. One needs a social component . . . the acceptance of the legitimate dominance of labour over capital, and the democratic rights of the General Assembly" (personal communication, August 10, 1982).

Labour-Management Relations

Management in the cooperatives seeks a participatory style as its ideal, but in reality, management styles range widely. Some managers are authoritarian while others have a highly participatory approach. Those who have a participatory style, see even this as inadequate for ensuring a participatory work environment.

The cooperatives do provide a system of checks on the power of management. Managers are hired under a four-year renewable contract. Should a firm encounter problems with a manager, the supervisory board can dismiss him or her. A cooperative can also veto a budget or other policies through the general assembly. The effectiveness of these checks varies from one cooperative to another.

Sixty-four percent of the managers interviewed were dissatisfied with the level of participation in their co-op. This may reflect a discrepancy between the managers' ideal level of participation and the actual level, rather than an inadequate level of real participation. Tannenbaum, Kavcic, Rosner, Vianello, & Weiser (1974) found such a discrepancy in their study of industrial plants in the kibbutzim of Israel, in Yugoslavia, and the United States. Many of the Mondragon managers cited limitations such as the lack of motivation and abilities of workers and the inadequacy of existing structures for participation, especially the social council.

Most of the co-ops do not offer any ongoing cooperative education for members. The average worker lacks the skills to read the budgets which he or she approves in the annual meeting of the general assembly.[1]

In many cases, management does not experience major differences from private industry in the daily operation of their firms. There are some exceptions where a workforce is well organized and controls the supervisory board. Despite the similarities to private industry, managers often spoke of the management of the cooperatives as being "transparent." For some, this was seen as a problem, an intrusion. For others, it was considered an essential part of cooperative management. Yet in general, management has the authority to administer the co-ops as it sees fit to ensure their financial success.

Bradley and Gelb (1983), in their study of Mondragon, found 59% of the members they surveyed perceived only slight differences between themselves and management. Throughout the interviews with managers in 1982, there was a great deal of concern expressed by them about their relationships with labour. The quality of relations varies with the firm; and age and size of the workforce, are also factors.

Younger workers are better educated and more militant politically. They do not have their parents' memories of the civil war nor their appreciation of how much the co-ops have improved their standard of living. Older workers are more willing to trust management to work in their interests while younger workers are more inclined to question them.

Most small firms have good relations. This is reinforced by social gatherings and the accessibility of managers to the workers. Medium to large firms tend to have greater problems with political polarization in the workforce. In the extreme case, these divisions have been a determining factor in the selection of members for the supervisory board.

In the larger firms, managers are isolated from the workers. They have little understanding of the problems from a shop-floor perspective, unless they have a number of friends who are workers or an effective president of the board to keep them informed.

The social life of Mondragon has in the past served to reduce that isolation. The *cuadrilla*, a group of friends who regularly meet in the evening and on weekends to go for drinks and other social activities, was the centre of social life outside the family. In the older generation of managers, the *cuadrilla* has ensured that managers are exposed to a worker's perspective. Since few people had the opportunity to go to school beyond high school, the older *cuadrillas* have a more heterogeneous composition of workers and professionals.

The data suggests the younger managers often lack this tie to workers for two reasons (see Table 1). Many younger managers prefer to spend their spare time with their families rather than with their *cuadrillas*. Those who are active in a *cuadrilla* often have a group of friends who are also college educated. The net result is that managers have fewer occasions to meet informally with worker/members.

Managers see the worker/members as more demanding of them than are workers in private industry. In most co-ops, management must "punch in" on the time clock along with everyone else, and has few, if any perks. Most managers work 10 or more hours a day. Even though the co-ops close for vacations in August, a number of the managers indicated they worked a portion of their vacation. The absence of such perks serves to minimize the social and economic differences between workers and managers.

Despite the long hours, most managers indicated they would prefer to stay in the cooperatives rather than leave for better paying jobs elsewhere. While they considered the worker/members more demanding than workers elsewhere, they considered labour-management relations to be relatively better than in other firms.

TABLE 1

Managers Who Are Active in a Cuadrilla

Age		Active	Inactive
Under 30	n = 4	3	1
30-39	n = 23	11	12
40 and over	n = 17	13	4

THE ECONOMIC CRISIS OF THE 1970s

The Management Crisis

The years of rapid growth appear to be over for the co-ops. The recession of the '70s and early '80s has had an impact throughout the co-ops. Yet the problems go beyond those of the recession. The oldest and largest of the firms are confronting issues related to their status as "mature industries." In the cooperatives, labour is a fixed cost. When a company is faced with excess inventory or the need to retool or to automate in order to remain competitive, the options available to management are governed by this altered role of labour in the structure of the firm. A manager can lay off workers or reduce work hours, but labour receives 80% of their *anticipo* while they are laid off. Should management wish to automate a plant, new jobs must be found for those workers who would be displaced.

The management crisis is best summarized by the general manager of the *Caja Laboral Popular*, Jose Maria Ormaechea.

> We have determined in the last few years, that many managers are inadequate. During a period of economic growth, there were many managers who could handle themselves comfortably even with some professional shortcomings . . . . At the hour when the management of the cooperative becomes difficult, it has shown us that many managers lack abilities. The problem is not just one of management but also of a lack of technology, markets, and the cost of capital (personal communication, August 10, 1982).

A number of managers are struggling with the problems of developing new markets in a period of slow growth. They are also concerned with how the anticipated entrance of Spain into the European Economic Community will affect them. Some co-ops have already established themselves in the European market and anticipate few problems. Those firms that rely heavily on the domestic market are the most vulnerable.

Despite these challenges (or perhaps because of them), three-fourths of the managers said they enjoyed what they were doing. While many indicated they had no intention of leaving, they frequently spoke of others who had "burned out"; lost their motivation for their work. As the general manager of one large firm said:

> It is inevitable due to our economic situation; the labour of the general manager and the management teams is thankless, hard, and demanding. And it consumes people . . . . The sales are difficult to obtain and rarely produce positive results. So this puts pressure on the entire management team and especially the commercial managers, those who are most immediately confronting the market. The challenge is there . . . that it not be an isolating labour . . . because one can drown in a personal subcrisis and become burned out.

When a manager "burns out," the cooperative system often has the ability to recycle him or her. According to a CLP staff member in the empresarial division, burnout "is a fairly common phenomenon in the group. Our co-ops are characterized by the quantity of managers that burnout. It is difficult to be a good administrator and also a leader of the (cooperative) community. When one is unsuccessful at either of these roles, the manager fails." People can be moved from a front-line position to a staff role in the bank or one of the cooperative groups if an opening exists or can be created. In some instances, people are moved to another co-op. Not everyone who experiences burnout is recycled. Some leave the co-ops. They may need time to "see other alternatives but the door is left open if they want to return."

Turnover in management is a problem. The extent to which changes occurred among management personnel in the group, as reflected in the directory on top management for the cooperatives in 1982, was approximately 10%. The directory listed 576 top management posts, excluding presidents. Of those positions, there were 56 changes in management personnel. About half of those changes were due to the departure of people from the co-ops. Other changes were due to the transfer of people within the system, in some cases as a result of the establishment of new cooperative groups, and the hiving off of two cooperatives from existing co-ops.

In the course of the research, it became clear that people leave for a variety of reasons. Some leave to pursue their professional advancement if a better opportunity arises outside of the co-ops. Others have left to work in the newly formed Basque government.

Most managers remain out of a dedication to a system which they feel better serves the needs of themselves, their coworkers, and their communities. The majority of the managers could go elsewhere if they chose to leave. They have the credentials and the experience to be successful elsewhere.

In the past, the co-ops have preferred to promote people from within the system. Outstanding young technicians are still able to advance themselves professionally in this way. Still, there has periodically been a need to look for management from outside the group. The cooperatives have found it increasingly difficult to hire new experienced managers from outside. There was a scarcity of qualified management people in Spain in 1982 and the cooperatives cannot always compete on an open market for managers due to the pay ratio which in 1982 was 1:3 between the highest and lowest paid members of the cooperatives. On three occasions, management searches were carried out for over a year without success. This was a major factor in the decision to change the pay ratio from 1:3 to 1:4.5 in 1983.

The Changing of the Guard

The co-ops are at a transition point in their history. Mondragon's leaders have been concerned about their ability to continue to lead effectively. They recognize they are not supermanagers. Since 1956, they have successfully launched more than 90 cooperatives. They have been successful entrepreneurs who built on the expertise they had within their industry to grow within it and related industries. The co-ops have developed competent business people with an ability to effectively balance pragmatic concerns against the requirements of a cooperative structure. A new generation of managers is gaining prominence as the first generation recognizes the need for new business expertise at the helm.

Mondragon's leadership is facing a changing environment both internally and in its markets. The demands of labour are likely to increase as better educated workers increase in number. The pressures in the business environment are also likely to pull managers out of the office in search of new markets. Ways must be found to reduce the isolation of managers from workers, to enable labour and management to see their shared values and objectives.

The managers in the Mondragon co-ops have gone a long way toward ensuring a more equitable workplace. Differences between labour and management will persist. Yet as long as they are able to attract people like those currently in the leadership, the cooperatives will continue to grow and learn from their ability to look critically at themselves.

Managing Co-ops in Crisis

The post-World War II period was, as Peter Drucker (1980, pp. 8-9) points out, "a period of unprecedented economic growth, the period of fastest and broadest growth the world economy has ever seen. (It was) also a period of high predictability." The Mondragon system shared in the benefits of that period of rapid growth while maintaining a commitment to its humanistic and democratic values. When the crisis of the early 1970s struck, the cooperatives found changes were necessary to ensure their survival. Changes have occurred. In some cases, the changes have strengthened and reinforced the cooperative values. In others, it has weakened them.

The Economic Environment

The Basque country is at an historic crossroad. The region once provided work for all who chose to come, but it can no longer do so. Unemployment soared in the Basque region and Spain during the 1970s. Between 1972 and 1981, the unemployment rate rose from under four percent to over 16% (Euskadi, 1981). There were 1,510,000 jobs lost in Spain during that period. This meant an annual loss of approximately 252,000 jobs. Jobs lost in the Basque country accounted for about 23,800 per year for the period 1976-1981, a total of 119,000 jobs (Caja Laboral Popular, 1982).

The cooperatives have not escaped unscathed from the recession. The economic hard times have been felt throughout the system, as is reflected in the following statements by management personnel:

> The crisis has changed things and the group (cooperative system) has been greatly affected. There are several cooperatives in a critical situation in large part due to this turn of events. And the development of the cooperative system has moderated, I would say to the extent of stagnancy.
>
> A management consultant in
> the Caja Laboral Popular, 1982.

> The effect of the crisis in the cooperatives is the same as in any other firm. The problem is the capacity of a co-op to react to the crisis. I believe it is extremely interesting because we will really see if the cooperative has elements in its constitution that permits it to endure and overcome the crisis better than a traditional corporation or firm. I believe such firms in positive economic situations obviously have merit and have a concrete aspect to illuminate new solutions. But in any case, a co-op is an enterprise and in consequence not only has positive aspects from the point of view of

new alternatives of participation (having overcome the labour-capital dichotomy), economic buoyancy, and clearly has the internal elements to overcome the situation of crisis. This obviously depends fundamentally on the specific situation of each cooperative since evidently it depends on which sector the cooperative is in. Some are obviously in much more difficult situations than others . . . there are several cooperatives that will have to make some hard decisions and the social community (of the firm) needs to understand them—which is not easy. . . . In my opinion, those firms that have the greatest capacity to make sacrifices will survive the crisis . . . .

> The general director of
> a cooperative group, 1982.

Actually, the group has endured the crisis better than other economic groups and largely because they are co-ops. This is due to the solidarity between cooperatives and because the social-labour crisis has affected the cooperatives much less than elsewhere in the country.

> The manager of a
> medium-sized firm, 1982.

But one thing of which I am certain is that now so much effort which went to creating new things (firms) is now devoted to maintaining existing co-ops and the conversion of established private firms in bad circumstances to cooperatives.

> The president of a
> small cooperative, 1982.

. . . as a community, we have taken some tough measures, such as changes in the work schedule, double shifts . . . . The response to all these measures of an austere nature has been good and the collectivity as such, always responds to the shortfall.

> A plant manager in
> a large firm, 1982.

I am preoccupied . . . that we have to accustom ourselves to a process of no growth in our factories and that there will be a reduction and how will the reduction occur; and the factories will grow older. There has always been a process for rejuvenation through expansion of our facilities. And I believe we will see ourselves grow old . . . . No new blood is entering (the co-ops). And normally over the years, people would enter the cooperatives after they finished their studies . . . and this will stop for at least ten years . . . . I don't know how we will resolve that problem.

> The manager of a
> medium-sized firm, 1982.

The cooperatives, which have set job creation as a major goal, have found themselves unable to do more than maintain those jobs which they have already created. The cooperatives' primary industrial sectors are in heavy metalworking and furniture. Both sectors have been hit hard by the world recession. Due to a job freeze, there was a decline in the number of cooperators from the 1980 high of 18,733 to 18,461 in 1981. The reduction in jobs (272 posts) was brought about primarily through attrition in the industrial cooperatives.

What is remarkable is that the cooperatives have been able to avoid the plant closings and job losses experienced by other firms in the region. The cooperatives might have promoted new jobs in the service sector but they see their commitment remaining within manufacturing and agriculture. That goal remains unchanged.

THE COOPERATIVE RESPONSE

The cooperatives have maintained essentially full employment through a series of measures, including a major expansion into export markets; and solidarity and cooperation between co-ops in instituting a job freeze, deploying excess workers to other firms, and allocating capital resources.

The Market Strategy

The shift to foreign markets has meant an increase in exports from 1,343 million pesetas to 19,512 million in 1981. Exports accounted for 12.6% of sales in 1972. As of 1981, exports were 23.4% of total sales (Table 2). Domestic sales increased by only 15% that same year.

The change in markets has implications beyond its immediate importance to the economic viability of the cooperatives. Those cooperatives which have well established foreign markets are likely to benefit from the entrance of Spain into the European Economic Community (EEC) when and if it occurs. The cooperatives that are operating primarily in the Spanish market have not been exposed to outside competition since there has been a longstanding policy of protectionism which has given a competitive edge to Spanish firms. The cooperatives in agribusiness are also expected to benefit from joining the EEC.

TABLE 2

Exports as a Percentage of Sales

Year	Exports/Sales
1972	12.58
1973	12.49
1974	11.13
1975	11.9
1976	12.12
1977	12.06
1978	13.49
1979	15.83
1980	19.66
1981	23.39

Source: CLP (1981). *Memoria*, pp. 60-61.

Labour as a Fixed Cost

Cooperatives do not have the same ability to manipulate their labour costs as do conventional firms. In noncooperative firms, management decides how many workers it will hire at the going rate based on the firm's expected sales for that year. During recessionary times, many workers are laid off since the expected output is low. The Mondragon firms are fortunate in that their size has provided them a way to address the fluctuations of the market, not only at the level of the individual firm, but at the level of the cooperative group and the system.

At a systemic level, the cooperatives have addressed the problems of the changing market since July, 1980, through a job freeze; the shifting of office workers into blue-collar work (*Directizacion de Mano de Obra Indirecta*); an agreement to shift workers from their cooperatives to others during periods of adversity (*Convenio Inter-cooperativo Sobre el Desempleo*); and the adoption of flexible calendars. Each cooperative can hire up to 10% of its workforce from other cooperatives and from outside the cooperatives. This was increased from five percent in the mid-1970s. In this way, the cooperatives have been able to maintain their commitment to full employment.

The system of shifting workers to other cooperatives is not free of problems but has ensured employment and eased the drain on the resources of firms in financial trouble. One thousand, one hundred and eighty workers (approximately six percent of the work force) moved to other cooperatives during the period July, 1980, to February, 1981 (Gutierrez-Johnson, 1982). Approximately 400 workers were employed in other cooperatives between May, 1981, and May, 1982, (Gardner, 1982).

The following three accounts describe the worker-exchange system from a management perspective in firms sending workers to other firms. All three reflect the need to establish a system of selecting workers that is fair, yet which ensures workers with essential skills are retained.

> Frankly, there was a condition which facilitated it. We had during some years a reduction in the work week and of earnings. When the possibility arose that another cooperative needed people, we went to them and arrived at an accord. They needed 20 people. Since we had a reduced work week, people had the opportunity to earn more money there than here. The first time we were able to identify 20 volunteers without major problems. This was the first time.
>
> There were other demands and no more volunteers. Then, they had to call people and tell them . . . .
> Clamp: *How long have people been working elsewhere?*
> For two years.
> Clamp: *And are they kept informed?*
> Yes. Every two months there is a meeting to brief them on the firm's progress and to listen to their problems.
>
> > The director of personnel in
> > a large cooperative firm, 1982.

In a second cooperative, they found that the transfer of workers is easier in principle than in practice.

> . . . at the end of 1981, in October, the first six people left; then four more to a total of 11 that have been outside for three or four months. Currently there are five persons working in other cooperatives.
> Clamp: *How was the decision made as to who would go?*
> The first that went had been told that there were too many people and some would have to leave . . . A plan was made of what they would earn; in what conditions they would have to work. And those who went at first, volunteered themselves. In fact, today, they are still working there. They were all from the same section. Their reasons for doing it varied . . . . Some said "if you have to go to work elsewhere, I prefer to remain in my own town . . ." And so they volunteered for three months.
>
> Others, because they weren't from here and their families are in Galicia, would have a full week of vacation which suited them very well. Our cooperative doesn't have that calendar, so they

opted to work three months, saying: "I will earn the same, etc. and have a week of vacation."

After those volunteers, no one else offered to go and so the director of production prepared a list . . . . Anyone whose skills were considered indispensible (26 people) remained free in one section of the firm. Another list was prepared of 36 persons from the other section. The group of 26 were told to elect two or three from a group of three or four. Everyone was called together and told who was on the list and why. Not everyone was content and convinced, but they were told the reasons why some had been chosen as possible candidates. The selection was then made . . . . People were given 15 days advanced noticed before the change.

> The director of personnel in
> a medium-sized firm, 1982.

The process in one of the Ularco cooperatives, where there have been a number of workers transferred to other cooperatives, is the most complex of the procedures described.

. . . three years ago, 40 to 50 people were sent out (to other cooperatives). This month we will send 15 people to other cooperatives. By the end of the year, I expect that another 30 to 40 people will have to go, and more next year since we are not profitable . . . .

How does one determine who goes? Now what happens is that there are rules developed which you will encounter in some other cooperatives as well, where they have the rule that if there is a need to reduce the number of work posts, it must be approved by a technical committee that determines which posts are affected. Then the plan is presented to a social control committee which includes the participation of members of the social council. They examine the extent to which a layoff is warranted and then the board decides whether to lay off workers or not.

Afterwards, where there is more than one person in the same post, one needs to have criteria that is a function of professionalism or seniority etc. . . . .

The last time went reasonably well. The one thing which can happen and inevitably does is that production workers quickly notice that office workers are not affected by this.

> The general manager of a
> large firm in the Ularco group, 1982.

A number of managers and nonmanagerial members assume that workers are concerned exclusively with the bread-and-butter issues of job security and good pay and benefits. This system seems much better to them than the periodic layoffs experienced in many (though not all) conventional firms.

Workers in the Mondragon cooperatives are increasingly more critical of apparent inequities between labour and management. The present research suggests a possible explanation for some of the conflict. There are serious differences between workers and managers in some of the cooperatives. The greater criticism is in part related to the higher level of education and often more leftist politics of younger workers. Another factor is the length of work experience in the cooperatives. Older workers, who joined during the period of economic prosperity, are more inclined to see the cooperatives as an end in themselves and to be more trusting of management. Younger workers tend to see the cooperatives as a means to an end and are more distrustful of management. When the cooperatives are prosperous, the expectations of both groups are satisfied; when a recession occurs, conflicts increase due to their different expectations. Further research is necessary to test this hypothesis.

Management accounts of the system of transferring workers suggest that there have been problems due to the unwillingness of the majority of workers to volunteer for even short transfers. A white paper written by workers in one of the Ularco cooperatives provides a perspective on why some workers have been critical of the system. Along with the system of job valoration and pay scales, the transfer system is seen as a means of social control of workers by managers. They argue that this institutionalizes a "system of fear." Management "can determine who works a lot or not, based on whether one talks or not, if one is sympathetic to management or not" (White paper, n.d.). Their distrust stems in part from the fact that white-collar workers have not been transferred elsewhere. The burden of the cutbacks have been disproportionately born by blue-collar workers.

The cooperative where these criticisms surfaced has sought to address the concerns raised by the white paper. Efforts were made to redirect white-collar workers to equalize the burden of the recession. The general manager of the cooperative acknowledged the workers' concern as legitimate. Yet, he argued it is more difficult to determine who can be shifted from professional levels into production.

> Where such a shift is to occur with white-collar workers, it needs to be for a longer period of time because one may be sacrificing much more at a professional level. It is not to our advantage to sacrifice a strong technician and then to discover within two months that he/she is needed. The process of assessing our indirect labour needs is much slower and requires other means of assessing it. That does not mean that it will not be done because it would be wrong not to, from a business perspective.

Another manager in the Ularco system supports this view:

> Yes it is traumatic to be transferred from office work to produc-
> tion—especially for some types of people—for example, a
> 50-year-old office worker who has spent all his/her life working in
> an office and then is transferred to an assembly line . . . there are
> some who are not transferred to production work but are
> relocated in another equivalent post.

A CLP department head who was critical of this transfer of office
workers had the following objections.

> The phenomena of regulating production work has been a blow to
> many people. People that were set in their jobs suddenly had to go
> to the assembly line, change their job, lower their indexes, etc.
> This has hurt many people psychologically, not only because they
> had to go to the assembly line, but also it has broken their preset
> work values. They view their entrance into the cooperatives as
> "manipulated." I don't believe it was a manipulation but a
> necessary conversion. But they understand it as a cruel manipula-
> tion of people . . . .

Antagonism toward management does not explain why all
workers are unwilling to transfer voluntarily. Transferred workers
also experience stress due to changes in the type of work they do and
the separation from their friends and community. The director of personnel in one firm that has received a large number of workers from
other cooperatives related the following experience.

> Everyone has suffered a great deal at the outset, especially
> workers over age 30. They suffer a great deal because they come
> feeling a terrible uncertainty. They often are men who have been
> in the same post for many years. (Here) they go from one day to
> another with new people. Our people have received them well.
> They have no problems and now I see people from different
> towns have remained friends after they worked here together. It is
> the uncertainty that makes people suffer so much.
>
> I even had a case where a man was affected psychologically
> and we had to send him back to his co-op because he was so
> disturbed by it. Many times one of our youths of 20 or 25 years
> knows a post, and will be asked to teach a 40-year-old man from
> another cooperative. This can be a problem at the outset, but
> overall it has been a very good experience.
>
> The director of personnel in
> a medium-sized cooperative, 1982.

A transferred worker employed at the *Caja Laboral* explained
that she had not worked in her own cooperative for a couple of years.

Her firm had placed her and nine other workers on an indefinite layoff. When the cooperative can locate work for them, they work where they are sent and are paid their travel costs as well as their full salary. When she is not employed, she receives 80% of her salary.

She is worried that things will get worse and has no idea when or if she will ever work in her cooperative again. The possibility of joining another cooperative, she observed, is unlikely since "no cooperative wants new members. They cannot afford to hire anyone except from time to time."

Managers see this as a good but imperfect solution.

> Evidently with the establishment of this mechanism of solidarity, no one pretends that those who transfer workers are angels, nor those who receive them.
>
> A staff member of Ularco, 1982.

Not all workers who are transferred are "bad" workers. The cooperatives which have received workers from other co-ops have found some "good" and "bad" workers.

> There have been problems because in some sites, the "worst" workers were sent . . . . In other cases, people were sent without a clear explanation why. And this creates problems . . . . But this is better than sending people into the street.
>
> The general manager of one of
> the cooperative groups, 1982.

Overall, the experience with this system has been positive. Cooperative managers, especially outside of the Upper Deva valley, see the importance of solidarity, yet encounter pressure from their members and local politicians to provide work for local people. They recognize that someday they may need to turn to the other cooperatives for similar help, though in practice it has been difficult to gain local acceptance for the exchange.

> What percentage do we have of personnel from outside? Twenty-six percent.
>
> There are people here who are 60 years old or over, that have children who are 17 or older and are unemployed . . . . And the member asks: "I work here, generated wealth; I have capital. I have money here and the result is that my children are out of work. For whom am I providing work? To give it to members of other co-ops?" This is constantly coming up. Or with *Auzo Lagun* (the women's co-op), we have 80 or more women working here. The workers see them and say: "There are women here from *Auzo Lagun* . . . who are married and working etc., etc. And they work part-time. Many of them are older; their families are grown

and married. Therefore, they have two salaries . . . ." It is difficult to resolve.

The personnel director of
a large cooperative, 1982.

I want to make clear that the motivation of the group of 12 people that formed the cooperative here was to seek a solution to the unemployment in these three municipalities . . . . With 30,000 inhabitants, there are 1,500 unemployed, that is, 1,500 last year . . . . This year there will be more. The people from here ask that we hire local people. The cooperatives ask us to do otherwise.

The manager of a
small cooperative, 1982.

In the community and the members' homes, there are children, family members who are unemployed and on the street . . . . I am bringing people from other areas . . . . We can't say that we are resolving the local unemployment problem. But we can say if one day we are in a crisis, who will solve our unemployment problem? Those who are unemployed on the street or the other co-ops that in that moment we had said to come here and work?

The personnel director of
a medium-sized firm, 1982.

Initially this accord was well received in general terms as something that would help everyone. The problem presented to us here was by one faction that disagreed with us when we brought personnel in from other co-ops. (They said) that we were resolving the problems of communities 20, 25, or 30 kilometers away when we had done nothing about the problems here. It was then responded to even to the level of the municipal government. The mayor publically expounded on the topic as a solution to the problems of other towns at the expense of the local towns . . . which I believe was one of the most stupid things that the mayor could have said . . . . I, in particular, continue to consider it a good thing and it would be absurd to reject a proposal of this sort.

The general manager of the
same medium-sized firm, 1982.

The process of transferring workers is an important innovation for ensuring the stability of the firms. It is a measure that is consistent with the principle of cooperative solidarity. The problems which have arisen around this system reflect the need for labour and management to play active roles in the process of selecting workers for transfer. Where transfers are determined only by management, workers are likely to see it as a "system of fear" that serves a social control function.

Where workers did organize to protest the transfers, management demonstrated a willingness to involve the social council and to establish a clearly defined process. This eliminated worker concerns that transfers might be used as a means of punishing "troublesome" workers.

The cooperatives have adapted to the recession in ways beyond the shifting of workers. The importance of solidarity among the cooperatives was recognized early in the formation of the cooperatives. The recession has served to reinforce its importance. Renewed efforts were underway in 1982 to strengthen the existing cooperative groups and to make new groups operational.

The Ularco group has standardized the net surplus (profits) since 1965 when it was established. This means 100% of the profits are distributed equally amongst all workers of Ularco member cooperatives. Workers in each of the Ularco cooperatives had to approve such an accord. The other cooperative groups have not had time to develop intercooperative solidarity to the same extent. Five of them were founded in 1978; another five in 1980, and two more in 1981. Learko, a group founded in 1978, is slowly standardizing its net surplus up to a limit of 70%.

> For 1981, we are (standardized) for 20%; in 1982, 30%; and 1983, 40%; and in this way to 70% . . . .
> First, the amounts to be returned to members, the retained earnings and the social fund is determined. Then the individual capital gains of all the cooperatives (in a group) and say for example, let's take 30%. So if here we have 20 million pesetas and here it was five and let's say here it was 18; 30% of each would be six million of the first one; 1.5 million from the next, and 5.4 of the third. And what do we do with that? We distribute it equally. And by 1986, we will do it with 70% of the earnings.
>
> The general director of
> a cooperative group, 1982.

Another measure for protecting the cooperatives in recessionary times is the creation of a sinking fund for emergencies. Danona, a furniture manufacturer, drew on such a fund to recoup losses from a fire in 1978. Like many other cooperatives, Danona has at times addressed the recessionary problem of excess inventory with a shortened work week. Depending on the cooperative's situation, workers may recoup the hours within a year.

There has been a decline in the rate of growth in earnings in many cooperatives. Many are attempting to increase their capital reserves by requiring new member contributions to capital. Labour costs were reduced by 3.6% (against total sales) in the period 1978-1981 (Caja

Laboral Popular, 1981). Bradley and Gelb, in a forthcoming article, "Mixed Economy" versus "Cooperative Adjustment," found that in Ularco, workers experienced an 11% pay cut in 1980. Two months' wages were capitalized. "In 1981, 1982, and 1983 respectively, the group paid only 90.8, 93.0 and 93.5 percent of CLP scales" (p. 22). Their findings support this study's conclusion that pay scales in the cooperatives have fallen sharply compared to those outside the cooperatives. This in turn has made more capital available to the bank to help firms which are in trouble. The need to increase the self-financing of the cooperatives has risen due to the adoption of new policies in the CLP in 1981. One of these policies states that the CLP will not assume a risk greater than a set percentage of the firm's assets (generally 100%). This has resulted in a critical situation in about 20% of the cooperatives. According to Bradley and Gelb's (in press) recent study,

> At the same time as five cooperatives have been closed or are closing, five new ones are being launched despite the generally difficult circumstances of the Spanish economy . . . the closing cooperatives represent cases in which the CLP's share of assets has risen to over 60 percent and there is no hope of resuscitation through an austerity/capital restructuring program. Nine cooperatives, mostly small, are now undergoing such programs and in total 26 cooperatives are experiencing intervention in their management by the CLP. Where a cooperative closes, workers lose their financial investment but are given preference in hiring where temporary or permanent jobs are available. They are considered "insiders" and receive unemployment compensation from Lagun-Aro (pp. 29-30).

This change was considered necessary to reduce the level of financial risk assumed by the bank (Aguinano, 1982). An explanation for the changes was provided by a bank staff member.

> We had been giving credit and it wasn't returned. Another credit would be given to repay the first one and so on. Last year for the first time, an independent auditor came and said, "You are counting these as good loans when they aren't, because you will never collect the 200, 500 or 700 million that you have given to this firm. Therefore you cannot call this one of your active ones when it doesn't exist. This firm has lost it. Therefore, of the two billion of credits that we have given, 700 million is bad debt because A.A. (the auditor) says so and refuses to sign it . . . .
> A CLP staff member, 1982.

Despite the unpopularity of these measures in some quarters, the cooperatives have successfully maintained full employment and a modest rate of growth. The fact that the cooperatives have done this elicits admiration from even the most critical of its members.

The Changing Bank Role

The bank has established stricter conditions for CLP-affiliated cooperatives with regard to the initial capital contribution of members in new cooperatives, the compliance of the cooperatives with the contract of association, and affiliation with cooperative groups. Guidelines were also published for the relationship between the CLP and cooperatives in trouble. Included in the guidelines are requirements that the firm undergo some severe financial changes, and develop a plan to restore itself to profitability within 10 years. These policy changes are all intended to shift the financial burden more fully back onto the cooperatives and cooperative groups.

The bank has in many respects played a social welfare role for a number of cooperatives in the past. The extent of the recession has raised questions about the appropriateness of that role. The bank's role, one can hypothesize, is affected by the external economic environment. When the economy is growing, the CLP serves primarily an entrepreneurial and banking function. During periods of recession, the CLP fulfills a social welfare and banking function. The cooperatives in turn experience a loss of autonomy as the bank's financial involvement with a firm increases.

The CLP provided credit to new cooperatives and those in short-term financial difficulties at eight percent in 1983. The market rate was 15%. In more serious cases, the bank provided interest-free loans. Since the bank must pay a competitive rate to its depositors, the overall effect is that of a subsidy to these co-ops by other co-ops in the system, according to Bradley and Gelb (in press).

There is widespread concern that the bank's role needs to be reexamined. There is a proposal to spin off the entrepreneurial division as central services to a cooperative congress. The bank would then have solely a conventional banking function. The risk in this proposal is that the bank could lose sight of its commitment to serve the cooperatives.

The bank has since its inception maintained a very definite commitment to serve the cooperatives. Ormaechea, the general manager, is tremendously influential in its operation and has ensured a high level of commitment. Yet, he is not subject to the four-year contract negotiated with managers in other cooperatives. The combination of his long tenure and the central function of finance, has resulted in his being perceived as inordinately powerful. As a result, there is much support for the increased role of the cooperative groups as a vehicle for the cooperatives to help themselves. The data does not indicate whether the reorganization of the bank would be widely supported by management in the cooperatives.

Those firms which deal with the bank through their cooperative groups have found this preferable to working directly with the bank. Managers in several of the small cooperatives objected to the necessity of having to meet personally with Ormaechea, the bank's general manager, each time they needed to negotiate a loan. They all indicated they would prefer a less paternalistic approach to the negotiation of loans.

CONCLUSION

The experience of the Mondragon cooperators, as this discussion has highlighted, has been one of an extremely dynamic and fluid organizational system. While they remain guided by their cooperative values and the need for good business practices, they have changed the system when conditions required it. Rather than rigidly adhering to rules and structures, they have engaged in a system-wide debate on proposed interventions. This has ensured effective participation of all the cooperatives in the intervention process. It has also fostered a critical self-appraisal of proposed changes. Not all changes are wholly successful, as this discussion has indicated. The social councils have not ensured a greater level of rank and file participation as they had intended. The recycling of workers which has addressed the problems of short-term layoffs still raises questions regarding the problems experienced by workers who are transferred to other firms.

The recession was a painful and difficult time for the cooperatives. The various interventions were successful in the sense that they ensured workers steady employment while protecting the business interests of the various firms. The overall effect on the system has been to increase the degree of cooperation between cooperatives (the recycling of labour and the sharing of profits/losses) while decentralizing more of the financial decision-making to the cooperative group level.

NOTES

1. This was determined on the basis of informal conversations with people during the course of the research.

REFERENCES

Aguinano, J. (1982). *El movimiento cooperativo de Mondragon*. Paper presented at a conference of socialists in Holland for the political party *Euskadiko Eskerra*.

Bradley, K. & Gelb, A. (in press). "Mixed economy" versus "cooperative adjustment": Mondragon's experience through Spain's recession. *Harvard Business Review*.

Bradley, K., & Gelb, A. (1983). *Cooperation at work: The Mondragon experience*. London: Heinemann Educational Books.

Caja Laboral Popular. (1982). *El desempleo en el Pais Vasco*.

Caja Laboral Popular. (1981). *Memoria*.

Craig, J.G. (1980). Managing cooperative organizations. *Working paper no. 4*. Saskatoon: The Co-operative College of Canada.

Drucker, P. (1980). *Managing in Turbulent Times*. London: Pan Books.

Euskadi. (1981). *Boletin de coyuntura y estadistica del Pais Vasco (No. 7)*. Elaborado por Camera Oficial de Comercio, Industria y Navegacion de Guipuzcoa, Camera Oficial de Comercio, Industria y Navegacion de Bilbao.

Gardner, D. (1982, June 10). Cooperative experiment a success. *Financial Times*, p. III.

Gutierrez-Johnson, A. (1982). *Industrial democracy in action*. Unpublished Doctoral dissertation, Cornell University.

Tannenbaum, A.S., Kavcic, B., Rosner, M., Vianello, M., & Wieser, G. (1974). *Hierarchy in organizations*. San Francisco: Jossey-Bass.

White paper from workers in an Ularco cooperative (n.d.).

Alexander Lockhart

14
COMMUNITY-BASED DEVELOPMENT AND CONVENTIONAL ECONOMICS IN THE CANADIAN NORTH

INTRODUCTION

Despite overwhelming evidence that orthodox economic develop-ment theory has become dangerously maladapted to contemporary social and environmental realities, this vestige of a more innocent stage in the evolution of economic model building continues to dominate developmental decision making throughout the Western world. The results, measured in terms of the statistics of human dislocation and environmental disaster, are everywhere apparent. Alternative development models are evolving, of which community-based development appears to hold the greatest potential for achieving some fundamental change in our socio-economic survival strategy. Advocates of community-based development share the view that social accounting is at least as important as economic record keeping in evaluating costs and benefits; that smaller-scale, decentralized development aimed at the maximization of self-sufficiency is more supportive of human survival needs than are the dependency-producing dynamics of centralized economic consolidation; and that without a return to a community focus in developmental planning and action, neither the individual's psychological nor the nation state's political integrity can much longer survive the destructive dynamics of economic consolidation and cultural homogenization (Ross & Usher, 1986).

Whenever these contending economic philosophies confront each other, one is inevitably reminded of the fable of David and Goliath. This is nowhere more apparent than in the Canadian North where the struggle between community-based economies and mega-project development has taken on truly epic dimensions. As a means of setting the stage for a more detailed discussion of David's battle with Goliath in the Canadian North, a brief summary of the character traits of each is in order.

THE CONVENTIONAL
ECONOMIC DEVELOPMENT WISDOM

Conventional economics texts invariably identify three basic factors that enter into the economic development equation. These are land, labour, and capital. Most go on to stress that "modern" development only can occur after the "traditional" restrictions of culturally particular community allegiance are systematically replaced with institutions committed to individual mobility and the "convergence" of social values into a "one-dimensional," universalistic value framework (e.g., Rostow, 1960; Kerr, Dunlop, Harbison, & Myers, 1964). Only in this way, it is argued, can economic production factors be freed from social and political inhibitions so as to ensure their optimal utilization and maximum growth. Particular stress is placed on the argument that if capital is to be allocated efficiently, it must be free to move wherever it can most rapidly multiply itself through the accumulation of profits. While there is rarely any discussion of how fairly production benefits are divided between inhabitants of the peripheral region from which so much new wealth is extracted and those from the economic centres which dominate world order development, the presumption of progress for all is implicit within this orthodox developmental model (Wallerstein, 1974).

By the same token, this same model of promiscuous development argues that those who sell their labour should be free from community obligations to go wherever the pay is highest. At first glance this would seem only fair in relation to capital's freedom to move about without any sense of obligation to the social base that produced it. However, on closer examination it appears that this attempt to argue the individual advantages to be derived from being a free agent serves only to disguise the personal crises experienced by those who have lost their fail-safe community supports and therefore must move on, or go under, whenever a footloose developer seeks greener pastures.

Indeed, the degree to which the assumptive roots of this economic theory deny the functionality of the communal and celebrate the authority of the individual created serious ideological inconsistencies when the joint stock company systematically replaced individual entrepreneurship as the primary instrument of modern industrial development. In order to rationalize the new organizational reality with the old individualist ideology, these inherently collective enterprises were legally defined as "corporate" bodies (meaning joined as in one individual). But whereas communitarian collectivism implies a balanced reciprocity between individual rights and collective obligations, corporate collectivism seeks to maximize the rights of those fortunate few who pool their narrowly vested economic interests, while at the same time minimizing their obligations to any wider community of interests.

Given this, what do these same orthodox economics texts say about the third developmental factor, that of the land and the human communities that are bound to the land? Since geography, whether viewed physically, socially, or politically, could hardly be conceived of as an item of capricious mobility, conventional economic development theory considers the land, and those riches which lie upon or within it, as a commodity which may be "freely" appropriated and as easily abandoned when quick gain commercial values have been exploited. To be sure, the notion that resource utilization rents may be charged has always been accepted in classical economic theory. But, to the extent that these renters are permitted to come and go as they please, they enjoy an inevitable advantage over those who seek fair compensation for the local depletions and foregone opportunities that alien development typically produces. Nor do transient resource renters acquire much empathy for the interests of those with a sense of long-term stewardship. As for the personal disruptions and social pathologies that externally imposed development may create within communities suffering these negative impacts, orthodox development models simply label these social aberrations as "externalities" that lie conveniently outside the economic cost-benefit determination formulas.

Of course, not all economists would admit to such a fundamentalist interpretation of the *homo economus* gospel. But, as Bennett has noted in the introduction to this collection, the limits of reformism are most definitively encountered as those who would "tinker" approach the boundaries of the established system's assumptive framework. Indeed, it is when these boundaries are transgressed that science converges with religion in its predisposition to excommunicate heretics. As a consequence, it is not until we broaden the notion of development from the confines of narrow economic scientism in order to include those "other-than-by-bread-alone" factors which have always served to empower our actions and enrich our lives, that we are able even to approach the more inclusive question of human development.

THE COMMUNITY-BASED
DEVELOPMENT ALTERNATIVE

The concept of community-based development differs dramatically from the orthodox economic development model. Whereas the conventional development wisdom identifies the individual's wellbeing in terms of transient corporate interests—interests which, as already noted, have sought to loosen the individual's sense of social connectedness—the community-based development perspective identifies individual wellbeing specifically in terms of the collective identification of community needs and wants. The critical concept that distinguishes community-based from corporately-based development lies in an understanding of "community" as more than a bedroom and service annex to alien commercial interests. Such a notion of community begins with the recognition of the crucial role that the building of shared commitments to the common well-being plays in the attainment of social health and individual satisfaction.

At the heart of the community-based developmental understanding of community lie three equally important process variables. These have been aptly categorized by Matthews (1976 & 1983) as *economic viability, social vitality*, and *political validity*.

In their efforts to develop an operational model for identifying and evaluating community processes, Blishen & Lockhart (1979) utilized a similar set of process variables which, in essence, were defined as follows:

Economic viability refers to the ability of a community, as a community, to sustain the material needs of its members over time. Though such viability may be achieved in a number of ways, it is in all cases dependent upon the creation of an adequate level of material productivity and long-term continuity to ensure the survival and stability of the social system of which it is a part.

Social vitality refers to the process through which individuals engage in reciprocal relations in order to satisfy social needs, share knowledge, resolve problems, and as a consequence of all this, pursue some common understanding of life meaning. To achieve these social requisites, a community must come to share a set of core values, beliefs, and identities. Without this sharing, there can be no basis for mutual trust or a collective sense of security.

Political efficacy is the process of achieving some commonly acceptable basis of power mobilization and distribution through which decisions concerning individual claims and public welfare are made and as a consequence of which collective initiatives and reactions are mobilized.

If there is any single characteristic that separates the Goliath of orthodox economic development from the David of community-based development, it is that the former rejects these processes as relevant to its fundamental goal of rapid economic growth through profit maximization. In contrast, community-based models explicitly recognize that human satisfaction requires integrity and consistency within and between these fundamental components of social survival.

By understanding the critical importance of each of these three community *process* variables in the determination of developmental priorities, it quickly becomes apparent that those who argue for narrowly *product*-defined development must be recognized as promoting not the economics of self-sufficiency and renewal but of dependency and depletion. Alternatively, those seeking to pursue a more self-reliant, sustained, and diversified approach to development must seek to harness those vital processes through which locally particular social and political experience are brought into focus with the more conventional economic feasibility considerations. It is only when these processes are harnessed that the inevitable tension between a community's need for conservation and preservation, on the one hand, and growth and change, on the other, can achieve optimal resolution.

In short, community-based development, which is primarily dependent upon an understanding of ongoing community processes, scans the totality of human needs, potentials, and limitations. It seeks to liberate the creative energies, to focus the adaptive potentials, and to tap the special knowledge of culturally rooted people who are committed to making their place a better place, and in so doing also to create a better region, nation, and world. The community-based developmental aproach is above all a self-reliant approach. It is not, as its technocratic detractors would have us think, synonymous with the static "traditionalism" that makes those who pursue it dependent upon subsidy because it denies hard-nosed economic principles. On the contrary, community-based development, precisely because it emphasizes a long-range social commitment, is far more sensitive to economic viability than the short-term, boom-bust forms of developmental thinking. Indeed, wherever community-based development has been consciously pursued, it is quality of life, not quantity of consumption, that becomes the critical social factor. And it is the potential for locally ensured livelihoods, not the job promises of outsiders, that is held to be the most relevant economic variable. Thus a community-based development strategy recognizes the real economic advantages and securities to be gained from an organic blending of smaller and larger, traditional and modern forms of enterprise within the *enabling* environment of local commitment rather than the *disabling* context of outside control. Further, such a strategy anticipates the creative forces arising out of the diversity of locally determined needs and wants as well as the real "relative advantage" to be gained from utilizing the community's unique understandings of what the local social and physical ecology can, or cannot, sustain.

While it should be recognized that human development everywhere requires community, nowhere is this more apparent than in the remote North where environmental conditions make life intolerable without a sense of physical rootedness, social bonding, cultural continuity, and economic security—all the things that externally imposed development in the North has not, and seemingly cannot, provide.

NORTHERN DEVELOPMENT ISSUES

To begin to understand the northern development conundrum, we must go beyond a notion of the North as an underdeveloped resource reserve with some residual aboriginal claim problems that are temporarily inhibiting it from being brought on stream as a source of support for the ever-expanding demands of a consumer driven Southern economy. The Canadian North is a culturally diverse, socially rich, politically innovative and, until heavily impacted by "modern" developmental forces, unquestionably one of the most self-reliant regions in the world. Indeed, from a Northern perspective the bitter irony is that the more new "development" has been promoted from outside, the more the region's established population (both indigenous and long-stay Euro-Canadian) have been rendered marginal (Rea, 1976). Recognizing that with this kind of development comes economic dependency, social disintegration, and political paralysis, virtually all long-stay northerners, whatever their other differences (of which there are many), perceive themselves as fundamentally different from southern Canadians and to be undergoing a form of exploitation characteristic of an earlier period of colonization (Dacks, 1981).

It is therefore incumbent upon those seeking self-reliant alternatives to our current dependency-producing development orthodoxies to understand the profoundly different, but also profoundly instructive, characteristics of northern community life. What are some of these differences?

As one travels north, the population density decreases

dramatically from just over 2000 per 100 square miles for all of Ontario (which contains a large segment of the middle north) to three per 100 square miles for the Northwest Territories. Combining Hamelin's (1978) three levels of "Nordicity" (the middle, far, and extreme North), the total northern region contains no more than a million people. In the extreme north, where Natives are in the majority, the population is less than a tenth of this total. Though small in proportion to the southern population, these Native northerners are also the most fertile and hence fastest growing ethnic group in the nation.

In terms of settlement patterns, over 70% of northerners live in small communities, for the most part with populations between 200 and 2000 (Science Council of Canada, 1977). Isolated community life is therefore a major feature of northern existence, a feature reinforced by the infrastructural limits placed on transportation by geography and climate.

In considering the natural environment, there is a tendency to confuse size with strength. That nature is abundant is perhaps the most obvious feature of the North. But this fact should not overshadow the inherent fragility which climate imposes on natural renewal and variation. It is the renewable resources that have to be given pride of place if northerners are to ensure a viable future for themselves. Thus the removal of non-renewable resources must always be balanced against the impact of such exploitation upon the tenuous renewable resource chain as well as on a clear understanding of the North's own future needs for such irreplaceable resources.

Economically, the contemporary North contains both a "traditional" and a "wage" economy. This in itself is no bad thing. Indeed, any realistic notion of self-reliance in the northern context demands a blending of these two economic systems. What makes the two components of the North's economy so perniciously incompatible is the extent to which the wage economy is externally controlled and narrowly focused upon non-renewable resource extraction. As it currently functions, this wage economy is either prejudiced against the participation of those who wish also to pursue some traditional economic activity or, to the extent that it seeks to accommodate such individuals, serves to destroy the very basis of community life and thus to increase individual alienation and social pathology. Dacks (1981, p. 21) describes this process as follows:

> . . . wage labour individualizes economic activity. Whereas hunting, fishing, and trapping involve varying degrees of cooperation among the members of a family ((or community)), who share the fruits of their common labours, wage employment means a paycheck for a single individual for whom sharing means giving without receiving in

return anything equally tangible. As a result, wage employment can lead the individual to see his interests in competition with the interests of others with whom he would normally wish to share. This feeling can erode the sense of community so basic to native social organization.

This reflects the third world "dual economy" developmental pattern in which the indigenous population is presented with an either/or choice of marginalization within the traditional community-based socio-economy or co-optation within an unstable individualized high risk socio-economy.

Culturally, the North embodies a wide range of values and life-styles of which the most obvious Native/Euro-Canadian distinctions are both over-emphasized and under-representative of the real diversity. But to note this is not to argue that northern society is "pluralistic" in the sense that diverse interests and life-styles co-exist within some larger homogeneous whole. On the contrary, most of the North's cultural variety is distributed within internally homogeneous, but mutually heterogeneous communities. Clearly, if community-based development is, as has been argued here, the best guarantee of achieving self-reliance while maintaining cultural diversity, then it is in the context of Northern community aspirations that its greatest demonstration potential may be found. For not only is the North a land of village states, each with its own strongly felt need for independent development, but it is also a land where the social traditions do not support prolonged conflicts between diverse interests. As a consequence, there is a great deal of respect for the autonomy of others and a willingness bred of necessity to forge viable compromises through consensus building processes.

While cultural diversity characterizes Northern populations, it is also fair to note those common features that derive from shared environmental imperatives. These include: a deeply rooted sense that the land provides spiritual as well as material sustenance; the recognition that psychological as well as physical survival requires strong community ties; the notion that a "hard life" is not synonymous with an "impoverished life"; and perhaps above all, the certainty that if there is to be a future, northerners will have to make it for themselves.

It was just such a recognition that motivated the Berger Commission investigation into the potential social impacts of the proposed Mackenzie Valley pipe line on the communities that lay in its path. In arguing against the popular image of the North as "the resource frontier," Berger (1979, vii) stressed that it was first and foremost a "homeland" for those who had put their roots down long before the energy hungry southern society took any interest. While he could not avoid concluding that the only sure way of protecting both the northern environment and its people was not to build the pipeline at all, Berger tempered this conclusion by recommending that if development was perceived to be so critical to the national interest that it must be considered anyway, the next best course was to declare a 10-year moratorium. This, he hoped, would allow the affected communities time to prepare for the impact.

This recommendation focused attention on the lack of adequate conceptual models through which the unique characteristics of northern communities might be relevantly assessed. In the debate over appropriate approaches that followed, Blishen and Lockhart (1979) argued that any predictive model-building intended to inform social policy decisions about the likely effects of impending developmental impacts on Northern communities should be abstracted from this northern environment itself. A proposal was then made to study a cross-section of northern communities directly in terms of their social process variables.

The eight northern communities selected for the pilot study, which was funded by the Department of Indian and Northern Affairs, were representative of both native and non-native populations and included long-established settlements as well as newer, instant resource industry towns. The results revealed that if the objective indicators that separated those communities with higher levels of dependency from those which had maintained a higher level of self-sufficiency were correlated with the more subjective community process variables, the characteristics of these process variables revealed a consistent pattern.

Interestingly, the nature of this pattern rather accurately reflected the social theoretical observations of Toennies (1957), Durkheim (1947), Polanyi (1957, 1968), and other early observers of the societal effects of the industrial revolution. Indeed, what these northern community comparisons revealed was that the more the vital processes of a community reflected the socially bonded, inter-personal "reciprocity" networks of pre-industrial society, the more self-sufficient and hence, impact resistant, the community had proven itself to be. Alternatively, the more a community's internal processes reflected the highly segmented, economically mediated, "contract" relationships of modern urban industrial society, the more the community lacked the capacity to mobilize internal resources to deal with impact problems and/or devise local alternatives to passively accepting dependency-producing external control. Blishen and Lockhart summarized the quite extensive social theoretical literature on the differences between these community types as follows:

The inter-personally connected community, as an ideal type, is portrayed as having a population characterized by face-to-face interactions. Social integrity is believed to result from a high level of mutual agreement about values and a strongly socialized sense of reciprocal obligations. While the model does not require that each individual in the community know all others personally, interconnected informal personal networks serve as an effective mechanism for acquiring critical information about the institutional environment, contacting key agents within this environment, distributing surplus products, and sharing skills and resources when and where this is necessary. Thus, individual members of such a community come to understand the broad functioning of their social group and they are able to exercise some direct control over it through collective participation in its functioning. Effective membership and acceptance in these communities is based primarily on demonstrating allegiance to local values and being willing to enter into the prevailing reciprocal obligations. Formalities such as certification and bureaucratic gatekeeping mechanisms tend to be ignored or subverted because personal relationships and obligations are more important. Individual knowledge of, and access to, the resources and opportunities which are available locally is thus dependent upon a demonstrated commitment to one's collective obligations. For those who meet such obligations, relatively high levels of material security and economic independence can emerge, provided these individuals are also willing to develop pluralized rather than specialized skills and are flexible in their response to changing circumstances. Excessive amounts of individual accumulation of wealth are not, however, likely to occur within such a community order. This is because those who may prove more successful at utilizing their social networks to economic advantage will in turn be subjected to heightened pressures to meet reciprocal community obligations . . . .

By contrast, the economically determined inter-dependent community as an ideal type is portrayed in terms of the concept of the "Mass Society." It is held to be a product of the industrial revolution and urbanization, and this community type is characterized by a very extensive division of labour and highly structured sets of roles. Within this complex institutional matrix, interactions in all but the immediate primary groups of the family and close acquaintances tend to be mediated through formal organizational processes. Because of this complex specialization, and because the institutional order tends to inhibit and in some cases forbid individuals from sharing wealth, knowledge, skills or resources on a reciprocal basis, there is a high degree of dependence upon commercially and bureaucratically organized products and services. Thus individuals in this form of community are rendered economically inter-dependent but socially isolated. There are greater opportunities for both success and failure at the individual level than in the socially bonded com-

TABLE 1
Community Process Scales

Social Vitality

Highly		Highly
Privatized		Cooperative
Relations	−5 −4 −3 −2 −1 0 +1 +2 +3 +4 +5	Relations

Economic Viability

Highly		Highly
Dependent on		Independent of
Externals	−5 −4 −3 −2 −1 0 =1 +2 +3 +4 +5	Externals

Political Efficacy

Low Level of		High Level of
Local		Local
Participation	−5 −4 −3 −2 −1 0 +1 +2 +3 +4 +5	Participation

Source: This table is adapted from Blishen & Lockhart (1979).

munity. It also tends to create an environment in which all, regardless of their degree of personal success, tend to become caught up in the "privatization syndrome." This is a withdrawal into a more personalistic pre-occupation with ambition and gratification which is untempered by a sense of collective obligation and broader social consequences. Social control mechanisms therefore become progressively extrinsic in form. This leads to a second behavioural manifestation, the "psychopathology of powerlessness," which is a rejection of the belief that it is possible for ordinary people to control or even influence their own destinies through any form of participatory politics (1979, pp. 143-145).

Given their obvious contextual relevance, Blishen and Lockhart applied these social dichotomies to the three basic community process variables already discussed so as to provide a relative location scale upon which the assessments could be made. In essence, the three process variable scaling appear in Table 1 above.

So scaled, the three community process variables provide a continuum between the theoretical limits of self-sufficiency and dependency. The actual locations of real communities are determined through an interview schedule applied to a sample of community members. Answers to these interview questions allow indexing on a set of pre-tested social, economic, and political process indicators. The final position assigned to a community on each of the three locations scales is arrived at by taking the mean values of the distribution of those indicators.

While this is not the appropriate place to detail the methodology, a listing of the major indicator headings adapted from Blishen and Lockhart should provide some useful insights:

Social Vitality

Mutual assistance norms
Knowledge acquisition norms
Social problem identification norms
Social leadership definitions
Social deviance definitions, boundaries
Conflict resolution norms, mechanisms
Status recognition and mobility norms, mechanisms
Proprietorial norms, limits, requirements
Group identification, socialization and rejection norms, mechanisms

Economic Viability

Learning and skill acquisition, recognition norms
Attitudes toward various criteria of competence
Attitudes toward what represents economic security, stability
Perceptions of economic opportunity
Perceptions of economic inequality, reciprocity
Perceptions of what represents socially productive, unproductive work
Perceptions of the relationship between work and economic reward
Perceptions of essential, non-essential, undesirable consumption
Perceptions of the relative value of local vs. external initiatives
Perception of inhibitors to, facilitators of local initiatives
Perceptions of the criteria of economic success, failure
Range and valuation of various forms of acceptable exchange
Range and valuation of various resource access and restriction

Political Efficacy

Acceptable and unacceptable participation norms
Dominant and recessive communication norms
Mediation and resolution norms applied internally, externally
Authority attainment legitimation norms

Opinion formation structures
Decision routes
Appeal and reversal mechanisms
Involvement and apathy indices

A comparison of the actual locations that resulted from developing and testing the instruments on the eight pilot study communities is reproduced in Table 2 below.

TABLE 2
Key Variable Comparison by Community

Community	Social Vitality	Economic Viability	Political Efficacy	Compentency Index
A	+5	+5	+5	+15
B	+4	-3	+4	+5
C	+4	-4	+5	+5
D	+3	-2	-2	-1
E	+1	-4	-5	-8
F	-2	-5	-3	-10
G	-4	-4	-4	-12
H	-5	-5	-5	-15

Source: This table is adapted from Blishen & Lockhart (1979).

Two brief comments need to be made with respect to Table 2. First, communities A and H were intentionally chosen for pilot test purposes because of the ample prior documentation that each represented an extreme example of positive and negative community life. As in all scaling efforts, the value assignments are distributed relatively within the selected range and hence carry no absolute value implications.

Second, the concept of the "competent community" was borrowed from Cottrell (1976) and refers to the ability of a community "to nourish some interest, meet some need, or render some service . . . . (The competent community) is capable of co-ordinated collective action" (p. 546). As utilized in the model, the concept was operationalized by summing the mean indicator values assigned to each of the three process variables for each community. While subsequent analysis of the results (see below) strongly suggests that some weighting should be applied, the unweighted value offers a rough estimate of the capacity of a community to deal with external impacts and/or develop its own community-based development alternatives.

Although a full report of the pilot project findings is available elsewhere (Blishen & Lockhart, 1979), the following summary is relevant to our current discussion.

1. While externally initiated development did not necessarily produce a deterioration in a community's economic viability, it did so wherever social vitality and/or political efficacy was already low. Of the three variables, social vitality was found to be the most assertive and could compensate for low economic viability and/or political efficacy up to a point. However, it was observed that as the negative values for economic and political factors increased, the positive value for social vitality decreased.

2. If social vitality is the strongest of the three variables, economic viability is the most fragile. It was found that social vitality and political efficacy were both necessary for a community to regain economic viability after it had been lost.

3. It was noted in particular that those communities with the highest aggregate compentency values also showed the least propensity to seek or accept externally referenced development planning, had the least faith in formally organized professional services, and the most notable success in limiting the negative effects of past impacts by forcing changes that were within the limits of community tolerance.

4. Finally, it was concluded that political efficacy was the most deterministic of how a community responded to impacts. The presence of positive political efficacy, particularly in combination with high social vitality, could turn an impact to community advantage or attract impacts that would have a positive community effect.

As already noted, the model was originally conceived in the *reactive* context of the need for a social impact assessment instrument that would be sensitive to Northern realities at a time when the social problems of Northern development had became a national issue. However, it should surprise no one that such a normatively based approach had very little influence upon a new field of social science application that was attempting to legitimate itself amongst those who were fundamentally supportive of orthodox development. Thus by the time that the model was presented at the First International Conference on Social Impact Assessment (Lockhart, 1982b), it had already been adapted and applied in the *proactive* context of locally initiated development projects.

MODEL APPLICATIONS

The application of the above evaluation model has proved valuable in facilitating community-based development in several ways. First, the model highlights the importance of identifying social and political developmental needs as an integral part of the economic development planning exercise. This is particularly important where the decision to engage in a local developmental initiative is motivated by the abrupt demise of the principal industry upon which a community has become dependent. Under such circumstances, it is likely that the historical pattern of economic dependency has conditioned the community's social and political processes in the direction of privitization and apathy. Since community-based development above all requires collective action, it is crucial to focus upon social and political process rehabilitation as an integral part of economic reconstruction.

By way of example, the local decision to employ our community-based approach was, in several cases, taken only after an attempt to attract some comparable replacement to a departing industrial juggernaut had failed. These examples of "smokestack-chasing" were characterized by an auction-like situation where several communities tried to outbid each other by offering the corporate object of their competitive affection ever more concessions in the areas of resource rents, taxes, and local capital subsidies. To the extent that such concessions could only further undercut the potential for locally controlled development, the losers in such bidding battles had the potential of becoming the ultimate winners. The essential point here is that the shift in local economic development planning from smokestack-chasing to community initiative also requires a shift in facilitation and planning approaches. The essential point here is that the shift in local economic development, the losers in such bidding battles had the potential of becoming the ultimate winners. The essential point here is that the shift in local economic development planning from smokestack-chasing to community initiative also requires a shift in facilitation and planning approaches. The community evaluation model thus provides a heuristic device through which the shift in mind-set from the logic of dependency to the logic of self-sufficiency can be achieved.

A second benefit that has become apparent in applying the evaluation model is its capacity to raise the community's own understanding of the importance of project compatibility with local cultural characteristics. It is ironic, but nevertheless true, that the greater the degree of cultural consistency within a community, the less culture is recognized as the great energizer of action that it is. Like the fish being the last to discover water, members of strongly integrated communities often fail to perceive the character of the cultural ties that bind. Unless these normative artifacts undergo a field-to-figure shift in the consciousness of those who possess them, there is a real danger that the choice of economic solution may only create serious social problems.

A salient example comes from one application where the community had, on the recommendation of an orthodox feasibility study, all but decided to build a conventional, high volume fish processing plant. However, after applying the evaluation model, the community members became acutely aware that both their work culture traditions and the established structure of authority legitimation were diametrically opposed to the work process and management imperatives inherent within the plant technology and related management system. On the basis of this realization, an alternative high quality low volume fish processing operation was developed. This alternative utilized the same resource base but in such a way as to mesh well with the local work culture norms (social vitality variable), and authority structures (political efficacy variable). In addition it offered greater economic viability through a higher value added ratio, greater utilization of the diversity of existing community knowledge and skills, and lower dependency upon alien marketing structures.

A third value that has emerged, more from the application logic than from the model's conceptual structure, relates to what Paulo Freire (1978) argues as the most important characteristic of community-based development (i.e., its capacity to empower those who have for so long wallowed in the apathy and self-doubt attending prolonged ecnomic dependency). Such empowerment results from a collective learning process where those who have been overly intimidated by the professional credentialism of outside "expertise" discover that they are the ones who possess the essential knowledge resources required for gaining control over their own destinies.

Unlike the narrowly focused, fragmented, and highly individualized technical study frameworks employed by outside professionals, the community evaluation model begins by making use of the collective knowledge of community members themselves. Only after this informal knowledge base is developed, and the self-confidence derived from it consolidated, are outside experts called upon to provide any useful additional information. Thus the evaluation model not only seeks to extract and render vital community knowledge in ways that specifically inform subsequent decision-making, but it does so through methods which allow the possessors to recognize their own centrality in the developmental planning and implementation process.

If these empowerment outcomes are to be achieved, the relationship between community insiders and outside process facilitators, as well as the information collecting and reporting methods themselves, become crucial. While a full discourse on the "action research" and "action learning" methodologies cannot be undertaken here, the following extracts from a report on the application of the model in a northern Native community development context should provide some basic insights.

With regard to the relationship between insiders and outsiders:

> . . . In essence, the terms of reference of the contract between the Tribal Council and their outside consultants were that the latter should assist . . . in attaining a clear understanding of the range of socio-economic development needs and aspirations within the seven constituent Band communities; and . . . help the Council design the most effective organizational structure through which it could facilitate such development . . . .
>
> . . . three prime tasks were identified. First, it was recognized that the . . . community process model was a viable basis for undertaking community evaluation research but that the detailed design would require extensive local level relevance and acceptability testing. Second, each of the seven Bands would select their own researchers from within their communities. These researchers would then undergo a common training program . . . . And third, the determination of the "ownership" of the research process and results would be pursued as an on-going part of the information gathering and decision-making . . . .
>
> . . . [Thus] the consultants were to aid the client in developing a *process* rather than delivering a *product*; this process would involve continuous learning and evaluation . . . ; the clients would at all times maintain control over this process . . . ; and the consultants would take a fresh look at their mandate at each of the in-process decision points . . . (Lockhart, 1982a, pp. 163-164).

With regard to the information exchange process:

> The research phase . . . was to serve two functions. The most obvious was the "information out" function, i.e., the determination of the socio-economic development needs and priorities of each of the Band communities. In essence, this was to be achieved by using the community process model as a basis for developing an [evaluation] framework that would identify the existing socio-economic profile of the community at the objective level and the ideally desired profile at the subjective level. The difference between these two profiles would then define the direction and extent of future development needs and priorities . . . .

But the research exercise was also intended to serve an "information input" function. By virtue of its pervasive presence [and participation requisites] within each community, the research project would alert the community to the fact that . . . from the outset [the development project was] community centred, community controlled and ultimately community dependent if it were to succeed.

In other words, the research had to be designed in such a way as to ensure that the "respondents" were not left with the impression that they could simply turn over development project initiative and responsibility to the Tribal Council and then blame them later for failures (Lockhart, 1982a, p. 165).

It hardly needs to be noted that such terms and methods stand in sharp contrast to the conventional employment of expertise in pursuit of orthodox economic development planning and promotion. To begin, the definition of the "problem" to be solved and the solution strategy to be employed was not pre-defined by, nor pre-allocated to, specific knowledge constituencies. By utilizing the different, but equally valid knowledge frames of outsiders and insiders, the tendency to substitute the outside consultant's narrow competency-determined agenda for the client's broader needs agenda is effectively precluded. This also undercuts any tendency for the client to surrender ownership of the problem to outsiders by progressively contracting more and more solution responsibility to those who do not have to live with the results. Finally, by treating the abstract, technical, and universalistic knowledge frames of the consultants and the concrete, experiential, and particular knowledge frames of the clients as equally valid, critically important mutual learning occurs in the only context that can possibly provide the relevant test of validity—the community itself.

Economic dependency, like any other form of dependency, is addictive. To kick the habit, it is absolutely important that those who are afflicted engage in a participatory learning process through which they gain confidence in their own knowledge and ability to take hold of their destinies for themselves. This is not likely to occur if development planning is dominated by a professional expertise mind-set that demands trust in the knowledge of strangers but denies the validity of one's own knowledge.

FROM DIAGNOSIS TO PROGNOSIS

Our effort to create an evaluation model useful in facilitating the community-based alternative to the corporate development orthodoxy is now a decade old. Sufficient application experience has been accumulated to allow some assessment of what we have learned and where we need to go from here.

The first and perhaps most important lesson is that well informed community-based development can meet both the social and economic accounting criteria of success. Further, interest in the community-based developmental alternatives has grown rapidly, not only in the "underdeveloped" hinterlands, such as the Canadian North where it has particular relevance, but also in the heartland of modern industrial society. Given the current restructuring of world order economics, this interest is not hard to understand. This restructuring, or perhaps it should be labelled *destructuring*, ensures that orthodox development will be less and less able to provide either the employment necessary to maintain any community's population or the socially necessary (as distinct from economically profitable) goods and services required by that population. Indeed, as the latest forms of large corporate development emerge, it is becoming quite clear that technological and organizational displacement no longer mean moving from regions of deindustrialization to regions of new industrialization (the so-called "growth pole" theory), but rather from the mainstream economy to some underground economy that conventional economists don't understand, or if they do, don't want to talk about.

But once pushed out of the highly institutionalized mainstream, the options are few: a dislocated person can try to make it in one of the few remaining back-eddies of individual entrepreneurship that have so far escaped the notice of the large corporate sector; can struggle to stay afloat in the marginalized part-time work ghettoes that are but a hair's breadth away from total welfare dependency; or can try to find a nitch in the so-called "underground" (meaning real demand) market networks where the poor cater to the poor by exchanging goods and services at affordable cash-or-kind values through the avoidance of institutionalized monopoly, restrictive practice regulation, and monitary reporting. But it is only the community-based development alternative that has focused upon a systematic search for progressive alternatives rather than retreatist adaptations.

While the growing interest in, and success of, community-based economic development is encouraging, it is important to note that this alternative development concept has *not* so far been significantly recognized within the dominant command institutions of our society. To be sure, an occasional government department has dabbled in the semantics, but only long enough for the forces of orthodoxy to reassert their hegemony. The efforts of a few locally controlled cooperative financial institutions notwithstanding, such as British Columbia's Van City Savings, the mainstream sources of venture capital are either unwilling or incapable of adjusting to community-based viability criteria. This failure to learn persists despite the fact that such criteria have been well documented as at least as good predictors of investment returns as the conventional assessment indicators.

But perhaps most disturbing of all has been the attitude that prevails within the relevant university-based disciplines. While traces of interest can certainly be found in academe, those academics who pursue community-based development approaches still find their work defined as lying outside the conventional research funding envelopes. So long as this research support base is denied, the concepts themselves will inevitably remain marginal to the mainstream teaching operation (Lockhart & McCaskill, 1987). If this seminal source of new knowledge development and dissemination through training practitioners is not nourished, the ability to transform pilot projects of the kind discussed here into a broader practice will simply not be available at the point when the need does become more widely apparent.

The only major institutional sector recently to have taken a serious interest in community-based alternative development has been organized labour. Given the union movement's historic commitment to defending working people against the social irresponsibility of capital, this support would seem consistent with their traditions. But organized labour has not found the adjustment from conventional economic to community-based thinking easy. Indeed, the union movement was forced long ago to pattern its own organizational system in the shape of its principal adversary. As a consequence, large, centralist, bureaucratically structured and economically focused unions emerged as the winning prototype for the very good reason that this structure was the only one that could effectively counter corporate exploitation of labour. As a consequence, until recently very little of what community-based development advocates talked about could be understood by unionists, and what was understood was often held in deep suspicion. However, as world order corporate development is now driven by either labour displacing technology or by moving the residual labour-intensive production to the newly industrialized low-wage countries, labour's strategy of fighting one Goliath with another is no longer very effective. As a consequence, the Canadian Labour Congress at its 1986 convention, adopted a positive stance toward exploring the union movement's most productive role in facilitating community-based development. Several of the Congresses' provincial affiliates had already established support mechanisms and at least one major industrial union is sponsoring a community-based development initiative.

Since there are always some who seek to convert any genuinely innovative alternative to a buzz word mystification of business as usual, organized labour will have to be on guard against those whose vision of the community-based developmental alternative is limited to legitimizing the downsizing of the existing corporate system at the expense of labour. Should community-based development become identified with such efforts to pour sour, old wine into new bottles, then its real capacity to fundamentally restructure the relationship between economic, social, and political processes will be seriously undercut.

For these reasons, then, community-based development advocacy must now transform its own thinking from a self-consciously "alternative" practice to a more aggressively interventionary social movement seeking to penetrate the institutional mainstream. Without a definitive presence within critical areas of economic and social planning, without a strong contingent of well trained facilitators who are at least as accessible as the orthodoxy promoting professional consultancy, and without a recognized place within the academic core of the research and training system, community-based development will, like the make-work projects of the 1970s, be forever constrained to the band-aid role of industrial casualty management.

NOTE

1. Parts of this chapter were originally included in my contribution to: *Strategies for Canadian Economic Self-Reliance* published by the Canadian Centre for Policy Alternatives (Lockhart, 1985), whose support I gratefully acknowledge.

REFERENCES

Berger, T.R. (1979). *Northern frontier, northern homeland, the report of the Mackenzie Valley Pipeline Inquiry: Vol. I & II.* Ottawa: Ministry of Supply and Services.

Blishen, B. & Lockhart, A. (1979). *Socio-economic impact model for northern development.* Ottawa: Department of Indian and Northern Affairs.

Cottrell, L. (1976). The competent community. In B.H. Kaplan, R.N. Wilson, & A.H. Leighton (Eds.), *Further explorations in social psychiatry.* New York: Basic Books, pp. 195-209.

Dacks, G. (1981). *A choice of futures: Politics in the Canadian north.* Toronto: Methuen.

Durkheim, E. (1947). *The division of labour in society*. Glencoe: The Free Press.

Freire, P. (1978). *Pedagogy in process: Letters to Guinea Bissau*. New York: Seabury.

Hamelin, L.E. (1978). *Canadian nordicity*. Montreal: Harvest Home.

Kerr, C., Dunlop, J., Harbision, F., & Myers, C. (1964). *Industrialism and industrial man*. New York: Oxford University Press.

Lockhart, A. (1982a). The insider-outsider dialectic in native socio-economic development: A case study in process understanding. *The Canadian Journal of Native Studies, 2* (1), 159-168.

Lockhart, A. (1982b). Paper presented at the First International Conference on Social Impact Assessment, Vancouver, B.C., October 24-27, 1982.

Lockhart, A. (1985). Northern development policy: Self-reliance versus dependency. In *Strategies for Canadian economic self-reliance*. Ottawa: Canadian Centre for Policy Alternatives.

Lockhart, A., & McCaskill, D. (In press). Toward an integrated, community-based, partnership model of native development and training. *The Canadian Journal of Native Studies*.

Matthews, R. (1976). *"There's no better place than here": Social change in three Newfoundland communities*. Toronto: Peter Martin.

Matthews, R. (1983). *The creation of regional dependency*. Toronto: University of Toronto Press.

Polanyi, K. (1957). *The great transformation*. Boston: Beacon Press.

Polanyi, K. (1968). In G. Dalton (Ed.), *Primitive, archaic and modern economies*. Garden City: Anchor Books.

Rea, K.J. (1976). *The political economy of northern development*. Ottawa: Science Council of Canada.

Ross, D., & Usher, P. (1986). *From the roots up: Economic development as if community mattered*. New York: Bootstrap Press.

Rostow, W.S. (1960). *The stages of economic growth*. Cambridge, MA: Harvard University Press.

Science Council of Canada. (1977). *Northward looking: A strategy and a science policy for northern development, Report No. 26*. Ottawa: Supply and Services Canada.

Toennies, F. (1957). *Community and society*. New York: Harper & Row.

Wallerstein, I. (1974). *The modern world system*. New York: Academic Press.

AUTHOR INDEX

SUBJECT INDEX

ABOUT THE CONTRIBUTORS

Edward M. Bennett is Professor, Department of Psychology, Wilfrid Laurier University, Ontario. He is the Co-founder and Co-editor of the *Canadian Journal of Community Mental Health*, a past President of the Ontario Division, Canadian Mental Health Association and a past Director of Community Psychology Training, Wilfrid Laurier University. Dr. Bennett has been actively engaged in community-based research and development work for over 20 years.

Stephen D. Berger is Professor, School of Human Services, New Hampshire College, New Hampshire. He served as Director of the Human Services Program when it was at Franconia College (1976-1978), and as founding Director of the Graduate Programs at the School of Human Services (1979-1984).

Françoise Boudreau, Ph.D., is an Associate Professor, Department of Sociology and Anthropology, University of Guelph, Ontario. She has done extensive research on mental health policy in the Provinces of Québec and Ontario. She is currently a consultant on the Comité de lecture sur la Politique de la Santé Mentale of the Ministry of Health and Social Services of the Province of Québec.

Christina A. Clamp is Associate Professor, the School of Human Services, New Hampshire College, New Hampshire, and an Associate of the Program on Nonviolent Sanctions, Center for International Affairs, Harvard University, Cambridge, Massachusetts. She has worked on research in Spain, Guatemala and India, specializing in cooperative community economic development, and nonviolent action against repressive governments.

Gail Czukar is an Ontario Lawyer who also has an M.A. in Community Psychology from Wilfrid Laurier University. She has worked with developmentally disabled persons and ex-psychiatric inmates over the past 15 years to develop options for community living. She was Legal Education Coordinator and litigation lawyer at the Advocacy Resource Centre for the Handicapped from 1985-86. Now living in the Ottawa area, she is participating in the development of a national cross-disability organization to litigate Charter and human rights test cases.

Ira Goldenberg has been active in social intervention work for over 20 years. He was Assistant Professor of Psychology, Yale University, 1964-1970, and Associate Professor of Education and Clinical Psychology, Harvard University, 1970-1975. He served as President, Franconia College, 1975-1978. He also served as Dean of the School of Human Services at New Hampshire College, 1978-1982, and as Vice-President for Academic Affairs, New Hampshire College, 1982-1987. His books include, *Oppression and social intervention: Essays on the human condition and the problem of change.* He is currently writing a book of selected essays on the problems of social action.

David Hallman is a Program officer for Social Issues and Justice in the national office of the United Church of Canada. He received a graduate degree in Community Psychology from Wilfrid Laurier University in 1974 and has worked for government and voluntary agencies in the areas of mental retardation, community development and family services. With the United Church, he is involved in advocacy and resource and leadership development related to a variety of social issues, including the environment, marketing of pharmaceuticals, and AIDS (acquired immune deficiency syndrome).

Patricia Hughes' political involvement as a feminist for over fifteen years includes an active commitment to the pro-choice movement. She received a Ph.D. in Political Economy and taught political science for four years. She is now a lawyer in Toronto, Ontario. Having worked as a researcher for the Abella Commission on Employment Equity and as counsel for the Ontario Ministry of the Attorney General, she is currently a Vice-Chair of the Ontario Labour Relations Board.

Louise Lévesque is Professor, Faculty of Nursing, University of Montreal, Quebec. She teaches two seminars at the graduate level in gerontology-geriatrics. Her research is with the aged. She is particularly concerned with the problem of the cognitively impaired elderly and their families, and their care both in the institution and in the community.

Alexander Lockhart is a Professor of Sociology and was the founding Director of the Frost Centre for Canadian Heritage and Development Studies at Trent University, Ontario. Originally from Northern British Columbia, he has worked extensively with the B.C. Research Council, as well as with Native and Community Organizations in researching and applying social impact assessment and community-based evaluation and development models in a wide range of northern locations. Professor Lockhart has also acted as a research associate and policy consultant for a number of Federal and Provincial Government agencies.

Donald Mason is an attorney with wide experience in the field of community economic development. He has worked for Florida Rural Legal Services and maintained a private practice with a specialty in corporate and real estate law. He is currently a faculty member in the Community Economic Development Program at New Hampshire College.

David Osher is an organizer and social historian who taught at Franconia College from 1971-1978 and in the School of Human Services from 1978-1987. He was Dean of Studies at Franconia College from 1974-1978. He has served as Associate Dean of the School of Human Services at New Hampshire College from 1978-1982, and as Dean from 1982-1987.

Maurice Payette is Professor, Department of Psychology, University of Sherbrooke, Quebec. He is a contributing author of a French-language book, *Becoming a consultant*. Professor Payette is actively involved in the training of change agents in a graduate program which focuses on the consultation process. As a community development consultant he has worked with many diverse community settings.

Mary Reidy is Assistant Professor, Faculty of Nursing, University of Montreal, Quebec. She teaches research methodology, theory development and program development in community health at the graduate level. Her research is with the aged and their families, and with young families in the community. She is currently interested in the health of the elderly woman and her role as caregiver.

Michael Swack has extensive consulting and teaching experience in the areas of community economic development and development finance. He is the Director of the Community Economic Development Program at New Hampshire College, President of the Institute for Community Economics and Chairman of the New Hampshire Community Development Finance Authority.

Bruce Tefft is Associate Professor and Director of Clinical Training, Department of Psychology, University of Manitoba, Manitoba. He founded the Community Coalition On Mental Health and serves in several capacities both provincially and nationally for the Canadian Mental Health Association. His interests include community mental health policy, program development and research. He is writing a book on public attitudes, beliefs and behavioural intentions toward the mentally disabled and community mental health facilities.

STUDIES IN HEALTH AND HUMAN SERVICES

71959

HM
101
.S6932
1987

Social intervention,
theory and practice